D0707389

The Jossey-Bass Nonprofit & Public Management Series also includes:

Financial & Strategic Management for Nonprofit Organizations:
A Comprehensive Reference to Legal, Financial, Management, and Operations Rules and
Guidelines for Nonprofits, Third Edition
Herrington J. Bryce

The Budget-Building Book for Nonprofits
Murray Dropkin and Bill La Touche

Saving Money in Nonprofit Organizations:
More Than 100 Money-Saving Ideas, Tips, and Strategies for Reducing Expenses Without
Cutting Your Budget
Gregory J. Dabel

Philanthropy and Law in Asia:
A Comparative Study of the Nonprofit Legal Systems in Ten Asia Pacific Societies
Thomas Silk, Editor

Creating Your Employee Handbook
Leyna Bernstein

The Five Strategies for Fundraising Success
Mal Warwick

Conducting a Successful Capital Campaign, Second Edition
Kent E. Dove

The Fundraising Planner:
A Working Model for Raising the Dollars You Need
Terry and Doug Schaff

Transforming Fundraising:
A Practical Guide to Evaluating and Strengthening Fundraising to Grow with Change
Judith Nichols

Winning Grants Step-by-Step:
Complete Workbook for Planning, Developing, and Writing Successful Proposals
Support Centers of America

Unified Financial Reporting System for Not-for-Profit Organizations

A Comprehensive Guide to
Unifying GAAP, IRS Form 990, and
Other Financial Reports Using a
Unified Chart of Accounts

Russy D. Sumariwalla
Wilson C. Levis
Foreword by Jan Masaoka

Sponsored by CompassPoint Nonprofit Services
A Product of the Project 990 in 2000

 JOSSEY-BASS
A Wiley Company
San Francisco

Jossey-Bass books and products are available through most bookstores. To contact Jossey-Bass directly, call (888) 378-2537, fax to (800) 605-2665, or visit our website at www.josseybass.com.

Substantial discounts on bulk quantities of Jossey-Bass books are available to corporations, professional associations, and other organizations. For details and discount information, contact the special sales department at Jossey-Bass.

 Printed in the United States of America on acid-free, recycled stock that meets or exceeds the minimum GPO and EPA requirements for recycled paper.

Library of Congress Cataloging-in-Publication Data

Sumariwalla, Russy D.
    Unified financial reporting system for not-for-profit organizations: a comprehensive guide to unifying GAAP, IRS Form 990, and other financial reports using a unified chart of accounts/Russy D. Sumariwalla, Wilson C. Levis; foreword by Jan Masaoka.—
1st ed.
        p.   cm.—(The Jossey-Bass nonprofit and public management series)
    Includes bibliographical references and index.
    ISBN 0-7879-5213-3 (alk. paper)
    1. Nonprofit organizations—United States—Accounting—Handbooks, manuals, etc. 2. Financial statements—United States—Handbooks, manuals, etc. I. Levis, Wilson C. II. Title. III. Series.

HF5686.N56 S86 2000
657'.98—dc21

00-042115

PB Printing   10 9 8 7 6 5 4 3 2 1   FIRST EDITION

Contents

Figures, Tables, Exhibits, and Worksheet   vii

Foreword   xi

Acknowledgments   xv

The Authors   xvii

Technical Advisory Group   xix

Participating Organizations   xxi

Introduction   xxiii

PART 1   INTRODUCTION, OVERVIEW, AND PERSPECTIVE

1   What Is a Not-for-Profit Organization?   3

2   America's Not-for-Profit Sector   8

3   The Pivotal Role of IRS Form 990 in Financial Reporting   14

4   Information Technology and Financial Reporting   19

PART 2   KEY BUILDING BLOCKS OF A UNIFIED FINANCIAL REPORTING SYSTEM

5   Unified Chart of Accounts   25

6   Activity-Level Accounting and Reporting for Revenue and Expenses   40

7   Functionalized Trial Balance Report   55

8   Allocation of Expenses   68

9   Staff Time Recording and Reporting   94

PART 3   UNIFIED INTERNAL AND EXTERNAL FINANCIAL REPORTS ALIGNED WITH FORM 990

10   Financial Reports: Overview   105

11   GAAP Financial Statements   108

12 IRS Form 990 Financial Statements   132

13 Uniform Government Grant Reports   143

14 Corporate and Foundation Grant Budgeting and Reporting   160

15 Reporting to United Ways and Other Grant Makers   168

16 Financial Reporting for Internal Management Purposes   178

     Conclusion   189

RESOURCES

A IRS Form 990 and Schedule A for 1999   197

B Content of Unified Chart of Accounts by Account Number   211

C Cross-Referencing Your Not-for-Profit Organization's Chart
of Accounts to the Unified Chart of Accounts:
Cross-Reference Worksheet and Keyword Index   221

D Examples of Employee Time Sheets   241

E Summary of State Registration and Filing Requirements for
Not-for-Profit Organizations   259

F National Taxonomy of Exempt Entities: Activity Codes   265

G Voluntary Standard-Setting and Evaluation Groups for
Not-for-Profit Organizations   291

H A Brief History of Financial Accounting and
Reporting Standards for Not-for-Profit Organizations   325

I Accountability for Service Efforts and Accomplishments   333

J Selected Form 990 and Management and
Technical Assistance Web Sites   335

     Notes   337

     Bibliography   341

     Index   349

Figures, Tables, Exhibits, and Worksheet

FIGURES

Figure Intro.1   Unified Not-for-Profit Financial Reporting System with the
Click of a Mouse   xxiv

Figure 6.1   Functional-Basis Financial Package of a Not-for-Profit
Human Service Organization   41

Figure 6.2   The Budget Process   53

TABLES

Table 1.1   Types of Exempt Organizations Under Internal Revenue
Code Section 501(c)   6

Table 5.1   Unified Chart of Accounts for Not-for-Profit Organizations
(Cross-Referenced to Selected Reporting Requirements)   31

Table 5.2   Revenue and Expense Coding by Activity   36

Table 5.3   Simplified Charts of Accounts for Smaller Organizations
(Cross-Referenced to Form 990 and Unified Chart of Accounts)   37

Table 6.1   Revenue and Expense Activity Code Table   43

Table 6.2   Simplified Activity Coding System for Smaller Organizations
(Cross-Referenced to Form 990 and Unified Chart of Accounts)   44

Table 6.3   Sample Budget by Activity   50

Table 7.1   Functionalized Trial Balance Report (Cross-Referenced to
Sample GAAP Financial Statements): Balance Sheet   58

Table 7.2   Functionalized Trial Balance Report (Cross-Referenced to
Sample GAAP Financial Statements): Revenues   60

Table 7.3   Functionalized Trial Balance Report (Cross-Referenced to
Sample GAAP Financial Statements): Expenses   62

Table 7.4   Simplified Functionalized Trial Balance Report for
Smaller Organizations: Revenues and Expenses   64

Table 7.5   Simplified Functionalized Trial Balance Report for
Smaller Organizations: Balance Sheet   66

Table 7.6   Simplified Functionalized Trial Balance Report for
Smaller Organizations: Changes in Cash-Based Net Assets   67

Table 8.1   Three Types of Costs Distributed to Four Classes of Activities   71

Table 8.2   Allocation Percentages Based on Direct Costs   72

Table 8.3   Reporting Requirements Cross-Referenced to the
Four Activity Classes   73

Table 8.4   Organizational Administration Versus Program Administration   78

Table 8.5   Allocation Variables by Object Expense Category   83

Table 8.6   Simplified Common Cost Pool Allocation for
Smaller Organizations   92

Table 9.1   Simplified Monthly Time Sheet for Employees of
Smaller Organizations   98

Table 9.2   Monthly Staff Time Distribution by Activity   99

Table 9.3   Monthly Staff Salary Distribution by Activity   100

Table 9.4   Year-to-Date Staff Salary Distribution by Activity   101

Table 12.1 IRS Form 990, Part I: Statement of Revenue, Expenses, and
Changes in Net Assets or Fund Balances   134

Table 12.2 IRS Form 990, Part II: Statement of Functional Expenses   135

Table 12.3 IRS Form 990, Part III: Statement of Program
Service Accomplishments   136

Table 12.4 IRS Form 990, Part IV: Balance Sheets   137

Table 12.5 IRS Form 990, Parts IV-A and IV-B: Reconciliation of
Revenue and Expenses per Books to Revenue and
Expenses per Return   138

Table 12.6 IRS Form 990, Part VII: Analysis of Income-Producing Activities   139

Table 13.1 Tennessee Policy 03 Uniform Reporting Alignment
Reference Table: Schedule A, Part 1   147

Table 13.2 Tennessee Policy 03 Uniform Reporting Alignment
Reference Table: Schedule B, Part 1   149

Table 14.1 Standard Corporate and Foundation Grant Budget and
Report Format (Cross-Referenced to Form 990 and Standard
Not-for-Profit Accounting Systems)   166

Table 15.1 1998 Black Book Standards Financial Categories
(Cross-Referenced to Form 990 and Other Standard

Not-for-Profit Accounting Systems): Assets, Liabilities,
and Net Assets 172

Table 15.2 1998 Black Book Standards Financial Categories
(Cross-Referenced to Form 990 and Other Standard Not-for-Profit
Accounting Systems): Revenues, Gains, and Other Support 174

Table 15.3 1998 Black Book Standards Financial Categories
(Cross-Referenced to Form 990 and Other Standard Not-for-Profit
Accounting Systems): Object Expenses 176

Table 16.1 Yearly Budget: Adult Activity Center 181

Table 16.2 Year-End Revenue and Expense Report (Actual):
Adult Activity Center 182

Table 16.3 Budget-to-Actual Report: Adult Activity Center 183

Table 16.4 Revenue and Expense Categories for Internal Budgeting and
Reporting (Cross-Referenced to Form 990, Unified Chart of Accounts,
and Sample GAAP Financial Statements) 184

Table 16.5 Overall Budget-to-Actual Report for Internal Management 185

Table B.1 Content of Unified Chart of Account: Account Number Index 212

Table C.1 Unified Chart of Accounts Keyword Index 229

Table D.1 Monthly Time Sheet 242

Table D.2 Monthly Staff Time Distribution Report by
Activity (in Hours) 244

Table D.3 Monthly Staff Time Distribution Report by
Activity (in Percentages) 246

Table D.4 Monthly Staff Salary Distribution Report by
Activity (in Dollars) 248

Table D.5 Prior Month Year-to-Date Time Distribution Report by
Activity (in Hours) 250

Table D.6 Year-End Staff Time Distribution Report by
Activity (in Hours) 252

Table D.7 Year-End Staff Time Distribution Report by
Activity (in Percentages) 254

Table D.8 Year-End Staff Salary Distribution Report by
Activity (in Dollars) 256

Table E.1 State Registration and Filing Requirements 260

Table F.1 National Taxonomy of Exempt Entities: Common
Activity Codes 268

Table J.1 Technical Assistance Web Sites 336

EXHIBITS

Exhibit 3.1   Quality Form 990 Resolution   16

Exhibit 11.1   Statement of Financial Position   115

Exhibit 11.2   Statement of Activities   116

Exhibit 11.3   Statement of Functional Expenses   118

Exhibit 11.4   Statement of Cash Flows   119

Exhibit 11.5   Simplified Statement of Financial Position for
Smaller Organizations   129

Exhibit 11.6   Simplified Statement of Activities for Smaller Organizations   130

Exhibit 11.7   Simplified Statement of Functional Expenses for
Smaller Organizations   131

Exhibit 13.1   Uniform Government Grant Report Form Using Tennessee
Policy 03 Format: Schedule A, Part 1   146

Exhibit 13.2   Uniform Government Grant Report Form Using Tennessee
Policy 03 Format: Schedule B, Part 1   148

Exhibit 13.3   Uniform Government Grant Report Using Tennessee
Policy 03 Format   150

Exhibit 14.1   Grant Budget: Seniors Project   165

Exhibit 14.2   Grant Budget and Report: Seniors Project
(Grant 204, Activity Code 420)   167

Exhibit A.1   IRS Form 990 and Schedule A for 1999   198

Exhibit G.1   National Charities Information Bureau Standards
in Philanthropy   295

Exhibit G.2   Philanthropic Advisory Service of the Council of
Better Business Bureaus Standards for Charitable Solicitations   301

Exhibit G.3   Evangelical Council for Financial Accountability Standards of
Accountability   305

Exhibit G.4   Maryland Association of Nonprofit Organizations Standards for
Excellence   308

Exhibit G.5   Charities Review Council of Minnesota Accountability Standards   318

WORKSHEET

Worksheet C.1   Worksheet for Cross-Referencing Your Organization's Chart
of Accounts to the Unified Chart of Accounts   223

Foreword

AMERICA'S NOT-FOR-PROFIT SECTOR is alive and well at the turn of a new century and a new millennium. Never before have so many Americans contributed so much of their time and resources to our nation's voluntary institutions, making them among the most dynamic, vital, and vibrant in the world. In particular the last quarter of the twentieth century witnessed extraordinary growth in the voluntary sector. A recent Internal Revenue Service study reveals that during the 1975–1995 period the real assets and revenues of the voluntary sector organizations filing information returns with the IRS more than tripled, to $1.9 trillion and $899 billion, respectively—compared with the real growth in gross domestic product (GDP) of 74 percent during the same period.[1] This is part of a global trend of unprecedented increase in numbers and types of voluntary associations around the world.

But the glass is only two-thirds full. Two issues continue to plague the voluntary sector: the quality of data and the accountability of voluntary organizations. Over the years many problems related to information on the sector have come to light. The authors of this manual, along with others, have worked tirelessly for over twenty years to help remedy the situation. Progress has been made but not so much that we can say, "Mission accomplished." As access to information about not-for-profit organizations becomes available at the click of a mouse, there is a new sense of urgency that this information be accurate and complete. Nothing less will do.

In the hope of addressing the twin issues of accuracy and accountability, on October 14, 1998, we launched "990 in 2000"—a three-year sector-wide project to improve the quality of reporting on IRS Form 990 and to strengthen the public accountability of not-for-profit organizations. The project was designed to accomplish three objectives: to engage the sector leadership in a discussion of data- and accountability-related issues and develop practical responses; to develop a not-for-profit financial reporting guide to help organizations improve the quality of their 990 and other financial reports and lower the costs of such reporting; and to create an accessible training and technical assistance network of individuals and organizations to foster accurate and accountable public reporting.

To engage the sector leadership in addressing these issues, we participated with many others in creating the 990 Nonprofit Accountability Collaborative (990-NAC). This work is ongoing and is expected to continue as part of a larger data quality project at the Center on Nonprofits and Philanthropy at The Urban Institute. With the publication of this guide we have accomplished the second objective. The training and technical assistance network is in the planning and development stage at the time of this writing.

This manual follows in the footsteps of *Accounting and Financial Reporting for Not-for-Profit Recipients of Grant Funds in Tennessee*. Bill Levis was deeply involved in the development of that guide, and the concept of a *unified* financial reporting system comes from that effort. A substantial amount of the material in this guide has been reproduced with the permission of the State of Tennessee. Russy Sumariwalla and Bill Levis between them command over fifty years' experience and expertise in not-for-profit data quality and accountability matters. Sumariwalla is the author of several books on not-for-profit organizations, including two editions of United Way of America's accounting and budgeting publications. A technical advisory group composed of leading specialists in not-for-profit accounting advised Sumariwalla and Levis on this project. We are fortunate to have had such expert guidance, and we wish to express our appreciation for their help.

This guide is different from standard publications on not-for-profit accounting and financial reporting. It provides a wealth of supporting information related to not-for-profit accounting and financial reporting and also places financial reporting in the larger context of public accountability on the part of these organizations. It explains why IRS Form 990 and other financial reports are so critical to maintaining public trust in America's not-for-profit sector.

Neither the 990 in 2000 project nor this publication would have been possible without the generous support of our funders. We sincerely thank the Lilly Endowment, Charles Stewart Mott Foundation, Rockefeller Brothers Fund, and William Randolph Hearst Foundation for their trust in our work. We are hopeful that by the end of the year 2000 there will be a noticeable improvement in not-for-profit financial reporting and account-ability. However, we will continue this effort beyond the year 2000—until substantial progress is made and a very high level of data quality and accountability becomes evident in not-for-profit financial reporting.

July 2000   Jan Masaoka
                                             Executive Director
                                             CompassPoint Nonprofit Services
                                             San Francisco, California

This guide is dedicated to the women and men
who have contributed to the development
of the generally accepted accounting principles
for not-for-profit organizations over the past half
century.
In particular we pay tribute to those who have contributed
to the creation and continuing evolution of
*The Black Book Standards of Accounting and
Financial Reporting for
Voluntary Health and Welfare Organizations.*

Acknowledgments

A PUBLICATION PROJECT of this scope is never accomplished without the help of an army of friends and colleagues. So we start with a blanket thank-you to each and every one of you who directly or indirectly assisted us with this guide or the 990 in 2000 project. You know who you are.

At the same time we would like to acknowledge the special contribution of certain individuals. First, we thank Jan Masaoka, executive director of CompassPoint Nonprofit Services (formerly known as the Support Center for Nonprofit Management—Nonprofit Development Center), who had the vision and courage to take a gamble on us and agreed to house the 990 in 2000 project at CompassPoint. The 990 in 2000 project was literally born one fine morning in Jan's San Francisco Bay area office. Jan quickly realized the importance of what the project was about and its potential long-term impact on America's nonprofit sector. Thank you, Jan.

Next, we thank our funders, without whose faith and confidence in us the project would not have seen the light of day. Our thanks to the Lilly Endowment, Charles Stewart Mott Foundation, Rockefeller Brothers Fund, and William Randolph Hearst Foundation for making this project a reality.

Third, we owe a deep debt of gratitude to all the individuals who participated in developing *Accounting and Financial Reporting for Not-for-Profit Recipients of Grant Funds in Tennessee*. We have so liberally drawn from the Tennessee guide that it would be accurate to characterize this manual as the "offspring" of that guide. Those familiar with the Tennessee guide will recognize how much we have borrowed. In particular we thank Margaret De Boe and Don Berkheimer for their contributions to the conceptual framework for activity-level accounting and financial reporting developed in the Tennessee guide and incorporated in this guide. Thanks are also due to Fred Adom of the State of Tennessee's Department of Finance and Administration for his contributions.

We were very fortunate to obtain the volunteer services of a distinguished technical advisory group—a "Who's Who" in not-for-profit accounting and reporting (their names are listed in a later section). This group reviewed a voluminous draft of the manuscript of this guide and spent one full day with us in Washington, D.C., offering their guidance. In particular we wish to recognize Gale Case, Dick Larkin, Mary Foster, and Liz Schaffer, who provided substantive input on several parts of this guide in addition to reviewing the draft and attending the Washington, D.C., meeting. Liz Schaffer was also kind enough to help us with additional material on smaller organizations. We thank all the members of the technical advisory group for their generous assistance.

We thank Elizabeth Boris, director of the Center on Nonprofits and Philanthropy at The Urban Institute, and Sandra Gray, vice president of leadership and international initiatives at INDEPENDENT SECTOR, for their wholehearted support of this project and for agreeing to cosponsor 990-NAC. Linda Lampkin, manager at the National Center for Charitable Statistics, provided valuable assistance with project coordination in Washington, D.C., and continues to serve in that capacity. We are grateful to Linda and her associate, Karin Willner, for the good work they are doing. We thank William Massey, president of the National Charities Information Bureau; Bennett Weiner, vice president and director of the Philanthropic Advisory Service of the Council of Better Business Bureaus; Paul Nelson, president of the Evangelical Council for Financial Accountability; Peter Berns, executive director of the Maryland Association of Nonprofit Organizations; and Richard Cowles, executive director, and Zina Poletz, senior research associate, of the Charities Review Council of St. Paul, Minnesota, for their kindness in allowing us to reproduce their written standards in this text. And we thank Frederick Schoff, senior vice president at the Foundation Center, for the use of the center's grants classification system.

We do not know what we would have done without the outstanding and continuing help, with manuscript development and in other areas, of Pardis Parsa, executive assistant at CompassPoint Nonprofit Services in San Francisco. We also thank Richard Fowler at CompassPoint for his help with this project.

Finally, we thank Jossey-Bass Publishers for their enthusiastic support of this project. In particular, we are grateful to Alan Schrader, Dorothy Hearst, Johanna Vondeling, Rachel Anderson, and Mark Colucci for their patience, understanding, and professionalism.

July 2000

Russy D. Sumariwalla
Pacifica, California
Wilson C. (Bill) Levis
White Plains, New York

The Authors

RUSSY D. SUMARIWALLA has been a keen student and observer of the not-for-profit scene for almost forty years. Prior to his retirement as president and chief executive officer of United Way International, he was senior vice president of the Research, Development, and Program Evaluation Division and senior fellow of the United Way Strategic Institute at United Way of America. Sumariwalla is the author of the 1974 and 1989 editions of United Way of America's *Accounting and Financial Reporting Guide* and has written over two hundred papers, reports, studies, and books on not-for-profit management, philanthropy, volunteerism, planning, budgeting, needs assessment, evaluation, and services classification. He created the original version of the National Taxonomy of Exempt Entities and was cofounder and the first executive director of the National Center for Charitable Statistics. Since his retirement, he has served as a consultant to various national and international not-for-profit organizations. He is currently cochair of The Aspen Institute Nonprofit Sector Research Fund and a senior research associate with the Center on Nonprofits and Philanthropy at The Urban Institute in Washington, D.C.

WILSON C. (BILL) LEVIS is senior associate at the National Center for Charitable Statistics, Center for Nonprofits and Philanthropy, The Urban Institute, and manager of the Nonprofit Management Group at the School of Public Affairs, Baruch College, City University of New York. At Baruch he conducted projects related to improving the quality of Form 990 and other not-for-profit reporting, including development of the 1994 Model Chart of Accounts for not-for-profit organizations, cross-referenced to Form 990 and other uniform reporting requirements. From 1994 to 1998 Levis assisted the Tennessee Department of Finance and Administration and the Office of the Comptroller with revision of the Tennessee

Department of Finance and Administration's Policy 03, Uniform Reporting Requirements for Grant Recipients, and *Accounting and Financial Reporting for Not-for-Profit Recipients of Grant Funds in Tennessee.* Levis was vice president for administration and special projects at the National Charities Information Bureau. His responsibilities included accounting, financial reporting, and special projects. Levis developed and directed several special projects, including the National Center for Charitable Statistics Project, the Uniform Federal/State Form 990 Project, and the Computer-Based Charity Registration and Auditing System. His volunteer affiliations include Applied Research and Development International and Cause Effective, a nonprofit resource development center.

Technical Advisory Group

THE VARIOUS MEMBERS of the Technical Advisory Group reviewed a draft of the manuscript of this guide and provided valuable comments, suggestions, and technical advice.

Fred Adom, CPA
Middle Tennessee Director, Program Accountability Review
Chair, Tennessee Taskforce on Uniform Grant Reporting (Policy 03)

Christopher H. Amundsen
Chief Administrative Officer
United Way of America

Douglas A. Bakken
Executive Director
Ball Brothers Foundation
Indiana Donors Alliance

Donald E. Berkheimer
Treasurer and Member of the Board
National Grants Management Association

Jack Campbell
Chief Financial Officer
American Red Cross

Gale L. Case, CPA, CFE
Rothstein, Kass & Company, P.C.
Chair, California Nonprofit Quality Reporting Collaborative

Stan Corfman, CPA
Director, City Center of Music and Drama

Margaret A. De Boe, CPA
Shareholder/Director, Nonprofit Specialty Group
Rubino & McGeehin, Chartered Certified Public Accountants
Chair, Greater Washington Society of CPAs Quality Reporting
    Subcommittee

Mary F. Foster
Partner, Deloitte & Touche LLP

Robert Gardiner
Senior Reviewer (Retired)
Exempt Organizations Division
Internal Revenue Service

Richard F. Larkin
Director, Not-for-Profit Industry Services Group
PricewaterhouseCoopers LLP

Robert C. Nauert
Vice President of Finance and Administration
Chicago Historical Society
Chair, Museum Management Committee, American Association of
    Museums

Elizabeth N. Schaffer
Financial Management Consultant
CompassPoint Nonprofit Services

Ronald L. Speck
Senior Cost Policy Officer
Office of the Assistant Secretary for Management and Budget
U.S. Department of Health and Human Services

Peter Swords
Executive Director, Nonprofit Coordinating Committee of New York

Jody Wahl
National Association of State Charity Officials

Participating Organizations

THE FOLLOWING ORGANIZATIONS participated in the Form 990 Nonprofit Accountability Collaborative under the auspices of the 990 in 2000 project.

Alliance for Nonprofit Management

American Association of Museums

American Diabetes Association

Association for Healthcare Philanthropy

Association of Direct Response Fundraising Counsel

California Association of Nonprofits

California Society of CPAs

Coalition for Nonprofit Health Care

CompassPoint Nonprofit Services (sponsor)

Council of Better Business Bureaus, Inc.

Council on Foundations

Evangelical Council for Financial Accountability

The Foundation Center

Greater Washington Society of CPAs

Healthcare Financial Management Association

INDEPENDENT SECTOR (sponsor)

The Indiana University Center on Philanthropy

Multi-State Filer Project

Note: Participation in the Form 990 Nonprofit Accountability Collaborative does not necessarily signify endorsement of this guide.

National Assembly of Health and Human Service Organizations

National Assembly of State Arts Agencies

National Association of State Charity Officials

National Center for Nonprofit Boards

National Charities Information Bureau

National Council of Nonprofit Associations

National Federation of Nonprofits

National Grants Management Association

National Health Council

National Society of Fund Raising Executives

Nonprofit Coordinating Committee of New York

Nonprofit Sector Research Fund, The Aspen Institute

OMB Watch

Philanthropic Research, Inc.

State of Tennessee, Task Force on Uniform Grant Reporting

The Union Institute

United Way of America

The Urban Institute Center on Nonprofits and Philanthropy (sponsor)

Introduction

THIS GUIDE to unified financial reporting is designed with a threefold purpose: to improve the quality of financial reporting by not-for-profit organizations, to reduce the costs and other burdens of financial reporting, and to enhance the accountability of and public trust in America's not-for-profit sector. We realize that financial reports can and will never tell the whole story of a not-for-profit organization's operations, effectiveness, and accomplishments. But we are convinced that when prepared accurately, truthfully, and in a timely manner, a not-for-profit organization's financial reports and IRS Form 990 can go a long way toward achieving that goal. It is also our hope that this guide will promote uniformity in financial reporting across the not-for-profit sector and comparability among like organizations.

The central theme of this manual is that not-for-profit organizations that have to prepare financial statements for a variety of audiences—funders, government agencies, boards of directors, and the public at large—can do so more efficiently and at a lower cost with appropriate software and the procedures presented in these pages. The core strategic concept is the use of a *unified chart of accounts* (UCOA). The guide shows how, by aligning your not-for-profit organization's chart of accounts with the UCOA presented in this manual, you can produce various financial reports, including those required by generally accepted accounting principles (GAAP) and IRS Form 990, for boards of directors, management, funders, and the public at large. Using the UCOA, you can develop a single functionalized trial balance report from which you can produce the necessary reports "with the click of a mouse" (see Figure Intro.1).

FIGURE INTRO. 1

Unified Not-for-Profit Financial Reporting System with the Click of a Mouse

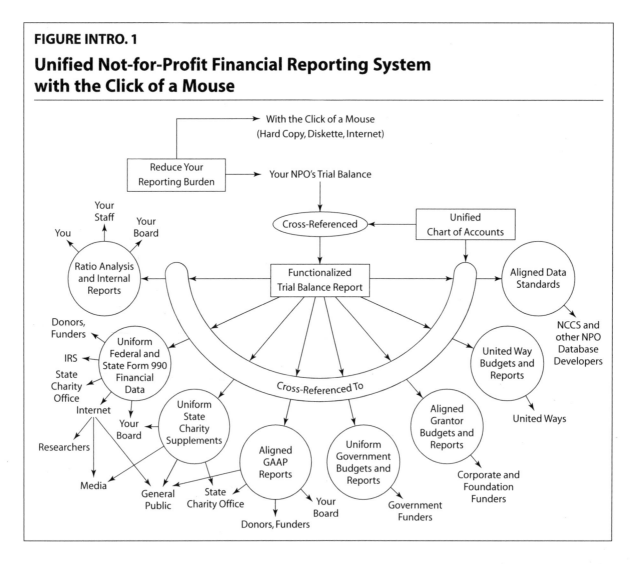

Who Should Use This Guide?

This guide is not intended as a manual on accounting for not-for-profit organizations; it is *not* an accounting guide. It does not pretend to promulgate accounting principles or standards, which is the sole domain of the Financial Accounting Standards Board (FASB). (FASB has been the recognized authority for establishing accounting principles since 1973. For details see Resource H.) Excellent accounting and financial reporting guides for not-for-profit organizations are already available (several are listed in the Bibliography). The primary focus of this guide is on *unified financial reporting* to the various recipients of financial statements and on the types of reports not-for-profit organizations will need for proper financial reporting.

This guide is designed primarily for accountants, bookkeepers, financial managers, chief financial officers, auditors, and volunteer treasurers of not-for-profit organizations. However, many others, including chief executive officers, board members, government charities regulators, voluntary charities monitors, software developers, researchers, students, and faculties of not-for-profit organization accounting and reporting may find this guide a useful reference. In short, it is a tool for those who generate financial information on not-for-profit organizations and those who use that information.

Not every reader will need to read this guide from cover to cover. The reader may pick and choose relevant chapters or sections. At first glance this manual may appear overly complicated and overwhelming—particularly to those associated with relatively small not-for-profit organizations. Nevertheless, we believe that even small not-for-profit organizations will find much of the material in this guide useful, especially those required to file IRS Form 990 (those with annual revenue of $100,000 or more and total assets at year end of $250,000 or more must file the form). Where feasible, we provide special guidance for smaller organizations. The annual Combined Federal Campaign (CFC), in which many not-for-profit entities participate, requires not-for-profit organizations to submit audits by a certified public accountant (CPA), as do several states' charities regulations. Organizations subject to these requirements will also find this manual beneficial.

A Message to Software Developers

This guide is intended for use by accounting software developers to enhance their software systems and products, save their not-for-profit clients time and money, and improve the quality of internal and external reporting by their clients. Such product enhancements include enabling not-for-profit organizations to align their charts of accounts with the UCOA presented in Chapter Five and produce a functionalized trial balance report and all reports presented in Chapter Eleven of this guide— with the click of a mouse.

Organization of This Guide

Part One is intentionally designed for a broad spectrum of not-for-profit staff and volunteers. Our purpose here is to provide a *context* for not-for-profit organization financial reporting. We believe it is important for the users of this guide to know a little about the unique nature of not-for-profit organizations and the critical role they play in our lives. We also believe it is important to discuss briefly why financial reporting—including Form 990—is so important to our understanding of America's not-for-profit sector and to the accountability of not-for-profit organizations. Most publications on technical subjects such as accounting and financial reporting do not deal with such issues. Part One covers the following topics:

- The definition of a not-for-profit organization
- The role of the not-for-profit sector in our society
- Financial reporting and accountability
- The stewardship responsibility of volunteer treasurers and chief executive officers
- The growing importance of Form 990 reports
- Information technology and financial reporting

In Part Two we address what we consider the key building blocks of a financial reporting system:

- UCOA
- Activity-level, or functional, accounting and reporting for revenue and expenses
- Functionalized trial balance reports
- Allocation of expenses
- Staff time recording and reporting

In Part Three we discuss relevant financial statements and reports and present examples. The statements and reports include

- A complete set of required financial statements in compliance with GAAP
- Form 990 financial statements
- Government grant budgets and reports
- Corporate and foundation grant reports
- Reporting to United Ways and other grant makers
- Internal management reports

Following Part Three, the Resources section provides a large body of supportive material, references, and information we believe will be helpful to the users of this guide. The Resources cover such important topics as

- State registration and filing requirements
- Service efforts and accomplishments
- Voluntary standard-setting and evaluation groups
- History of not-for-profit accounting standards

• Sources of management and technical assistance

Although we have tried to be as inclusive as possible, this is by no means an exhaustive treatment of not-for-profit accounting and financial reporting. In summing up what this manual is and is not, it bears repeating that it is not intended to teach elementary accounting or bookkeeping. It assumes the reader will have some familiarity with accounting and financial reporting.

To some readers the guide may sound a bit prescriptive; this is not intentional. Outside of the specific standards and GAAP promulgated by FASB and the American Institute of Certified Public Accountants (AICPA), which must be observed by practicing accountants and auditors and may be required by some governmental authorities, the policies and practices recommended in this guide are just that—recommendations. Readers will decide for themselves which to follow and which to ignore. All we can hope is that they find our presentation helpful and that they benefit from the recommendations we offer in the following pages.

Part One

Introduction, Overview, and Perspective

Chapter 1

What Is a Not-for-Profit Organization?

FOR PURPOSES OF THIS GUIDE, we are using the FASB definition of a not-for-profit organization.[1] By this definition a not-for-profit organization is an entity that receives contributions of significant amounts of resources from resource providers who do not expect commensurate or proportionate pecuniary return, that operates for purposes other than to provide goods or services at a profit, and that does not have ownership interests like those of a business enterprise. These characteristics may be present in varying degrees, and they need not all be present in order for an entity to qualify as a not-for-profit organization under this definition. For example, an organization may receive all of its revenue from exchange transactions and none from contributions and still meet the requirements of the FASB definition. This definition of a not-for-profit organization explicitly excludes organizations such as mutual insurance companies, credit unions, farm and rural electric cooperatives, and employee benefit plans. However, it includes all entities previously covered by the AICPA industry audit guides and statements of position (SOPs) concerning not-for-profit organizations:

- *Audits of Voluntary Health and Welfare Organizations*
- *Audits of Colleges and Universities*
- *Audits of Certain Nonprofit Organizations*
- SOP 74-8, *Financial Accounting and Reporting by Colleges and Universities*
- SOP 78-10, *Accounting Principles and Reporting Practices for Certain Nonprofit Organizations*

AICPA's *Audit and Accounting Guide: Not for Profit Organizations* includes under this broad definition the following types of organizations, provided they are nongovernmental and organized on a not-for-profit basis:[2]

Cemetery organizations

Civic and community organizations

Colleges and universities

Elementary and secondary schools

Environmental and animal welfare organizations

Federated fundraising organizations

Fraternal organizations

Labor unions

Libraries

Museums

Other cultural organizations

Performing arts organizations

Political parties

Political action committees

Private and community foundations

Professional associations

Public broadcasting stations

Religious organizations

Research and scientific organizations

Social and country clubs

Trade associations

Voluntary health and welfare organizations

Zoological and botanical societies

Not-for-profit organizations that provide health care services are not covered by AICPA's *Audit and Accounting Guide: Not for Profit Organizations* but should follow AICPA's *Audit and Accounting Guide: Health Care Organizations.*

Governmental organizations are excluded from the FASB definition of not-for-profit organizations. FASB defines governmental organizations as follows:

> *Public corporations and bodies corporate and politic are governmental organizations. Other organizations are*

governmental organizations if they have one or more of the following characteristics:

   a. Popular election of officers or appointment (or approval) of a controlling majority of the members of the organization's governing body by officials of one or more state or local governments;

   b. The potential for unilateral dissolution by a government with the net assets reverting to a government; or

   c. The power to enact and enforce a tax levy.

Furthermore, organizations are presumed to be governmental if they have the ability to issue directly (rather than through state or municipal authority) debt that pays interest exempt from federal taxation. However, organizations possessing only that ability (to issue tax-exempt debt) and none of the other governmental characteristics may rebut the presumption that they are governmental if their determination is supported by compelling, relevant evidence.[3]

In sum, the accounting and financial reporting information included here applies to all not-for-profit organizations covered by AICPA's *Audit and Accounting Guide: Not for Profit Organizations.* It is our hope, however, that all tax-exempt organizations covered by section 501(c) of the Internal Revenue Code (IRC) will find this manual a useful reference. Table 1.1 lists the various types of tax-exempt organizations under IRC 501(c).

We have chosen to use the term *not-for-profit* in this manual over the more common term *nonprofit.* Although a bit more cumbersome, *not-for-profit* more accurately describes the real characteristics of the types of entities under discussion. To some laypersons *nonprofit* may imply that the entity either does not or may not retain any surplus or show excess of revenue over expenses in any particular period, which is certainly not true. A not-for-profit organization may obtain revenues in excess of its expenses—and in fact many do—as long as it is neither organized nor operated for the financial benefit of any individual or group of individuals. Our choice is consistent with both AICPA and FASB, as well as leading authors in the field, who have adopted *not-for-profit* as the term of choice.

TABLE 1.1

Types of Exempt Organizations Under Internal Revenue Code Section 501(c)

Internal Revenue Code Section	Description of Organization	General Nature of Activities
501(c)(1)	Corporations organized under Act of Congress	Instrumentalities of the United States
501(c)(2)	Title holding corporation for an exempt organization (e.g., Masonic building corporations)	Holds title to property of an exempt organization
501(c)(3)	Charitable, religious, educational, scientific, and literary organizations (including private foundations) and organizations that foster national or international amateur sports competitions, prevent cruelty to children and animals, and test for public safety (e.g., Yale University, Kaiser Foundation Health Plan, United Way, Ford Foundation)	Promotes public welfare (as opposed to private interests) primarily through charitable, religious, educational, scientific, or literary activities
501(c)(4)	Civic leagues, social welfare organizations, and local associations of employees (e.g., Lions Clubs, Rotary Clubs, volunteer fire departments)	Promotes community welfare and activities from which net earnings are devoted to charitable, educational, or recreational purposes
501(c)(5)	Labor, agricultural, and horticultural purpose organizations (e.g., Major League Baseball Players Association, United Auto Workers)	Educational or instructive groups whose purpose is to improve conditions or work, products, and efficiency
501(c)(6)	Business leagues, chambers of commerce, and real estate boards (e.g., National Football League, American Bar Association)	Works toward improvement of business conditions in one or more lines of business
501(c)(7)	Social and recreational clubs (e.g., Metropolitan Club, sorority and fraternity chapters)	Pleasure, recreational, and social activities
501(c)(8)	Fraternal beneficiary societies and associations (e. g., B'nai B'rith, Loyal Order of Moose)	Provides for payment of life, sickness, accident, or other benefits to members
501(c)(9)	Voluntary employee beneficiary associations (including Federal employees' voluntary beneficiary associations formerly covered under 501(c)(10)) (e. g., U.S. Steel and Carnegie Pension Plan, National Education Association Members Insurance Trust)	Provides for payment of life, sickness, accident, or other benefits to members
501(c)(10)	Domestic fraternal societies (e. g., Knights Templar)	Devotes net earnings to charitable, fraternal, and other specified purposes,

(Continued)

TABLE 1.1

Types of Exempt Organizations Under Internal Revenue Code Section 501(c) *(Continued)*

Internal Revenue Code Section	Description of Organization	General Nature of Activities
		without life, sickness, or accident benefits to members
501(c)(11)	Teachers' retirement fund associations	Fiduciary association that provides payment of retirement benefits
501(c)(12)	Local benevolent life insurance associations, mutual ditch or irrigation companies, mutual or cooperative telephone companies, and like organizations	Activities of a mutually beneficial nature implied by the description of the class of organization
501(c)(13)	Cemetery companies	Provides burials and incidental related activities to members
501(c)(14)	State-chartered credit unions and mutual reserve funds	Provides loans to members
501(c)(15)	Certain mutual insurance companies or associations	Provides insurance to members substantially at cost
501(c)(16)	Farmers cooperatives organized to finance crop operations	Finances crop operations in conjunction with activities of a marketing or purchasing association
501(c)(17)	Supplemental unemployment benefit trusts	Fiduciary agent that pays supplemental unemployment compensation benefits
501(c)(18)	Employee-funded pension trusts	Provides for payments of benefits under a pension plan funded by employees
501(c)(19)	War veterans organizations (e. g., American Legion Posts)	Provides services and activities for war veterans

Note: *A small number of other organizations are also exempt under subsections 501(c)(20)–(25). These include: prepaid legal service funds exempt under 501(c)(20); black lung benefit trusts exempt under 501(c)(21); withdrawal liability payment funds exempt under 501(c)(22); associations of past and present members of the armed forces founded before 1880, exempt under 501(c)(23); trusts described in section 4049 of the Employee Retirement Income Security Act of 1974 exempt under 501(c)(24); and title-holding corporations or trusts with no more than 35 shareholders or beneficiaries and only one class of stock or benefit interest exempt under 501(c)(25). Those organizations exempt under 501(c)(20) were only exempt for reporting years before June 20, 1992.*

Source: *Alicia Meckstroth and Paul Arnsberger, "A 20-Year Review of the Nonprofit Sector, 1975–1995," in Statistics of Income Bulletin, Fall 1998, Internal Revenue Service (Washington, D.C.: U.S. Government Printing Office, 1998), p. 162.*

Chapter 2

America's Not-for-Profit Sector

All who wish to understand the strength and vibrancy of democratic institutions at home in America or abroad in the rest of the world would do well to keep constantly in mind that the great variety of not-for-profit organizations—religion, social welfare, private education higher and lower, private health organizations, the rich variety of advocacy in behalf of every area of public policy and then some, the arts, think tanks, the many kinds of foundations—constitute, despite all of their differences, one *sector* distinct from both government and the for-profit sector. What all such organizations share is an explicit commitment to serve the public interest as seen through the many-faceted prism of free minds deliberating and associating together. Their commitment to exclusively public-benefiting ends distinguishes them from their for-profit fellow private sector compatriots, while their exclusive reliance on voluntariness stamps them as fundamentally different from the public sector, which alone has the power to coerce cooperation and obedience.[1]

THE NOT-FOR-PROFIT SECTOR is known by different names: the *voluntary, charitable, eleemosynary, independent,* or *third* sector; more recently it has come to be called *civil society.* The sector is vast, vibrant, and all-embracing—it touches every aspect of human life and planetary concern. It embraces literally millions of small, unincorporated groups as well as some of the most distinguished institutions of education, culture, and health and human services, such as Harvard University, the Metropolitan Museum of Art, and the American Red Cross.

According to the latest figures available, over 1.2 million organizations are registered with the IRS as tax exempt. Contributions to charitable organizations, including religious organizations, were estimated at $190.16 billion in 1999.[2] In 1998, 109 million Americans were estimated to have volunteered approximately 19.9 billion hours; the total estimated assigned dollar value of the donated time was $225.9 billion.[3] The sector also represents a significant economic force in America. It employs almost 10 percent of the workforce and contributes at least 7 percent of America's GDP.[4] A recent IRS study indicates that the sector has experienced phenomenal growth:

> *Nonprofit organizations, strengthened by charitable giving and volunteering, make positive differences in communities, states, and the nation by providing goods and services, often using innovative strategies. While nonprofit organizations lack the resources and are not structured to meet all of America's needs, they do play an important role in addressing needs and in enhancing community strength, vitality, and diversity. During the 20-year period from 1975 to 1995, the real assets and revenues of nonprofit organizations filing information returns with the IRS more than tripled, to 1.9 trillion and $899 billion, respectively. This compares to real growth in gross domestic product (GDP) of 74 percent during the same 20-year period.[5]*

Despite the sector's tremendous scope and all-encompassing dimensions, its impact on American life and culture remains one of America's most undervalued assets and least understood phenomena. Why is this discussion on America's not-for-profit sector relevant to a guide on financial reporting?

Financial Reporting and Accountability

> *All of the organizations in the sector depend to a greater or lesser degree on the support of the public, through donations, patronage or tax benefits enacted by government. Continued public support depends on continued public trust in the bona fides of the not-for-profit sector. That trust can be gradually undermined by instances of fiscal irresponsibility, mismanagement, wastefulness, and fraud within the sector, as well as by the huge recent increase in assets held by not-for-profit organizations. The present accountability-enforcing arrangements of the state and*

federal governments are entirely inadequate, as they currently function, to detect, deter, and punish illegal actions by a tiny number of organizations, which, if not appropriately dealt with, could poison the well of public good will toward not-for-profit organizations.[6]

Strengthening the accountability of America's not-for-profit organizations was one of the motivations for creating this guide. As one learned scholar of the sector and a keen observer of the not-for-profit scene recently observed, "The greatest threat to the not-for-profit sector is the betrayal of public trust, the disappointment of public confidence."[7] Public confidence and trust in not-for-profit organizations is of paramount importance if the sector is to survive and continue to enrich our lives. Indeed, public trust is the lifeblood of not-for-profit organizations.

Truthful, accurate, and timely financial reporting by not-for-profit organizations is only one way they can fulfill their obligation of accountability to the public. But in the absence of other readily available mechanisms, such reporting remains one of the most potent ways not-for-profit organizations can "tell their stories," justify their tax-exempt status, and satisfy their contributors. Much has been written about accountability—or lack of it—on the part of not-for-profit organizations (see the Bibliography for several examples). A few well-publicized scandals have already damaged the credibility and respectability of not-for-profit organizations in recent times, something we can ill afford. Implementing the recommendations made in this manual can assist not-for-profit organizations in fulfilling their duty of accountability to donors, clients, governments, and the public at large.

Stewardship Responsibility of Volunteer Treasurers and Chief Executive Officers

A report of the AICPA study group on the objectives of financial statements included some pertinent observations on the relationship between the notion of stewardship responsibility and a not-for-profit organization's financial reports: "Whoever has a responsibility to others for his actions and their consequences is accountable to them. That responsibility may derive from law, contract, organization policy, or moral obligation. Accountability is a broad term that encompasses stewardship. Stewardship refers to the efficient administration of resources and the execution of plans for conserving and consuming them. *Reporting on management's stewardship has long been recognized as a principal purpose of financial statements.*"[8]

Not-for-profit organizations' boards of directors, trustees, or governors and their executive directors, managers, or presidents retain the ultimate authority and responsibility over the governance and management of their organizations.[9] They are stewards of the public trust. They are responsible for the prudent and effective use of resources. The treasurer of the board is specifically charged with overseeing the financial management and the chief financial officer of the organization. The treasurer may or may not be an accountant, but it is essential that the treasurer have a basic understanding of financial reporting. According to the *Financial and Accounting Guide for Not-for-Profit Organizations*:

> *The treasurer has significant responsibilities, including the following:*
>
> 1. *Keeping financial records*
>
> 2. *Preparing accurate and meaningful financial statements*
>
> 3. *Budgeting and anticipating financial problems*
>
> 4. *Safeguarding and managing the organization's financial assets*
>
> 5. *Complying with Federal and state reporting requirements*
>
> *While this list certainly is not all-inclusive, most of the financial problems the treasurer will face are associated with these five major areas.*[10]

Increasingly, board members are being held liable not only for the organization's financial mismanagement but also for their own conduct in their capacity as board members or trustees. An example of the most egregious kind is still evolving.[11] The case involves the 115-year-old, $10 billion Kamehameha Schools/Bishop Estate in Hawaii. On May 7, 1999, a probate court judge accepted the interim resignation of one of the trustees and ordered the temporary resignation of four other trustees on the ground that their continuation in office would jeopardize the tax-exempt status of the estate, costing the estate millions of dollars in federal taxes and possibly making the estate liable for state and county taxes as well. The IRS had threatened to revoke the tax exemption of the trust. In recent years, the annual fee paid to each of the five trustees ballooned beyond $1 million. The trustees had come under increasing public criticism for a long list of abuses, including mismanagement, conflict of interest, "self-inurement," and enrichment of their cronies.

Cases such as this, though exceptional, are cause for grave concern among all who care about the credibility of the not-for-profit sector. It takes only a few such incidents to damage the reputation of the entire sector. Trustees, directors, and governors of not-for-profit organizations should take special note of this case and remind themselves of their stewardship responsibility.

Many not-for-profit organizations do not consider it essential to conduct a special orientation or briefing for current or future board members. If they are not already familiar with the principles and procedures of not-for-profit financial reporting, board members—the volunteer treasurer in particular—should be trained in reading and understanding financial statements and IRS Form 990. The National Center for Nonprofit Boards (NCNB) in Washington, D.C., has produced a number of very useful publications on the subject. Local support centers and other management support organizations regularly provide training to not-for-profit boards of directors. It is also important that chief executives of not-for-profit organizations keep the board abreast of changes in the regulatory environment as they occur.

Accountability for Financial Information: The Role of Audits

Not-for-profit organizations are often required by their own governing bodies, by funding sources, or by governmental agencies to have an independent financial audit of the organization conducted annually by a certified public accountant (CPA) or some other qualified public accountant. The audit should cover all fiscal events that occurred during a specified period.

A financial audit consists of various procedures a professional accountant may use to test transactions and internal controls so as to form an opinion on the accuracy of the presentation of the organization's financial statements for the period covered by the audit. It is not an examination of every financial transaction; it is rather a series of tests conducted to allow the accountant to determine how effectively the records were kept and how reliable the organization's internal controls are. The results of these tests permit the auditor to express an opinion on the financial position of the organization. The audit is conducted in accordance with generally accepted auditing standards in effect at the time the audit is performed. These standards include ten commonly accepted auditing principles as well as the AICPA Statements on Auditing Standards that interpret those principles. Regulatory authorities may have additional requirements applicable to organizations under their jurisdiction. For example, some not-for-profit organizations may be subject to the requirements of the U.S. Office of Management and Budget (OMB).

As noted, the purpose of an audit is to enable an independent auditor to express an opinion on the fairness of the financial statements and their compliance with GAAP. Discovery of irregularities may or may not occur as a direct consequence of an audit. The auditor's examination is not designed for the purpose of discovering them, nor can it be relied on to disclose mismanagement or wrongdoing. The auditor nonetheless does assist management in meeting its responsibility for safeguarding assets by suggesting improvements in the internal accounting controls and procedures to reduce opportunities for errors and mishandling and the likelihood of their occurring.

Significance of the Auditor's Opinion

The auditor's opinion is the culmination of an audit. As an independent expert, the auditor conducts an intensive review and investigation of an organization's financial statements, referring to supporting documents and actual assets when necessary. It is important to remember that although auditors are responsible for their opinion on the presentation of financial statements, responsibility for the *content* of financial statements ultimately rests with an organization's management. The word *opinion* was carefully chosen as the best term to describe the conclusions reached through an audit—they are an opinion and nothing more. The fact that the opinion is an informed professional one, arrived at by an expert after performing a careful and critical examination, gives it additional value, but nonetheless it remains an opinion. The auditor does not give guarantees or assurances that financial statements are accurate or reliable. And because the auditor does not examine all transactions, the normal audit cannot be relied on to detect fraud or similar irregularities. With these caveats in mind, board members should consider it normal, prudent, and part of their responsibility as guardians of the organization's assets to require an annual audit of the organization's financial statements by a CPA. A financial audit by a CPA is also one of the best ways a not-for-profit organization can render a bona fide report on its stewardship of the organization's assets to funders, government agencies, and the public at large.

Chapter 3

The Pivotal Role of IRS Form 990 in Financial Reporting

IRS FORM 990 is central to this guide—for several reasons. First, it is the information return that all not-for-profit organizations (except those with under $25,000 in annual gross receipts, churches, and certain other religious organizations) must file with the IRS annually. It is one of the reports required by law, with penalties for those who neglect to file. The law does not require typical annual reports from not-for-profit organizations. Even financial audits by independent accountants are not required by law except in special circumstances. But Form 990 must be filed if a not-for-profit organization wants to retain its tax-exempt status.

Second, Form 990 serves as the basic annual report to over thirty-five state charities offices. Prior to the 1980s, most states required a separate report to be filed with state charities regulation offices, and states used different forms to obtain similar information. The IRS, state charities regulators, and representatives of the not-for-profit sector collaborated in an effort to promote changes to Form 990 so that states would accept it in lieu of their own information returns. This effort was most beneficial to not-for-profit organizations who raised funds across the nation and had to file different returns in different states.

Third, Form 990 serves as the fundamental data source for not-for-profit sector research, and it provides data in a relatively uniform, consistent format. Most of what we know about America's not-for-profit sector is based on information from Form 990. It is the only information available on many not-for-profit organizations.

Fourth, the information contained in Form 990 is mostly consistent with GAAP. In addition, it provides information not found in audited financial

---

Note: This chapter is to be read in conjunction with Chapter Eleven and Resource A.

statements of not-for-profit organizations. The information in Form 990 is different from that found in GAAP reports and is used for different purposes. It covers both qualitative and quantitative data and, when prepared accurately, completely, and truthfully, is a treasure trove of information. It is conceptually comparable to the reports that registered for-profit corporations are required to file with the Securities and Exchange Commission.

Finally, Form 990 is a public report and potentially a powerful means of ensuring and demonstrating accountability.[1] Not only must not-for-profit organizations file this report with the IRS, but they are also required to make it available to anyone who demands to see it. On June 8, 1999, new IRS regulations regarding not-for-profit organization disclosure came into effect, making Form 990 even more public, and copies of some not-for-profit organizations' Forms 990 are now accessible at the click of a mouse, on the organizations' Web sites.[2] In the foreseeable future any interested party will also be able to obtain a copy of the Form 990 of any not-for-profit organization from a Form 990 Web site.[3]

For all of these reasons it makes sense for not-for-profit organizations to use a unified financial reporting system aligned with Form 990 and GAAP as promulgated by AICPA and FASB.

Awareness of Form 990's importance and of problems associated with Form 990 returns has increased over the years. In 1998, recognizing the pivotal role of Form 990 in public disclosure and accountability, the Greater Washington Society of CPAs (GWSCPA) and the California Society of CPAs (CalCPA) adopted a "Quality Form 990 Resolution." This resolution was reviewed and edited extensively by more than fifty sectorwide participants at the 1998 Annual Form 990 meeting. It urges key constituencies to take action to improve the quality of information reported on Form 990, reflects on the current state of Form 990 returns. Several other CPA societies and major national organizations are considering adoption of this resolution. The full text of the resolution is presented in Exhibit 3.1.

EXHIBIT 3.1

Quality Form 990 Resolution

Co-sponsored by

The Greater Washington Society of CPAs

And the California Society of CPAs.

October 14, 1998

"Quality" means readability, reliability, comparability,
consistency, completeness, accuracy, timeliness,
decision-usefulness, accessibility, and cost-effectiveness.

Whereas there is broad nonprofit sector support for public disclosure and accountability; and

Whereas while audited financial statements of nonprofit organizations provide comprehensive financial information and disclosures and offer the highest level of assurance by independent auditors, many non-profit organizations that must file Forms 990 with IRS do not have their financial statements audited, and, consequently, the data source that provides the broadest and most accessible base of information about the nonprofit sector is Form 990; and

Whereas federal and state laws require (a) public disclosure by way of the uniform federal/state Form 990 and other reports; (b) that Forms 990 be prepared in accordance with the instructions; and (c) that nonprofit organizations make their Forms 990 readily available to the public; and

Whereas many of the nonprofit sector standards and codes of ethics require compliance with the law; and

Whereas fiduciary duties imposed by state law on board members require compliance with the law; and

Whereas for over 30 years, leading nonprofit sector groups have lobbied in support of federal and state public disclosure laws including the 1996 amendments to federal law requiring increased accessibility to Forms 990 (widely-available provisions) and increased penalties for non-compliance with the Form 990 instructions and/or disclosure requirements; and

Whereas Form 990 is increasingly becoming the primary instrument for public accountability by nonprofits especially via the Internet (e.g., as a way of meeting the new IRS widely-available disclosure regulations); and

Whereas nonprofit organizations need their Forms 990 to present their organizations as fairly, accurately, and completely as possible, especially to prospective contributors; and

(Continued)

EXHIBIT 3.1

Quality Form 990 Resolution *(Continued)*

Whereas Form 990 is the principal source of data on the nonprofit sector that is used for (a) public policy purposes of all kinds, (b) comparative statistics for governance and management, (c) sector advocacy, (d) research of all kinds, and (e) marketing useful products and services by for-profit and nonprofit organizations to the sector; and

Whereas reports by users of Forms 990 and studies of the quality of Forms 990 filed with IRS and state charity offices indicate that numerous errors are made by nonprofit sector organizations and their accountants in the preparation of Forms 990; and

Whereas there is extensive noncompliance with respect to the disclosure requirements of Section 6104(e) of the Internal Revenue Code which requires nonprofits to make their Forms 990 readily available to the general public;

Therefore, let it be resolved that, to improve the quality of Form 990 reporting and reduce the cost and burden, the sponsors of this resolution make *12 quality Form 990 recommendations*:

1. That the **accounting profession** employ the necessary quality assurance procedures to be able to prepare Forms 990 efficiently, accurately, completely, consistently, and on a timely basis; and establish procedures that assure the proper and timely disclosure of Forms 990;

2. That **nonprofit organizations** assure that their Forms 990 are prepared by competent professionals accurately, completely, consistently, and on a timely basis; have their Forms 990 reviewed, before they are filed, by officers or a committee of their board of directors and, when there are significant changes from prior Forms 990, by knowledgeable legal counsel; have their boards of directors learn how to read and understand Form 990 and use it as an essential internal control document for fulfilling fiduciary duty; and implement procedures to assure proper and timely disclosure of their Forms 990;

3. That **national, state, and local nonprofit sector and subsector organizations, umbrella groups, and other associations of nonprofit organizations,** as part of their ethics, standards, accountability, and public policy programs, encourage their respective constituents to prepare their Forms 990 accurately, completely, consistently, and on a timely basis, and to properly disclose their Forms 990 by adopting and implementing those parts of this *Quality Form 990 Resolution* that are relevant to them;

4. That **IRS** pursue electronic filing of Forms 990 and placing of all the public sections of Forms 990 for all filers on an IRS Form 990 Web Site and promote its use world wide;

5. That **IRS** and **state charity officials** seek the participation of the nonprofit sector and professional groups in federal and state efforts to identify and publicize common reporting errors and to enforce compliance with public disclosure laws related to Forms 990;

(Continued)

EXHIBIT 3.1

Quality Form 990 Resolution *(Continued)*

6. That **accounting software suppliers** develop and provide software products and services, including implementation of the model chart of accounts for not-for-profit organizations, that enable users of their software to prepare Forms 990 accurately, completely, consistently, and on a timely basis;

7. That nonprofit **academic centers** and **technical assistance providers** develop and provide educational and training tools and services that enable their nonprofit financial management students and clients to be able to prepare Forms 990 accurately, completely, consistently, and on a timely basis, and to understand and comply with the requirements for proper and timely disclosure of Forms 990;

8. That **institutional donors (e.g., corporations, foundations, United Ways, federal and state government agencies)** include Forms 990 (along with audited financial reports when available) in their application guidelines and grant reporting requirements and encourage their grantees to comply with Form 990 reporting and disclosure requirements;

9. That **charity review groups** request and use copies of Forms 990 as a routine part of their review, evaluation, and reporting activities and encourage the nonprofits they report on to comply with Form 990 reporting and disclosure requirements;

10. That **information centers**—via the Internet and otherwise—request and use copies of Forms 990 as a routine part of their data collection and reporting activities, and encourage the nonprofits they report on to comply with the Form 990 reporting and disclosure requirements;

11. That national, state, and local nonprofit sector **advocates** of ethical practices and full public disclosure and accountability, together with their public policy counterparts, organize Quality Reporting Collaboratives—by state and by subsector—that involve the accounting, legal, and fund-raising professions, technical assistance providers, academic centers, software suppliers, charity review groups, grantmakers, state charity officials, nonprofit database developers and users, and groups interested in assuring that Forms 990 are reliable and comparable, are prepared consistently, completely, and accurately, and are properly disclosed to the public in a timely fashion; and

12. That corporate and foundation **funders** interested in and concerned about nonprofit accountability, ethical behavior, public policy, and/or oversight consider funding programs and projects that implement various aspects of these recommendations for improving the quality and reducing the cost and burden of Form 990 reporting.

Chapter 4

Information Technology and Financial Reporting

INFORMATION TECHNOLOGY offers not-for-profit organizations the potential for tremendous improvements in the efficiency and effectiveness of accounting and financial reporting. Even relatively small not-for-profit organizations should consider taking advantage of available technology to enhance their accounting and reporting systems.

Accounting Software

Regardless of their size, not-for-profit organizations can benefit from computer software that ensures accurate and efficient operation of accounting and financial reporting systems.[1] Accounting software can be used to simplify maintenance of the general ledger, improve the accuracy, completeness, timeliness, and usefulness of all financial reports, enter accounting data one time to meet all of an organization's accounting and financial reporting needs, and save time by eliminating all or most of the manual record keeping and calculations otherwise necessary.

Most of today's accounting software allows the user to maintain transaction files from which all the month-end, year-to-date, and year-end journals, general and subsidiary ledgers, trial balances, and other financial reports can be generated. These accounting programs typically only require the user to code transactions according to a chart of accounts—rather than posting or recording transactions in a separate journal or ledger for each account as is done in manual bookkeeping. The software uses the coding to post transactions to the appropriate accounts. If its chart of accounts is consistent with the UCOA presented in this guide, an organization can easily and effectively use the activity-level revenue and expense coding techniques explained in Chapter Six of this guide as a basis for coding transactions.

These software programs automatically double-code single transactions—and thus automatically perform double-entry bookkeeping. The bookkeeper does not have to make two separate entries in journals, ledgers, or trial balances for each transaction as is required in manual bookkeeping. Each transaction is entered into the system only once rather than posted manually to multiple journals and ledgers. When journals, ledgers, or trial balances are needed, the software generates them as standard reports based on the information in the coded transaction files. There is no need to maintain separate journals, ledgers, or trial balances as is necessary in manual accounting.

Fully integrated accounting software includes all aspects of accrual basis accounting, such as accounts payable and accounts receivable; entry and automatic allocation of payroll data and time-and-effort activity reports by employee for each pay period; and maintenance of various payroll, activity, and central service department cost pools, with automatic allocation on multiple bases at the time reports are processed.

Even without an integrated computer-based accounting system, using a computer spreadsheet such as Lotus 1-2-3 or Excel to prepare trial balances can be a significant time-saver. Spreadsheets can also be used to produce many other financial reports and are especially useful if an organization's other accounting software cannot produce reports in the desired format. (All of the sample financial reports in this guide were originally prepared using computer spreadsheets.) If an organization uses computer spreadsheets, they become part of the organization's official books and records.

The more popular general-purpose business accounting software products available in most computer stores today do not have adequate cost allocation or report-formatting features to meet not-for-profit reporting requirements. Small and midsize not-for-profit organizations that employ such systems can produce reports using spreadsheet software to do cost allocation and tailored reporting. This technique requires a high degree of skill.

Sophisticated not-for-profit accounting software systems with comprehensive, fully integrated payroll record keeping and analysis, cost allocation, accounts receivable, accounts payable, and other features produce standard and tailored reports directly from the coded transaction file. This can eliminate the need for spreadsheet software and the cumbersome task of getting data from the accounting system to the spreadsheet. Sophisticated accounting software does not produce reports from a trial balance. But it can generate a trial balance that the organization or its auditor can use to verify that all of the reports produced can be reconciled with the same trial balance (as is the case with the trial balance report illustrated in Chapter Seven). *Sophisticated* does not mean *complicated* from a user standpoint. In fact these systems are designed to be used by the average bookkeeper with limited additional training.

Small not-for-profit organizations may find it cost effective to hire outside services that have sophisticated accounting software and skilled professional and support staff. The outside service can provide a not-for-profit organization with rudimentary accounting software for day-to-day entry of coded transactions for receipts and disbursements. Such services can perform all or most of the month-end accounting and reporting and can help with reports to government funding agencies. These services can also prepare the financial records for the year-end audit. Such outsourcing eliminates the need for full-time, on-staff expertise, which can be impractical when these tasks are only performed a few days each month or once a year. Payroll processing can also be outsourced to payroll services that regularly update their software according to changes in IRS, state, and local tax rules, prepare all the necessary governmental tax reports, calculate staff time and salary distribution by activity, and offer a variety of other useful services.

The sample charts of accounts presented in Chapter Five can be used either for transaction coding in an accounting software system or for designing a manual bookkeeping system. In both cases the level of detail must be such that all the required internal and external reports can be prepared without having to go back to supporting documentation in the hard-copy records for more detailed breakdowns. Further, in either case the supporting hard-copy documentation (such as invoices for accounts payable and transmittals for accounts receivable payments) must always be coded according to the chart of accounts.

The traditional accounting system requirement of a separate set of general ledger revenue and expense accounts for each activity can be problematic in manual accounting and financial reporting systems when an organization has more than two or three activities. Basically, the general ledger must have separate revenue and expense accounts for each active combination of line item account and activity. An "active" account is one with any financial transaction during the current or prior period.

In a manual general ledger and subsidiary ledgers, there is usually a separate ledger page for each account. (As noted earlier, most accounting software systems maintain transaction files coded by account, eliminating the need for cumbersome separate ledger pages.) A not-for-profit organization may choose to have a separate page for each account in a manual general ledger. In this case revenue and expense transactions for the various activities related to one account are posted on the same page in the general ledger. However, this approach requires manual extraction and calculation of revenues and expenses by activity when an activity-level trial balance is needed for preparation of financial reports. If the not-for-profit organization has more than a few activities, computerization is almost mandatory.

A computerized system of recording financial data and preparing reports is highly desirable and recommended, even for relatively small organizations. It can facilitate the tasks of keeping records and preparing financial statements, reports to state and federal grantors, and Form 990. In addition, computerization enables an organization to submit reports on diskette, by e-mail, or on the World Wide Web. An increasing number of report recipients prefer electronic submission of reports.

Part Two

Key Building Blocks of a Unified Financial Reporting System

Chapter 5

Unified Chart of Accounts

A CHART OF ACCOUNTS rests at the heart of a financial accounting and reporting system. It provides the structure for the general ledger, from which a period-ending trial balance is prepared. The trial balance is the source of data for virtually all internal and external financial reporting.

The UCOA and functionalized trial balance report presented in this guide are cross-referenced to and consistent with various reporting requirements, including those for

- IRS Form 990

- FASB Statement no. 117

- AICPA's *Audit and Accounting Guide: Not for Profit Organizations*

- OMB Circular A-122

- Tennessee Uniform Reporting Policy Statement no. 03

It is impossible for a single chart of accounts to meet the needs of a not-for-profit organization's multiple external and internal reports when financial elements of those reports are different and when terminology and definitions for similar data elements are different. Unified financial reporting and the use of a UCOA can solve this problem and increase the quality and reduce the cost of all reporting.

Regardless of its size or complexity, every organization needs some sort of a chart of accounts to systematically and meaningfully portray its financial transactions and financial condition. The larger and more complex an organization, the more detailed its chart of accounts. Smaller, less complex organizations need a commensurately less complex chart of accounts. (In this chapter, in addition to the UCOA, we present several simplified charts of accounts specially designed for smaller organizations.) However, all organizations must track certain key elements of a financial reporting system: assets, liabilities, net assets, revenue, and expenses.

A chart of accounts is a system for identifying and classifying accounts and transactions by the type of account or the nature of the transaction (that is, what occurred) and by the activity or function involved (that is, the purpose for which the transaction occurred). Some sort of coding scheme, although not absolutely necessary, is generally used to bring logic, order, and structure to the chart of accounts.

A not-for-profit organization's accounting system should enable it to record financial information systematically and consistently, with adequate supporting documents. It should include internal controls to provide reasonable assurance that the organization's assets are properly safeguarded, that financial transactions are carefully recorded, and that transactions are carried out as authorized (see Chapter Six for a summary of internal controls). A not-for-profit organization's accounting system must be designed to enable it to develop internal budgets and periodic reports for its staff and board of directors, design budgets and reports for funders and grantors in accordance with reporting standards, prepare GAAP financial statements, and file uniform Form 990 returns.

In sum the basic purpose of a chart of accounts is to enable a not-for-profit organization to classify and record transactions one time at a level of detail necessary to produce all required reports. A not-for-profit organization's accounting system for internal management and reporting to funders is usually more detailed than required for external financial reporting. Therefore adequate accounting systems in place for internal and grant reporting will likely be sufficient to meet the needs of external financial reporting requirements.

Nonprofit Accounts Coding System: XXXX-XXX

The coding system used in this guide is the Nonprofit Accounts Coding System (NACS), used in the State of Tennessee's *Accounting and Financial Reporting for Not-for-Profit Recipients of Grant Funds in Tennessee.* In the NACS, a seven-digit code is assigned to each account. The first four digits identify the account type—asset, liability, net asset (equity), revenue, or expense—and the specific account within its account category.

The three digits following the hyphen serve as an *activity code* for revenue and expense account transactions. Activity codes are assigned to revenue transactions to identify a specific grant, service fee category, or other funding source category. Those assigned to expense transactions identify a specific activity, program, project, service provided, or other cost objective.

Activity codes are the revenue and expense transaction codes that the not-for-profit organization has determined are needed in order for its accounting system to satisfy its various revenue and expense budgeting and reporting requirements. For example, the use of activity codes enables the not-for-profit organization to produce expense or revenue reports by activity conducted, service provided, program service area (a group of program services), department, function, grant, project, cost center, net asset classification (including total net assets), and performance measurement categories. (See Chapter Six for a more detailed discussion of activity codes used in this manual; see Resource F for information on the suggested nonprofit services identification system activity codes.)

The UCOA featured in this chapter is based on NACS and is intended to be flexible enough to meet all of the internal and grantor accounting and reporting needs of not-for-profit organizations. The UCOA is cross-referenced to the sample financial statements found in Part Three. The functionalized trial balance report, presented in Chapter Seven, uses NACS and the UCOA to demonstrate that many internal, and most external, reporting requirements can be met with a single year-end adjusted trial balance report.

Outline of UCOA

In the UCOA used in this guide the *first* digit of the four-digit account number indicates the account type: 1 for assets, 2 for liabilities, 3 for net assets, 4–6 for revenue, and 7–9 for expenses. The *second through fourth* digits of the account number designate the specific account category—for example, bank checking (asset) account, government grants (revenue) account, or salary (expense) account.

Balance Sheet Accounts

Balance sheet accounts use only the four-digit account number. Net asset accounts are subdivided into four categories (general unrestricted, fixed unrestricted, temporarily restricted, and permanently restricted) that can be distinguished by the *second* digit of the account number. Balance sheet accounts, then, are coded as follows:

Balance Sheet Accounts

Account Number	Account Type
1XXX	Asset
2XXX	Liability
3XXX	Net Asset

Net Asset Accounts

Account Number (or Range)	Net Asset Type
30XX	General unrestricted
31XX	General unrestricted
32XX	Fixed unrestricted
33XX	Temporarily restricted for program
34XX	Temporarily restricted for fixed asset acquisition
35XX	Temporarily restricted for time
36XX	Temporarily restricted, add if necessary (AIN)
37XX	Temporarily restricted, AIN
38XX	Temporarily restricted, AIN
39XX	Permanently restricted

Revenue and Expense Accounts

Revenue and expense accounts use the four-digit account number *plus* a three-digit activity code number attached to the account number by a hyphen. Revenue accounts fall into two general categories (contributed and earned) that can be distinguished by the *first* digit of the account number. Revenue and expense accounts are coded as shown here:

Account Number	Account Type
4XXX-XXX	Revenue (contributed)
5XXX-XXX	Revenue (earned)
6XXX-XXX	Revenue (earned)
7XXX-XXX	Expense
8XXX-XXX	Expense
9XXX-XXX	Expense

Specific Account Numbers

Understanding this system of account categories will allow a not-for-profit organization to create a chart of accounts that suits its particular needs by referring to the UCOA presented in this chapter. The following examples illustrate the coding principles discussed so far:

Account Number	Account
1010	Cash in bank—operating (asset)
4530-XXX	Government grants—state (revenue)

7220-XXX	Other salaries and wages (expense)
8010-XXX	Rent (expense)
8310-XXX	Travel (expense)

Organizations can assign separate control accounts as needed for maintaining balances for each contract, grant, project, activity, or group of activities. They can assign a separate unearned or deferred revenue control account code number for each contract and assign a separate net asset control account number for each temporarily restricted grant or unrestricted project. In the UCOA, for example, 3010 is an unrestricted net asset control account for general operating transactions, and 3310 is a temporarily restricted net asset control account for temporarily restricted transactions. Based on the UCOA, control accounts could be established as follows:

Account Number	Account
2311	Deferred revenue control account for contract 101
2312	Deferred revenue control account for contract 102
2313	Deferred revenue control account for contract 103
3010	Unrestricted control account for general activities
3310	Temporarily restricted control account for grant 204

Note that GAAP reporting generally does not require assets and liabilities to be classified by donor restriction or by their relationship to net assets. However, if for internal management purposes your organization wants to designate whether assets and liabilities are related to unrestricted, temporarily restricted, or permanently restricted net assets, a fifth digit can be added to asset and liability accounts. For example:

Asset or Liability Account Number	Asset or Liability Type
XXXX-1	Unrestricted (includes land, building, and equipment)
XXXX-2	Temporarily restricted (such as restricted grants and contributions)
XXXX-3	Permanently restricted (usually endowment)

Specific Activity Codes

The three-digit suffix attached to revenue and expense account numbers (the activity code) designates the unique activity related to particular revenue and expense transactions. These are the activity codes used in this guide:

Activity Code Range	**Activity**
100–499	Program-related
500–699	Management and general
700–899	Fundraising
900–999	Cost pool (multiactivity)

Cost pool codes represent costs that benefit more than one activity. For example:

Activity Code	**Cost Pool**
910	Central service
920	Common—by expense account
930	Common—other
980	Capital or fixed asset purchases

Take the "employee leave" common cost pool for account 7220 (Other salaries and wages) as an example. Employee leave expense transactions would be coded 7220–920. Consider next a direct salary expense transaction related to a meals-at-home service under a nutrition grant to a senior citizens' center. If the unique activity code for this service under this grant is 220 and the expense account affected is 7220, the transaction would be coded 7220-220.

When using NACS it is essential that an organization maintain a revenue and expense activity code table that cross-references the activity codes to its various reporting requirements (see Chapter Six, Table 6.1). The single activity-level coding technique eliminates the need for coding each revenue and expense transaction with multiple activity-level codes for different reporting requirements. (See Chapter Six for a discussion of the multiple activity-level coding alternative, which is traditionally used by larger organizations with more complex reporting needs.)

Proposed Unified Chart of Accounts

Table 5.1 shows the UCOA we propose for not-for-profit organizations.

For not-for-profit organizations that have fewer reporting requirements, the UCOA may be too detailed and overly complex. In Table 5.3 three simplified alternatives are presented, each of which is extracted from and consistent with the UCOA. Each could be modified to include additional detail and complexity as the organization grows and changes.

TABLE 5.1

Unified Chart of Accounts for Not-for-Profit Organizations (Cross-Referenced to Selected Reporting Requirements)

Account Number	Account	Sample GAAP Financial Statements[a]	OMB A-122 Cost Principle[b]	United Way Accounts Coding System[c]	Tennessee Policy 03 Templates[d]	Form 990 (Line Number)[e]
	Balance Sheet or Statement of Financial Position Accounts (1000–3999)					
	Asset Accounts (1000–1999)					
	Cash:					
1010	Cash in bank—operating	1	n/a	1000–1099	n/a	45
1020	Cash in bank—payroll	1	n/a	1000–1099	n/a	45
1040	Petty cash	1	n/a	1000–1099	n/a	45
1070	Savings and temporary cash investments	2	n/a	1100–1199	n/a	46
	Accounts receivable:					
1110	Accounts receivable	3	n/a	1200–1299	n/a	47a
1190	Allowance for doubtful accounts	3 (contra)	n/a	1200–1299	n/a	47b
	Contributions receivable:					
1210	Pledges receivable	4	n/a	1300–1399	n/a	48a
1220	Allowance for doubtful pledges	4 (contra)	n/a	1300–1399	n/a	48b
1230	Discounts on long-term pledges	n/a (contra)	n/a	1300–1399	n/a	48b
1240	Grants receivable	5	n/a	1300–1399	n/a	49
1250	Discounts on long-term grants	n/a (contra)	n/a	1300–1399	n/a	49
	Other receivables:					
1270	Receivables due from trustees and employees	3	n/a	1200–1299	n/a	50
1280	Other short-term notes and loans receivable	3	n/a	1200–1299	n/a	51a
1290	Allowance for doubtful notes and loans	3 (contra)	n/a	1200–1299	n/a	51b
	Other assets:					
1310	Inventories for sale	6	n/a	1400–1499	n/a	52
1320	Inventories for use	6	n/a	1400–1499	n/a	52
1350	Prepaid expenses and deferred charges	7	n/a	1500–1599	n/a	53
1360	Refundable deposits	7	n/a	1500–1599	n/a	53
	Investments:					
1410	Marketable securities held for operations	8	n/a	1700–1799	n/a	54
1420	Marketable securities held in perpetuity	8	n/a	1700–1799	n/a	54
1430	Land held for investment	n/a	n/a	1800–1899	n/a	55a
1440	Buildings held for investment	n/a	n/a	1800–1899	n/a	55a
1450	Accumulated depreciation for 1440	n/a (contra)	n/a	1800–1899	n/a	55b
1480	Other investments	9	n/a	1900–1999	n/a	56
	Fixed operating assets:					
1510	Land	11	n/a	1800–1899	n/a	57a
1520	Buildings	12	n/a	1800–1899	n/a	57a
1530	Accumulated depreciation for 1520	12 (contra)	n/a	1800–1899	n/a	57b
1540	Leasehold improvements	13	n/a	1800–1899	n/a	57a
1550	Accumulated amortization for 1540	13 (contra)	n/a	1800–1899	n/a	57b
1560	Furniture, fixtures, and equipment	14	n/a	1800–1899	n/a	57a
1570	Accumulated depreciation for 1560	14 (contra)	n/a	1800–1899	n/a	57b
1580	Vehicles	14	n/a	1800–1899	n/a	57a
1590	Accumulated depreciation for 1580	14 (contra)	n/a	1800–1899	n/a	57b
1650	Construction in progress	n/a	n/a	1800–1899	n/a	57a
1700	Other long-term assets	n/a	n/a	1900–1999	n/a	58
1750	Split-interest agreements	n/a	n/a	1900–1999	n/a	58
1800	Collections of works of art and similar assets	n/a	n/a	1900–1999	n/a	58
1900	Funds held in trust by others	n/a	n/a	1900–1999	n/a	58
	Total Assets	15	n/a	sum	n/a	59

(Continued)

TABLE 5.1

Unified Chart of Accounts for Not-for-Profit Organizations (Cross-Referenced to Selected Reporting Requirements) *(Continued)*

Account Number	Account	Sample GAAP Financial Statements[a]	OMB A-122 Cost Principle[b]	United Way Accounts Coding System[c]	Tennessee Policy 03 Templates[d]	Form 990 (Line Number)[e]
	Liability Accounts (2000–2999)					
	Accounts payable and accrued expenses:					
2010	Accounts payable	21	n/a	2000–2099	n/a	60
2110	Accrued expenses—payroll	22	n/a	2100–2199	n/a	60
2120	Accrued expenses—compensated absences	23	n/a	2100–2199	n/a	60
2130	Accrued expenses—payroll taxes	23	n/a	2100–2199	n/a	60
2150	Accrued expenses—other	24	n/a	2100–2199	n/a	60
2200	Grants and allocations payable	n/a	n/a	2200–2399	n/a	61
	Unearned and deferred revenue:					
2310	Control accounts for contracts	25	n/a	n/a	n/a	62
2311	Control account for contract 101	25	n/a	n/a	n/a	62
2312	Control account for contract 102	25	n/a	n/a	n/a	62
2313	Control account for contract 103	25	n/a	n/a	n/a	62
2350	Other unearned and deferred revenue	25	n/a	2500–2599	n/a	62
2400	Refundable advances	n/a	n/a	2500–2599	n/a	65
	Short-term notes and loans payable:					
2510	Loans from trustees and employees	n/a	n/a	2400–2499	n/a	63
2550	Other short-term notes and loans payable	n/a	n/a	2400–2499	n/a	64b
2600	Liabilities related to split-interest agreements	n/a	n/a	2400–2499	n/a	65
	Long-term bonds, notes, and loans payable:					
2710	Bonds payable	n/a	n/a	2600–2699	n/a	64a
2730	Mortgages payable	27	n/a	2600–2699	n/a	64b
2750	Obligations under capital leases	n/a	n/a	2600–2699	n/a	64b
2770	Other long-term bonds, notes, and loans payable	n/a	n/a	2600–2699	n/a	64b
2800	Liabilities for government-owned fixed assets	n/a	n/a	2600–2699	n/a	65
2900	Funds held on behalf of others—custodial	n/a	n/a	2600–2699	n/a	65
	Total Liabilities	28	n/a	sum	n/a	66
	Net Asset Accounts (3000–3999)					
	Unrestricted net assets (3000–3299):					
3010	Available for general activities	29	n/a	3000–3999	n/a	21, 67
3020	Board-designated for special purposes	31	n/a	3000–3999	n/a	21, 67
3030	Board-designated endowment	30	n/a	3000–3999	n/a	21, 67
	Fixed operating assets—net					
3210	Land—held for use, operating	32	n/a	3000–3999	n/a	21, 67
3220	Buildings—held for use, operating	32	n/a	3000–3999	n/a	21, 67
3230	Leasehold improvements	32	n/a	3000–3999	n/a	21, 67
3240	Furniture and equipment	32	n/a	3000–3999	n/a	21, 67
	Total Unrestricted Net Assets	33	n/a	sum	n/a	21, 67
	Temporarily restricted net assets (3300–3899):					
3300	Control accounts for program restrictions	34	req	3000–3999	req (B-58)	21, 68
3310	Control account for restricted grant 204	34	req	3000–3999	req (B-58)	21, 68
3400	Control accounts for fixed asset acquisition restrictions	n/a	req	3000–3900	req (B-58)	21, 68
3500	Control accounts for time restrictions	n/a	req	3000–3900	req (B-58)	21, 68
	Permanently restricted net assets (3900–3999):					
3910	Endowment	35	n/a	3000–3999	n/a	21, 69
	Total Net Assets	36	n/a	sum	n/a	21, 73
	Total Liabilities and Net Assets	37	n/a	sum	n/a	74

(Continued)

TABLE 5.1

Unified Chart of Accounts for Not-for-Profit Organizations (Cross-Referenced to Selected Reporting Requirements) *(Continued)*

Account Number	Account	Sample GAAP Financial Statements[a]	OMB A-122 Cost Principle[b]	United Way Accounts Coding System[c]	Tennessee Policy 03 Templates[d]	Form 990 (Line Number)[e]
	Revenues, Gains, and Other Support (4000–6999)					
	Contributions, Support					
	Contributions received directly (public support):					
4010-XXX	From individuals and small businesses	51	n/a	4000–4099	B-37	1a
4050-XXX	Special fundraising events—gift portion	52	n/a	4200–4299	B-37	1a, 9a
4070-XXX	Legacies and bequests	53	n/a	4300–4399	B-37	1a
4080-XXX	Estimated uncollectible pledges for 4000–4070	51 (contra)	n/a	4000–4099	B-37	1a (contra)
4090-XXX	Discounts on long-term pledges for 4000–4070	n/a (contra)	n/a	4000–4099	B-37	1a (contra)
4110-XXX	Donated services or use of facilities—GAAP	54	match/in-kind	4000–4099	B-38, A-24	part III and 82
4120-XXX	Donated services or use of facilities—non-GAAP[f]		match/in-kind	n/a	B-38, A-24	part III and 82
4130-XXX	Other gifts in kind	55	match/in-kind	4000–4099	B-38, A-24	1a
4140-XXX	Donated works of art and similar assets	n/a	match/in-kind	4000–4099	B-38, A-24	1a
4210-XXX	Corporate and other business grants	51	match/$	4000–4199	B-37	1a
4230-XXX	Foundation and trust grants	51	match/$	4000–4199	B-37	1a
4250-XXX	Grants from other not-for-profit organizations	51	match/$	4000–4199	B-37	1a
4270-XXX	Discounts on long-term pledges for 4210–4250	n/a (contra)	match/$	4000–4199	B-37	1a (contra)
4310-XXX	Contributions from split-interest agreements	n/a	n/a	4000–4199	B-37	1a
4350-XXX	Change in value of split-interest agreements	n/a	n/a	4000–4199	n/a	20
	Contributions received indirectly (allocations):					
4410-XXX	Allocated by federated fundraising organizations	56	match/$	4700–4799	B-37, 42	1b
4420-XXX	From affiliated organizations	n/a	match/$	4500–4599	B-37, 42	1b
4430-XXX	From other fundraising agencies	n/a	match/$	4800–4899	B-37, 42	1b
	Government grants (equivalent to contributions):					
4510-XXX	Grants from government agencies	n/a	grant/match	5500–5999	n/a	1c
4520-XXX	Government grants—federal	n/a	grant/match	5500–5999	B-31, 34	1c
4530-XXX	Government grants—state	n/a	grant/match	5500–5999	B-32, 35	1c
4540-XXX	Government grants—other	n/a	grant/match	5500–5999	B-36	1c
	Other Revenues, Gains					
	Revenue from government agencies:					
5010-XXX	Contracts or fees from government agencies	58	n/a	5000–5499	B-39	2, 93g
5020-XXX	Government contracts—federal	58	grant/match	5000–5499	B-31, 34	2, 93g
5030-XXX	Government contracts—state	58	grant/match	5000–5499	B-32, 35	2, 93g
5040-XXX	Government contracts—other	58	grant/match	5000–5499	B-36	2, 93g
	Revenue from program service sales and fees:					
5110-XXX	Sales of program-related publications	59	n/a	6300–6499	B-39	2, 93a
5150-XXX	Other sales to public, program-related inventory	59	n/a	6300–6499	B-39	2, 93a
5180-XXX	Estimated uncollectible revenue for 5110–5150	59 (contra)	n/a	6200–6399	B-39	2, 93b
5210-XXX	Other program service sales and fees	59	match/$	6200–6299	B-39	2, 93b
5280-XXX	Estimated uncollectible revenue for 5210	59 (contra)	match/$	6200–6399	B-39	2, 93b
	Revenue from dues:					
5310-XXX	Membership and dues—individuals	n/a	n/a	6000–6099	B-40	3, 94
5320-XXX	Assessments and dues—member units	n/a	n/a	6100–6199	B-40	3, 94
	Revenue from investments:					
5410-XXX	Interest on savings and temporary cash investments	60	n/a	6500–6599	B-40	4, 95
5420-XXX	Dividends and interest from securities	61	n/a	6500–6599	B-40	5, 96
5510-XXX	Gross rents	n/a	n/a	6500–6599	B-40	6a, 98
5520-XXX	Related rental expense (deduct from 5510)	n/a (contra)	n/a	6500–6599	B-40	6b, 98
5610-XXX	Other investment income	n/a	n/a	6500–6599	B-40	7

(Continued)

TABLE 5.1

Unified Chart of Accounts for Not-for-Profit Organizations (Cross-Referenced to Selected Reporting Requirements) *(Continued)*

Account Number	Account	Sample GAAP Financial Statements[a]	OMB A-122 Cost Principle[b]	United Way Accounts Coding System[c]	Tennessee Policy 03 Templates[d]	Form 990 (Line Number)[e]
5810-XXX	Unrealized gain (loss) on value of investments	63	n/a	6600–6699	n/a	20
5910-XXX	Gross amount from sale of securities	62	n/a	6600–6699	B-40	8a(A), 100
5920-XXX	Cost and sales expense (deduct from 5910)	62 (contra)	n/a	6600–6699	B-40	8b(A), 100
	Revenue from other sources:					
6110-XXX	Gross amount from sale of other assets	n/a	allowed/appr/35	6600–6699	B-40	8a(B), 100
6120-XXX	Other cost and sales expense (deduct from 6110)	n/a (contra)	allowed/appr/35	6600–6699	B-40	8b(B), 100
6180-XXX	Unrealized gain (loss) on value of other assets	n/a	n/a	6600–6699	n/a	20
6210-XXX	Special events—gross revenue excluding gifts	52	n/a	4200–4299	B-40	9a, 101
6310-XXX	Gross sales to public, non-program-related	n/a	n/a	6400–6499	B-40	10a, 102
6320-XXX	Cost of goods sold (deduct from 6310)	n/a (contra)	n/a	6400–6499	B-40	10b, 102
6510-XXX	Revenue from advertising in publications	64	n/a	6900–6999	B-40	11, 103
6520-XXX	Revenue from affiliations with other entities	64	n/a	6900–6999	B-40	11, 103
6810-XXX	Other revenue	64	n/a	6900–6999	B-40	11, 103
	Net assets released from restriction:[g]					
6910-XXX	Satisfaction of program restrictions	65	n/a	n/a	n/a	n/a
6920-XXX	Satisfaction of fixed asset acquisition restrictions	n/a	n/a	n/a	n/a	n/a
6930-XXX	Expirations of time restrictions	n/a	n/a	n/a	n/a	n/a
	Total Revenues, Gains, and	66	sum	sum	sum	12
	Other Support					
	Object Expense Categories (7000–9999)[h]					
	Grants, Contracts, and Direct Assistance					
7010-XXX	Program-related contracts to other entities	135	not/8	9100–9199	A-15	22
7020-XXX	Grants to other organizations	n/a	allowed	9100–9199	n/a	22
7030-XXX	Allocations to affiliated organizations	n/a	not/8	9100–9199	n/a	22
7040-XXX	Awards and grants to individuals	135	allowed/30	9100–9199	A-15	22
7050-XXX	Specific assistance to individuals	136	allowed/30	8900–8999	A-16	23
	Salaries and Related Expenses					
7210-XXX	Salaries of officers, directors, etc.	121	allowed/6, 28, 45	7000–7099	A-1	25
7220-XXX	Other salaries and wages	121	allowed/6, 28, 45	7000–7099	A-1	26
7310-XXX	Pension plan contributions	122	allowed/6	7100–7199	A-2	27
7320-XXX	Other employee benefits	122	allowed/6, 28, 45	7100–7199	A-2	28
7410-XXX	Payroll taxes, etc.	122	allowed/6	7200–7299	A-2	29
	Other Expenses					
7510-XXX	Professional fundraising fees	124	not/19	8000–8099	n/a	30
7520-XXX	Accounting fees	124	allowed/35	8000–8099	A-4	31
7530-XXX	Legal fees	124	allowed/appr/35	8000–8099	A-4	32
7540-XXX	Other professional fees	124	allowed/35, 40	8000–8099	A-4	43
7550-XXX	Contract temporary help	124	allowed/34	8000–8099	A-4	43
7580-XXX	Donated professional services—GAAP	124	not/match/10	8000–8099	A-24	part III and 82
7590-XXX	Donated professional services—non-GAAP	(not GAAP)	not/match/10	n/a	A-24	part III and 82
7710-XXX	Supplies	125	allowed/24	8100–8199	A-5	33
7720-XXX	Donated materials and supplies	125	not/match/10	8100–8199	A-24	33
7810-XXX	Telephone	126	allowed/5, 22, 23	8200–8299	A-6	34
7910-XXX	Postage and shipping	127	allowed/5, 23, 49, 50	8300–8399	A-7	35
7920-XXX	Mailing services	127	allowed/5	8300–8399	A-7	35
	Occupancy Expenses					
8010-XXX	Rent (including parking space rental)	128	allowed/22, 42, 46	8400–8499	A-8	36
8020-XXX	Utilities	128	allowed/22, 42, 46	8400–8499	A-8	36

(Continued)

TABLE 5.1

Unified Chart of Accounts for Not-for-Profit Organizations (Cross-Referenced to Selected Reporting Requirements) *(Continued)*

Account Number	Account	Sample GAAP Financial Statements[a]	OMB A-122 Cost Principle[b]	United Way Accounts Coding System[c]	Tennessee Policy 03 Templates[d]	Form 990 (Line Number)[e]
8030-XXX	Real estate taxes	128	allowed/22, 42, 46	8400–8499	A-8	36
8040-XXX	Personal property taxes	128	allowed/22, 42, 46	8400–8499	A-8	36
8050-XXX	Interest on mortgages	128	allowed/19	8400–8499	A-8	36
8080-XXX	Donated use of facilities and utilities—GAAP	128	not/match/10	8400–8499	A-24	part III and 82
8090-XXX	Donated use of facilities and utilities—non-GAAP	(not GAAP)	not/match/10	n/a	A-24	part III and 82
8110-XXX	Equipment rental and maintenance	129	allowed/23, 43	8500–8600	A-9	37
8210-XXX	Printing and duplicating	130	allowed/23, 34, 37, 38	8600–8699	A-10	38
8220-XXX	Publications published by others	130	allowed/25, 38	8600–8699	A-10	38
8230-XXX	Publications published by organization	n/a	allowed/appr/37, 20	8600–8699	A-10	38
8310-XXX	Travel	131	allowed/22, 41, 50	8700–8799	A-11	39
8510-XXX	Conferences, conventions, and meetings	132	allowed/24, 25, 49	8800–8899	A-12	40
8610-XXX	Interest—general	133	not/19	9200–9299	A-13	41
8650-XXX	Depreciation—allowable	137	allowed/9	9500–9599	A-17	42
8660-XXX	Depreciation—not allowable	137	not/9	9500–9599	A-17	42
8710-XXX	Insurance—excluding employee-related	134	allowed/4, 18	9300–9399	A-14	43
8810-XXX	Membership dues	138	allowed/26	9400–9499	A-18	43
8820-XXX	Staff development	138	allowed/49	9400–9499	A-18	43
9010-XXX	List rental	n/a	not/19	9400–9499	A-18	43
9020-XXX	Outside computer services	n/a	allowed/35	8000–8099	A-18	43
9100-XXX	Bad debt expense	n/a	not/2	9400–9499	n/a	43
9110-XXX	Sales taxes	n/a	not/47	9400–9499	n/a	43
9120-XXX	Unrelated business income taxes (UBIT)	n/a	not/47	9400–9499	n/a	43
9150-XXX	Other taxes	n/a	not/47	9400–9499	n/a	43
9210-XXX	Fines, penalties, and judgments—organization	n/a	allowed/appr/14	9400–9499	A-18	43
9230-XXX	Incorporation and other organizational expenses	n/a	allowed/appr/27	9400–9499	A-18	43
9250-XXX	Advertising	n/a	allowed/1	9400–9499	A-18	43
9290-XXX	Contingency provisions	n/a	not/7	9400–9499	n/a	43
9300-XXX	Other expenses	138	allowed/appr	9400–9499	A-18	43
	Total Functional Expenses	146	sum	sum	A-19	44
9810-XXX	Capital purchases—land	capitalized	allowed/appr/13	LB&E	A-20	capitalized
9820-XXX	Capital purchases—building	capitalized	allowed/appr/13	LB&E	A-20	capitalized
9830-XXX	Capital purchases—equipment	capitalized	allowed/appr/13	LB&E	A-20	capitalized
9840-XXX	Capital purchases—vehicles	capitalized	allowed/appr/13	LB&E	A-20	capitalized
9910-XXX	Payments to affiliates	n/a	not/00	9600–9699	n/a	16

Note: Other account number cross-reference tables in this manual: Table 8.5—Allocation Variables by Object Expense Category (Chapter Eight); Table 13.1—Tennessee Policy 03 Uniform Reporting Alignment Reference

Table: *Schedule A, Part 1, and Table 13.2—Tennessee Policy 03 Uniform Reporting Alignment Reference Table: Schedule B, Part 1 (Chapter Thirteen); Table 14.1—Standard Corporate and Foundation Grant Budget and Report Format (Chapter Fourteen).*

Key: *contra = amounts are to be deducted from the designated account; n/a = not applicable; req = use of this account is required by the reporting standard (line number in the reporting standard is indicated in parentheses); GAAP = generally accepted accounting principles; match, match/$, match/in-kind = amounts in the accounts qualify as matching funds per OMB Circular A-122; allowed = allowable for reimbursement per OMB Circular A-122; not = not allowable for reimbursement per OMB Circular A-122; appr = subject to approval by the funding agency; LB&E = fixed assets (land, buildings, and equipment).*

[a]*Reference number in the sample GAAP financial statements (see Chapter Eleven, Exhibits 11.1–11.4).*

[b]*Cost principle number in OMB Circular A-122.*

[c]*Account number in United Way of America Accounts Coding System (see Chapter Fifteen).*

[d]*Schedule and line item number in Tennessee Policy 03 forms and templates (see Chapter Thirteen, Exhibits 13.1–13.3).*

[e]*Line number on IRS Form 990 (see Chapter Twelve and Resource A).*

[f]*Used for donated services or use of facilities that are acceptable in-kind matching funds under government contracts but that are not allowed for GAAP reporting.*

[g]*Accounts used for year-end adjustments for GAAP reporting (see Chapter Eleven, Exhibit 11.2).*

[h]*For definitions of object expense categories, see Resource B.*

TABLE 5.2

Revenue and Expense Coding by Activity

Activity Code	Activity	Sample GAAP Financial Statements[a]		OMB A-122 Cost Principle[b]	United Way Accounts Coding System[c]	Tennessee Policy 03 Templates[d]	Form 990 (Line Number)[e]
		Exhibit 11.2	Exhibit 11.3				
XXXX-100 to 199	Program department A	81A	139A	n/a	001-899	n/a	IIIa
XXXX-200 to 299	Program department B	82A	139B	n/a	001-899	n/a	IIIb
XXXX-300 to 399	Program department C	83A	139C	n/a	001-899	n/a	IIIc
XXXX-400 to 449	Program department D	84A	139D	n/a	001-899	n/a	IIId
XXXX-450 to 499	Other program service activities	84A	139D	n/a	001-899	n/a	13, IIB, IIIe, IIIf
	Total program services	85A	139E	n/a	sum	sum	sum
XXXX-500 to 699	Management and general department	86A	139F	varies	900-949	varies	14, IIC
XXXX-510	Management and general department—general	86A	139F	allowed/indirect	900-949	A-22	14, IIC
XXXX-520	Management and general department—unallowable (A-122)	86A	139F	not/12, 36, 41	900-949	n/a	14, IIC
XXXX-610	Management and general special event production	52 (contra)	n/a	not/00	900-949	n/a	9b
XXXX-620	Management and general special event promotion	86A	n/a	not/00	900-949	n/a	9b
XXXX-700 to 899	Fundraising department	87A	139G	not/19	900-949	n/a	15, IID
XXXX-900 to 999	Cost pools	internal	allocated	use permitted	allocated	optional	allocated
XXXX-910	Central services cost pool	internal	allocated	use permitted	allocated	optional	allocated
XXXX-920	Common cost pool by account	internal	allocated	use permitted	allocated	optional	allocated
XXXX-930	Common cost pool—other	internal	allocated	use permitted	allocated	optional	allocated
XXXX-980	Capital or fixed asset purchases pool	internal	capitalized	use permitted	capitalized	optional	capitalized

Note: Four Xs (XXXX-) take the place of the account number in the Activity Code column.

[a]*Reference number in the sample GAAP financial statements (see Chapter Eleven, Exhibits 11.2 and 11.3).*

[b]*Cost principle number in OMB Circular A-122.*

[c]*Function code number in United Way of America Accounts Coding System (see Chapter Fifteen).*

[d]*Schedule and line item number in Tennessee Policy 03 forms and templates (see Chapter Thirteen, Exhibits 13.1–13.3).*

[e]*Line number on IRS Form 990 (see Chapter Twelve and Resource A).*

TABLE 5.3

Simplified Charts of Accounts for Smaller Organizations (Cross-Referenced to Form 990 and Unified Chart of Accounts)

Level One (All Volunteer, Cash Basis)		Level Two (Salaried Staff, Cash Basis)		Level Three (Salaried Staff, Accrual Basis)		Cross-References	
Account Number	Account	Account Number	Account	Account Number	Account	Form 990 (Line Number)[a]	Unified Chart of Accounts (Account Number)[b]
Asset Accounts			*Asset Accounts*		*Asset Accounts*		*Asset Accounts*
1010	Cash in bank—operating	1010	Cash in bank—operating	1010	Cash in bank—operating	45	1010
1070	Savings and temporary cash investments	1070	Savings and temporary cash investments	1070	Savings and cash investments	46	1070
				1110	Accounts receivable	47	1110
				1560	Furniture, fixtures, and equipment	57a	1560
				1570	Accumulated depreciation for 1560	57b	1570
	Total assets		*Total assets*		*Total assets*	59	sum
	Liability Accounts		*Liability Accounts*		*Liability Accounts*		*Liability Accounts*
	[None, cash basis]		[None, cash basis]	2010	Accounts payable	60	2010
	Net Asset Accounts		*Net Asset Accounts*		*Net Asset Accounts*		*Net Asset Accounts*
3010	Unrestricted, available for general activities	3010	Unrestricted, available for general activities	3010	Unrestricted, available for general activities	67	3010
				3210	Unrestricted, furniture and equipment—	67	3210
		3310	Temporarily restricted for activity 120	3310	Temporarily restricted for activity 120	68	3310
		3320	Temporarily restricted activity 220	3320	Temporarily restricted activity 220	68	3320
	Total net assets		*Total net assets*		*Total net assets*	73	sum
	Total liabilities and net assets		*Total liabilities and net assets*		*Total liabilities and net assets*	74	sum

(Continued)

TABLE 5.3

Simplified Charts of Accounts for Smaller Organizations (Cross-Referenced to Form 990 and Unified Chart of Accounts) (Continued)

Account Number	Level One (All Volunteer, Cash Basis) Account	Account Number	Level Two (Salaried Staff, Cash Basis) Account	Account Number	Level Three (Salaried Staff, Accrual Basis) Account	Cross-References Form 990 (Line Number)[a]	Cross-References Unified Chart of Accounts (Account Number)[b]
	Revenue Accounts		*Revenue Accounts*		*Revenue Accounts*	*Revenue Accounts*	
4010	Contributions from individuals	4010	Contributions from individuals	4010	Contributions from individuals	1a	4010
		4230	Foundation grants	4230	Foundation grants	1a	4230
		4510	Government grants	4510	Government grants	1c	4510
5210	Program service fees and sales	5210	Program service fees and sales	5210	Program service fees and sales	2	5210
				5310	Membership dues—individuals	3	5310
5410	Interest on savings and temporary cash investments	5410	Interest on savings and temporary cash investments	5410	Interest on savings and temporary cash investments	4	5410
6810	Other revenue	6810	Other revenue	6810	Other revenue	11	6810
	Total revenue		*Total revenue*		*Total revenue*	12	sum
	Personnel Expense Accounts		*Personnel Expense Accounts*		*Personnel Expense Accounts*	*Personnel Expense Accounts*	
	[None, all volunteer]	7210	Salaries of officers, directors, etc.	7210	Salaries of officers, directors, etc.	25	7210
		7220	Other salaries and wages	7220	Other salaries and wages	26	7220
		7310	Pension plan contributions	7310	Pension plan contributions	27	7310
		7320	Other employee benefits	7320	Other employee benefits	28	7320
		7410	Payroll taxes	7410	Payroll taxes	29	7410
			Total payroll		*Total payroll*	sum	sum
		7540	Professional fees	7540	Professional fees	43	7540
			Total personnel expenses		*Total personnel expenses*	sum	sum

Nonpersonnel Expense Accounts		Nonpersonnel Expense Accounts		Nonpersonnel Expense Accounts		
7710	Supplies	7710	Supplies	33	7710	Supplies
7810	Telephone	7810	Telephone	34	7810	Telephone
7910	Postage and shipping	7910	Postage and shipping	35	7910	Postage and shipping
	[Office space donated]	8010	Occupancy	36	8010	Occupancy
8110	Equipment rental and maintenance	8110	Equipment rental and maintenance	37	8110	Equipment rental and maintenance
8210	Printing and publications	8210	Printing and publications	38	8210	Printing and publications
8310	Travel	8310	Travel	39	8310	Travel
		8510	Conferences and meetings	40	8510	Conferences and meetings
		8610		41	8610	Interest
	[Capital purchases not capitalized]	8650	[Capital purchases not capitalized]	42	8650	Depreciation
9300	Other nonpersonnel expenses	9300	Other nonpersonnel expenses	43	9300	Other nonpersonnel expenses
	[Capital purchases not capitalized]	9830	[Capital purchases not capitalized]	n/a	9830	Capital purchases—equipment
	Total nonpersonnel expenses		Total nonpersonnel expenses	sum		Total nonpersonnel expenses
	Total expenses		Total expenses	44	sum	Total expenses
	14 accounts		26 accounts			35 accounts
						UCOA has 151 accounts

[a]Line number on IRS Form 990 (see Chapter Twelve and Resource A).

[b]See Table 5.1.

Chapter 6

Activity-Level Accounting and Reporting for Revenue and Expenses

ACTIVITY-LEVEL ACCOUNTING focuses on identifying and linking all costs associated with one or more activities (program, service, and so on) of the organization. It focuses on the *purpose* for which resources are provided and expenses are incurred. It helps management make prudent decisions about the use of resources by measuring the efficiency and effectiveness of each *activity* that incurs costs. It is an invaluable management tool for program evaluation, expansion, reduction, elimination, or merger. It is a useful tool not only for management but also for resource providers, who can use it to evaluate whether the organization deserves continued or additional support. Limited resources coupled with high expectations regarding accomplishments make it critical to change the way not-for-profit organizations account for costs at the activity level and the way they deploy their resources.

Activity-level accounting is a two-dimensional system. The first dimension consists of accounts that identify the standard revenue and expense classifications, such as contributions, fees, or investment income, and standard expense classifications, such as salaries, occupancy, or telephone service. The second dimension identifies the purpose for which resources were received or expended. This system is illustrated in Figure 6.1.

An activity is a specific service, purpose, or cost objective for which an organization needs a separate measurement of expense or revenue. It is the lowest (most specific) level of detail desired or the lowest grouping of revenues and expenses required by the organization's accounting system. It is the most detailed level for assessing an organization's outputs (results and accomplishments) against its inputs (efforts).

The number of activities to be tracked is largely at the discretion of management. GAAP requires only a distinction between program services, management and general, and fundraising expenses. More detailed

FIGURE 6.1

Functional-Basis Financial Package of a Not-for-Profit Human Service Organization

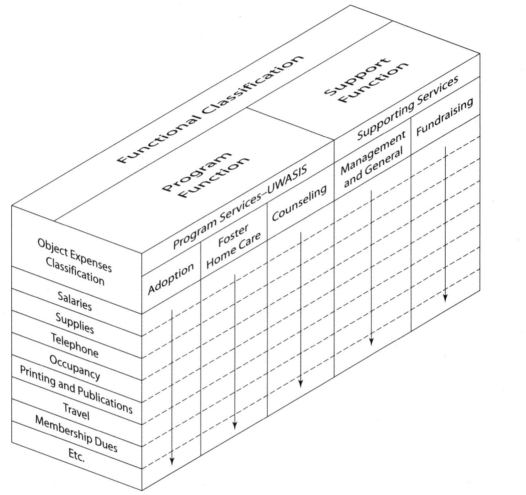

Source: *United Way of America,* Accounting and Financial Reporting: A Guide for United Ways and Not-for-Profit Human Service Organizations, *2nd ed. (Alexandria, Va.: United Way of America, 1989), p. 159.* Duplicated by permission, United Way of America.

breakdowns should be based on the information that management needs in order to carry out its managerial and fiduciary duties. In addition, some funders may require information about activities subsidized by their funds.

Activity-level accounting entails activity-level coding and grouping of all revenue and expense transactions. Multilevel revenue and expense reporting consists of selecting and grouping those activities required for each report and aggregating activity-level accounting information accordingly.

Activity reports showing how each employee actually spent work time are the basis of allocation of salaries to federally funded grants. It is in this connection that we discuss activity-level accounting, activity-level transaction coding, and activity-level employee time and effort reporting.

Activity-Level Transaction Coding

Financial transactions to be recorded in the organization's accounting system must be coded at a level of detail such that all required internal and external reports can be prepared from a single monthly or end-of-period trial balance. One should not have to go back to supporting documentation in the bookkeeping records for more detailed breakdowns required for particular reports. For purposes of this guide the activity level is defined by the level of detail required for internal and external reports. Cost pools are maintained at the activity level and related costs are allocated among benefiting activities to determine the total costs of each activity.

Nonprofit Accounts Coding System Single Activity-Level Coding Technique

When designing its chart of accounts an organization selects the accounts (and account numbers) it will need as well as the *activity codes* it will need for coding revenue and expense transactions. As explained in Chapter Five, the three-digit activity code appended to revenue and expense account numbers (for instance, the "220" in "7120-220") designates the specific activity that earned revenue or incurred expense. Revenue and expenses are accounted for by coding revenue and expense transactions at the activity level. In the single activity-level coding technique (used for smaller, less complex organizations), the activity level is the level of detail at which the accounting system records information on (1) specific grants and other sources of revenue, (2) the way employees, consultants, and volunteers spend their time, and (3) utilization of other resources, such as equipment, space, supplies, telephone service, and so on. (Larger, more complex organizations use the traditional multiple activity-level coding alternative, described later in this chapter.)

Revenue and Expense Activity Code Tables

To use the NACS single activity-level coding technique, an organization needs to set up a *revenue and expense activity code table* with the activity codes that are valid for its accounting system. This table cross-references an organization's activity codes to various reporting requirements, such as net asset control accounts; functions, departments, and programs; donor restrictions and net asset classifications; and projects, grants, or cost centers.

Table 6.1 is an example of a revenue and expense activity code table. (Table 6.1 contains the activity codes used in the various sample

TABLE 6.1

Revenue and Expense Activity Code Table

Activity	Activity Code	Control Account	Function or Department	Funding Source	Restriction	Project, Grant, or Cost Center
Adult center	100	3010	Program A		unrestricted	general
Congregate meals	120	2311	Program A	Commission on Aging	unrestricted	contract 101
Nutrition education	130	2312	Program A	Commission on Aging	unrestricted	contract 102
Residential services	200	3010	Program B		unrestricted	general
Meals at home	220	2311	Program B	Commission on Aging	unrestricted	contract 101
Rehab center	300	3010	Program C		unrestricted	general
Rehab services	320	2313	Program C	Department of Health	unrestricted	contract 103
Seniors project	420	3310	Program D	XYZ Foundation	temporary	grant 204
Executive office	510	3010	Management and general[a]		unrestricted	general
Fundraising	710	3010	Fundraising		unrestricted	general
MIS	910	n/a	Central service pool		n/a	n/a
Common cost pools by account	920	n/a	n/a		n/a	n/a

[a]*Management and general is the recommended indirect or administrative cost pool option.*

financial reports in this guide.) This sample table cross-references the activity codes to a few selected reporting requirements. However, there is no limit to the number of internal and external reporting requirements that can be included in an organization's revenue and expense activity code table.

All not-for-profit organizations that file Form 990 have at least three basic activities: (1) program, (2) fundraising, (3) management and general. Based on this premise three simplified alternative activity coding systems for smaller organizations are presented in Table 6.2. Each of these alternatives is extracted from and consistent with the UCOA used in this manual. Each could be modified to include additional detail and complexity as organizational growth and particular funding sources may require. In many

TABLE 6.2

Simplified Activity Coding System for Smaller Organizations (Cross-Referenced to Form 990 and Unified Chart of Accounts)

| | Level One | | Level Two | | Level Three | | Cross-References | |
| | | | | | | | Form 990 (Line Number) | Unified Chart of Accounts (Account Number) |
Code Number	Activity	Code Number	Activity	Code Number	Activity		
100	Program A	100	Program A	100	Program A	IIIa, IIB	100
		120	Special project A, donor restricted 3310	120	Special project A, donor restricted 3310	IIIa, IIB	120
200	Program B	200	Program B	200	Program B	IIIb, IIB	200
		220	Special project B, donor restricted 3320	220	Special project B, donor restricted 3320	IIIb, IIB	220
510	Management and general	510	Management and general	510	Management and general	14/IIC	510
710	Fundraising	710	Fundraising	710	Fundraising	15/IID	710
		920	Common cost pool by account	920	Common cost pool by account	n/a [allocated]	920
				980	Capital purchases pool	n/a	980
	4 activities		7 activities		8 activities	up to 1,000 activities	

cases the coding system requirements are determined by the sources of funding that the organization typically receives. For example, organizations that are solely supported by membership dues or tuition will have no need to code expenses to specific restricted revenue sources. Other organizations that receive foundation grants or disburse scholarships may need to associate expenses with specific restricted revenue sources.

The revenue and expense activity code table (Table 6.1) indicates which activities to include when extracting data from the period-ending adjusted functionalized trial balance report for use in various other reports, such as revenue and expense reports, profit and loss statements, budgets, and budget-to-actual (BTA) comparison reports. Note that allocation of central service and common cost pool expenses is performed when the trial balance report is produced. The following list shows which activity codes to include for various other reports.

Subject of Report	Activity Code to Include
Program department A	100, 120, 130
Commission on Aging (funding source)	120, 130, 220

Contract 101	120, 220
Adult center	100
Restricted grant 204	420
All program services	100–420
Management and general function	510
Fundraising	710

When revenue and expense reports cannot be produced with existing activity codes, some activity codes are split into two or more codes, as needed, to meet reporting requirements. For example, when two departments can share grant funds, two activity codes would be needed for that grant, as is the case with contract 101 in Table 6.1.

Multiple Activity-Level Coding Alternative

A two-dimensional account coding system with accounts and activities is required to accommodate the reporting requirements in this guide. An organization can achieve activity-level accounting and reporting through the use of the NACS single activity-level coding technique or a multiple activity-level coding alternative.

Larger organizations usually have more complex accounting and reporting requirements. Thus they usually need to use the traditional multiple activity-level coding alternative and have separate codes for such things as department, project, funding source, and restriction in their account coding system. For example, a larger organization might establish the following four-part multiple activity-level coding system (XX-XX-XX-X) rather than use the NACS single activity-level coding technique (XXX):

- Part 1: Department codes

    01—Program A

    02—Program B

    03—Program C

    04—Program D

    21—Management and general

    31—Fundraising

    71—Management information systems central service cost pool

    91—Account cost pools

- Part 2: Project codes

  01—General

  11—Contract 101

  12—Contract 102

  13—Contract 103

  14—Project 204

- Part 3: Funding source codes

  01—General fund

  41—Commission on Aging

  42—Department of Health

  43—XYZ Foundation

- Part 4: Restriction codes

  1—Unrestricted

  2—Temporarily restricted

  3—Permanently restricted

All together, there are 480 possible combinations of activity-level coding in this four-part scheme. There could be even more departments, projects, and funding sources for very large organizations, and the number of possible combinations could be even greater. In the simple illustration in this guide, only twelve activity-level combinations are valid. In larger organizations there could be several hundred valid combinations. The following is a cross-reference of the NACS activity codes in Table 6.1 to the four-part multiple activity-level codes.

NACS Activity Code	Corresponding Four-Part Code
100	01-01-01-1
120	01-11-41-1
130	01-12-41-1
200	02-01-01-1
220	01-12-41-1
300	03-01-01-1
320	01-13-42-1
420	04-14-43-2
510	21-01-01-1

710	31-01-01-1
910	71-00-01-0
920	91-00-01-0

Either system can meet the same internal and external reporting requirements. If all 480 combinations were to be treated as valid and actually needed for coding revenue and expense transactions, an organization could either use the four-part multiple activity-level coding scheme or establish 480 NACS activity codes with a corresponding activity code table.

The NACS account coding system, with its single activity-level coding technique, yields codes that are seven digits long (XXXX-XXX). Codes in the four-part system would be eleven digits long (XXXX-XX-XX-XX-X). (In both cases the first four digits consist of the account number.) Some multiple activity-level account coding systems use as many as fifteen or twenty digits to accommodate the accounting and reporting needs of the organization.

Multiple activity-level coding systems have certain advantages, especially for larger organizations. They do not require changes to activity code tables as is required in a single activity-level coding system every time a new department-project-source combination is used. If the organization's software has a report-generating capability, it may be easier to program with a multiple activity-level coding system. Also, an organization can have better control over which combinations would be valid for such things as staff time reporting and distribution of expenses among activities.

Whether a not-for-profit organization uses a multiple activity-level coding system or the single activity-level coding technique illustrated in this guide, the concepts for a functionalized trial balance report from which all the internal and external reports can be produced still apply.

Chart of Accounts and Revenue and Expense Budgeting and Reporting

It is important to understand how a two-dimensional coding system such as NACS, with its account numbers and activity codes, relates to internal and external revenue and expense budgets and reports. An organization's NACS activity codes enable it to group activities to produce revenue and expense reports by

- Net asset control account (for tracking net asset balances related to specific grants and projects)

- Function, department, or program

- Project, grant, or cost center
- Specific activity or service
- Donor restriction
- Performance objective or service statistic category

Revenue and expense reports generally present a list of revenues followed by a list of related expenses and end with the excess or deficit of total revenues over total expenses. In the business world such reports are called *P&L reports* (profit and loss reports); in this guide such reports are referred to as *R&E reports* (revenue and expense reports) instead. Many business accounting software systems include the capability to produce P&L reports by project, department, customer, product, and so on. An organization that uses one of these business software systems can use the P&L report option to produce not-for-profit R&E reports. (See Chapter Sixteen.)

R&E reports of not-for-profit organizations are designed by specifying combinations of revenue and expense accounts and activity codes. In an R&E report accounts or combinations of accounts are usually represented by rows, and the names of the accounts are listed down the left side of the report. When useful, the account number or code is included next to the account name. Activities, or combinations of activities grouped into categories (such as departments or grants), are usually represented by columns with descriptors of the activities or groups of activities as column headings across the top. When useful, the NACS activity code or grant number is included under the column descriptor. If there are two or more columns (representing two or more functions, departments, grants, projects, cost centers, or activities), the report usually includes a total column down the right side.

The revenue and expense sections of the end-of-period functionalized trial balance report list every *active* account down the left side and every *valid* activity code across the top. (All of the sample reports in this manual that present revenue or expense information extract the data needed from the functionalized trial balance report. See Chapter Seven.)

Many R&E reports to resource providers and reports used internally include BTA comparisons. For resource providers the budget approved for each grant is compared with actual expenses for each grant. For internal management purposes BTA reports may be needed for each activity, function and department, project and grant, and for the overall organization. When preparing budgets for resource providers or for internal purposes, a not-for-profit organization should always use the revenue and expense accounts and activity codes in its chart of accounts. Otherwise, the accounting system will not be able to produce BTA reports. This is especially true when budgeting for salaries. The process described in Chapter Nine and Resource D for distributing salaries among activity codes can be adapted for use in budgeting for salaries.

Budgeting

This guide is *not* about budgeting, which is an important enough topic to warrant a separate manual of its own. A number of good books on budgeting are available (see the Bibliography for several listings). However, because of the close connection between the processes of budgeting, accounting, and reporting, a few words about budgeting are in order.

In not-for-profit organizations, small or large, budgeting is one of the most important functions of management. A well-crafted budget tied to the organization's objectives is usually a sure sign of the agency's maturity and sophistication. Thus investment of time and resources in preparing budgets may pay high dividends later.

What is budgeting? In short, budgeting is about prudent deployment of scarce resources in pursuit of an organization's mission, goals, and specific objectives for a specific time period. Budgeting is especially important to not-for-profit organizations because it concerns the use of donated resources—other people's money—for public benefit.

The single most important element in budgeting is *planning*—planning for the accomplishment of specific objectives set by the organization's board within a specific time frame. A second critical element is use of the budget as a tool to control the financial activities of the organization. Even the best made budget is of little value if not used regularly to monitor the finances of the organization over the budget's fiscal period. The *Financial and Accounting Guide for Not-for-Profit Organizations* provides useful observations on this subject:

> A budget is a "plan of action." It represents the organization's blueprint
> for coming months, or years expressed in monetary terms. This means
> the organization must have specific goals before it can prepare a budget.
> If it doesn't know where it is going, it is going to be very difficult for the
> organization to do any meaningful planning. All too often the process is
> reversed and it is in the process of preparing the budget that the goals are
> determined.
>
> The first function of a budget is to record, in monetary terms, what
> the realistic goals or objectives of the organization are for the coming year
> (or years). The budget is the financial plan of action that results from the
> board's decisions as to the program for the future.

TABLE 6.3

Sample Budget by Activity

Account Number	Revenue or Expense	Program A General (100)	Program A Project A (120)	Program B General (200)	Program B Project B (220)	Total Program	Management and General (510)	Fundraising (710)	Total Budget
	Revenue								
4010	Contributions from individuals					0		140,000	140,000
4230	Foundation grants			12,000		12,000			12,000
4510	Government grants		25,000			25,000			25,000
5210	Program service fees and sales	75,000				75,000			75,000
5410	Interest on savings and temporary cash investments					0	8,000		8,000
6810	Other revenue					0			0
	Total revenue	75,000	25,000	0	12,000	112,000	8,000	140,000	260,000
	Personnel expenses								
7210	Salaries of officers, directors, etc.	15,000	8,000	5,000		28,000	6,000	8,000	42,000
7220	Other salaries and wages	60,000	13,000	18,000	7,000	98,000	3,500	6,000	107,500
	Activity salaries and wages as percent of total	50.2%	14.0%	15.4%	4.7%	84.3%	6.4%	9.4%	100.0%
7310	Pension plan contributions[a]	7,500	2,100	2,300	700	12,600	950	1,400	14,950
7330	Other employee benefits[a]	3,750	1,050	1,150	350	6,300	475	700	7,475
7410	Payroll taxes, etc.[a]	6,000	1,680	1,840	560	10,080	760	1,120	11,960
	Total payroll	92,251	25,830	28,290	8,610	154,981	11,685	17,220	183,886
7540	Professional fees						3,500		3,500
	Total personnel expenses	92,251	25,830	28,290	8,610	154,981	15,185	17,220	187,386

Nonpersonnel expenses

Code									
7710	Supplies	6,000	1,200	1,600	200	9,000	800	600	10,400
7810	Telephone	1,800	500	700	200	3,200	800	1,200	5,200
7910	Postage and shipping	500	200	300	100	1,100	400	1,200	2,700
8010	Rent	9,000	2,300	2,500	900	14,700	1,200	1,100	17,000
8110	Equipment rental and maintenance	4,300	1,000	1,200	500	7,000	600	700	8,300
8210	Printing and publications	3,600	1,500	2,500	500	8,100	800	1,400	10,300
8310	Travel	1,800	1,000	1,200	300	4,300	900	600	5,800
8510	Conferences and meetings	600		600		1,200	1,500	400	3,100
9300	Other nonpersonnel expenses	2,000	1,000	200	200	3,400	200	200	3,800
	Total nonpersonnel expenses	29,600	8,700	10,800	2,900	52,000	7,200	7,400	66,600
	Total expenses	121,851	34,530	39,090	11,510	206,981	22,385	24,620	253,986

F.Y. 20X2 Overall Cash-Based Budget Excess (Deficit) 6,014

Note: *Three-digit activity codes are shown in parentheses in column headings where applicable.*

[a]Percentages of salaries and wages, based on prior-year figures, are used to compute budget figures for pension plan contributions (100%), other employee benefits (5%), and payroll taxes (8%).

The second function of a budget is to provide a tool to monitor the financial activities throughout the year. Properly used, the budget can provide a benchmark or comparison point that will be an early warning to the board that their financial goals may not be met. For a budget to provide this type of information and control, four elements must be present:

1. *The budget must be well-conceived and have been prepared or approved by the board.*

2. *The budget must be broken down into periods corresponding to the periodic financial statements.*

3. *Financial statements must be prepared on a timely basis throughout the year and a comparison made to the budget with explanations of significant deviations (or lack of deviation where one might be expected).*

4. *The board must be prepared to take action where the comparison in Step 3 indicates a problem.[1]*

It is essential that not-for-profit organizations use the same chart of accounts for budgeting and accounting—preferably the UCOA presented in this manual. We recommend activity (program-functional) budgeting—in order to allow for comparison to the activity accounting and reporting discussed in this chapter and elsewhere throughout this guide. Activity budgeting will facilitate line-by-line and item-by-item comparison of actual revenue and expenditures to the budgeted figures. Table 6.3 shows a simple example of a budget by activity for a smaller organization. We also recommend the ten-step program-planning and budgeting process presented in Figure 6.2 (excerpted from the Support Center for Nonprofit Management's training material on budgeting).

Key Internal Controls

For accurate tracking of revenues and expenses and for proper monitoring of an organization's adherence to its budget, a system of sound *internal controls* is essential. Indeed, the integrity of an accounting and financial reporting system overall depends largely on the soundness of its internal controls. Even the best accounting system would collapse sooner or later if adequate internal controls were not enforced. Not-for-profit organizations have a responsibility to ensure that adequate internal controls are set up to protect their solvency and to reduce opportunities for fraud to an absolute minimum.

Internal control is a set of procedures and cross-checks that, in the absence of collusion, minimize the likelihood of misappropriation of assets

FIGURE 6.2

The Budget Process

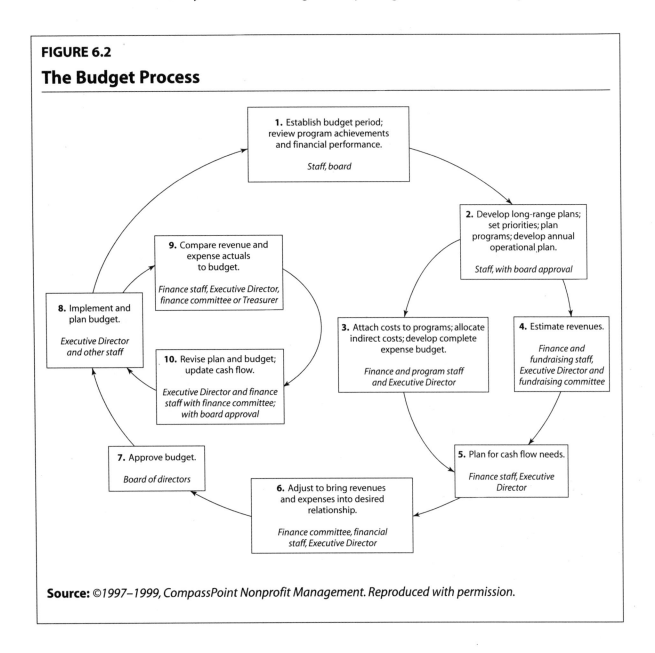

1. Establish budget period; review program achievements and financial performance.

Staff, board

2. Develop long-range plans; set priorities; plan programs; develop annual operational plan.

Staff, with board approval

3. Attach costs to programs; allocate indirect costs; develop complete expense budget.

Finance and program staff and Executive Director

4. Estimate revenues.

Finance and fundraising staff, Executive Director and fundraising committee

5. Plan for cash flow needs.

Finance staff, Executive Director

6. Adjust to bring revenues and expenses into desired relationship.

Finance committee, financial staff, Executive Director

7. Approve budget.

Board of directors

8. Implement and plan budget.

Executive Director and other staff

9. Compare revenue and expense actuals to budget.

Finance staff, Executive Director, finance committee or Treasurer

10. Revise plan and budget; update cash flow.

Executive Director and finance staff with finance committee; with board approval

Source: ©1997–1999, CompassPoint Nonprofit Management. Reproduced with permission.

or misstatement of accounts and that maximize the likelihood of detecting any such misappropriation or misstatement. Good internal controls, although no guarantee against embezzlement, may aid in its prompt discovery. Among the most important are the following specific types of basic internal controls that emphasize physical control over the organization's assets (mostly cash): control over receipts, control over receivables, control over investments, control over cash disbursements, insurance and bonding, safekeeping of records and cash on hand, and control for meeting the requirements of donors and funders.

The *Financial and Accounting Guide for Not-for-Profit Organizations* lists eleven rules of internal control applicable to most not-for-profit organizations:

1. Prenumbered receipts should be issued for all money when it is first received. A duplicated copy should be accounted for, and a comparison eventually made between the aggregate of the receipts issued and the amount deposited in the bank.

2. Cash collections should be under the control of two people whenever possible, particularly when it is not practicable to issue receipts.

3. Two people should open all mail and make a list of all receipts received each day. This list should subsequently be compared with the bank deposit by someone not handling the money. Receipts in the form of checks should be restrictively endorsed promptly upon receipt.

4. All receipts should be deposited in the bank, intact and on a timely basis.

5. All disbursements should be made by check, and supporting documentation (which would include an appropriate "approval" procedure and evidence of receipt of goods or services) should be kept for each disbursement.

6. If the treasurer or check signer is also the person who writes checks, two signatures should be required on all checks.

7. A person other than the bookkeeper should receive bank statements directly from the bank and should reconcile them promptly; the reconciliation should be reviewed at a higher level, and evidence of such review (signature and date) should be made.

8. Someone other than the bookkeeper should authorize all write-offs of accounts receivable or other assets.

9. Marketable securities should be kept in a bank safe deposit box or held by a bank as custodian.

10. Fixed asset records should be maintained, and an inventory taken periodically.

11. Excess cash should be maintained in a separate bank account. Withdrawals from this account should require two signatures.[2]

Chapter 7

Functionalized Trial Balance Report

REGARDLESS OF THE METHOD used, the objective of the financial reporting system is to end up with a single functionalized trial balance report from which the not-for-profit organization can prepare all of its period-ending reports. In this chapter we present an example of how a functionalized trial balance report is developed and how spreadsheet software can be used during the report preparation cycle. We have also included an example of a simplified functionalized trial balance report for smaller organizations.

To prepare the various sample financial reports in this guide uniformly and consistently, a sample *functionalized trial balance report* has been developed using the accounts in the UCOA (see Chapter Five, Table 5.1), the twelve sample activity codes in the Revenue and Expense Activity Code Table (see Chapter Six, Table 6.1), and an assumption that the organization has ten employees and an annual budget of $750,000. These illustrations may be too simplified for the accounting, reporting, and software requirements of midsize and large not-for-profit organizations with budgets of over $1 million. Such organizations will have significantly more employees for payroll processing and will have more activities whose revenues and expenses will need to be tracked.

The sample functionalized trial balance report was developed in several steps:

1. Salaries can represent 50 percent or more of the expenses of not-for-profit organizations. In addition, salaries can provide the basis for allocation of many or most of the other items of expense. Thus the first step in developing the sample trial balance was to establish amounts for salaries (account numbers 7210 and 7220 in the UCOA and the trial balance) and to distribute these amounts by the twelve sample activity codes. The salary figures (by activity code) found in the trial balance were established by

developing a sample list of ten employees along with their individual salaries and by developing a procedure for determining how each of them distributed their time among the twelve areas represented by the twelve activity codes. (The details of this step in the process are provided in Chapter Nine and Resource D.)

2. The second step established both direct and common costs for all of the other expense categories—distributed by the twelve activity codes (see Chapter Eight for definitions of direct costs and common costs). Expense amounts directly identifiable with a single activity were charged to that activity code. Amounts for common expenses that benefited more than one activity were accumulated in cost pools for each account and then allocated to the activity categories on the basis of salaries (see Resource D, including Table D.7). To simplify the illustration, other bases, such as square footage for occupancy and usage for equipment rental and maintenance, were not employed. In general, salary percentages can often be the basis for most allocations among categories of activity unless clearly inappropriate allocations result.

3. The third step established amounts for various sources of revenue (accounts) by activity code. The revenues by activity code are consistent with the corresponding expenses by activity code.

4. The fourth step established amounts for the assets and liabilities sections of the trial balance, again consistent with the revenue and expense sections.

5. The fifth step established amounts for the net assets section, consistent with the rest of the trial balance.

6. During the process of using the single functionalized trial balance report to develop the various sample financial reports found in this guide, some final adjustments were made to the figures in the trial balance. Even so, all the sample reports in this manual have been prepared from the single functionalized trial balance report.

Not-for-profit organizations can follow the procedure just outlined using spreadsheet software, such as Excel or Lotus 1-2-3. A separate spreadsheet is created for each report or group of reports. One section (a "sheet" in Excel) in each spreadsheet contains a copy of the functionalized trial balance report. One or more other sections contain the desired reports. Data for each cell in each report are extracted by formula from the corresponding cells in the functionalized trial balance section. All of the sample reports in Part Three are cross-referenced to the functionalized trial balance in this chapter for the express purpose of enabling not-for-profit organizations to do this.

Accounting software with report-generating capabilities can be programmed to produce the desired reports directly from the accounting system's transaction database, eliminating the need for spreadsheet software. Further, as mentioned in Part One, we hope that not-for-profit accounting software vendors will enhance their products with features that will do all of this with the click of a mouse.

Tables 7.1–7.3 show the sample adjusted functionalized trial balance report for June 30, 20X2, cross-referenced to the sample GAAP financial statements (see Chapter Eleven). This report includes all of the financial data required for the sample GAAP financial statements, IRS Form 990 financial statements (see Chapter Twelve), and uniform government grant reporting forms and electronic templates (see Chapter Thirteen). Every figure in every sample financial statement and schedule can be traced to one or more corresponding amounts in this trial balance report by using the unified chart of accounts with its cross-reference to various reporting requirements (see Chapter 5, Table 5.1). This sample report assumes that no grant requires matching expenses (federal and state grants may have matching requirements).

From the figures in Tables 7.4 and 7.5 the organization can calculate the changes in its net assets for the fiscal year (see Table 7.6). (We have deviated from normal accounting order, by displaying revenue and expenses before assets and liabilities, in order to fit the following tables into the book properly.)

TABLE 7.1

Functionalized Trial Balance Report (Cross-Referenced to Sample GAAP Financial Statements): Balance Sheet
June 30, 20X2 and 20X1

Account Number	Balance Sheet Account	Sample GAAP Financial Statement, Exhibit 11.1 (Line Number)	20X2 Debit/(Credit)	20X1 Debit/(Credit)
	Assets			
1010	Cash in bank—operating	1	$ 9,480	$ 5,078
1020	Cash in bank—payroll	1	14,143	9,523
1040	Petty cash	1	100	100
1070	Savings and temporary cash investments	2	55,000	95,000
1110	Accounts receivable	3	13,789	7,893
1190	Allowance for doubtful accounts	3 (contra)	(1,103)	(631)
1210	Pledges receivable	4	5,000	
1220	Allowance for doubtful pledges	4 (contra)	(200)	
1240	Grants receivable	5	57,996	7,047
1270	Receivables due from trustees and employees	3		
1280	Other short-term notes and loans receivable	3		
1290	Allowance for doubtful notes and loans	3 (contra)		
1310	Inventories for sale	6	3,852	4,687
1350	Prepaid expenses and deferred charges	7	7,398	6,489
1410	Investments—marketable securities	8	40,000	
1480	Other investments	9	1,143	
1510	Land—held for use, operating	11	34,247	34,247
1520	Buildings—held for use, operating	12	134,000	134,000
1530	Accumulated depreciation for 1520	12 (contra)	(43,945)	(35,583)
1540	Leasehold improvements	13	54,278	54,278
1550	Accumulated amortization for 1540	13 (contra)	1(22,698)	(19,545)
1560	Furniture, fixtures, and equipment	14	137,834	137,834
1570	Accumulated depreciation for 1560	14 (contra)	(43,754)	(35,529)
	Total Assets		$450,617	$410,831

(Continued)

TABLE 7.1

Functionalized Trial Balance Report (Cross-Referenced to Sample GAAP Financial Statements): Balance Sheet
June 30, 20X2 and 20X1 *(Continued)*

Account Number	Balance Sheet Account	Sample GAAP Financial Statement, Exhibit 11.1 (Line Number)	20 X 2 Credit/(Debit)	20 X 1 Credit/(Debit)
	Liabilities			
2010	Accounts payable	21	$ 5,476	$ 6,024
2110	Accrued expenses—payroll	22	12,541	13,795
2130	Accrued expenses—payroll taxes	23	3,276	3,604
2150	Accrued expenses—other	24	894	1,143
2311	Control account for contract 101	25		
2312	Control account for contract 102	25		
2313	Control account for contract 103	25		
2350	Other unearned and deferred revenue	25	17,850	15,870
2730	Mortgages payable	27	69,834	73,679
	Total Liabilities		$109,871	$114,115
	Net Assets			
	Unrestricted Net Assets			
3010	Available for general activities	29	$134,260	$100,693
3020	Board-designated for special purposes	31		
3030	Board-designated for reserves	30		
	Fixed Operating Assets—Net			
3210	Land—held for use, operating	32	34,247	34,247
3220	Buildings—held for use, operating	32	20,221	24,738
3230	Leasehold improvements	32	31,580	34,733
3240	Furniture and equipment	32	94,080	102,305
	Total Unrestricted Net Assets		$314,388	$296,716
	Temporarily Restricted Net Assets			
3310	Control account for restricted grant 204	34	26,357	
	Permanently Restricted Net Assets			
3910	Endowment	35		
	Total Net Assets		$340,745	$296,716
	Total Liabilities and Net Assets		$450,616	$410,831
	Control Change in Net Asses		$ 44,029	$0

TABLE 7.2

Functionalized Trial Balance Report (Cross-Referenced to Sample GAAP Financial Statements): Revenues

Account Number	Activity Code	Revenue, Gain, or Other Support	Sample GAAP Financial Statement, Exhibit 11.2 (Line Number)	Program A: Nongrant Activities[a] (100, A)	Program A: Grant 101 (120, A)	Program A: Grant 102 (130, A)	Program B: Nongrant Activities[a] (200, A)
4010-	XXX	From individuals and small businesses	51	$	$	$	$
4050-	XXX	Special fundraising events—gift portion	52				
4070-	XXX	Legacies and bequests	53				
4080-	XXX	Estimated uncollectible pledges (for 4000–4070)	51 (contra)				
4110-	XXX	Donated services or use of facilities—GAAP	54	13,000			
4120-	XXX	Donated services or use of facilities—non-GAAP	(not GAAP)	21,500			18,500
4130-	XXX	Other gifts in kind	55	8,795			
4210-	XXX	Corporate and other business grants	51	60,000			30,000
4230-	XXX	Foundation and trust grants	51				
4410-	XXX	Allocated by federated fundraising organizations	56				
4520-	XXX	Government grants—federal	58		254,444	33,322	
4530-	XXX	Government grants—state	58				
4540-	XXX	Government grants—other	58				
5020-	XXX	Government contracts—federal	n/a				
5030-	XXX	Government contracts—state	n/a				
5040-	XXX	Government contracts—other	n/a				
5150-	XXX	Sales to public, program-related inventory	59				
5210-	XXX	Other program service sales and fees	59	33,689			26,934
5410-	XXX	Interest on savings and temporary cash investments	60				
5420-	XXX	Dividends and interest from securities	61				
5910-	XXX	Gross amounts from sale of securities	62				
5920-	XXX	Cost and sales expense (deduct from 5910)	62 (contra)				
6110-	XXX	Gross amounts from sale of other assets	62				
6120-	XXX	Other cost and sales expenses (deduct from 6110)	62 (contra)				
6180-	XXX	Unrealized gain (loss) on value of other assets	63				
6210-	XXX	Special events—gross revenue excluding gifts	52				
6810-	XXX	Other revenue	64				
6910-	XXX	Net assets released from restriction	66				
		Total revenue		$136,984	$254,444	$33,322	$75,434

Note: *The three-digit activity code and the letter of the relevant column in Exhibit 11.2 (Sample GAAP Statement of Activities) are shown in parentheses in column headings where applicable. Amounts are for the year ended June 30, 20X2.*

[a]*Activity classifications may be more or less detailed, depending on the entity's needs. Generally activities are "action" oriented, such as food service (grant 101), rehabilitation services (grant 102), and education services (grant 103). For ease of following, grant numbers rather than names are used to identify activities.*

Program B: Grant 101 (220, A)	Program C: Nongrant Activities[a] (300, A)	Program C: Grant 103 (320, A)	Program D: Grant 204 (420, B)	Total Program	Management and General (510, A)	Fundraising (710)	20X2 Total
$	$	$	$	$	$	$12,358	$12,358
				13,000			13,000
				40,000			40,000
				8,795			8,795
	43,000			133,000			133,000
			50,000	50,000			50,000
					18,500		18,500
77,878		30,307		395,951			395,951
	10,478			71,101			71,101
					7,423		7,423
$77,878	$53,478	$30,307	$50,000	$711,847	$25,923	$12,358	$750,128
						GAAP	$710,128
						Form 990	$697,128

TABLE 7.3

Functionalized Trial Balance Report (Cross-Referenced to Sample GAAP Financial Statements): Expenses

Account Number	Activity Code	Object Expense	Sample GAAP Financial Statement Exhibit 11.3 (Line Number)	Program A: Nongrant Activities (100, A81, A)	Program A: Grant 101 (120, A81, A)	Program A: Grant 102 (130, A81, A)	Program B: Unrestricted (200, A82, B)
7010-	XXX	Program-related contracts to other entities	135	$	$ 6,246	$	$
7040-	XXX	Awards and grants to individuals	135				
7050-	XXX	Specific assistance to individuals	136				
7210-	XXX	Salaries of officers, directors etc.	121	14,368	39,718	2,364	16,369
7220-	XXX	Other salaries and wages	121	63,780	91,848	11,437	13,421
7310-	XXX	Pension plan contributions	122	6,951	9,187	962	2,112
7320-	XXX	Other employee benefits	122	5,958	7,875	825	1,810
7410-	XXX	Payroll taxes etc.	122	9,434	12,468	1,306	2,866
7510-	XXX	Professional fundraising fees	124				
7520-	XXX	Accounting fees	124				
7530-	XXX	Legal fees	124				
7540-	XXX	Other professional fees	124	274	977	102	83
7550-	XXX	Contract temporary help	124		3,487		
7590-	XXX	Donated professional services—non-GAAP	124	21,500			18,500
7710-	XXX	Supplies	125	961	9,109	1,145	292
7720-	XXX	Donated materials and supplies	125	8,795			
7810-	XXX	Telephone	126	754	2,690	282	229
7910-	XXX	Postage and shipping	127	261	931	97	79
7920-	XXX	Mailing services	127				
8010-	XXX	Rent	128	897	3,202	335	273
8050-	XXX	Interest on mortgage	128	642	2,291	240	195
8080-	XXX	Donated use of facilities and utilities—GAAP	128	13,000			
8110-	XXX	Equipment rental and maintenance	129	789	7,504	295	240
8210-	XXX	Printing and duplicating	130	1,432	9,696	535	435
8220-	XXX	Publications published by others	130	70	249	26	21
8310-	XXX	Travel	131		678	8,576	
8510-	XXX	Conferences, conventions, and meetings	132	635	319	33	725
8610-	XXX	Interest—general	133				
8650-	XXX	Depreciation	137	2,305	8,225	861	700
8710-	XXX	Insurance—excluding employee-related	134	1,267	4,522	474	385
8810-	XXX	Membership dues	138	215	87	9	147
8820-	XXX	Staff development	138	600	472	49	829
9300-	XXX	Other expenses	138	89	876	33	27
9830-	XXX	Capital purchases—equipment	capitalized				
		Total direct expenses and assets released from restrictions		$154,977	$222,657	$ 29,986	$ 59,738
		Decrease or increase in net assets		$(17,993)	$ 31,787	$ 3,336	$ 15,696
		For grants: maximum administrative expense allowed			$ 31,787	$ 3,336	
		Total expenses			$254,444	$33,321	
		Excess (deficit)			$0	$0	

Note: *The three-digit activity codes, the relevant column and line in Exhibit 11.2 (Sample GAAP Statement of Activities), and the relevant column in Exhibit 11.3 (Sample GAAP Statement of Functional Expenses), respectively, are shown in parentheses in column headings where applicable. Amounts are for the year ended June 30, 20X2.*

Program B: Grant 101 (220, A82, B)	Program C: Nongrant Activities (300, A83, C)	Program C: Grant 103 (320, A83, C)	Program D: Grant 204 (420, A84, D)	Total Program	Management and General (510, A86, F)	Fundraising (710, A87, G)	Central Services (910, Allocated, Allocated)	Account Cost Pool (920, Allocated, Allocated)	20X2 Total
$	$	$	$	$ 6,246	$	$	$	$	$ 6,246
			5,432	5,432					5,432
4,547				77,366	33,451	4,183			115,000
38,046	16,806	17,331	12,079	264,748	5,252				270,000
3,003	1,167	1,239	864	25,485	2,713	293			28,491
2,575	1,000	1,062	741	21,846	2,326	251			24,423
4,075	1,584	1,682	1,173	34,588	3,682	397			38,667
					11,564				11,564
320	46	132	92	2,026	289	31			2,346
				3,487					3,487
				40,000					40,000
4,597	7,730	463	323	24,620	3,989	109			28,718
				8,795					8,795
879	126	363	253	5,576	794	86			6,456
304	43	126	88	1,929	275	486			2,690
1,046	150	432	301	6,636	946	102			7,684
749	108	309	216	4,750	676	73			5,499
				13,000					13,000
920	132	380	265	10,525	831	90			11,446
1,670	240	689	481	15,178	5,205	931			21,314
81	12	34	23	516	428	8			952
				9,254					9,254
104	15	43	30	1,904	2,672	10			4,586
2,688	387	1,109	774	17,049	2,429	262			19,740
1,478	213	610	426	9,375	1,336	144			10,855
29	4	12	8	511	761	3			1,275
154	457	64	44	2,669	1,496	15			4,180
323	15	43	30	1,436	2,553	10			3,999
$67,588	$30,235	$26,123	$23,643	$614,947	$83,668	$ 7,484	$0	$0	$706,099
$10,290	$23,243	$ 4,184	$26,357	$ 96,900	$(45,387)	$ (7,484)	$0	$0	$ 44,029
$10,291		$ 4,187		$ 49,601	$(49,601)				$0
$77,878		$30,310							$666,099
								GAAP	$666,099
								Form 990	$653,099

TABLE 7.4

Simplified Functionalized Trial Balance Report for Smaller Organizations: Revenues and Expenses

Account Number	Revenue or Expense	Program Service Activities			
		Program A		Program B	
		General (100)	Project A (120)	General (200)	Project B (220)
	Revenue				
4010	Contributions from individuals	$	$	$	$
4230	Foundation grants				12,000
4510	Government grants		25,000		
5210	Program service fees and sales	82,678			
5410	Interest on savings and temporary cash investments				
6810	Other revenue				
	Total revenue	$ 82,678	$25,000	$0	$12,000
	Expenses				
7210	Salaries of officers, directors, etc.	$ 16,339	$7,895	$3,578	$206
7220	Other salaries and wages	64,638	13,478	12,567	7,384
7310	Pension plan contributions	8,098	2,137	1,615	759
7320	Other employee benefits	4,049	1,069	807	379
7410	Payroll taxes	6,478	1,710	1,292	607
7540	Professional fees				
7710	Supplies	6,527	890	1,267	330
7810	Telephone	2,294	642	678	332
7910	Postage and shipping	1,084	250	367	68
8010	Occupancy	9,991	2,637	1,992	936
8110	Equipment rental and maintenance	3,583	842	1,256	396
8210	Printing and publications	4,042	1,619	2,735	303
8310	Travel	2,355	998	1,057	139
8510	Conferences and meetings	765	0	456	0
9300	Other nonpersonnel expenses	345	832	56	160
	Total expenses	$130,588	$35,000	$29,723	$12,000

Note: This report is for fiscal year 20X2. The three-digit activity code is given in parentheses in column headings where applicable.

[a]The common cost pool for each account has been allocated to activities on a pro rata basis using salaries (see percentages).

Management and General (510)	Fundraising (710)	Total Revenue of Expense	Common Cost Pool[a]
$	$134,579	$134,579	
		12,000	
		25,000	
		82,678	
8,679		8,679	
$ 8,679	$134,579	$262,936	
$ 7,124	$ 6,890	$ 42,033	$ 4,101
3,658	7,268	108,994	23,950
1,078	1,416	15,103	15,103
539	708	7,551	7,551
863	1,133	12,082	12,082
3,890		3,890	
546	1,345	10,905	4,327
465	509	4,920	3,785
367	1,190	3,326	1,357
1,330	1,747	18,634	18,634
546	789	7,412	5,478
578	1,767	11,043	2,478
1,123	657	6,329	678
1,980	567	3,768	
673	200	2,266	
$24,760	$ 26,185	$258,256	$ 99,524

TABLE 7.5

Simplified Functionalized Trial Balance Report for Smaller Organizations: Balance Sheet

Account Number	Account	20X2	20X1
Asset			
1010	Cash in bank—operating	$ 8,746	$ 18,764
1070	Savings and temporary cash investments	104,699	90,001
	Total assets	$ 113,445	$ 108,765
Liabilities [None, cash-based]		0	0
Net assets			
3010	Unrestricted—available for general activities	$ 113,445	$ 98,765
3310	Temporarily restricted for activity 120	0	10,000
3320	Temporarily restricted for activity 220	0	0
	Total net assets	$ 113,445	$ 108,765
	Total liabilities and net assets	$ 113,445	$ 108,765

Note: *This report is for fiscal year 20X2.*

TABLE 7.6

Simplified Functionalized Trial Balance Report for Smaller Organizations: Changes in Cash-Based Net Assets

20X2 Trial Balance Item	Amount
Total revenue[a]	$ 262,936
Total expenses[a]	(258,256)
Overall cash-based actual excess/(deficit)	$ 4,680
Other changes in cash-based net assets	0
Beginning cash-based net assets[b]	108,765
Ending cash-based net assets[b]	$ 113,445

[a]See Table 7.4.
[b]See Table 7.5.

Chapter 8

Allocation of Expenses

ALLOCATION OF EXPENSES ranks high among the most vexing issues encountered in accounting and financial reporting of not-for-profit organizations. In the world of for-profit organizations, cost accounting standards are well established and routinely observed. In the not-for-profit world it is a different story, particularly when it comes to *allocation* of an expense category (for example, salaries) to two or more distinct *functions* or *cost objectives*.

For government contractors—both for-profit and not-for-profit—cost accounting standards are critically important. All government agencies, as well as their contractors and subcontractors, are required to follow the standards promulgated by the Cost Accounting Standards Board (CASB), an independent board created by the government in 1988.[1] However, OMB Circular A-122 *(Cost Principles for Nonprofit Organizations)*, although not entirely exempting not-for-profit organizations from CASB standards, states, "It is unlikely that the type of grantees covered by this Circular would have contracts large enough to be covered by the CASB. In the event that they do, however, the regulations of the CASB would apply."[2]

This chapter seeks to clarify the important issue of cost allocation in not-for-profit accounting and reporting by explaining the often confusing terminology, specifying the requirements and standards promulgated by various authoritative bodies, and describing various cost allocation methods. Not everything in this chapter may be useful to all readers, and therefore readers may wish to skip certain sections. The following is an outline of this chapter:

I. Terminology and definitions

    A. Cost accumulation

    B. Cost distribution

    C. Cost objectives

    D. Types of costs distributed to cost objectives
       1. Direct costs
       2. Common costs and cost pools
          a. Common cost pools by account
          b. Service department cost pools
    E. Management and general expenses
    F. Classifying administrative activities
II. Requirements for cost allocation
    A. GAAP requirement for cost allocation
    B. IRS and state regulatory requirements for cost allocation
    C. OMB Circular A-122 requirements for cost allocation
III. Cost allocation methods
    A. Cost allocation objectives and recommended policies
    B. Activity-level cost allocation
    C. Dimensions of cost allocation methods
       1. Object expense category
       2. Types of cost pools
       3. Timing
       4. Bases for allocation
       5. Suggested allocation bases for Table 8.1
    D. Reducing the burden of cost allocation by using only one or two bases
    E. Cost pool allocation for smaller organizations
    F. Reporting costs of joint activities that include a fundraising appeal
       1. The purpose criterion
       2. The audience criterion
       3. The content criterion
       4. Disclosure of allocation of joint costs

Terminology and Definitions

The terminology and definitions used in this section are consistent with OMB Circular A-122, IRS Form 990, FASB Statement no. 117, and AICPA's *Audit and Accounting Guide: Not for Profit Organizations* (1998).

Cost accounting consists of *accumulation* of costs by their natural expense classification and *distribution* of these costs to cost *objectives*. Cost distribution consists of direct assignment of costs to specific cost objectives and, when direct assignment is not possible, *allocation* of common costs to multiple cost objectives on some basis.

Cost Accumulation

Before costs are distributed to cost objectives, they are accumulated by account expense categories (also referred to as *natural expense classifications* and *object expense categories*), such as salaries, occupancy, telephone, postage and shipping, printing and duplication, and supplies. Costs are assigned directly to specific accounts without reference to cost objectives.

Cost Distribution

Cost distribution in not-for-profit organizations is the distribution of account costs (such as salaries or supplies) to cost objectives (such as regions, organizations, functions, departments, programs, grants, projects, contracts, cost centers, services, and activities). A cost objective is any activity for which a separate measure of costs is desired. In activity accounting all account costs are distributed to activity-level cost objectives. Activities are assigned to various summary-level cost objectives, and costs for summary-level cost objectives are determined by totaling the costs of the activities assigned to each summary-level cost objective.

Three broad types or categories of costs are distributed to four general classes of activities. The four classes of activities (cost objectives) are

1. Program services (including grants)

2. Fundraising

3. Management and general (M&G)

4. Central service departments

Three types of costs are distributed to these activities:

1. Direct costs

2. Common costs

   2a. Common costs by account

   - Employee leave costs
   - Employee fringe benefit costs
   - Other common costs by account

   2b. Common costs by central service department

3. M&G costs

Direct costs relate to and are assigned directly to only one of the cost objectives, and cost allocation is not involved.

Note that M&G and central service departments are *both* activities (cost objectives) *and* types of costs. In other words they are classes of cost objectives that, when appropriate, become types of costs that can be allocated to other activities, such as program services, grants, or fundraising.

Table 8.1 illustrates how three types of costs totaling $1.1 million can be distributed among four classes of activities. Some $600,000 is directly identifiable with a single class of activity and has been assigned directly to the four activity classes as *direct costs*. The remaining $500,000 is accounted for in the various common cost pools by account. In Table 8.1, the total common costs of $500,000 have been allocated to the four activity classes on the basis of direct costs by activity as a percentage of total direct costs (see allocation line A in Table 8.2).

Central service costs are also common costs and shared by the other three classes of activity. The total central service costs of $92,000 have been allocated to these three activities on the basis of direct costs by activity as a percentage of total direct costs less central service direct costs (line B in Table 8.2).

TABLE 8.1

Three Types of Costs Distributed to Four Classes of Activities

Cost Type	Activity Class				Total
	Program	**Fundraising**	**Management and General**	**Central Service**	
1. Direct costs (salaries, printing, travel, etc.)	400	100	50	50	600
2. Common costs					
2a. Common cost pools by account (up to 50; for example, occupancy)	333	83	42	42	500
Total direct costs and account cost pools	733	183	92	92	1,100
2b. Service department cost pools (for example, information systems)	67	17	8	(92)	
Total direct costs, account cost pools, and service department cost pools	800	200	100		1,100
3. Management and general cost pool	80	20	(100)[a]		
Total costs	880	220			1,100

Note: *Dollar amounts are in thousands.*

[a]*In GAAP reporting, management and general expenses are not allocated to other functions. However, such expenses are usually classified as organizational administrative costs and allocated for purposes of reimbursement under government grants and contracts.*

TABLE 8.2

Allocation Percentages Based on Direct Costs

	Total	Program	Fundraising	Management and General	Central Service
Direct costs (thousands of dollars)	600	400	100	50	50
Percentage allocation basis: Direct activity costs as a percentage of					
A. Total direct costs	100.0	66.7	16.7	8.3	8.3
B. Direct costs less central service	100.0	72.7	18.2	9.1	
C. Direct costs less central service and management and general	100.0	80.0	20.0		

The $100,000 total M&G costs have also been allocated to the two remaining classes of activity, program and fundraising. This allocation is on the basis of direct cost by activity as a percentage of total direct costs less the direct costs of central service and M&G (line C in Table 8.2). Table 8.3 shows the relationship between reporting requirements and the four classes of activities.

Cost Objectives

OMB Circular A-122 provides the following definition of cost objective: "Cost objective means a function, organizational subdivision, contract, grant, or other work unit for which cost data are desired and for which provision is made to accumulate and measure the cost of processes, projects, jobs, and capitalized projects."[3]

FASB Statement no. 117 describes three of the four classes of cost objectives, or *functional categories*—M&G, program, and fundraising:

> 26. *To help donors [including federal, state, and local government agencies], creditors, and others in assessing an organization's service efforts, including the costs of its services and how it uses resources, a statement of activities or notes to financial statements shall provide information about expenses reported by their functional classification such as major classes of program services and supporting activities. Voluntary health and welfare organizations shall report that information as well as information by their natural classification, such as salaries, rent, electricity, interest expense, depreciation, awards and grants to others, and professional fees, in a matrix format in a separate financial statement. Other not-for-profit organizations are encouraged, but not required, to provide information about expenses by their natural classification.*

TABLE 8.3

Reporting Requirements Cross-Referenced to the Four Activity Classes

Requirement	Program	Fundraising	Management and General	Central Service
OMB Circular A-122	Grants and services	Not allowed	Administrative	Allocated and indirect cost rate[a]
GAAP	Program(s)	Fundraising	Management and general	Allocated
IRS Form 990	Program(s)	Fundraising	Management and general	Allocated
Internal management	Department(s)	Department(s)	Department(s)	Department(s)

[a]*The types of costs used for indirect cost rates can include organizational administrative costs (management and general) only, administrative costs (management and general) plus portions of common costs in any combination, or administrative costs (management and general) plus all common costs.*

27. *Program services are the activities that result in goods and services being distributed to beneficiaries, customers, or members that fulfill the purposes or mission for which the organization exists. Those services are the major purpose for which the organizations exists. Those services are the major purpose for and the major output of the organization and often relate to several major programs. For example, a large university may have programs for student instruction, research, and patient care, among others. Similarly, a health and welfare organization may have programs for health or family services, research, disaster relief, and public education, among others.*

28. *Supporting services are all activities of a not-for-profit organization other than program services. Generally, they include management and general, fund-raising, and membership-development activities. Management and general activities include oversight, business management, general record keeping, budgeting, financing, and related administrative activities, and all management and administration except for direct conduct of program services or fund-raising activities. Fund-raising activities include publicizing and conducting fund-raising campaigns; maintaining donor mailing lists; conducting special fund-raising events; preparing and distributing fund-raising manuals, instructions, and other materials, and conducting other activities involved with soliciting contributions from individuals, foundations, government agencies, and others. Membership-development activities*

include soliciting for prospective members and membership dues, membership relations, and similar activities.[4]

Types of Costs Distributed to Cost Objectives

OMB Circular A-122 specifies three basic types of costs: (1) direct costs, (2) "joint" (common) costs, (3) "general administrative" (M&G) costs. In GAAP reporting, M&G expenses are shown separately from program services and fundraising expenses. However, M&G expenses may be allocated to other activities or projects for purposes of reimbursement under government grants and contracts and in determining the full costs of all program service and fundraising activities.

Direct Costs

Direct costs are costs that can be identified specifically and exclusively with one particular activity or cost objective. Direct costs are assigned directly to the single activity; cost allocation is not involved. Direct costs are usually assigned to their respective single activities at the same time they are accumulated for, and assigned to, their expense account categories.

OMB Circular A-122 provides the following definition of direct costs:

B. Direct costs

   1. Direct costs are those that can be identified specifically with a particular final cost objective, i.e., a particular project, service, or other direct activity of an organization. However, a cost may not be assigned to an award as a direct cost if any other cost incurred for the same purpose, in like circumstance, has been allocated to an award as an indirect cost. Costs identified specifically with awards are direct costs of the awards and are to be assigned directly thereto. Costs identified specifically with other final cost objectives of the organization are direct costs of those cost objectives and are not to be assigned to other awards directly or indirectly.

   2. Any direct cost of a minor amount may be treated as an indirect cost for reasons of practicality where the accounting treatment for that item of cost is consistently applied to all cost objectives.[5]

Often an itemized invoice will show several different categories of line item account expense. For example, an invoice from an outside copying service could include duplicating fees and charges for a supply of copy paper for internal use. Duplication fees are charged to printing and duplicating, whereas copy paper costs are charged to supplies. In such a situation the expense transaction is divided into separate transactions for each expense account category, and each separate transaction is posted to the appropriate expense account. This is a distribution of direct cost expenses among line item accounts and is *not* cost allocation.

Common Costs and Cost Pools

Common costs are also referred to as *joint costs* and *shared costs*. Common costs are costs that benefit more than one activity. Note that common costs are only part of *allocable costs,* which consist of common costs plus administrative (M&G) costs. Further, administrative (M&G) costs are not allocated to the fundraising and various program functions for GAAP and IRS Form 990 reporting. However, for purposes of reimbursement under government grants and contracts, such allocation is allowable.

Common costs are accumulated in interim cost pools. The cost pools can be allocated to various activities or cost objectives either permanently (when the general ledger is updated at the end of each month) or provisionally (on a monthly basis for reporting purposes only and permanently when the general ledger is updated at the end of the year and the year-to-date cost pools are closed).

The use of cumulative, year-to-date cost pools for all of an organization's common costs can result in fairer and more consistent allocations. For example, vacation salaries and various types of insurance coverage are more fairly allocated on the basis of a full year than on the basis of one month. The use of cumulative cost pools can also reduce the accounting and reporting burden for smaller organizations. Cost pools can be used for expenses for employee leave or other out-of-service salary, employee benefits, employer's payroll taxes, occupancy, some categories of supplies, and other categories of object expense.

Common costs can be further classified as either common costs by line item account or common costs by central service department. Common cost pools by account might include an employee leave cost pool, an employee fringe benefit cost pool, and other common cost pools by account.

Common Cost Pools by Account

Common cost pooling by account is accomplished by specifying a single activity code that creates a separate cost pool for employee leave, employee fringe benefits, and any other account category that can incur common costs. The account number for any expense category and the cost pool activity code together constitute the cost pool number for that expense category. There are nearly fifty line item or expense account categories in the sample UCOA, and most of them can have common costs, which are charged to their respective common cost pools.

Although common cost pools for individual accounts require an activity code, the activity code does not represent a cost objective. Rather, individual account cost pools contain accumulations of costs that are allocated to other activity codes related to various cost objectives. The allocation step must be done before most internal, and all external, reports can be prepared.

Individual account cost pools may be allocated line by line to activities on a single basis for all accounts, on bases that vary from one account to another, or as a summary common cost account on a single basis. Examples of single bases are direct-staff salaries, direct-staff hours, total direct costs, or modified total direct costs (for example, total direct costs less pass through funds).

Cost pools are allocated in the following sequence: (1) employee leave cost pool, (2) employee fringe benefit cost pool, (3) all other line item or individual account common cost pools, (4) service department cost pools, and when applicable (5) the M&G cost pool.

Service Department Cost Pools

As noted earlier, service department cost pools are both a type of cost and one of the classes of cost objectives. Service department cost pools are established by specifying separate activity codes for each service department. Examples of service departments are printing and duplicating, data processing or management information systems, mailing and shipping, and storage. A central service department can incur costs related to any expense account category. Service department cost pools are allocated their pro rata share of the various individual account cost pools. Service department cost pools are then allocated to the other activities or cost objectives on one or more bases. Whereas larger organizations can have several central service departments, midsize organizations generally have only one or two central services, if any. Smaller organizations usually do not have any.

Although service department cost pools require an activity code, the activity code does not represent the final cost objective for most reporting requirements. Service department cost pools are generally allocated to activities related to various other cost objectives. Of course for many of the reports for the service department manager, top management, and the board of directors and for many of the reports used in the budgeting process, the service department cost pool is itself a cost objective.

Service department cost pools are allocated line by line to activities on a single basis for all accounts (or on bases that vary from one account to another) or as a total service department cost account on a single basis. Examples of single bases are direct-staff salaries or direct-staff hours. At the end of this chapter we present an example of a simplified common cost pool allocation for smaller organizations.

Management and General Expenses

As noted earlier, M&G expenses are both a type of cost and one of the classes of activities (cost objectives). M&G costs are costs that are incurred in organizing and operating the organization itself, that benefit the agency or *organization as a whole*, and that cannot be identified with specific programs or the fundraising function. They are reported on IRS Form 990 in part II, column C, and as "management and general" in GAAP statements of functional expenses.

IRS Form 990 instructions define *management and general* as follows:

Use column (C) to report the organization's expenses for overall function and management, rather than for its direct conduct of fundraising activities or program services. Overall management usually includes the salaries and expenses of the chief officer of the organization and that officer's staff. If part of their time is spent directly supervising program services and fundraising activities, their salaries and expenses should be allocated among those functions.

Other expenses to report in column (C) include those for meetings of the board of directors or similar group; committee and staff meetings (unless held in connection with specific program services or fundraising activities); general legal services; accounting (including patient accounting and billing); general liability insurance; office management; auditing, personnel, and other centralized services; preparation, publication, and distribution of an annual report; and investment expenses. . . .

You should report only general expenses in column (C). Do not use this column to report costs of special meetings or other activities that relate to fundraising or specific program services.

The AICPA *Audit and Accounting Guide: Not for Profit Organizations* also provides for allocation of executive salaries and expenses to program services and fundraising. The AICPA guide states, "The costs of oversight and management usually include the salaries and expenses of the governing board, the chief executive officer of the organization, and the supporting staff. (If such staff spend a portion of their time directly supervising program services or categories of other supporting services, however, their salaries and expenses should be allocated among those functions.)"[6]

An organization must have a reliable, properly structured system for recording staff time in order to be able to allocate a portion of the salaries of the chief officer and supporting staff to functions other than management and general (see Chapter Nine for staff time reporting).

Classifying Administrative Activities

When classifying administrative activities, it is important to distinguish between staff time and expenses spent on the administrative activities of the organization and staff time and expenses spent on administrative activities related to various programs, grants, or fundraising functions. Administrative activities related to programs, grants, or fundraising can be directly identified with those cost objectives, and related costs should be allocated accordingly. Costs related to administrative activities of the *entire* organization should be allocated to M&G. Table 8.4 compares the activities of organizational administration (M&G) with those of program administration. This same comparison can be applied to administrative activities related to management of grants, fundraising, and central service departments.

Requirements for Cost Allocation

This section summarizes the cost allocation requirements of FASB and AICPA, IRS Form 990, and OMB Circular A-122.

GAAP Requirement for Cost Allocation

FASB Statement no. 117 requires health and welfare organizations to provide a statement of functional expenses and encourages other not-for-profit organizations to do so. Although cost allocation becomes necessary to account for and prepare such a statement, FASB Statement no. 117 does not address cost allocation. Instead it refers to current AICPA requirements and alludes to IRS Form 990. FASB Statement no. 117 states:

TABLE 8.4

Organizational Administration Versus Program Administration

Organizational Administration (Management and General)	Program Administration
Organizational management and coordination	Program management and coordination
Organizational planning and evaluation	Program planning and evaluation
Organizational budgeting	Program budgeting
Central purchasing of organization-related supplies	Purchases made by a program department for program-related supplies
A central switchboard activity	A program department answering service
Organizational personnel activities	Program staff hiring, firing, performance reviews, and so on

The Board indicated in the Exposure Draft that it believes that current specialized accounting and reporting principles and practices that require certain organizations to provide information about their expenses by both functional and natural classifications are not inconsistent with the requirements of this statement. Thus, those specialized requirements continue in effect. It also noted that not-for-profit organizations often provide that information in regulatory filings to the Internal Revenue Service and certain state agencies, which are available to the public.[7]

On the topic of cost allocation AICPA's *Audit and Accounting Guide: Not for Profit Organizations* states:

Classification of Expenses Related to More Than One Function

13.42 *Some expenses are directly related to, and can be assigned to, a single major program or service or a single supporting activity. Other expenses relate to more than one program or supporting activity, or to a combination of programs and supporting services. These expenses should be allocated among the appropriate functions. Examples include salaries of persons who perform more than one kind of service and the rental of a building used for various programs and supporting activities.*

13.43 *Direct identification of specific expense (also referred to as assigning expenses) is the preferable method of charging expenses to various functions. If an expense can be specifically identified with a program or supporting service, it should be assigned to that function. For example, travel costs incurred in connection with a program activity should be assigned to that program.[8]*

A footnote to paragraph 13.44 of the same publication suggests that "the guidance found in U.S. Office of Management and Budget Circular A-122 may also be helpful in allocating costs."[9]

IRS and State Regulatory Requirements for Cost Allocation

IRS Form 990, also required by more than thirty-five state charities registration offices across the country, requires cost allocation for preparing Part II, Statement of Functional Expenses. The following is an excerpt from Form 990 instructions for Part II:

In Part II, the organization's expenses are designated by object classification (e.g., salaries, legal fees, supplies, etc.) and allocated into 3 functions: program services (column (B)); management and general (column (C)); and fundraising (column (D)). . . .

Use the organization's normal accounting method to report total expenses in column (A) and to segregate them into functions under columns (B), (C), and (D) [i.e., GAAP functional expense allocation methods are acceptable for IRS Form 990]. . . . The amounts reported should be accurate and the method of allocation documented in the organization's records.

Report, in the appropriate column, expenses that are directly attributable to a particular functional category. In general, allocate expenses that relate to more than one functional category. For example, allocate employees' salaries on the basis of each employee's time. For some shared expenses such as occupancy, supplies, and epreciation of office equipment, use an appropriate basis for each kind of cost. However, you should report some other shared expenses in column (C) only.

OMB Circular A-122 Requirements for Cost Allocation

OMB Circular A-122 (*Cost Principles for Nonprofit Organizations*) requires the use of an approved method of cost allocation. OMB Circular A-122's *direct allocation method* is quoted here:

4. *Direct allocation method.*

    a. *Some nonprofit organizations treat all costs as direct costs except general administration and general expenses. These organizations generally separate their costs into three basic categories: (i) General administration and general expenses, (ii) fund raising, and (iii) other direct functions (including projects performed under Federal awards). Joint costs, such as depreciation, rental costs, operation and maintenance of facilities, telephone expenses, and the like are prorated individually as direct costs to each category and to each award or other activity using a base most appropriate to the particular cost being prorated.*

    b. *This method is acceptable, provided each joint cost is prorated using a base which accurately measures the benefits provided to each award or other activity. The bases must be established in accordance with reasonable criteria, and be supported by current data.*[10]

This method is consistent with the functional expense reporting requirements of FASB Statement no. 117, AICPA's *Audit and Accounting Guide: Not for Profit Organizations,* and IRS Form 990. This method is also compatible with *The Black Book Standards of Accounting and Financial Reporting for Voluntary Health and Welfare Organizations* issued jointly by the National

Assembly of National Voluntary Health and Social Welfare Organizations and the National Health Council (1998).

Cost Allocation Methods

Regardless of the cost allocation method an organization employs, the objective is to end up with a single functionalized trial balance report from which you can prepare all your period-ending reports. For purposes of this discussion of cost allocation methods, organizations incur two general categories of costs: direct costs that apply to, benefit, or can otherwise be identified with a single function, department, project, or grant; and common costs that apply to more than one function, department, project, or grant and therefore require allocation on some basis. *Indirect costs*, as related to government indirect cost rates, can be M&G costs only or M&G costs plus all or any portion of the common costs.

Cost Allocation Objectives and Recommended Policies

The *objectives* of a cost allocation methodology are to provide reasonable allocations of expenses and to avoid establishing costly and burdensome allocation procedures. The same cost allocation method, consistent with GAAP, should be employed for all accounting and financial reporting, including government grant budgeting and reporting, IRS Form 990, and GAAP statements of functional expenses. This policy ensures that, regardless of the cost allocation method an organization uses, it will end up with a single functionalized trial balance report from which all of its period-ending reports can be prepared. The cost allocation method should be used consistently from year to year and from activity to activity. Reliable time records should be maintained for each employee for each pay period based on actual detailed time reports or other contemporaneous determination of the actual activity of each employee.

Activity-Level Cost Allocation

Common costs can be allocated to detail-level cost objectives. In this guide the most detailed cost objectives measured by the accounting system are referred to as *activity-level* costs objectives. Activity-level cost allocation, the primary method discussed here, means that all allocations of common costs to cost objectives are made at the activity level (that is, the detailed level) and that costs of activities are aggregated as needed to obtain summary-level distributions of costs to cost centers, contracts, projects, grants, programs, departments, functions, organizations, and regions. This approach avoids multiple and differing methods of cost allocation for the various summary-level cost distributions.

Dimensions of Cost Allocation Methods

Cost allocation methods vary according to the object expense category involved, the type of cost pool employed, the timing of the allocation, and the basis that is used. Table 8.5 shows how these four allocation variables are applied to the common cost pools for each expense account, to the service department cost pools, and to management and general costs.

Object Expense Category

Most of the object expense categories can involve allocable expenses. Each object expense category can involve allocations at different times, have one or more bases, and use one or more types of cost pool. The categories in the UCOA presented in this manual have been tailored to ensure that various cost allocation methods can be employed.

Types of Cost Pools

Allocations can be significantly simplified when grouped and accounted for in cost pools. Listed below are the types of cost pools in the sequence in which they should be performed, with one or two suggested bases noted in parentheses.

1. Employee leave line item common cost pool; for example, vacation, sick leave, holidays, and other out-of-service hours (basis: direct-staff in-service salaries or hours worked)

2. Employee fringe line item common cost pool; for example, pension, benefits, taxes; may need a second such cost pool to accommodate items not allowed to be charged to government grants (basis: direct-staff salaries)

3. Line item common cost pools for other object expense categories; for example, occupancy, supplies, telephone, and depreciation (simple basis: direct-staff salaries or hours or modified total direct costs, which excludes subcontracts, capital expenditures, and other pass-throughs; variable basis: by line item, if justified)

4. Common cost pools for service departments, such as data processing, printing and duplicating, or mail room (basis: direct-staff salaries or modified total direct costs)

5. M&G cost pool can be allocated for grant reporting but not for GAAP or IRS Form 990 reporting (basis: direct-staff salaries or modified total direct costs)

TABLE 8.5

Allocation Variables by Object Expense Category

Account Number	Object Expense	Initial Recording in Books	Month-End Report Processing	Year-End Report Processing	Use of Cost Pool	Suggested Allocation Bases[a]	Form 990 (Line Number)
	Grants, Contracts, and Direct Assistance						
7010-XXX	Program-related contracts to other entities	Direct/program	No	No	Unusual	1 (all program)	22
7020-XXX	Grants to other organizations	Direct/program	No	No	Unusual	1 (all program)	22
7030-XXX	Allocations to affiliated organizations	Direct/program	No	No	Unusual	1 (all program)	22
7040-XXX	Awards and grants to individuals	Direct/program	No	No	Unusual	1 (all program)	22
7050-XXX	Specific assistance to individuals	Direct/program	No	No	Unusual	1 (all program)	23
	Salaries and Related Expenses						
7210-XXX	Salaries of officers, directors, etc., in service	Always/pay period	No	No	Unusual	1, 2	25
	Salaries of officers, directors, etc., out of service	Optional/pay period	Optional	Optional	Yes	1, 3	25
7220-XXX	Other salaries and wages, in service	Always/pay period	No	No	Unusual	1, 2	26
	Other salaries and wages, out of service	Optional/pay period	Optional	Optional	Yes	1, 3	26
7310-XXX	Pension plan contributions	Optional	Optional	Optional	Yes	1, 3	27
7320-XXX	Other employee benefits	Optional	Optional	Optional	Yes	1, 3	28
7410-XXX	Payroll taxes, etc.	Optional	Optional	Optional	Yes	1, 3	29
	Other Expenses						
7510-XXX	Professional fundraising fees	Direct/ fundraising	No	No	No	1 (fundraising)	30
7520-XXX	Accounting fees	Direct/M&G	No	No	Unusual	1, 7, 8, 9	31
7530-XXX	Legal fees	Direct/usually M&G	No	No	Unusual	1, 7, 8, 9	32
7540-XXX	Other professional fees	Optional	Optional	Optional	Yes	1, 3, 7, 8, 9	43
7550-XXX	Contract temporary help	Optional	Optional	Optional	Yes	1, 2, 7, 8, 9	43

(Continued)

TABLE 8.5

Allocation Variables by Object Expense Category *(Continued)*

Account Number	Object Expense	Initial Recording In Books	Month-End Report Processing	Year-End Report Processing	Use of Cost Pool	Suggested Allocation Bases[a]	Form 990 (Line Number)
7580-XXX	Donated professional services—GAAP	Optional	Optional	Optional	Yes	1, 7, 8, 9	Part III
7590-XXX	Donated professional services—non-GAAP	Optional	Optional	Optional	Yes	1, 7, 8, 9	Part III
7710-XXX	Supplies	Optional	Optional	Optional	Yes	1, 3, 7, 8, 9	33
7720-XXX	Donated materials and supplies	Optional	Optional	Optional	Yes	1, 3, 7, 8, 9	33
7810-XXX	Telephone	Optional	Optional	Optional	Yes	1, 6, 3, 7, 8, 9	34
7910-XXX	Postage and shipping	Optional	Optional	Optional	Yes	1, 3, 6, 7, 8, 9	35
7920-XXX	Mailing services	Optional	Optional	Optional	Yes	1, 3, 6, 7, 8, 9	35
8010-XXX	Rent	Optional	Optional	Optional	Yes	1, 6, 3, 7, 8, 9	36
8020-XXX	Utilities	Optional	Optional	Optional	Yes	1, 6, 3, 7, 8, 9	36
8030-XXX	Real estate taxes	Optional	Optional	Optional	Yes	1, 6, 3, 7, 8, 9	36
8040-XXX	Personal property taxes	Optional	Optional	Optional	Yes	1, 6, 3, 7, 8, 9	36
8050-XXX	Interest on mortgages	Optional	Optional	Optional	Yes	1, 6, 3, 7, 8, 9	36
8080-XXX	Donated use of facilities and utilities—GAAP	Optional	Optional	Optional	Yes	1, 6, 3, 7, 8, 9	Part III
8090-XXX	Donated use of facilities and utilities—non-GAAP	Optional	Optional	Optional	Yes	1, 6, 3, 7, 8, 9	Part III
8110-XXX	Equipment rental and maintenance	Optional	Optional	Optional	Yes	1, 6, 3, 7, 8, 9	37
8210-XXX	Printing and duplicating	Optional	Optional	Optional	Yes	1, 7, 3, 8, 9	38
8220-XXX	Publications published by others	Optional	Optional	Optional	Yes	1, 7, 3, 8, 9	38
8230-XXX	Publications published by organization	Optional	Optional	Optional	Yes	1, 7, 3, 8, 9	38
8310-XXX	Travel	Optional	Optional	Optional	Yes	1, 7, 3, 8, 9	39
8510-XXX	Conferences, conventions, and meetings	Optional	Optional	Optional	Yes	1, 7, 3, 8, 9	40
8610-XXX	Interest—general	Optional	Optional	Optional	Yes	1, 3, 7, 8, 9	41

(Continued)

TABLE 8.5

Allocation Variables by Object Expense Category *(Continued)*

Account Number	Object Expense	Initial Recording in Books	Month-End Report Processing	Year-End Report Processing	Use of Cost Pool	Suggested Allocation Bases[a]	Form 990 (Line Number)
8650-XXX	Depreciation—allowable	Optional	Optional	Optional	Yes	1, 6, 3, 7, 8, 9	42
8660-XXX	Depreciation—not allowable	Optional	Optional	Optional	Yes	1, 6, 3, 7, 8, 9	42
8710-XXX	Insurance—excluding employee-related	Optional	Optional	Optional	Yes	1, 3, 7, 8, 9	43
8810-XXX	Membership dues	Optional	Optional	Optional	Yes	1, 7, 8, 9	43
8820-XXX	Staff development	Optional	Optional	Optional	Yes	1, 3, 7, 8, 9	43
9010-XXX	List rental	Optional	Optional	Optional	Yes	1, 7, 8, 9	43
9020-XXX	Outside computer services	Optional	Optional	Optional	Yes	1, 3, 7, 8, 9	43
9100-XXX	Bad debt expense	Direct/program	No	No	No	1	43
9110-XXX	Sales taxes	Optional	Optional	Optional	Yes	1, 7	43
9120-XXX	Unrelated business income tax (UBIT)	Optional	Optional	Optional	Yes	1, 7	43
9150-XXX	Other taxes	Optional	Optional	Optional	Yes	1, 7	43
9210-XXX	Fines, penalties, and judgments—organization	Optional	Optional	Optional	Yes	1	43
9230-XXX	Incorporation and other organization expenses	Direct/usually M&G	No	No	Unusual	1, 3, 4, 5, 7, 8, 9	43
9250-XXX	Advertising	Optional	Optional	Optional	Yes	1, 7	43
9290-XXX	Contingency provisions	Optional	Optional	Optional	Yes	1, 7	43
9300-XXX	Other expenses	Optional	Optional	Optional	Yes	1, 3, 7, 8, 9	43
9810-XXX	Capital purchases—land	Optional	Optional	Optional	Yes	Capitalized	Capitalized
9820-XXX	Capital purchases—buildings	Optional	Optional	Optional	Yes	Capitalized	Capitalized
9830-XXX	Capital purchases—equipment	Optional	Optional	Optional	Yes	Capitalized	Capitalized
9840-XXX	Capital purchases—vehicles	Optional	Optional	Optional	Yes	Capitalized	Capitalized
9910-XXX	Payments to affiliates	Unusual	No	No	No	N/A	16
XXX-910	Service department cost pools	No	Optional	Optional	Central service pool	1, 3, 4, 6, 7, 8, 9	N/A
XXX-510	Administrative (M&G) costs	No	Optional	Optional	Administrative pool	1, 3, 4, 5, 7, 8, 9	44(C)

[a]*See "Suggested Allocation Bases for Table 8.5" on p. 88. "Optional" means that allocations can take place at that time.*

To ensure that common costs are distributed fairly and evenly among functions and grants, cost pools are often maintained on a year-to-date, cumulative basis rather than allocated and recorded in the accounting records monthly. Final cost pool allocations are made at year end or at the end of a grant period. Provisional cost allocations are made during the year or during a grant period for interim reporting purposes only. Grants or contracts with periods that end during the organization's fiscal year will not have final allocated costs until year end.

In general, cost pool allocations can be more economical and reliable than transaction-by-transaction allocations, which can be cumbersome and costly, even with computer software. The major exception is direct-staff in-service salary and wages, where detailed salary transactions for each employee must be allocated at least monthly, based on reliable and credible staff time records.

Timing

Costs can be allocated at three points in time: when the transaction is *initially* coded and recorded in the accounting system, during *month-end* report processing, or during *year-end* processing.

Different object expense categories can involve expense allocations at different times. For example, in-service salaries for each employee should always be allocated when the payroll data are initially coded and recorded for a pay period. Out-of-service salaries (such as for vacation, holidays, or sick leave) are recorded in a common cost pool for allocation at the end of each month or, more equitably, at the end of the year. Depreciation is usually calculated and allocated during year-end processing (with provisional allocations for monthly reporting if necessary).

All direct costs should be charged directly to the specific activity or cost objective when the expense transaction is initially coded and recorded. Exceptions should be temporarily coded as suspense transactions, with final activity coding to be applied during month-end processing.

Bases for Allocation

The AICPA *Audit and Accounting Guide: Not for Profit Organizations* provides an outline of suggested bases for allocation for various categories of object expenses:

> *13.44 If direct identification (that is, assignment) is impossible or impracticable, an allocation is appropriate. The techniques used to allocate are common to all entities, for-profit and not-for-profit alike. A reasonable allocation of expenses among an organization's functions may be*

made on a variety of bases. Objective methods of allocating expenses are preferable to subjective methods.

13.45   *The allocation may be based on related financial or non-financial data. For example, the expenses associated with occupying and maintaining a building, such as depreciation, utilities, maintenance, and insurance, may be allocated based on the square footage of space occupied by each program and supporting service. If floor plans are not available and the measurement of the occupied space is impractical, an estimate of the relative portion of the building occupied by each function may be made. Occupying and maintaining a building is not a separate supporting service. Interest costs, including interest on a building's mortgage, should be allocated to specific programs or supporting services to the extent possible; interest costs that cannot be allocated should be reported as part of the management and general function.*

13.46   *An organization should evaluate its expense allocation methods periodically. The evaluation may include, for example, a review of the time records or activity reports of key personnel, the use of space and the consumption of supplies and postage. The expense allocation methods should be reviewed by management and revised when necessary to reflect significant changes in the nature or level of the organization's current activities.*[11]

Allocations can be made on a single basis for all categories of object expenses or on multiple bases that vary by account or object category. When reliable, using a single basis for allocating common costs can be less burdensome.

In multifunded, multiple-fiscal-year environments, financial bases, such as direct salaries and modified total direct expenses, are easier to apply. They reflect the continuing change in funding and the relationship of each activity to the whole. As funding begins and ends, activities enter and leave the ongoing allocation process. Hours and units of service may also be practical bases. Static bases, such as square footage, number of telephones, and the like are often unreliable in a changing environment.

Many or most of the decisions regarding expense allocation bases can be made during the budgeting process when budgets for activities are established in a line item–by–activity format. That format is a matrix where object expense accounts are allocated across activities. Activity budgets are aggregated into budgets for various summary cost objectives, including departments, functions, programs, cost centers, grants, and projects.

Suggested Allocation Bases for Table 8.5

The "Suggested Allocation Bases" column in Table 8.5 uses reference numbers to indicate the allocation bases in the checklist that are relevant to each account. The numbers are sequenced in the recommended order of preference.

1. Expenses that can be identified directly with a single activity are charged 100 percent to the single activity.

    Expenses that are incurred for the benefit of more than one activity can be allocated on the basis of

2. *Direct-staff hours* (percentage of time spent by staff assigned to activities); or

3. *Direct-staff salaries* (percentage of total salary of staff assigned to activities); or

4. *Direct expenses* (percentage of total direct expenses for activities); or

5. *Modified total direct expenses* (percentage of total direct expenses for activities, less distorting expense items, such as equipment purchases, flow-through funds, or food under U.S. Department of Agriculture food programs); or

6. *Units of service* (percentage by units of service provided); or

7. *Usage* (percentage by usage of space, equipment, or other assets by activities); or

8. *Budget* (percentages used in the budget for activities); or

9. *Prior year* (percentages based on prior-year actual percentages for activities)

The *budget* and *prior year* options should be used only if using one of the other options is not feasible. According to OMB Circular A-122, budget estimates (estimates determined before the services are performed) do not qualify as support for charges to awards.[12]

Reducing the Burden of Cost Allocation by Using Only One or Two Bases

To reduce the complexity and burden of cost allocation for smaller not-for-profit organizations, direct-staff salaries and total direct costs (which include in-service direct-staff salaries) can often be the only bases used for allocation of every object expense category. These bases are fairly simple to calculate and apply.

There are several reasons why using direct-staff salaries as the single basis (or as one of two total direct cost bases) can be reliable and useful, especially when two-thirds or more of all expenses are personnel related.

First, salaries alone are often 50 percent or more of an organization's expenses. Second, all other payroll-related expenses are allocated on the basis of direct-staff salaries. And third, other categories of object expenses tend to vary according to staff salaries; examples include occupancy, equipment rental and maintenance, depreciation, and general insurance. This approach can provide a significant cost-saving option, especially for small to midsize organizations. Direct-staff salaries have been used as the single basis to develop the sample trial balance (see Chapter Seven), GAAP financial statements (see Chapter Eleven), and IRS Form 990 financial statements (see Chapter Twelve) presented in this guide.

Cost allocation can be simplified even further by accumulating the expenses of account and service department common cost pools into one or more overall cost centers for allocation purposes. Form 990 instructions for Part II, Statement of Functional Expenses, provides guidance on using cost centers for allocating cost pools:

> *Colleges, universities, hospitals, and other organizations that accumulate indirect [common] expenses in various cost centers (such as the expenses of operating and maintaining the physical plant) that are reallocated to the program services and other functional areas of the organization in single or multiple steps may find it easier to report these expenses in the following optional manner:*
>
> > First, *report the expenses of these indirect cost centers on lines 25 through 43 of column (C), Management and general, along with the expenses properly reportable in that column.*
> >
> > Second, *allocate the total expenses for each cost center to columns (B), (C), and (D) (Program services, Management and general, and Fundraising) as a separate item entry on line 43, Other expenses. Enter the name of the cost center on line 43. . . . If any part of the cost center's expenses are to be allocated to columns (B), Program services, and (D), Fundraising, enter these expenses as positive amounts in these columns and as single negative amounts in column (C), Management and general. Do not make any entries in column (A), Total, for these offsetting entries.*

When a single basis is employed, it provides the same allocation results as making line-by-line allocations but eliminates the cost and burden of following such procedures. (Note, however, that this approach will no longer allow the reader to understand the line-by-line costs of individual program activities and supporting service activities.) If this cost center approach to allocation is employed, it must also be used in the budgeting process as well. Otherwise, BTA reporting and analysis would not be possible.

Cost Pool Allocation for Smaller Organizations

All not-for-profit organizations that have more than one activity will have certain common costs that must be allocated to the organization's activities. Table 8.6 provides an illustration of the use of only one cost allocation basis and the single overall cost center approach for all of the common cost pools. The cost allocation basis used is Basis 3, Direct-Staff Salaries, and the percentages are listed in Table 8.6 in the "Activity salaries and wages as a percentage of total" line. To calculate these percentages, "Salaries of officers, directors, etc." is combined with "Other salaries and wages." The expenses for all common cost pools by account total $99,524. In the "Common cost pool allocation" line, the $99,524 is allocated to the activities using the corresponding percentages.

Reporting Costs of Joint Activities That Include a Fundraising Appeal

Finally, we come to one of the most intractable issues in not-for-profit accounting and reporting: allocation of joint costs involving the fundraising function. The GAAP governing this issue is promulgated in AICPA's Statement of Position 98-2, *Accounting for Costs of Activities of Not-for-Profit Organizations and State and Local Governmental Entities That Include Fund Raising* (SOP 98-2). This latest development of standards on this topic follows over twenty years of debate and discussion on how to treat the allocation of such joint costs. The following is a brief summary.

According to SOP 98-2:

- If the three criteria of *purpose, audience,* and *content* are met, the costs of joint activities that are identifiable with a particular function (that is, M&G, program, or fundraising) should be charged to that function and joint costs should be allocated accordingly between fundraising and the applicable program or the M&G function.

- If *any* of the three criteria (purpose, audience, or content) are not met, all costs of the activity should be reported as fundraising costs. An exception is the cost of goods or services provided in exchange transactions that are part of joint activities (for instance, a meal at a special event fundraiser), which should not be reported as fundraising.

- Certain financial statement disclosures are required if joint costs are allocated.

The Purpose Criterion

The purpose criterion is met if the purpose of the joint activity includes accomplishing either the M&G function or one or more program functions.

SOP 98-2 states that to accomplish program functions the activity should call for specific action by the audience (the client, recipient, or beneficiary) that will help accomplish the not-for-profit organization's mission.

The Audience Criterion

A rebuttable presumption exists that the audience criterion is not met if the audience includes prior donors or if the audience is chosen on the basis of its members' ability or likelihood to donate to the organization. This presumption can be rebutted if audience members are also chosen on the basis of

- Their need or potential to take the specific action recommended as the program component of the joint activity

- Their ability to take specific action to assist the organization in meeting its program goals

- Their status as the particular audience to which the organization must direct the M&G component of the joint activity or their reasonable potential to use the M&G component

The Content Criterion

The content criterion requires that the joint activity support either the M&G or program function of the organization. The joint activity is considered to support the program function if it calls for specific action by the recipient that will help accomplish the organization's mission. The joint activity is considered to support the M&G function if it fulfills one or more of the organization's M&G responsibilities through a component of the joint activity.

Disclosure of Allocation of Joint Costs

Not-for-profit organizations that allocate joint costs disclose in the notes to their financial statements

- The types of activities for which the joint cost were incurred

- A statement that such costs were allocated

- The total amount allocated in each period and the portion allocated to each functional category—program, M&G, and fundraising.

SOP 98-2 encourages, but does not require, that the amount of joint costs for each kind of joint activity be disclosed, if practical. Not-for-profit organizations that are heavily engaged in "public education" activities and that therefore of necessity must conduct joint activity are well advised to study SOP 98-2, which provides several examples of the application of the standards discussed in this section.

TABLE 8.6

Simplified Common Cost Pool Allocation for Smaller Organizations

Account Number	Revenue or Expense	Program Service Activities					Management and General (510)	Fundraising (710)	Common Cost Pool (920)	Total Expense
		Program A		Program B		Total Program				
		General (100)	Project A (120)	General (200)	Project B (220)					
	Personnel expenses									
7210	Salaries of officers, directors, etc.	14,140	7,315	3,140		24,595	6,831	6,506	4,101	42,033
7220	Other salaries and wages	51,797	10,089	10,007	6,180	78,073	1,948	5,023	23,950	108,994
	Activity salaries and wages as percentage of total[a]	53.6	14.2	10.7	5.0	68.0	7.1	9.4		100.0
7310	Pension plan contributions								15,103	15,103
7320	Other employee benefits								7,551	7,551
7410	Payroll taxes								12,082	12,082
	Total payroll	65,937	17,404	13,147	6,180	102,668	8,779	11,529	62,787	185,763
7540	Professional fees						3,890			3,890
	Total personnel expenses	65,937	17,404	13,147	6,180	102,668	12,669	11,529	62,787	189,653
	Nonpersonnel expenses									
7710	Supplies	4,207	278	804	113	5,402	237	939	4,327	10,905
7810	Telephone	265	106	273	142	786	195	154	3,785	4,920
7910	Postage and shipping	356	58	222		636	270	1,063	1,357	3,326
8010	Rent								18,634	18,634
8110	Equipment rental and maintenance	646	67	670	121	1,504	155	275	5,478	7,412
8210	Printing and publications	2,713	1,268	2,470	178	6,629	401	1,535	2,478	11,043
8310	Travel	1,991	902	985	105	3,983	1,075	593	678	6,329

TABLE 8.6
Simplified Common Cost Pool Allocation for Smaller Organizations *(Continued)*

Account Number	Revenue or Expense	Program Service Activities					Management and General (510)	Fundraising (710)	Common Cost Pool (920)	Total Expense
		Program A		Program B		Total Program				
		General (100)	Project A (120)	General (200)	Project B (220)					
8510	Conferences and meetings	765		456		1,221	1,980	567		3,768
9300	Other nonpersonnel expenses	345	832	56	160	1,393	673	200		2,266
	Total nonpersonnel expenses	11,288	3,511	5,936	819	21,554	4,986	5,326	36,737	68,603
	Total expenses before allocation	77,225	20,915	19,083	6,999	124,222	17,655	16,855	99,524	258,256
	Common cost pool allocation[a]	53,363	14,085	10,640	5,001	83,089	7,105	9,330	(99,524)	0
	Total expenses	130,588	35,000	29,723	12,000	207,311	24,760	26,185	0	258,256

Note: *All amounts are dollar amounts except those specifically designated as percentages.*

[a]*The common cost pool total is allocated to activities on a pro rata basis using salaries (see "Activity salaries and wages as percentage of total").*

Chapter 9

Staff Time Recording and Reporting

CLOSELY RELATED to the concept of cost allocation is the principle of staff time recording and reporting. Most not-for-profit organizations are labor intensive, particularly those engaged in human services or personal social services. In many cases over 50 percent of the organization's total expenses are accounted for in salaries, benefits, payroll taxes, and so on, for employees. In cases where an employee is assigned to perform just one service, function, or activity, 100 percent of the employee's time—and therefore cost—is assigned to that service, function, or activity. However, when employees are assigned to perform more than one function, then time reporting becomes essential.

Not-for-profit organizations should maintain reliable time records for each employee and each pay period, based on detailed time reports or other contemporaneous determination of the actual activity of each employee. All in-service, direct-staff salaries should be allocated based on direct-staff hours. All payroll-related expenses, and frequently many other categories of expense, are also allocated based on direct-staff salaries that have been allocated based on hours. Each employee's salary for each pay period is allocated to various activities based on time and attendance records. Year-to-date total direct-staff salaries are maintained in the accounting system by activity.

Not-for-profit organizations receiving funding from government sources and subject to the regulations of OMB Circular A-122 are specifically required to maintain detailed staff time records according to that circular:

Charges to awards for salaries and wages, whether treated as direct costs or indirect costs, will be based on documented payrolls approved by a responsible official(s) of the organization. The distribution of salaries and wages to awards must be supported by personnel activity reports . . . maintained for all staff members whose compensation is charged, in whole or in part, directly to awards. . . .

(a) *The reports must reflect an after-the-fact determination of the actual activity of each employee. Budget estimates (i.e., estimates determined before the services are performed) do not qualify as support for charges to awards.*

(b) *Each report must account for the total activity for which employees are compensated. . . .*

(d) *The reports must be prepared at least monthly and must coincide with one or more pay periods. . . .*

Charges for the salaries and wages of nonprofessional employees, in addition to the supporting documentation described [elsewhere], must also be supported by records indicating the total number of hours worked each day. . . .

Salaries and wages of employees used in meeting cost sharing or matching requirements on awards must be supported in the same manner.[1]

Time Records and Salary Allocations for Each Pay Period

A time sheet should be prepared and signed every payroll period for every employee (see Resource D, Table D.1, for an example). Even if the activity assignments are the same every payroll period, an organization needs a time sheet for its records. The time sheet is also needed to report any out-of-service time, such as vacation or sick leave. The time sheet objective for the pay period is to record the time an employee spends on any activity within a project or grant within a function or department.

Every payroll period, gross salaries and wages for each employee should be distributed to activities based on the percentage of time spent on each activity as evidenced by the time sheet for the related pay period. (When payroll-related expenses represent two-thirds or three-quarters of an organization's budget, direct-staff salaries may be reliable as the primary basis for cost allocations.)

Establishing Amounts for Salaries and Distributing Them by Activity

Accounting for salaries begins with monthly time distribution data from time sheets for each pay period and payroll data for each employee and ends with year-to-date amounts by activity code in the trial balance for the two salary account numbers 7210 and 7220.

This chapter includes sample schedules showing how expenses for various accounts can be distributed by activity code. A single monthly computer spreadsheet was used to produce the illustrations presented in this chapter. These examples show that the vast majority of the many accounting tasks can be performed by a computer—in this case using spreadsheet software.

Monthly Time Sheets for Employees

The sample functionalized trial balance report and various financial reports in this guide are based on the assumption that the organization employs after-the-fact determinations of how employees spent their time in terms of activity codes found in its chart of accounts—as required by OMB Circular A-122. The activities listed in the sample monthly time sheets for employees are the same as those in the simplified coding system, level 3, in Chapter Six (Table 6.2).

Methods for making these after-the-fact determinations of the use of staff time can vary from one employee to another depending on the circumstances. For employees whose time is always distributed in the same amounts to one or more activity codes, daily maintenance of time sheet records is not needed; the same preset time sheet can be used from one pay period to the next. For others periodic actual daily time records may be required, with adjustments to the preset time sheets as needed (for example, one-week testing on a quarterly basis or random moment or random week sampling). In some cases employees will need to keep daily time records. Depending on the nature of the work and the work assignments, the organization will choose a *tracking threshold* that determines the smallest increment of time tracked—commonly fifteen minutes, thirty minutes, or one hour.

Sample Employee Time Sheets

Table 9.1 illustrates the time sheet for one employee, in this case the executive director and chief executive officer. The total hours by activity for the month are converted to percentages, which are entered in the line for the executive director in Table 9.2, which shows how the percentages for the month by activity are entered into a report for the organization from all the employee time sheets. Table 9.3 shows how the percentages from Table 9.2 are applied to the monthly gross salaries for each employee in order to calculate the amount of direct-staff salaries for each employee distributed to each activity. The total salaries for the month by activity within account are tabulated. These totals are added to the "Prior month YTD salaries" in Table 9.4 to arrive at "Current month YTD salaries." Table 9.4 provides the current month year-to-date salaries by activity within account. (These are the figures used in Table 8.6.)

A more detailed discussion of time recording and reporting, including examples, can be found in Resource D.

TABLE 9.1
Simplified Monthly Time Sheet for Employees of Smaller Organizations

Activity	Activity Code	Day of Month															Period	
		1	2	3	4	5	6	7	8	9	10	11	12	13	14	15	Hours	Percent
Program A, general	100			4.0		4.0			8.0			8.0	4.0				28.0	31.8%
Program A, project A	120	8.0		4.0		4.0							4.0			8.0	28.0	31.8%
Program B, general	200									8.0							8.0	9.1%
Program B, project B	220																0.0	0.0%
Management and general	510		8.0								4.0						12.0	13.6%
Fundraising	710				8.0						4.0						12.0	13.6%
Common cost pool	920																0.0	0.0%
Total		8.0	8.0	8.0	8.0	8.0	0.0	0.0	8.0	8.0	8.0	8.0	8.0	0.0	0.0	8.0	88.0	100.0%

Activity	Activity Code	Day of Month															Period		Month	
		16	17	18	19	20	21	22	23	24	25	26	27	28	29	30	31	Hours	Percent	Hours	Percent
Program A, general	100		4.0		4.0				8.0						4.0		4.0	24.0	25.0%	52.0	28.3%
Program A, project A	120	8.0	4.0		4.0			8.0								8.0		32.0	33.3%	60.0	32.6%
Program B, general	200																	0.0	0.0%	8.0	4.3%
Program B, project B	220																	0.0	0.0%	0.0	0.0%
Management and general	510									4.0					4.0			8.0	8.3%	20.0	10.9%
Fundraising	710			8.0														8.0	8.3%	20.0	10.9%
Common cost pool	920									4.0	8.0	8.0					4.0	24.0	25.0%	24.0	13.0%
Total		8.0	8.0	8.0	8.0	0.0	0.0	8.0	8.0	8.0	8.0	8.0	0.0	0.0	8.0	8.0	8.0	96.0	100.0%	184.0	100.0%

TABLE 9.2

Monthly Staff Time Distribution by Activity

Account Number	Job Title	Percentage of Total Time Allocated to Each Activity							
		Program A		Program B		Management and General (510)	Fundraising (710)	Common Cost Pool (920)	Total
		General (100)	Project A (120)	General (200)	Project B (220)				
7210	Executive director or CEO[a]	28.3	32.6	4.3	0.0	10.9	10.9	13.0	100
7220	Office manager, bookkeeper					72.0	15.0	13.0	100
7220	Program director	70.0	5.0	12.0				13.0	100
7220	Assistant program director	87.0						13.0	100
7220	Administrative assistant	45.0				27.0	15.0	13.0	100
7220	Receptionist							100.0	100

Note: Data are taken from the monthly time sheet of each employee.

[a]The percentages used for Executive Director or CEO are from the illustrative time sheet (Table 9.1).

TABLE 9.3

Monthly Staff Salary Distribution by Activity

Account Number	Job Title	Gross Monthly Salary (Dollars)	Portion of Salary Allocated to Each Activity (Dollars)							
			Program A		Program B		Management and General (510)	Fundraising (710)	Common Cost Pool (920)	Total
			General (100)	Project A (120)	General (200)	Project B (220)				
7210	Executive director or CEO	3,503	990	1,142	152	0	381	381	457	3,503
	Total salary for officers	3,503	990	1,142	152	0	381	381	457	3,503
7210	Office manager, bookkeeper	1,880					1,354	282	244	1,880
7220	Program director	2,500	1,750	125	300	0			325	2,500
7220	Assistant program director	1,980	1,723			0			257	1,980
7220	Administrative assistant	1,470	662			0	397	221	191	1,470
7220	Receptionist	1,250				0			1,250	1,250
7220	Total salary—other	9,080	4,134	125	300	0	1,751	503	2,268	9,080
	Total salary for month	12,583	5,124	1,267	452	0	2,131	883	2,725	12,583

Note: *Data are taken from the monthly time sheet of each employee.*

TABLE 9.4

Year-to-Date Staff Salary Distribution by Activity

Account Number	Job Title	Portion of Salary Allocated to Each Activity (Dollars)							
		Program A		Program B		Management and General (510)	Fundraising (710)	Common Cost Pool (920)	Total
		General (100)	Project A (120)	General (200)	Project B (220)				
	Prior month year-to-date salaries[a]								
7210	Salaries of officers, directors, etc.	13,150	6,173	2,988	0	6,450	6,125	3,644	38,530
7220	Other salaries and wages	47,663	9,964	9,707	6,180	198	4,521	21,682	99,914
7220	Program director	2,500	1,750	125	300			325	2,500
	Current month year-to-date salaries[b]								
7210	Salaries of officers, directors, etc.	14,140	7,315	3,140	0	6,831	6,506	4,101	42,033
7220	Other salaries and wages	51,797	10,089	10,007	6,180	1,948	5,023	23,950	108,994

Note: *Data are taken from the monthly time sheet of each employee.*

[a]*Enter from prior month staff time/salary work sheet.*

[b]*Enter current month year-to-date figures in direct cost worksheet.*

Part Three

Unified Internal and External Financial Reports Aligned with Form 990

Chapter 10

Financial Reports: Overview

IN PART THREE we present and discuss unified internal and external financial reporting for not-for-profit organizations. The key term to note is *unified*. By enabling various financial statements and reports to be aligned with IRS Form 990, we are proposing the *unification* of financial reports using the UCOA and functionalized trial balance report presented in Part Two.

The basic purpose of financial statements is to tell the "financial story" of an organization: how the resources were acquired or where the resources came from, how and for what purposes the resources were spent, and, in the case of Part III of Form 990 financial statements, what efforts were exerted and what was accomplished with the resources. This is, of course, an oversimplification of the purposes of financial statements. Users of financial statements need to know and assess the financial health of the organization. How financially viable is the organization? What is the likelihood of its financial sustainability?

Decisions to contribute to not-for-profit organizations are not unlike decisions to invest in securities. Contributors make certain sacrifices in return for anticipated social benefits. Estimates of probable social benefits are based on a contributor's evaluation of a not-for-profit organization's ability to achieve its goals. Decision makers in not-for-profit organizations—like those in business enterprises—need to predict, compare, and evaluate benefits and sacrifices in terms of amount, timing, and related uncertainties. The benefits are almost always nonmonetary and therefore difficult to quantify. The decision process, however, is essentially similar to that of commercial enterprises. As the AICPA's *Objectives of Financial Statements* points out:

> *The measurement of potential or actual benefits resulting from sacrifices by not-for-profit organizations is especially difficult. Information about*

the number and cost of patient-days provided by a hospital is of limited value; consideration must be given to the quality of the care. The numbers of credit courses completed or degrees granted by a university means little without reference to the quality of that education. In government, spending on poverty programs or agricultural supports should be assessed in terms of changes in the poverty level or improvement in the agricultural economy. The cost of military aircraft—or, in fact, the efficiency of production—should be viewed in the context of the nation's defense strategies.

Still, the objectives of the financial statements of commercial enterprises can provide broad guidelines for the development of objectives in the not-for-profit sector. They can offer useful distinctions about the decision-making process and users' needs that deserve attention in any effort to develop financial statement objectives for not-for-profit organizations.

The evaluation of the attainment of long-range goals of a commercial enterprise prior to its dissolution provides a useful pattern for the evaluation of governmental and eleemosynary organizations. Financial statement users need information for assessing:

Past goal attainments of the organization.

The status of present efforts to attain goals.

The probability of future goal attainment.

Similarly, significant assumptions underlying judgments, interpretations, approximations, and probabilities for all information should be disclosed so that users can apply their own judgments and interpretations. . . . An objective of financial statements for governmental and not-for-profit organizations is to provide information useful for evaluating the effectiveness of the management of resources in achieving the organization's goals. Performance measures should be quantified in terms of identified goals.[1]

In the following chapters we present and discuss

- A complete set of financial statements required under GAAP

- IRS Form 990 financial statements

- Uniform government grants and reports

- Financial reports for corporate and foundation grants

- Reports to United Ways and other grant makers

- Periodic financial reports for internal management

All of these internal and external financial reports can be unified with the help of the UCOA and the functionalized trial balance report—with the click of a mouse.

Uniform State Charity Financial Summaries and Supplements

In 1981 the National Association of State Charity Officials (NASCO) and the IRS, with the assistance and cooperation of the not-for-profit sector, established the uniform federal-state Form 990 and for nearly twenty years have collaborated to improve Form 990 and minimize the differences between Form 990 and GAAP. Virtually all states with annual financial reporting requirements accept Form 990 in lieu of their own reporting forms, and many states find that Form 990 with its twenty-eight attached schedules provides adequate financial information. A number of state charities offices require supplemental schedules to be filed with Form 990. NASCO, the IRS, and the not-for-profit sector have for several years been developing uniform state charity supplements under the auspices of the Multi-State Filing Program. This work in progress has been successful in establishing unified charity registration requirements and is expected to establish standards for annual supplemental state reporting in the near future. (See Resource E for a summary of state registration and reporting requirements.)

Chapter 11

GAAP Financial Statements

FASB STATEMENT of Financial Accounting Standards no. 117 (FAS-117) describes the purpose of a set of financial statements as follows:

4. *The primary purpose of financial statements is to provide relevant information to meet the common interests of donors, members, creditors, and others who provide resources to not-for-profit organizations. Those external users of financial statements have common interests in assessing (a) the services an organization provides and its ability to continue to provide those services and (b) how managers discharge their stewardship responsibilities and other aspects of their performance.*

5. *More specifically, the purpose of financial statements, including accompanying notes, is to provide information about:*

   a. *The amount and nature of an organization's assets, liabilities, and net assets*

   b. *The effects of transactions and other events and circumstances that change the amount and nature of net assets*

   c. *The amount and kinds of inflows and outflows of economic resources during a period and the relation between the inflows and outflows*

   d. *How an organization obtains and spends cash, its borrowing and repayment of borrowing, and other factors that may affect its liquidity*

   e. *The service efforts of an organization.*[1]

Prior to the issuance of FAS-117, most not-for-profit organizations used the "fund accounting" model for their general-purpose GAAP financial statements. Under this fund accounting model not-for-profit organizations would sort their various funds into fund groups with similar characteristics, providing a high level of detail about such fund groups. This made financial statements of not-for-profit organizations different from each other and from those of for-profit organizations. Under FAS-117, financial statements of not-for-profit organizations present activities, financial position, and cash flows as a whole, which makes the presentation similar to the financial statements of for-profit entities. This is part of a larger effort in the accounting profession to bring greater congruence between accounting and reporting of for-profit and not-for-profit organizations.

FAS-117 requires all not-for-profit organizations to present the following set of financial statements:

- Statement of financial position

- Statement of activities

- Statement of cash flows

- Accompanying notes to financial statements

In addition, "voluntary health and welfare" organizations must also present a statement of functional expenses, which is encouraged but not required for other not-for-profit organizations.

Statement of Financial Position

According to FAS-117, "The primary purpose of a statement of financial position is to provide relevant information about an organization's assets, liabilities, and net assets and about their relationships to each other at a moment in time." The statement of financial position must report and focus on the not-for-profit organization as a whole and must report on the organization's total assets, liabilities, and net assets. The statement must contain the following elements:

- Total assets

- Total liabilities

- Unrestricted net assets

- Temporarily restricted net assets

- Permanently restricted net assets

- Total net assets

Assets are reported by homogeneous groups such as cash and cash equivalents, receivables, short-term loans, inventories, deposits and prepaid expenses, marketable securities, other long-term investments, and land, buildings, and equipment. Assets may be sequenced according to their liquidity. FAS-117 states that "Cash or other assets received with a *donor-imposed restriction* that limits their use to long-term purposes should not be classified with cash or other assets that are unrestricted and available for current use."

Liabilities are reported by groups such as accounts payable, accrued payroll, other accrued expenses, deferred and unearned revenue, funds due to grantors, short-term loans, mortgages, and other long-term liabilities. Liabilities may be sequenced according to the nearness of their maturity and resulting use of cash.

Net assets are reported by three groups—unrestricted net assets, temporarily restricted net assets, and permanently restricted net assets—based on the existence or absence of donor-imposed restrictions. Net assets are the same as *equity* (the term used in the statements of position of for-profit organizations). The term *net assets* is now used in lieu of *fund balances*. According to FAS-117:

> *This Statement does not use the terms fund balance or changes in fund balances because in current practice those terms are commonly used to refer to individual groups of assets and related liabilities rather than to an entity's net assets or changes in net assets taken as a whole. Reporting by fund groups is not a necessary part of external financial reporting; however, this Statement does not preclude providing disaggregated information by fund groups.*

Increases in *unrestricted net assets* generally result from unrestricted contributions and from other revenues from program service fees and sales, membership dues and assessments, interest and dividends, gains (or losses) on sales of assets, and other earned income. That is, revenues that do not involve donor-imposed restrictions result in increases in unrestricted net assets. All expenses incurred in providing services, producing and delivering goods, raising contributions, and performing administrative functions result in decreases in unrestricted net assets.

Separate line items may be reported within unrestricted net assets or in notes to financial statements to distinguish between unrestricted net assets that are available for current use, invested in fixed assets, invested in long-term investments (for example, board-designated endowment), or otherwise designated by the board. In this regard FAS-117 observes:

> *The only limits on the use of unrestricted net assets are the broad limits resulting from the nature of the organization, the environment in which it operates, and the purposes specified in its articles of incorporation or bylaws and limits resulting from contractual agreements with suppliers, creditors, and others entered into by the organization in the course of its business. Information about those contractual limits that are significant, including the existence of loan covenants, generally is provided in notes*

to financial statements. Similarly, information about self-imposed limits that may be useful, including information about voluntary resolutions by the governing board of an organization to designate a portion of its unrestricted net assets to function as an endowment (sometimes called a board-designated endowment), may be provided in notes to or on the face of financial statements.

Increases in *permanently restricted net assets* result from receiving contributions and other revenue with permanent donor-imposed restrictions. According to FAS-117:

Separate line items may be reported within permanently restricted net assets or in notes to financial statements to distinguish between permanent restrictions for holdings of (a) assets, such as land or works of art, donated with stipulations that they be used for a specified purpose, be preserved, and not be sold or (b) assets donated with stipulations that they be invested to provide a permanent source of income. The latter result from gifts and bequests that create permanent endowment funds.

Increases in *temporarily restricted net assets* result from receiving contributions or other revenue with temporary donor-imposed restrictions. Expenses that are related to temporary donor-imposed restricted purposes result in temporarily restricted net assets being released from restriction, increasing unrestricted net assets and decreasing temporarily restricted net assets. In short, reclassification occurs when restrictions are met. On this point FAS-117 observes:

Separate line items may be reported within temporarily restricted net assets or in notes to financial statements to distinguish between temporary restrictions for (a) support of particular operating activities, (b) investment for a specified term, (c) use in a specified future period, or (d) acquisition of long-lived assets. Donors' temporary restrictions may require that resources be used in a later period or after a specified date (time restrictions), or that resources be used for a specified purpose (purpose restrictions), or both. For example, gifts of cash and other assets with stipulations that they be invested to provide a source of income for a specified term and that the income be used for a specified purpose are both time and purpose restricted. Those gifts often are called term endowments.

Statement of Activities

Previously called "statement of support, revenue, expense, and changes in fund balances," the statement of activities includes information about contributions and other revenues, expenses, gains, losses, and the amount of change in net assets for the period. This statement also summarizes expenses for programs, management and general, and fundraising. According to FAS-117, the primary purpose of this statement is to provide relevant information about:

- The effects of transactions and other events and circumstances that change the amount and nature of net assets;
- The relationships of those transactions and other events and circumstances to each other; and
- How the organization's resources are used in providing various services or programs.

FAS-117 states:

18. . . . *The change in net assets should articulate to the net assets or equity reported in the statement of financial position. . . .*

19. *A statement of activities shall report the amount of change in permanently restricted net assets, temporarily restricted net assets, and unrestricted net assets for the period. Revenues, expenses, gains, and losses increase or decrease net assets and shall be classified as provided in paragraphs 20–23. Other events, such as expirations of donor-imposed restrictions, that simultaneously increase one class of net assets and decrease another (reclassifications) shall be reported as separate items. Information about revenues, expenses, gains, losses, and reclassifications generally is provided by aggregating items that possess similar characteristics into reasonably homogeneous groups. . . .*

Classification of Revenue, Expenses, Gains, and Losses

20. *A statement of activities shall report revenues as increases in unrestricted net assets unless the use of the assets received is limited by donor-imposed restrictions. For example, fees from rendering services and income from investments generally are unrestricted; however, income from donor-restricted permanent or term endowments may be donor restricted and increase either temporarily restricted net assets or permanently restricted net assets. A statement of activities shall report expenses as decreases in unrestricted net assets.*

21. *Pursuant to FASB Statement No. 116,* Accounting for Contributions Received and Contributions Made, *in the absence of a donor's explicit stipulation or circumstances surrounding the receipt of the contribution that make clear the donor's implicit restriction on use, contributions are reported as unrestricted revenues or gains* (unrestricted support), *which increase unrestricted net assets. Donor-restricted contributions are*

reported as restricted revenues or gains (restricted support), which increase temporarily restricted net assets or permanently restricted net assets depending on the type of restriction. However, donor-restricted contributions whose restrictions are met in the same reporting period may be reported as unrestricted support provided that an organization reports consistently from period to period and discloses its accounting policy.

22. *A statement of activities shall report gains and losses recognized on investments and other assets (or liabilities) as increases or decreases in unrestricted net assets unless their use is temporarily or permanently restricted by explicit donor stipulations or by law. For example, net gains on investment assets, to the extent recognized in financial statements, are reported as increases in unrestricted net assets unless their use is restricted to a specified purpose or future period. If the governing board determines that the relevant law requires the organization to retain permanently some portion of gains on investment assets of endowment funds, that amount shall be reported as an increase in permanently restricted net assets.*

23. *Classifying revenues, expenses, gains, and losses within classes of net assets does not preclude incorporating additional classifications within a statement of activities. For example, within a class or classes of changes in net assets, an organization may classify items as* operating and nonoperating, *expendable and nonexpendable, earned and unearned, recurring and nonrecurring, or in other ways. This Statement neither encourages nor discourages those further classifications. However, because terms such as* operating income, operating profit, operating surplus, operating deficit, *and* results of operations *are used with different meanings, if an intermediate measure of* operations *(for example, excess or deficit of operating revenues over expenses) is reported, it shall be in a financial statement that, at a minimum, reports the change in unrestricted net assets for the period. If an organization's use of the term* operations *is not apparent from the details provided on the face of the statement, a note to financial statements shall describe the nature of the reported measure of operations or the items excluded from operations.*

Statement of Cash Flows

Previously required only of for-profit entities, the statement of cash flows provides relevant information about cash receipts and cash payments of an organization during a reporting period. This statement must show:

- Cash flows from operating activities, including net cash used by operating activities

- Cash flows from investing activities, including net cash used by investing activities

- Cash flows from financing activities, including net cash used by financing activities

- Net increase or decrease in cash and cash equivalents

- Cash and cash equivalents at the beginning of the year

- Cash and cash equivalents at the end of the year, including a reconciliation of changes in net assets to net cash used by operating activities

Statement of Functional Expenses

Voluntary health and welfare organizations must continue to prepare a statement of functional expenses in a matrix presenting both functional expenses (expenses for each program, for management and general, and for fundraising) and object expenses (such as salaries, occupancy, and travel). FASB does not require, but does encourage, other not-for-profit organizations to prepare this statement.

In the statement of activities all not-for-profit organizations must show a summary of their functional expenses. In order to be able to do this they must account for functional expenses by object categories (that is, by natural classifications) even though they are not required to present this information in a GAAP statement of functional expenses. Moreover, not-for-profit organizations that have to file Form 990 are required to report expenses by object in Part II of that form. IRS section 501(c)(3) and 501(c)(4) organizations are also required to report their object expenses as allocated to program services, management and general, and fundraising.

In Exhibits 11.1 to 11.4 we present a complete set of the GAAP-required financial statements and accompanying disclosure notes. This set of statements is only one of several that FAS-117 suggests. We follow these with a second set of three sample financial statements for the benefit of smaller organizations. Note that the sequential numbers in the left column of Exhibits 11.1 to 11.4 and the capital letters under the column headings would not ordinarily appear in general-purpose GAAP financial statements; we include them to permit cross-referencing with the Unified Chart of Accounts in Table 5.1 and various other tables in this book.

EXHIBIT 11.1

Statement of Financial Position
June 30, 20X2 and 20X1

	Assets	Note Number	20X2	20X1
1	Cash and cash equivalents		$ 78,722	$109,700
3	Accounts receivable—general, less allowance	(11)	12,686	7,262
	of $1,103 and $631			
4	Pledges receivable, less allowance of $0	(3, 4, 11)		4,800
	and $200			
5	Grants and contracts receivable		57,996	7,047
6	Inventories for sale		3,852	4,687
7	Prepaid expenses and deferred charges		7,398	6,489
8	Investments—marketable securities	(7)	40,000	
9	Other investments			1,143
	Fixed assets			
11	Land	(8)	34,247	34,247
12	Buildings, less depreciation of $43,945 and $35,583	(8)	90,055	98,417
13	Building improvements, less depreciation	(8)	31,580	34,733
	of $22,698 and $19,545			
14	Furniture and equipment, less depreciation of $43,754 and $35,529	(8)	94,080	102,305
15	Total Assets		$450,616	$410,830
	Liabilities and Net Assets			
	Liabilities			
21	Accounts payable		$5,476	$6,024
22	Accrued expenses—payroll		12,541	13,795
23	Accrued expenses—payroll taxes		3,276	3,604
24	Accrued expenses—other		894	1,142
25	Unearned revenue		17,850	15,870
27	Mortgages payable	(14)	69,834	73,679
28	Total liabilities		$109,871	$114,114
	Net assets			
29	Unrestricted—available for general activities		$134,260	$100,693
30	Unrestricted—board designated endowment	(5)		
31	Unrestricted—board designated for special purposes			
32	Unrestricted—invested in fixed assets	(8)	180,128	196,023
33	Total unrestricted		$314,388	$296,716
34	Temporarily restricted for specific grants and activities	(3)	26,357	
35	Permanently restricted—donor restricted endowment	(3)		
36	Total net assets		$340,745	$296,716
37	Total liabilities and net assets		$450,616	$410,831

EXHIBIT 11.2

Statement of Activities
For Years Ended June 30, 20X2 and 20X1

Revenues, Gains, and Other Support	Note Number	Temporarily Unrestricted (A)	Permanently Restricted (B)	20X2 Restricted (C)	20X1 Total (D)	Total (E)
Public support received directly						
51 Contributions, net of estimated uncollectible pledges of $0 and $200	(3, 11)	$145,358	$50,000	$0	$195,358	$54,890
52 Special events, net of costs of direct benefit to participants of $0 and $8,500						9,234
53 Legacies and bequests						12,000
54 Donated services and use of facilities	(6)	13,000			13,000	8,900
55 Gifts in kind—tangible	(6)	8,795			8,795	7,845
Public support received indirectly						
56 United Way allocations		18,500			18,500	18,500
57 Total public support		$185,653	$50,000	$0	$235,653	$111,369
58 Government grants		$395,951	$0	$0	$395,951	$316,875
59 Program service fees and revenue		71,101			71,101	189,076
Other revenue						
60 Interest on savings and temporary cash investments	(7)	7,423			7,423	4,689
61 Endowment and other interest and dividends from securities	(7)					
62 Realized gain (loss) on investments	(7)					
63 Unrealized gain (loss) in value of investments	(7)					
64 Other revenue						3,600
65 Net assets released from restrictions	(3)	23,643	(23,643)			
66 Total revenues, gains, and other support		$683,771	$26,357	$0	$710,128	$625,609

(Continued)

EXHIBIT 11.2

Statement of Activities
For Years Ended June 30, 20X2 and 20X1 (*Continued*)

Revenues, Gains, and Other Support	Note Number	Temporarily Unrestricted (A)	Permanently Restricted (B)	20X2 Restricted (C)	20X1 Total (D)	Total (E)
Expenses and Changes in Net Assets Program service expenses						
81 A—Adult activity center		$386,120	$0	$0	$386,120	$334,854
82 B—Residential services		108,826			108,826	107,890
83 C—Rehabilitation services		56,358			56,358	51,600
84 D—Special projects		23,643			23,643	
85 Total program services		$574,947	$ 0	$0	$574,947	$494,344
Supporting service expense						
86 Management and general		$ 83,668	$ 0	$0	$ 83,668	$ 63,800
87 Fundraising		7,484			7,484	54,600
88 Total supporting services		$ 91,152	$ 0	$0	$ 91,152	$118,400
89 Total expenses		$666,099	$ 0	$0	$666,099	$612,744
90 Increase (decrease) in net assets		$ 17,672	$26,357	$0	$ 44,029	$ 12,865
91 Other changes in net assets						
92 Changes in net assets		$ 17,672	$26,357	$0	$ 44,029	$ 12,865
93 Net assets at beginning of year		296,716			296,716	283,851
94 Net assets at end of year		$ 314,388	$26,357	$0	$340,745	$296,716

EXHIBIT 11.3

Statement of Functional Expenses
For Years Ended June 30, 20X2 and 20X1

Expenses	Program Services					Supporting Services			Total Program and Supporting Services	
	Adult Activity Center (A)	Residential Services (B)	Rehabilitation Services (C)	Special Projects (D)	Total (E)	Management and General (F)	Fundraising (G)	Total (H)	20X2 Total (I)	20X1 Total (J)
121 Salaries and wages	$223,515	$ 72,383	$34,137	$12,079	$342,114	$38,703	$4,183	$42,886	$385,000	$300,857
122 Employee benefits and payroll taxes	54,966	16,441	7,734	2,778	81,919	8,721	941	9,662	91,581	71,368
123 Total personnel expenses	$278,481	$ 88,824	$41,871	$14,857	$424,033	$47,424	$5,124	$52,548	$476,581	$372,225
124 Professional fees	$ 4,840	$403	$ 178	$ 92	$ 5,513	$11,853	$ 31	$11,884	$ 17,397	$ 68,365
125 Supplies	20,010	4,889	8,193	323	33,415	3,989	109	4,098	37,513	40,487
126 Telephone	3,726	1,108	489	253	5,576	794	86	880	6,456	5,789
127 Postage and shipping	1,289	383	169	88	1,929	275	486	761	2,690	3,287
128 Occupancy	20,607	2,263	999	517	24,386	1,622	175	1,797	26,183	12,845
129 Rental and maintenance of equipment	8,588	1,160	512	265	10,525	831	90	921	11,446	9,487
130 Printing and publications	12,008	2,207	975	504	15,694	5,633	939	6,572	22,266	28,746
131 Travel and transportation	9,254				9,254				9,254	11,757
132 Conferences, conventions, and meetings	987	829	58	30	1,904	2,672	10	2,682	4,586	5,487
133 Interest										200
134 Insurance	6,263	1,863	823	426	9,375	1,336	144	1,480	10,855	9,845
135 Grants and awards	6,246			6,246	6,246				6,246	8,790
136 Specific assistance to individuals				5,432	5,432				5,432	6,489
137 Depreciation of buildings and equipment	11,391	3,388	1,496	774	17,049	2,429	262	2,691	19,740	17,467
138 Other nonpersonnel expenses	2,430	1,509	595	82	4,616	4,810	28	4,838	9,454	11,478
139 Total functional expenses	$386,120	$108,826	$56,358	$23,643	$574,947	$83,668	$7,484	$91,152	$666,099	$612,744

EXHIBIT 11.4

Statement of Cash Flows
For Years Ended June 30, 20X2 and 20X1

		20X2	20X1
	Reconciliation of change in net assets to net cash used by operating activities		
250	Change in net assets	$ 44,029	$ 12,865
	Adjustments to reconcile change in net assets to net cash used by operating activities		
251	Depreciation	19,740	17,467
252	Decrease (increase) in accounts receivable	(5,424)	(6,058)
253	Decrease (increase) in pledges receivable	4,800	(2,450)
254	Decrease (increase) in grants receivable	(50,949)	
255	Decrease (increase) in inventories for sale	835	(105)
256	Decrease (increase) in prepaid expenses and deferred charges	(909)	7,530
257	Decrease (increase) in other assets	1,143	24
258	Increase (decrease) in accounts payable and accrued expenses	(2,378)	(12,250)
259	Increase (decrease) in unearned revenue	1,980	(973)
260	Net cash used by operating activities	$ 12,867	$ 16,050
	Cash flows from investing activities		
261	Purchase of fixed assets	$	$
262	Proceeds from sale of investments		12,425
263	Purchase of investments	(40,000)	
264	Net cash used by investing activities	$ (40,000)	$ 12,425
	Cash flows from financing activities		
265	Payments on long-term debt	$ (3,845)	$ (3,845)
266	Net cash used by financing activities	$ (3,845)	$ (3,845)
267	Net increase (decrease) in cash and cash equivalents	$ (30,978)	$ 24,630
268	Cash and cash equivalents at beginning of year	109,700	85,070
269	Cash and cash equivalents at end of year	$ 78,722	$109,700

Note: *This example uses the indirect method.*

Accompanying Notes to Financial Statements

Notes to financial statements are generally essential to the complete understanding of any financial report. Following is a list of possible disclosures. The list is not intended to be all-inclusive and may be too detailed for many organizations. Any information necessary for the full understanding of your financial statements should be included in a note if it is not included on the face of the statements themselves. However, do not include any note that is not needed for a full understanding of your organization's financial report.

1. Summary of Significant Accounting Policies

This note should identify and describe all accounting principles followed by your organization that materially affect the presentation of its financial information. The policies described in the note may include

- Method of accounting

- Basis of accounting

- Capitalization policy for fixed assets

- Methods of depreciation

- Methods of inventory valuation

- Policy concerning the valuation of donated assets or services

- Methods of allocating expenses among functions, projects, and grants

- Policy regarding loss allowances for various types of receivables

- Other policy concerning vacation, sick leave, and other compensated absences

- Definition of cash and cash equivalents in the statement of cash flows

- Policy regarding implied time restrictions on long-lived assets received without donor restrictions

- Policy regarding the classification of donor-restricted revenues when the restrictions are met in the same reporting period as the donation

- Disclosures concerning the liquidity of contributions receivable

2. Donor-Restricted Contributions and Net Assets

Unless adequate information concerning donor-restricted contributions and net assets is disclosed in the financial statements, you should have a note describing the donor-restricted contributions your organization received during the period covered and the temporarily and permanently restricted net assets the organization had on the date of the statement of financial position. Information about donor-restricted contributions and net assets may be aggregated according to categories of donor restrictions. Include in this note

- Nature and description of the donor restriction

- Grant period, if applicable

- Amount of contribution increasing the restricted net asset

- Amount of expense released from restriction and decreasing the restricted net asset

- Beginning and ending balance in the restricted net asset account for the contribution for the reporting period

- Status of donor restriction as temporarily restricted or permanently restricted

3. Donor-Restricted Contributions and Cash

Unless adequate information about the nature and amount of limitations on the use of cash and cash equivalents is disclosed in the financial statements, such restrictions should be disclosed in the notes. Examples of situations requiring disclosure include special borrowing arrangements, requirements imposed by donors that cash be held in separate accounts, and known significant liquidity problems.

4. Contributions Receivable

Disclosures relating to the liquidity of the organization's contributions receivable should include the following:

- Contributions receivable pledged as collateral or otherwise limited as to use

- A schedule of unconditional promises to give (showing the total amount separated into amounts receivable in less than one year, in one to five years, and in more than five years), the related allowance for uncollectible promises receivable arising from subsequent decreases due to changes in the quantity or nature of assets expected to be received, and the unamortized discount

- The amount of conditional promises to give—in total and, with descriptions, the amount of each group of similar promises (for example, those conditioned on the development of new programs, the purchase or construction of new property and equipment, or on the raising of matching funds within a specified time period)

5. Board-Designated Unrestricted Endowment and Reserves

Unless adequate information concerning unrestricted net assets that your board has formally designated for investment in endowment or reserves is disclosed in the financial statements, it is recommended that you have a note describing the board-designated unrestricted endowment and reserves the organization had on the date of the statement of financial position. Information about board-designated unrestricted endowment and reserves may be aggregated according to categories of board designations. Include in this note

- Nature and description of the board designation

- Total amount of increase or decrease in the related board-designated unrestricted net asset account

- Beginning and ending balance in the account for the reporting period

6. Donated Materials and Services

With regard to donated materials and services, the notes should include disclosure of these items:

- Nature and extent of contributed services

- Program or activities for which the services were used

- Amount of contributed services recognized during the period

The entity is encouraged to report the fair value of contributed services received but not recognized, if it is practical to do so.

7. Investments

Generally, notes concerning investments should disclose the following:

- Basis of valuation on which investments are presented in the financial statements

- Types of investments held

- Amount of the investments at cost

- Amount of the investments at fair value

- Summary of realized and unrealized investment gains and losses

- Income derived from investments during the reporting period

Refer to FASB Statement no. 124 for further guidance on reporting investments in the financial statements and accompanying notes. See also FASB Statement no. 133, *Accounting for Derivative Instruments and Hedging Activities*.

8. Property, Equipment, and Depreciation

If the following information is not disclosed on the face of the financial statements, present it in a note, if applicable:

- Depreciation expense for the period
- Balances of major classes of depreciable assets at the date of the statement of financial position
- General description of the method or methods and estimated lives used for computing depreciation on major classes of depreciable assets

Separate disclosure should also be made of the following items:

- Nondepreciable assets
- Property and equipment not held for use in operations (for example, items held for sale or for investment purposes or construction in progress)
- Assets restricted by donors to investment in property and equipment
- Improvements to leased facilities and equipment
- Assets, and related obligations, recognized under capital leases (in conformity with FASB Statement no. 13, *Accounting for Leases*)
- Capitalized interest (in conformity with FASB Statements no. 34, *Capitalization of Interest Cost*, and no. 62, *Capitalization of Interest Cost in Situations Involving Certain Tax-Exempt Borrowings and Certain Gifts and Grants—An Amendment of FASB Statement No. 34*)
- Disclosures required by FASB Statement no. 121, *Accounting for the Impairment of Long-Lived Assets and for Long-Lived Assets to Be Disposed Of* (if applicable)

The notes to the financial statements should also include disclosures concerning the liquidity of the organization's property and equipment, including information about limitations on their use. For example, information should be provided about

- Property and equipment pledged as collateral or otherwise subject to lien
- Property and equipment acquired with restricted assets where title may revert to another party, such as a resource provider
- Donor or legal limitations on the use of or proceeds from the disposal of property and equipment

9. Functional Classification of Expenses

FAS-117 requires the presentation, in either a statement of activities or the notes to the financial statements, of information about expenses (but not losses) reported by their functional classification, such as major classes of program services and supporting activities and other disclosures required by AICPA Statement of Position 98-2 regarding joint costs.

10. Nonmonetary Transactions

If your organization has been involved in nonmonetary transactions during the reporting period, it should include in the notes to its financial statements

- The nature of such transactions
- The basis of accounting for the assets transferred
- Any gains or losses recognized on such transfers

11. Contingencies

Whenever it is reasonably possible that an asset has been impaired or that a liability has been incurred as of the date of the statement of financial position, a loss contingency must be reported in the notes to the financial statements. Litigation, unreported claims, and potential disallowances for noncompliance with grant or contractual agreements or donor-imposed restrictions are all examples of common loss contingencies that may need to be disclosed or accrued. Moreover, all guarantees of the indebtedness of others must be reported, even if the possibility of loss is considered to be remote. Other circumstances that may require disclosure include problems with the organization's tax-exempt status or the fact that a determination letter regarding that status has not been received.

12. Commitments

The nature and amount of any commitments should be disclosed in the financial statements. Some examples of commitments are assets pledged as security for loans, commitment of funds for the acquisition or construction of plant assets or for the reduction of liabilities, commitments under pension plans, or commitment of funds to maintain working capital.

The notes to the financial statements should include a schedule of unconditional promises to give that shows the total amount (separated into amounts payable in less than one year, in one to five years, and in more than five years) and the unamortized discount.

13. Leases

The following disclosures should be made for leases.

Capital Leases

Disclosures should include

- Current book value of assets recorded by major classes as of the date of each statement of financial position presented

- Future minimum lease payments as of the latest statement of financial position presented in the aggregate and for each of the five succeeding fiscal years with appropriate deductions therefrom for executory costs and imputed interest to reduce net minimum lease payments to present value
- Total future minimum sublease rentals under noncancelable subleases as of the date of the latest statement of financial position presented
- Total contingent rentals actually incurred for each period for which a statement of activities is presented

Operating Leases

For operating leases disclosure is required of rental expense for each period a statement of activities is presented (with separate amounts for minimum rentals, contingent rentals, and sublease rentals). For operating leases that have initial or remaining noncancelable lease terms in excess of one year, disclosures should include

- Future minimum rental payments required as of the latest statement of financial position presented in the aggregate and for each of the five succeeding fiscal years
- Total future minimum rentals under noncancelable subleases as of the latest statement of financial position presented

Also required is disclosure of a general description of the organization's leasing arrangements, including but not limited to

- Basis for determination of contingent rentals
- Terms of any renewal or purchase options or escalation clauses
- Restrictive covenants

14. Debt

Make adequate disclosure of interest rates, maturities (including the next five years' principal and interest payments and total aggregate thereafter), and other significant conditions of loans, mortgages, and other short- and long-term debt agreements. For each debt agreement, disclosures should include

- Purpose of the debt
- Explanation of sources of repayment, if not obvious from the description of the debt
- Debt due in less than one year, due in one to five years, and due in more than five years
- Description of land, buildings, equipment, or other assets pledged as security for the debt, including the book value of the assets as of the date of the statement of financial position

In addition, if short-term obligations are to be excluded from current liabilities pursuant to a debt refinancing agreement, then include these disclosures:

- General description of the financing agreement

- Terms of a new obligation incurred, or expected to be incurred, as a result of the refinancing

15. Violations of Finance-Related Legal and Contractual Provisions

Significant violations of finance-related legal and contractual provisions should be disclosed in the notes. Disclosure should include a description of the nature of the violation and its effect on the reporting organization. Potential violations that may require disclosure are

- Failure to adhere to the provisions of a debt resolution

- Failure to issue notes in compliance with controlling statutes

- Failure to adhere to controlling statutes governing the organization's operations

- Violations of grant contract provisions

16. Accounting Changes

Once you adopt an accounting principle, it normally should not be changed. You may, however, change from one accounting principle to another if the other accounting principle is "preferable." When such a change is made to a preferable accounting principle, the notes should disclose the nature of the change and justify why it is preferable. Also, the statement of activities should disclose the effect of the change in accounting principle on changes in net assets. It is not necessary to disclose the effects of changes in estimates made each period in the ordinary course of business (such as changes in estimates of uncollectible accounts). However, such disclosure is recommended if the change in estimate is material to the accurate understanding of the organization's financial position.

17. Financially Interrelated Organizations

If an organization has a financially related organization not appropriately included in the financial statements, the notes should disclose the existence of the related organization and the nature of the relationship.

18. Correction of an Error

The correction of an error (which includes a change from an unacceptable accounting principle to a generally accepted accounting principle) should be presented in the financial statements as a prior-period adjustment. The nature of the error in the previously issued financial statements and the effect of its correction on changes in net assets should be disclosed in the period that it is detected and corrected.

19. Pensions and Other Postemployment Employee Benefits

The disclosure requirements for these benefits vary according to the type of organization and the type of plan that is administered. If your organization offers any pensions or other postemployment employee benefits, you should be guided by the disclosure requirements set forth in the following FASB statements:

- No. 87, *Employers' Accounting for Pensions*

- No. 106, *Employer's Accounting for Postretirement Benefits Other Than Pensions*

- No. 112, *Employers' Accounting for Postemployment Benefits—an Amendment of FASB Statements No. 5 and 43*

- No. 132, *Employers' Disclosures About Pensions and Other Postretirement Benefits—an Amendment of FASB Statements No. 87, 88, and 106* for other changes in disclosure requirements

20. Subsequent Events

If it is evident that a liability has been incurred or an asset has been impaired after the date of the financial statements but before they are issued, disclosure of this information may be necessary. Disclosure may be needed even if it is only reasonably possible that a liability may have been incurred or an asset may have been impaired after the date of the financial statements. The disclosure of these subsequent events should include the nature of the loss and the amount of the loss or estimated loss contingency, a range of loss or possible loss, or a statement that such an estimate cannot be made. Typical events that should be considered for disclosure are

- Authorization of an act that has significant financial impact (for example, bond authorizations)

- Significant property damage due to natural causes such as tornado, flood, or fire

- Approval of a significant grant application

- Commencement of a new activity

- A situation causing the filing of a lawsuit for which the potential liability could be substantial

21. Use of Estimates

Preparation of financial statements in accordance with GAAP requires the use of management's estimates. The notes should also identify any estimates that meet the criteria for disclosure under AICPA Statement of Position 94-6.

22. Concentration of Risks

AICPA Statement of Position 94-6 outlines criteria that, if met, require disclosure in the financial statements regarding concentration of risks.

23. Other Disclosures to Consider

An organization might also disclose the following items in notes to its financial statements:

- Split-interest agreements

- Derivatives

- Investment disclosure required by FASB Statement no. 119, *Disclosure About Derivative Financial Instruments and Fair Value of Financial Instruments*

- Collection items

Simplified Financial Statements for Smaller Organizations

Not-for-profits organizations whose funders do not require audited financial statements often choose independently reviewed financial statements, which can offer a less expensive alternative. Whether audited or reviewed, statements prepared in the "standard" reporting formats allow users (board members, funders, and so on) to compare the reports of one not-for-profit organization to those of others. Specifically, statements of financial position that distinguish between unrestricted and restricted net assets (which Form 990 does not) are quite useful. See Exhibit 11.5 for an example of a statement of financial position suitable for smaller organizations.

Consistent with Form 990, the statement of activities segregates program costs from supporting costs. Exhibit 11.6 shows a simplified statement of activities as a model that smaller organizations can follow.

The statement of functional expenses provides additional detail on the program and supporting costs. Exhibit 11.7 presents a simplified statement of functional expenses appropriate for smaller organizations.

EXHIBIT 11.5

Simplified Statement of Financial Position for Smaller Organizations

Account	December 31, 20X2	December 31, 20X1
Asset accounts		
Cash in bank—operating	$ 8,746	$ 18,764
Savings and temporary cash investments	104,699	90,001
Total assets	$113,445	$108,765
Liability accounts [None, cash-based]	$ 0	$ 0
Net asset accounts		
Unrestricted—available for general activities	$113,445	$ 98,765
Temporarily restricted for project A		10,000
Temporarily restricted for project B		
Total net assets	$113,445	$108,765
Total liabilities and net assets	$113,445	$108,765

EXHIBIT 11.6

Simplified Statement of Activities for Smaller Organizations
For Years Ended December 31, 20X2 and 20X1

Revenues, Gains, and Other Support	Unrestricted	Temporarily Restricted	Permanently Restricted	20X2 Total	20X1 Total
Public support					
Contributions from individuals	$134,579			$134,579	$126,908
Foundation grants		$ 12,000		12,000	
Government grants		25,000		25,000	35,000
Total public support	$134,579	$ 37,000	$0	$171,579	$161,908
Other revenue					
Program service fees and sales	$ 82,678			$ 82,678	$ 88,790
Interest on savings and temporary cash investments	8,679			8,679	7,689
Other revenue					1,243
Net assets released from restriction	47,000	$(47,000)			
Total revenues, gains, and other support	$272,936	$(10,000)	$0	$262,936	$259,630
Expenses and Changes in Net Assets					
Program service expenses					
Program A	$165,588			$165,588	$156,352
Program B	41,723			41,723	32,567
Total program services	$207,311	$0	$0	$207,311	$188,919
Supporting service expenses					
Management and general	$ 24,760			$ 24,760	$ 27,850
Fundraising	26,185			26,185	21,567
Total supporting services	$ 50,945	$ 0	$0	$ 50,945	$ 49,417
Total expenses	$258,256	$ 0	$0	$258,256	$238,336
Increase (decrease) in net assets	$ 14,680	$(10,000)	$0	$4,680	$ 21,294
Other changes in net assets					
Changes in net assets	$ 14,680	$(10,000)	$0	$ 4,680	$ 21,294
Net assets at beginning of year	98,765	10,000		108,765	87,471
Net assets at end of year	$113,445	$ (0)	$0	$113,445	$108,765

EXHIBIT 11.7

Simplified Statement of Functional Expenses for Smaller Organizations
For Years Ended December 31, 20X2 and 20X1

Expense Category	Program Services			Supporting Services			Total Program and Supporting Services	
	Program A	Program B	Total	Management and General	Fund-raising	Total	20X2 Total	20X1 Total
Salaries of officers, directors, etc.	$ 24,234	$ 3,785	$ 28,019	$ 7,124	$ 6,890	$ 14,014	$ 42,033	$ 39,780
Other salaries and wages	78,117	19,951	98,068	3,658	7,268	10,926	108,994	98,673
Pension plan contributions	10,235	2,374	12,609	1,078	1,416	2,494	15,103	13,845
Other employee benefits	5,117	1,187	6,304	539	708	1,247	7,551	6,923
Payroll taxes	8,188	1,899	10,087	863	1,133	1,995	12,082	11,076
Total payroll expenses	$125,892	$29,195	$155,086	$13,261	$17,415	$30,677	185,763	$170,297
Professional fees				$ 3,890		$ 3,890	$ 3,890	$ 3,579
Supplies	$ 7,417	$ 1,597	$ 9,014	546	$ 1,345	1,891	10,905	11,254
Telephone	2,936	1,010	3,946	465	509	974	4,920	4,467
Postage and shipping	1,334	435	1,769	367	1,190	1,557	3,326	3,679
Rent	12,628	2,929	15,557	1,330	1,747	3,077	18,634	17,369
Equipment rental and maintenance	4,425	1,652	6,077	546	789	1,335	7,412	7,089
Printing and publications	5,660	3,037	8,698	578	1,767	2,345	11,043	9,057
Travel	3,352	1,197	4,549	1,123	657	1,780	6,329	6,178
Conferences and meetings	765	456	1,221	1,980	567	2,547	3,768	3,491
Other nonpersonnel expenses	1,177	216	1,393	673	200	873	2,266	1,876
Total functional expenses	$165,588	$41,723	$207,311	$24,760	$26,185	$50,945	$258,256	$238,336

Chapter 12

IRS Form 990 Financial Statements

THE INFORMATION REQUIRED for IRS Form 990 financial statements varies in only a few ways from the information required for GAAP statements covered in Chapter Eleven. Form 990 includes the following financial statements:

Form 990 Statement	GAAP Equivalent
Part I—Statement of Revenue, Expenses, and Changes in Net Assets	Statement of Activities
Part II—Statement of Functional Expenses	Statement of Functional Expenses
Part IV—Balance Sheets	Statement of Financial Position

The UCOA in Chapter Five is cross-referenced to Form 990 line items and functional categories and to the sample GAAP financial statements. The UCOA identifies the items that are treated differently by Form 990 and GAAP. The following are the main differences between Form 990 financial statements and GAAP financial statements:

1. The value of donated services and use of facilities reported as contributed revenue and expense in the GAAP statement of activities and statement of functional expenses cannot be reported as revenue and expense on Form 990, part I, Statement of Revenue, Expenses, and Changes in Net Assets, or part II, Statement of Functional Expenses. On Form 990 the value of these items may be reported on line 82.

2. The value of net unrealized gains or losses on investments reported with total revenues and total expenses in the GAAP statement of activities cannot be reported on Form 990, line 12, Total revenue, or line 17, Total expenses. On Form 990 the net amount of these items is reported on line 20, Other changes in net assets or fund balances.

3. Note that Form 990, parts IV-A and IV-B, must be completed for reconciliation of revenues and expenses per audited financial statements with revenues and expenses per Form 990. This includes items 1 and 2 above.

4. GAAP and Form 990 both require all not-for-profit entities to summarize the functional expense categories of program, management and general, and fundraising in the statement of activities (Part I on Form 990). However, GAAP requires only voluntary health and welfare organizations to present functional expenses in a matrix with object line items. Form 990, by contrast, requires every IRC section 501(c)(3) and 501(c)(4) not-for-profit organization that files the form to complete Part II, which is a matrix presentation of functional and object expenses. In addition, Part III of Form 990 calls for a description of the program services to which the organization devoted major funds, representing a summary of the not-for-profit organization's service efforts and accomplishments.

5. GAAP reports require a statement of cash flows; Form 990 does not.

6. GAAP reports require accrual basis reporting; Form 990 does not.

7. GAAP reports require detailed footnote disclosures; Form 990 does not.

8. GAAP reports require listing of revenues and changes in each class of net assets; Form 990 does not.

Following are examples of Form 990, Parts I through VII, using financial information from the functionalized trial balance report in Chapter Seven, based on the cross-references to Form 990 line items in the UCOA in Chapter Five.

Note that this guide does *not* address the following forms:

- Form 990-EZ (for use by organizations with gross receipts of less than $100,000 and total assets of $250,000 at the end of the year)

- Form 990-T, Exempt Organizations Business Income Tax Return

- Form 990-PF, Return of Private Foundations

Sample Statements: Form 990, Parts I–VII

Parts I through VII of Form 990 are presented in Tables 12.1 through 12.6.

Attachments and Explanations

In addition to the specified financial statements, Form 990 and Schedule A require a whole series of attachments and explanations for numerous line items, when applicable. The following is a list of explanations and

TABLE 12.1

IRS Form 990, Part I: Statement of Revenue, Expenses, and Changes in Net Assets or Fund Balances

Form 990 Line Number	Item			Revenue	If Line Not Zero
1	Contributions, gifts, grants, and similar amounts received:				
1a	Direct public support		$204,153		
1b	Indirect public support		18,500		
1c	Government contributions (grants)		395,951		
1d	Total (add lines 1a through 1c)			$618,604	Attach Schedule
2	Program service revenue (from Part VII, line 93)			71,101	
3	Membership dues and assessments			n/a	See Instructions
4	Interest on savings and temporary cash investments			7,423	
5	Dividends and interest from securities			0	
6a	Gross rents		n/a		
6b	Less: Rental expenses		n/a		
6c	Net rental income (loss)			n/a	
7	Other investment income			0	Describe
		(A) Securities	(B) Other		
8a	Gross amount from sale of assets other than inventory	0	0		
8b	Less: Cost or other basis and sales expense	0	0		
8c+d	Gain (loss)	0	0	0	Attach Schedule
9	Special events and activities:				
9a	Gross revenue (not including $ __0__ of contributions reported on line 1a)		0		
9b	Less: Direct expenses other than fundraising expenses		0		
9c	Net income or (loss) from special events			0	Attach Schedule
10a	Gross sales less returns and allowances		n/a		
10b	Less: Cost of goods sold		n/a		
10c	Gross profit (loss)			n/a	Attach Schedule
11	Other revenue (from Part VII, line 103)			0	Attach Schedule
12	Total revenue (add lines 1d, 2 5, 6c, 7, 8d, 9c, 10c, and 11)			$697,128	
13	Program services (from line 44, column (B))			$561,947	
14	Management and general (from line 44, column (C))			83,668	
15	Fundraising (from line 44, column (D))			7,484	
16	Payments to affiliates			n/a	Attach Schedule
17	Total expenses (add lines 16 and 44, column (A))			$653,099	
18	Excess (deficit) for the year (subtract line 17 from line 12)			$ 44,029	
19	Net assets or fund balances at beginning of year (from line 73, column (A))			296,716	
20	Other changes in net assets or fund balances*			0	Attach Explanation
21	Net assets or fund balances at end of year (add lines 18, 19, and 20)			$340,745	
	Note: *Form 990 will match GAAP report only if these are zero:*				
*	Unrealized gains (losses) are included in line 20				
82	Donated services and use of facilities		$ 13,000		

TABLE 12.2

IRS Form 990, Part II: Statement of Functional Expenses

Form 990 Line Number	Item	Total (A)	Program Services (B)	Management and General (C)	Fundraising (D)
22	Grants and allocations (attach (schedule) cash $_____ noncash $_____)	$ 6,246	$ 6,246	n/a	n/a
23	Specific assistance to individuals (attach schedule)	5,432	5,432	n/a	n/a
24	Benefits paid to or for members (attach schedule)	n/a	n/a	n/a	n/a
25	Compensation of officers, directors, etc.	115,000	77,366	33,451	4,183
26	Other salaries and wages	270,000	264,748	5,252	0
27	Pension plan contributions	28,491	25,485	2,713	293
28	Other employee benefits	24,421	21,844	2,326	251
29	Payroll taxes	38,666	34,587	3,682	397
30	Professional fundraising fees	0	n/a	n/a	0
31	Accounting fees	11,564	0	11,564	0
32	Legal fees	0	0	0	0
33	Supplies	37,514	33,416	3,989	109
34	Telephone	6,456	5,576	794	86
35	Postage and shipping	2,690	1,929	275	486
36	Occupancy	13,183	11,386	1,622	175
37	Equipment rental and maintenance	11,445	10,524	831	90
38	Printing and publications	22,268	15,695	5,634	939
29	Travel	9,254	9,254	0	0
40	Conferences, conventions, and meetings	4,587	1,905	2,672	10
41	Interest	0	0	0	0
42	Depreciation, depletion, etc. (attach schedule)	19,740	17,049	2,429	262
43	Other—insurance	10,854	9,374	1,336	144
43	Other—membership dues	1,275	511	761	3
43	Other—staff development	4,183	2,672	1,496	15
43	Other—other professional fees	2,345	2,025	289	31
43	Other—contract temporary help	3,487	3,487	0	0
43	Other expenses	3,998	1,436	2,552	10
44	Total functional expenses (add lines 22 through 43)	$653,099	$561,947	$83,668	$7,484

Note: *Totals for columns (B)–(D) are carried to lines 13–15.*

TABLE 12.3

IRS Form 990, Part III: Statement of Program Service Accomplishments

Form 990 Line Number	Item	From GAAP Report	Less Donated Services and Use of Facilities	Report in Part III	Grants and Allocations (Line 22)
a	Program A	$386,120	$13,000	$373,120	n/a
b	Program B	108,826	0	108,826	n/a
c	Program C	56,358	0	56,358	n/a
d	Program D	23,643	0	23,643	n/a
e	Other program services	n/a	n/a	n/a	n/a
f	Total (add lines a through e)	$574,947	$13,000	$561,947	$0
		(1)	(2)	(3)	

(1)	Disclose program-related donated services and use of facilities on line 82 and in Part III: Donated professional services (non-GAAP)	40,000
	Use of donated facilities and utilities (GAAP)	13,000
	Total	$53,000
(2)	Total reported in Part III, line f should equal line 44, column (B).	
(3)	Report detail in Part III, lines a through e. Total should equal line 22, column (A).	

TABLE 12.4

IRS Form 990, Part IV: Balance Sheets

Form 990 Line Number	Item	Beginning of Year (Column A)	End of Year (Column B)	If Line Not Zero
	Assets			
45	Cash—non-interest-bearing	$14,700	$23,722	
46	Savings and temporary cash investments	95,000	55,000	
47a	Accounts receivable	$13,789		
47b	Less: Allowance for doubtful accounts	1,103	7,262	12,686
48a	Pledges receivable	0		
48b	Less: Allowance for doubtful pledges	0	4,800	0
49	Grants receivable		7,047	57,996
50	Receivables from officers, directors, trustees, and employees		0	0	Attach Schedule
51a	Other notes and loans receivable	0			Attach Schedule
51b	Less: Allowance for doubtful notes and loans	0	0	0	
52	Inventories for sale or use		4,687	3,852	
53	Prepaid expenses and deferred charges		6,489	7,398	
54	Investments—securities			40,000	Attach Schedule
55a	Investments—land, buildings, and equipment: basis	n/a			
55b	Less: Accumulated depreciation	n/a	n/a	n/a	Attach Schedule
56	Investments—other		n/a	n/a	Attach Schedule
57a	Land, buildings, and equipment: basis	360,359			
57b	Less: Accumulated depreciation	110,397	269,702	249,962	Attach schedule
58	Other assets		1,143	0	Describe
59	Total assets (add lines 45 through 58; must equal line 74)		$410,830	$450,616	
	Liabilities			
60	Accounts payable and accrued expenses		$24,565	$22,187	
61	Grants payable		n/a	n/a	
62	Support and revenue designated for future periods		15,870	17,850	
63	Loans from officers, directors, Trustees, and employees		n/a	n/a	Attach Shedule
64a	Tax-exempt bond liabilities		n/a	n/a	Attach Schedule
64b	Mortgages and other notes payable		73,679	69,834	Attach Schedule
65	Other liabilities		n/a	n/a	Describe
66	Total liabilities (add lines 60 through 65)		$114,114	$109,871	
	Net Assets			
67	Unrestricted		$296,716	$314,388	
68	Temporarily restricted		0	26,357	
69	Permanently restricted (Form 990 lines 70 through 72 not applicable)		0	0	
73	Total net assets (add lines 67 through 69)		$296,716	$340,745	
74	(Column (A) must equal line 19, and (B) must equal line 21) Total liabilities and net assets (add lines 66 and 73)		$410,830	$450,616	

TABLE 12.5

IRS Form 990, Parts IV-A and IV-B: Reconciliation of Revenue and Expenses per Books to Revenue and Expenses per Return

Part IV-A: Reconciliation of Revenue per Audited Financial Statements with Revenue per Return

a Total revenue, gains, and other support per audited financial statements $710,128

b Amounts included on line a above but not on line 12, Form 990:

   (1) Net unrealized gains on investments $—

   (2) Donated services and use of facilities 13,000

   (3) Recoveries of prior year grants n/a

   (4) Other (specify) n/a

      Add amounts on lines 1 through 4 $ 13,000

c Line a above minus line b $697,128

d Amounts included on line 12, Form 990, but not on line a above:

   (1) Investment expenses not included on line 6b, Form 990 $ ____

   (2) Other (specify): ____

      Add amounts on lines 1 and 2 $ ____

e Total revenue per line 12, Form 990 (line c above plus line d) $697,128

Part IV-B: Reconciliation of Expenses per Audited Financial Statements with Expenses per Return

a Total expenses and losses per audited financial statements $666,099

b Amounts included on line a above but not on line 17, Form 990:

   (1) Donated services and use of facilities $13,000

   (2) Prior year adjustments reported on line 20, Form 990 ____

   (3) Losses reported on line 20, Form 990 ____

   (4) Other (specify) ____

      Add amounts on lines 1 through 4 $ 13,000

c Line a above minus line b $653,099

d Amounts included on line 17, Form 990, but not on line a above:

   (1) Investment expenses not included on line 6b, Form 990 $ ____

   (2) Other (specify): ____

      Add amounts on lines 1 and 2 $ ____

e Total expenses per line 17, Form 990 (line c above plus line d) $653,099

TABLE 12.6

IRS Form 990, Part VII: Analysis of Income-Producing Activities

Form 990 Line Number	Item	Unrelated Business Income			Excluded by Section 512, 513, or 514		Related or Exempt Function Income (e)
		Business Code (a)	Amount (b)		Exclusion Code (c)	Amount (d)	
93	Program service revenue:						
a	Other program service sales and fees						
b							$71,101
c	_____						
d	_____						
e	_____						
f	Medicare/Medicaid payments						
g	Fees and contracts from government agencies						
94	Membership dues and assessments						
95	Interest on savings and temporary cash investments					$ 7,423	
96	Dividends and interest from securities						
97	Net rental income or (loss) from real estate:						
a	Debt-financed property						
b	Not debt-financed property						
98	Net rental income or (loss) from personal property						
99	Other investment income						
100	Gain (loss) from sale of assets other than inventory						
101	Net income from special fundraising events						
102	Gross profit or (loss) from sales of inventory						
a	Other revenue _____						
b	_____						
c	_____						
d	_____						
e	_____						
104	Subtotal (add columns (b)(d) and (e))		n/a			$ 7,423	$ 71,101
105	Total (add line 104, columns (b), (d), and (e))						$ 78,524
							$ 697,128

Note: line 105 plus line 1d, Part I, should equal the amount on line 12, Part I

schedules that may have to be attached to Form 990. Items marked with an asterisk should not be filed with any state regulatory agency and should not be included with copies of Form 990 given to members of the public who request it.

Form 990

Line 1d: Schedule of contributors*

Line 7: Other investment income

Line 8: Sale of assets

Line 9: Special events

Line 10: Sale of inventory

Line 16: Payments to affiliates

Line 20: Changes in net assets

Line 22: Grants and allocations

Line 23: Assistance to individuals

Line 24: Benefits paid to members

Line 42: Depreciation

Part III, line e: Other program services

Line 50: Receivables from officers

Line 51: Other notes receivable

Line 54: Investments—securities

Line 55: Investments—land, buildings, and equipment

Line 56: Investments—other

Line 57: Land, buildings, and equipment

Line 58: Other assets

Line 63: Loans from officers

Line 64a: Tax-exempt bonds

Line 64b: Mortgages, other notes

Line 65: Other liabilities

Line 75: Officer compensation

Line 90: List of states filed

Schedule A, line 26b: Donors*

Schedule A, line 27a: Disqualified persons*

Schedule A, line 28: Grants*

Public Disclosure Requirements

The Form 990 financial statements have become even more important than before. This is because effective June 8, 1999, the federal requirement that the records of not-for-profit organizations be open and accessible to the public has been greatly expanded as part of the Tax Payer Bill of Rights. The following is a brief summary:

What Must Be Disclosed

Under the law tax-exempt organizations described in IRC sections 501(c) or 501(d) and exempt under section 501(a), with the exception of private foundations, have to provide copies of their three most recent annual returns (Form 990) and their exemption application (Form 1023) upon request in person at the organization's offices or within thirty days of any written request. The copies must be provided at no charge other than a reasonable fee for reproduction and mailing costs.

Copies of all schedules, attachments, and supporting documents filed with these forms must also be provided, except the names and addresses of contributors and Form 990-T, Exempt Organization Business Tax Return.

An organization does not have to provide a copy of its Form 1023 if that form was filed prior to July 15, 1987, unless the organization had a copy of the application on July 15, 1987. An organization not yet recognized as tax-exempt is not required to provide a copy of its pending form 1023.

Internet as an Alternative

A not-for-profit organization does not have to provide copies of Form 990 and Form 1023 if it has made those forms "widely available." The information can be posted on the organization's own Web site or as part of a database of similar documents, such as Philanthropic Research Inc.'s GuideStar Web site (www.guidestar.org). The documents must be in a format that allows Internet users to download at no cost and to view and print the documents in a manner that exactly reproduces the document filed with the IRS.

If the organization's Web site is used for posting the documents, the Web site must inform readers that the documents are available and explain how they can be downloaded. Documents also cannot be posted in a format that would require special computer hardware or software (other than software readily available to the public free of charge). An organization making its documents available on the Web must tell anyone requesting the information where the information can be found, including the Web address.

Time Frame

If the request is made in person, the copies generally must be provided on the same business day as the request, although a limited number of extensions are granted for "unusual circumstances." For example, if the organization has its entire managerial staff out of the office at a convention or meeting, it may take up to five days to fulfill an in-person request for a Form 990. If the request is made by mail, the organization must provide the copies within thirty days of receiving the request (or thirty days after receipt of payment, if the organization chooses to require advance payment for copies). An organization is allowed to retain an agent to respond to requests for its documents, but the organization retains responsibility for complying with the law and regulations as well as for associated penalties for failure to comply.

Harassment

It is harassment when requests are part of a single coordinated effort to disrupt the operations of a tax-exempt organization and not simply to collect information about the organization. An organization will not have to comply if it is found that there is a campaign to harass the organization and if compliance would not be deemed in the public interest. Not-for-profit organizations must apply to the IRS to determine if harassment has occurred. They may suspend compliance until a determination has been made. Requests from members of the news media or an increase in unrelated requests resulting from an article or story appearing in the news media will not be construed as harassment. Organizations may ignore multiple requests from a single individual or address without seeking a determination of harassment from the IRS and may disregard requests beyond the first two within any thirty-day period or the first four within any one-year period that come from the same person or same address.

Penalty for Noncompliance

Not-for-profit organizations that refuse to allow public inspection or to provide copies of returns face a penalty of $20 for every day they fall behind in providing the forms, up to a maximum of $10,000. The penalty for "willful failure" to follow the statute is $5,000.

Chapter 13

Uniform Government Grant Reports

ON AVERAGE over one-third of the budget of not-for-profit organizations comes from the government—local, state, or federal. For some not-for-profit organizations the dependence on government funding may reach 80 to 90 percent of their budget. This scope of funding translates into billions of dollars of tax revenue. Clearly government has the stewardship responsibility of obtaining accurate, complete, and meaningful reports from grantee organizations on the use of government resources. Governments at all levels have developed their own rules and regulations regarding financial reporting requirements for recipient organizations. The problem is that these requirements are not always consistent with those of the IRS, GAAP, or individual states. However, recent developments in Tennessee provide some hope for future movement toward uniformity and consistency among at least state government reporting requirements for not-for-profit organizations.

In this section we propose to showcase Tennessee as a model of state reporting that brings together the financial reporting requirements of disparate authoritative agencies: the IRS, AICPA, FASB, OMB, and the State of Tennessee. Several of the advisers on the writing of this guide helped the State of Tennessee align its uniform government grant-reporting requirements with Form 990 and GAAP. To our knowledge Tennessee is the only state to have developed this process. It is our hope that other states will consider adopting the Tennessee model. We believe this will greatly benefit the not-for-profit sector and ultimately the public at large.

Uniform Government Grant Reporting:
The Tennessee Prototype

In 1981, through the joint efforts of the IRS and NASCO, most state charity offices agreed to accept the revised, uniform Form 990 in lieu of their own unique financial reporting forms. Form 990 was also revised to follow most of the accounting guidance in FASB Statements no. 116 and no. 117. Promoting uniformity in the reporting requirements of the IRS, state charity offices, and GAAP has saved not-for-profit organizations hundreds of millions of dollars each year since 1981. Thanks to the Tennessee *Uniform Grant Budgeting and Reporting Program* initiative, the reporting requirements of federal and state government funding agencies provide an additional dimension—a significant result of the long-term cooperative efforts of the public and not-for-profit sectors to improve the quality of not-for-profit reporting while reducing the cost and burden to the organizations.

In 1997 the Tennessee Department of Finance and Administration (F&A) issued Policy 03, Uniform Reporting Requirements and Cost Allocation Plans for Subrecipients of Federal and State Grant Monies, to address inconsistencies in the reporting requirements among grantor agencies. Policy 03 requires the State of Tennessee's forty-seven departments and agencies to standardize their budgeting and reporting requirements for not-for-profit subrecipients of federal and state funding.

In 1998 Tennessee revised F&A Policy 03's budgeting and reporting requirements to be aligned with OMB Circulars A-122 and A-133, with GAAP, and with IRS Form 990. In addition the State of Tennessee Comptroller of the Treasury revised *Accounting and Financial Reporting for Not-for-Profit Recipients of Grant Funds in Tennessee* to incorporate F&A Policy 03 and to be consistent with

- OMB Circulars A-122, *Cost Principles for Nonprofit Organizations,* and A-133, *Audits of Institutions of Higher Education and Other Nonprofit Organizations*

- Uniform federal-state Form 990

- Annual financial reporting requirements of the Division of Charitable Solicitations, Tennessee Secretary of State

- GAAP established by FASB Statement no. 117 and AICPA's *Audit and Accounting Guide: Not for Profit Organizations*

National Groups Assisting Tennessee

The National Grants Management Association (NGMA) and the Greater Washington Society of CPAs (GWSCPA) formed task forces to provide assistance with revision of F&A Policy 03 and the Tennessee Comptroller's manual to ensure consistency with OMB circulars and GAAP. Participants serving on the NGMA and GWSCPA task forces and otherwise assisting with the Tennessee project included representatives from the IRS, NASCO, OMB, the U.S. Department of Health and Human Services, and the General Accounting Office as well as not-for-profit sector leaders and accountants who have been part of the federal-state uniform reporting collaborative efforts since 1981.

The sponsor of this guide and participants in the 990 in 2000 project (which include NGMA, GWSCPA, the IRS, NASCO, INDEPENDENT SECTOR, NCCS, and others) hope that other state and local governments, as well as federal funding agencies, will find it useful to follow the Tennessee model if they have not already established uniform grant-reporting requirements aligned with Form 990, GAAP, and OMB Circular A-122.

Further, it is likely that many federal, state, and local government agencies would be able, if asked by grant recipients, to accept grant budgets and reports aligned with Form 990, GAAP, and OMB Circular A-122 as prescribed in the Tennessee prototype.

Tennessee Reporting Requirements

F&A Policy 03 and the Tennessee comptroller's financial reporting manual for not-for-profit organizations established two mandatory uniform reporting requirements:

Requirement 1: The organization must comply with the uniform reporting requirements and guidelines for cost allocation plans set forth in F&A Policy 03.

The primary purpose of Tennessee's policy statement is to provide uniformity in the reporting of, and improve controls over, costs associated with the delivery of services by subrecipients of federal and state grant monies.

Requirement 2: The organization must use the same policies, procedures, and methods for all accounting, including cost allocation, and for all financial reporting, including grant reporting to state funding agencies, annual reporting to the secretary of state (including IRS Form 990), and general-purpose financial reporting.

Tables 13.1 and 13.2 and Exhibits 13.1 through 13.3 provide examples of uniform government grant reports using Policy 03 report formats. They are intended to demonstrate how uniform government grant budgeting and reporting can be aligned with Form 990 and GAAP. The figures used are from the functionalized trial balance report in Chapter Seven.

EXHIBIT 13.1

Uniform Government Grant Report Form Using Tennessee Policy 03 Format: Schedule A, Part 1

Schedule A, Part 1

CONTRACTOR/GRANTEE _____

Page _____ of _____ Pages

STATE OF TENNESSEE
PROGRAM EXPENSE REPORT
FEDERAL ID Number _____
REPORT PERIOD

CONTRACTING STATE AGENCY _____

CONTRACT NUMBER _____
GRANT PERIOD
PROGRAM NAME
SERVICE NAME

Schedule A
Line
Item

Number	Expense by Object:	Program A			Program B		
		Quarter-to-Date	Year-to-Date		Quarter-to-Date	Year-to-Date	
		TOTAL EXPENSES					
		TOTAL BUDGET					
1	Salaries and wages						
2	Employee benefits and payroll taxes						
3	Total personnel expenses						
4	Professional fees						
5	Supplies						
6	Telephone						
7	Postage and shipping						
8	Occupancy						
9	Equipment rental and maintenance						
10	Printing and publications						
11	Travel						
12	Conferences and meetings						
13	Interest						
14	Insurance						
15	Grants and awards						
16	Specific assistance to individuals						
17	Depreciation						
18	Other nonpersonnel expenses						
a							
b							
c							
d							
19	*Total nonpersonnel expenses*						
20	Reimbursable capital purchases						
21	*Total direct program expenses*						
22	Administrative expenses						
23	*Total direct and administrative expenses*						
24	In-kind expenses						
25	*Total expenses*						

TABLE 13.1

Tennessee Policy 03 Uniform Reporting Alignment Reference Table: Schedule A, Part 1

Schedule A Line Item Number	Expense by Object	Related A-122 Cost Principle	Related Uniform Form 990 Line Number	Related Unified Chart of Accounts Account Number	Sub-line Item or Attached Schedule When Required
1	Salaries and wages	6, 28, 45	Part II: 25, 26	7210, 7220	For example, 1.1—Client wages
2	Employee benefits and payroll taxes	6, 15, 45	Part II: 27, 28, 29	7310, 7320, 7410	Client benefits, taxes
3	Total personnel expenses	n/a	n/a		
4	Professional fees	20, 41, 49	Part II: 30, 31, 32, 43	7520, 7530, 7540, 7550	Prof/audit/contract
5	Supplies	24	Part II: 33	7710	For example, 5.1—Food
6	Telephone	5, 22	Part II: 34	7810	
7	Postage and shipping	5, 23, 50	Part II: 35	7910, 7920	
8	Occupancy	19, 23, 43, 46, 47	Part II: 36	8010–8050	
9	Equipment rental and maintenance	23, 43	Part II: 37	8110	
10	Printing and publications	26, 38	Part II: 38	8210–8230	
11	Travel	41, 51	Part II: 39	8310	
12	Conferences and meetings	24, 25, 49	Part II: 40	8510	
13	Interest	19	Part II: 41	8610	
14	Insurance	4, 18	Part II: 43	8710	
15	Grants and awards	30	Part II: 22	7010, 7040	
16	Specific assistance to individuals	30	Part II: 23	7050	
17	Depreciation	9	Part II: 42	8650	
18	Other nonpersonnel expenses	1, 2, 7, 14, 17, 26, 27, 29, 39, 41, 47	Part II: 43	8810–9300	Combined line items
a	Part II: 43				
b	Part II: 43				
c	Part II: 43				
d	Part II: 43				
19	Total nonpersonnel expenses	n/a	n/a	n/a	
20	Reimbursable capital purchases	13	Capitalized	9810–9830	Attached schedule
21	Total direct program expenses	n/a	Part II, Col B	n/a	
22	Administrative expenses	11, 12, 16, 19, 20, 21, 32, 33, 36, 40, 41, 43, 45, 47	Part II, Col C	n/a	
23	Total direct and administrative	n/a	n/a	n/a	
24	In-kind expenses	10	Part I; 1a, Part VI; 82	7580, 7590, 7720, 8080, 8090	Detail by expense category
25	Total expenses	n/a	n/a	n/a	

EXHIBIT 13.2

Uniform Government Grant Report Form Using Tennessee Policy 03 Format: Schedule B, Part 1

Schedule B, Part 1

CONTRACTOR/GRANTEE _____

Page ____ of ____ Pages

STATE OF TENNESSEE
PROGRAM REVENUE REPORT
REVENUE AND EXPENSE
____ BUDGET ____ REPORT

FEDERAL ID Number _____
REPORT PERIOD _____

CONTRACTING STATE AGENCY _____

CONTRACT NUMBER _____
GRANT PERIOD _____
PROGRAM NAME _____
SERVICE NAME _____

Schedule B Line Item Number	Sources of Revenue	Program A Quarter-to-Date	Program A Year-to-Date	Program B Quarter-to-Date	Program B Year-to-Date
	Reimbursable program funds:				
31	Reimbursable federal program funds				
32	Reimbursable state program funds				
33	*Total reimbursable program funds (equals Line 55)*				
	Matching revenue funds:				
34	Other federal funds				
35	Other state funds				
36	Other government funds				
37	Cash contributions (nongovernment)				
38	In-kind contributions (equals schedule A, Line 24)				
39	Program income				
40	Other matching revenue				
41	Total matching revenue funds				
42	Other program funds				
43	*Total revenue*				
	Reconciliation between total expenses and reimbursable expenses				
51	Total expenses (from Schedule A, Line 25)				
52	Subtract other unallowable expenses (contractual)				
53	Subtract excess administration (contractual)				
54	Subtract matching expenses (equals Line 41)				
55	Reimbursable expenses (Line 51 Less 52, 53, & 54) (equals Line 33)				
56	*Total reimbursement to date*				
57	Difference (line 55 less 56)				
58	Advances				
59	This reimbursement (Line 57 Less 58)				

TABLE 13.2

Tennessee Policy 03 Uniform Reporting Alignment Reference Table: Schedule B, Part 1

Schedule B Line Item Number	Sources of Revenue	Related Uniform Form 990 Line Number	Related Unified Chart of Accounts Account Number	Sub-line Item or Attached Schedule When Required
	Reimbursable program funds:			
31	Reimbursable federal program funds	Part I; 1c	4520, 5020	Detail, reconciliation schedule
32	Reimbursable state program funds	Part I; 1c	4530, 5030	Detail, reconciliation schedule
33	Total reimbursable program funds (Equals Line 55)		Sum	
	Matching revenue funds:			
34	Other federal funds	Part I; 1c	4520, 5020	Detail, reconciliation schedule
35	Other state funds	Part I; 1c	4530, 5030	Detail, reconciliation schedule
36	Other government funds	Part I; 1c	4540, 5040	Detail, reconciliation schedule
37	Cash contributions (nongovernment)	Part I; 1a, 1b	4010–4090, 4210–4430	
38	In-kind contributions (equals Schedule A, line 24)	Part I; 1a, Part VI; 82	4110–4140	Detail by expense category
39	Program income	Part I; 2	5110–5280	Detail
40	Other matching revenue	Part I; 3–11	5410–6810	Detail
41	Total matching revenue funds	n/a	Sum	
42	Other program funds	Part I; 1–11	4000–6810	For example, 42.1—Client fees
43	Total revenue	Part I; 12	Sum	
	Reconciliation between total expenses and reimbursable expenses:			
51	Total expenses (from Schedule A, line 25)	See Schedule A	See Schedule A	See Schedule A
52	Subtract other unallowable expenses (contractual)	n/a	n/a	
53	Subtract excess administration (contractual)	n/a	n/a	
54	Subtract matching expenses (equals line 41)	n/a	n/a	
55	Reimbursable expenses (line 51 less 52, 53, and 54; equals line 33)	n/a	n/a	
56	Total reimbursement to date	n/a	n/a	
57	Difference (line 55 less 56)	n/a	n/a	
58	Advances	n/a	n/a	
59	This reimbursement (line 57 less 58)	n/a	n/a	

EXHIBIT 13.3
Uniform Government Grant Report Using Tennessee Policy 03 Format

Schedule A, Part 1

CONTRACTOR/GRANTEE NOT-FOR-PROFIT ORGANIZATION

STATE OF TENNESSEE
PROGRAM EXPENSE REPORT
_X_ TOTAL EXPENSES
___ TOTAL BUDGET
Grant 101

FEDERAL ID Number _____ 62-888888888
REPORT PERIOD _____ 4/1/20x2—6/30/20x2
Grant 101

CONTRACTING STATE AGENCY _____ TN. Commission On Aging
CONTRACT NUMBER
GRANT PERIOD
PROGRAM NAME
SERVICE NAME

Schedule A

Line Item Number	Expenses by Object:	GR97695014 7/1/20x1—6/30/20x2 Adult Activity Center Congregate Meals Quarter-to-Date	GR97695014 7/1/20x1—6/30/20x2 Adult Activity Center Congregate Meals Year-to-Date	GR97695014 7/1/20x1—6/30/20x2 Residential Services Meals at Home Quarter-to-Date	GR97695014 7/1/20x1—6/30/20x2 Residential Services Meals at Home Year-to-Date
1	Salaries and wages	32,891.50	131,566.00	10,648.25	42,593.00
2	Employee benefits and payroll taxes	7,382.50	29,530.00	2,413.25	9,653.00
3	*Total personnel expenses*	40,274.00	161,096.00	13,061.50	52,246.00
4	Professional fees	871.75	3,487.00	—	—
5	Supplies	2,277.25	9,109.00	1,149.25	4,597.00
6	Telephone	672.50	2,690.00	219.75	879.00
7	Postage and shipping	232.75	931.00	76.00	304.00
8	Occupancy	1,373.25	5,493.00	448.75	1,795.00
9	Equipment rental and maintenance	1,876.00	7,504.00	230.00	920.00
10	Printing and publications	2,486.25	9,945.00	437.75	1,751.00
11	Travel	169.50	678.00	—	—
12	Conferences and meetings	197.75	791.00	64.50	258.00
13	Interest	—	—	—	—
14	Insurance	1,130.50	4,522.00	369.50	1,478.00
15	Grants and awards	1,561.50	6,246.00	—	—
16	Specific assistance to individuals	—	—	—	—
17	Depreciation	—	—	—	—
18	Other nonpersonnel expenses	2,056.25	8,225.00	672.00	2,688.00
a		266.00	1,064.00	87.25	349.00
b		219.00	876.00	80.75	323.00
c					
d					
19	*Total nonpersonnel expenses*	15,390.25	61,561.00	3,835.50	15,342.00
20	Reimbursable capital purchases				
21	*Total direct program expenses*	55,664.25	222,657.00	16,897.00	67,588.00
22	Administrative expenses	7,946.75	31,787.00	2,572.75	10,291.00
23	*Total direct and administrative expenses*	63,611.00	254,444.00	19,469.75	77,879.00
24	In-kind expenses				
25	*Total expenses*	63,611.00	254,444.00	19,469.75	77,879.00

EXHIBIT 13.3
Uniform Government Grant Report Using Tennessee Policy 03 Format (Continued)

Schedule B, Part 1

CONTRACTOR/GRANTEE NOT-FOR-PROFIT ORGANIZATION

CONTRACTING STATE AGENCY _____ TN. Commission On Aging

STATE OF TENNESSEE
PROGRAM REVENUE REPORT
REVENUE AND EXPENSE REPORT
___ BUDGET _X_ REPORT

FEDERAL ID Number _____ 62-888888888

REPORT PERIOD _____ 7/1/20x2—6/30/20x2

Page __1__ of __7__ Pages

		Grant 101	Grant 101	Grant 101	Grant 101
	CONTRACT NUMBER	GR97695014	GR97695014	GR97695014	GR97695014
	GRANT PERIOD	7/1/20x1—6/30/20x2	7/1/20x1—6/30/20x2	7/1/20x1—6/30/20x2	7/1/20x1—6/30/20x2
	PROGRAM NAME	Adult Activity Center	Adult Activity Center	Residential Services	Residential Services
	SERVICE NAME	Congregate Meals	Congregate Meals	Meals at Home	Meals at Home
Schedule B Line Item Number	Source of Revenue	Quarter-to-Date	Year-to-Date	Quarter-to-Date	Year-to-Date
	Reimbursable program funds:				
31	Reimbursable federal program funds	63,611.00	254,444.00	19,469.50	77,878.00
32	Reimbursable state program funds	—	—	—	—
33	Total reimbursable program funds (equals Line 55)	63,611.00	254,444.00	19,469.50	77,878.00
	Matching revenue funds:				
34	Other federal funds	—	—	—	—
35	Other state funds	—	—	—	—
36	Other government funds	—	—	—	—
37	Cash contributions (nongovernment)	—	—	—	—
38	In-kind contributions (equals Schedule A, Line 24)	—	—	—	—
39	Program income	—	—	—	—
40	Other matching revenue	—	—	—	—
41	*Total matching revenue funds*	—	—	—	—
42	Other program funds	63,611.00	254,444.00	19,469.50	77,878.00
43	*Total revenue*	63,611.00	254,444.00	19,469.50	77,878.00
	Reconciliation between total expenses and reimbursable expenses				
51	Total expenses (from Schedule A, Line 25)	63,611.00	254,444.00	19,469.75	77,879.00
52	Subtract other unallowable expenses (contractual)	—	—	—	—
53	Subtract excess administration (contractual)	—	—	—	—
54	Subtract matching expenses (equals Line 41)	—	—	—	—
55	Reimbursable expenses (Line 51 Less 52, 53, & 54) (equals Line 33)	63,611.00	254,444.00	19,469.75	77,879.00
56	*Total reimbursement to date*				
57	Difference (line 55 less 56)	63,611.00	254,444.00	19,469.75	77,879.00
58	Advances	—	—	—	—
59	This reimbursement (Line 57 Less 58)	63,611.00	254,444.00	19,469.75	77,879.00

(Continued)

EXHIBIT 13.3
Uniform Government Grant Report Using Tennessee Policy 03 Format (*Continued*)

Schedule A, Part 1

STATE OF TENNESSEE
PROGRAM EXPENSE REPORT
_X_ TOTAL EXPENSES
___ TOTAL BUDGET

Page _2_ of _7_ Pages

CONTRACTOR/GRANTEE NOT-FOR-PROFIT ORGANIZATION ___

FEDERAL ID Number _62-888888888_
REPORT PERIOD _7/1/20x1—6/30/20x2_

CONTRACTING STATE AGENCY ___ Dept. of Health

CONTRACT NUMBER
GRANT PERIOD
PROGRAM NAME
SERVICE NAME

Schedule A Line Item Number	Expense by Object:	Grant 103 — Z60781046 — 7/1/20x1—6/30/20x2 — Rehabilitation Center — Rehabilitation Serv. — Quarter-to-Date	Z60781046 — 7/1/20x1—6/30/20x2 — Rehabilitation Center — Rehabilitation Serv. — Year-to-Date	Grant 102 — GR97694013 — 7/1/20x1—6/30/20x2 — Adult Activity Center — Nutrition Education — Quarter-to-Date	GR97694013 — 7/1/20x1—6/30/20x2 — Adult Activity Center — Nutrition Education — Year-to-Date
1	Salaries and wages	4,3332	17,331.00	3,450.25	13,801.00
2	Employee benefits and payroll taxes	995.75	3,983.00	773.25	3,093.00
3	*Total personnel expenses*	5,328.50	21,314.00	4,223.50	16,894.00
4	Professional fees	—	—	—	—
5	Supplies	115.75	463.00	286.25	1,145.00
6	Telephone	90.75	363.00	70.50	282.00
7	Postage and shipping	31.50	126.00	24.25	97.00
8	Occupancy	185.25	741.00	143.75	575.00
9	Equipment rental and maintenance	95.00	380.00	73.75	295.00
10	Printing and publications	180.75	723.00	140.25	561.00
11	Travel	—	—	2,144.00	8,576.00
12	Conferences and meetings	26.75	107.00	20.50	82.00
13	Interest	—	—	—	—
14	Insurance	152.50	610.00	118.50	474.00
15	Grants and awards	—	—	—	—
16	Specific assistance to individuals	—	—	—	—
17	Depreciation	277.25	1,109.00	215.25	861.00
18	Other nonpersonnel expenses	—	—	—	—
a		36.00	144.00	27.75	111.00
b		10.75	43.00	8.25	33.00
c					
d					
19	*Total nonpersonnel expenses*	1,202.25	4,809.00	3,273.00	13,092.00
20	Reimbursable capital purchases				
21	*Total direct program expenses*	6,530.75	26,123.00	7,496.50	29,986.00
22	Administrative expenses	1,046.75	4,187.00		3,336.00
23	*Total direct and administrative expenses*	7,577.50	30,310.00	7,496.50	33,322.00
24	In-kind expenses				
25	*Total expenses*	7,577.50	30,310.00	7,496.50	33,322.00

EXHIBIT 13.3

Uniform Government Grant Report Using Tennessee Policy 03 Format *(Continued)*

Schedule B, Part 1

STATE OF TENNESSEE
PROGRAM REVENUE REPORT
REVENUE AND EXPENSE REPORT
BUDGET _X_ REPORT

Page _2_ of _7_ Pages

CONTRACTOR/GRANTEE NOT-FOR-PROFIT ORGANIZATION _____

CONTRACTING STATE AGENCY _____ Dept. of Health _____

FEDERAL ID Number _____ 62-888888888 _____

REPORT PERIOD _____ 7/1/20x2—6/30/20x2 _____

Line Item Number	Source of Revenue	Z60781046 — Grant 103 — 7/1/20x1—6/30/20x2 — Rehabilitation Center — Rehabilitation Services — Quarter-to-Date	Z60781046 — 7/1/20x1—6/30/20x2 — Rehabilitation Center — Rehabilitation Services — Year-to-Date	GR97694013 — Grant 102 — 7/1/20x1—6/30/20x2 — Adult Activity Center — Nutrition Education — Quarter-to-Date	GR97694013 — 7/1/20x2—6/30/20x2 — Adult Activity Center — Nutrition Education — Year-to-Date
	Reimbursable program funds:				
31	Reimbursable federal program funds	7,576.75	30,307.00	8,330.50	33,322.00
32	Reimbursable state program funds	—	—	—	—
33	Total reimbursable program funds (equals Line 55)	7,576.75	30,307.00	8,330.50	33,322.00
	Matching revenue funds:				
34	Other federal funds	—	—	—	—
35	Other state funds	—	—	—	—
36	Other government funds	—	—	—	—
37	Cash contributions (nongovernment)	—	—	—	—
38	In-kind contributions (equals Schedule A, Line 24)	—	—	—	—
39	Program income	—	—	—	—
40	Other matching revenue	—	—	—	—
41	Total matching revenue funds	—	—	—	—
42	Other program funds	7,576.75	30,307.00	8,330.50	33,322.00
43	*Total revenue*	7,577.50	30,310.00	8,330.50	33,322.00
	Reconciliation between total expenses and reimbursable expenses				
51	Total expenses (from Schedule A, Line 25)	7,577.50	30,310.00	8,330.50	33,322.00
52	Subtract other unallowable expenses (contractual)	—	—	—	—
53	Subtract excess administration (contractual)	—	—	—	—
54	Subtract matching expenses (equals Line 41)	7,577.50	30,310.00	8,330.50	33,322.00
55	Reimbursable expenses (Line 51 Less 52, 53, & 54) (equals Line 33)	7,577.50	30,310.00	8,330.50	33,322.00
56	Total reimbursement to date	7,577.50	30,310.00	8,330.50	33,322.00
57	Difference (line 55 less 56)	7,577.50	30,310.00	8,330.50	33,322.00
58	Advances	—	—	—	—
59	This reimbursement (Line 57 Less 58)	7,577.50	30,310.00	8,330.50	33,322.00

(Continued)

EXHIBIT 13.3
Uniform Government Grant Report Using Tennessee Policy 03 Format (Continued)

Schedule A, Part 1

STATE OF TENNESSEE
PROGRAM EXPENSE REPORT
__X__ TOTAL EXPENSES
_____ TOTAL BUDGET
Non Grant

CONTRACTOR/GRANTEE NOT-FOR-PROFIT ORGANIZATION _____

FEDERAL ID Number _____ 62-888888888
REPORT PERIOD _____ 7/1/20x1—6/30/20x2
Grant 204 (NonGrant)

CONTRACT NUMBER _____
GRANT PERIOD _____
PROGRAM NAME _____
SERVICE NAME _____

CONTRACTING STATE AGENCY _____

Schedule A Line Item Number	Expense by Object	7/1/20x1—6/30/20x2 Rehabilitation Center Rehabilitation Services Quarter-to-Date	7/1/20x1—6/30/20x2 Rehabilitation Center Rehabilitation Services Year-to-Date	7/1/20x1—6/30/20x2 Special Projects Seniors Project Quarter-to-Date	7/1/20x1—6/30/20x2 Special Projects Seniors Project Year-to-Date
1	Salaries and wages	4,201.50	16,806.00	3,019.75	12,079.00
2	Employee benefits and payroll taxes	937.75	3,751.00	694.50	2,778.00
3	*Total personnel expenses*	5,139.25	20,557.00	—	14,857.00
4	Professional fees	—	—	—	—
5	Supplies	1,932.50	7,730.00	80.75	323.00
6	Telephone	31.50	126.00	63.25	253.00
7	Postage and shipping	10.75	43.00	22.00	88.00
8	Occupancy	64.50	258.00	29.25	517.00
9	Equipment rental and maintenance	33.00	132.00	66.25	265.00
10	Printing and publications	63.00	252.00	126.00	504.00
11	Travel	—	—	—	—
12	Conferences and meetings	118.00	472.00	18.50	74.00
13	Interest	—	—	—	—
14	Insurance	53.25	213.00	106.50	426.00
15	Grants and awards	—	—	—	—
16	Specific assistance to individuals	—	—	1,358.00	5,432.00
17	Depreciation	96.75	87.00	193.50	774.00
18	Other nonpersonnel expenses				
a		12.50	50.00	25.00	100.00
b		3.75	15.00	7.50	30.00
c					
d					
19	*Total nonpersonnel expenses*	2,419.50	9,678.00	2,196.50	8,786.00
20	Reimbursable capital purchases	—	—	—	—
21	*Total direct program expenses*	7,558.75	30,235.00	5,910.75	23,643.00
22	Administrative expenses	—	—	—	—
23	*Total direct and administrative expenses*	7,558.75	30,235.00	5,910.75	23,643.00
24	In-kind expenses	558.75			
25	*Total expenses*	7,558.75	30,235.00	5,910.75	23,643.00

EXHIBIT 13.3

Uniform Government Grant Report Using Tennessee Policy 03 Format *(Continued)*

Schedule B, Part 1

Page _3_ of _7_ Pages

CONTRACTOR/GRANTEE VOLUNTARY NOT-FOR-PROFIT ORGANIZATION

FEDERAL ID Number 62-888888888

STATE OF TENNESSEE
PROGRAM REVENUE REPORT
REVENUE AND EXPENSE
BUDGET _X_ REPORT

REPORT PERIOD 7/1/20x2—6/30/20x2

CONTRACT NUMBER
GRANT PERIOD
PROGRAM NAME
SERVICE NAME

CONTRACTING STATE AGENCY

Line Item Number	Sources of Revenue	Non Grant 7/1/20x1—6/30/20x2 Rehabilitation Center Rehabilitation Services Quarter-to-Date	Non Grant 7/1/20x1—6/30/20x2 Rehabilitation Center Rehabilitation Services Year-to-Date	Grant 204 (NonGrant) 7/1/20x1—6/30/20x2 Special Projects Seniors Project Quarter-to-Date	Grant 204 (NonGrant) 7/1/20x1—6/30/20x2 Special Projects Seniors Project Year-to-Date
	Reimbursable program funds:				
31	Reimbursable federal program funds	—	—	—	—
32	Reimbursable state program funds	—	—	—	—
33	Total reimbursable program funds (equals Line 55)	—	—	—	—
	Matching revenue funds:				
34	Other federal funds	—	—	—	—
35	Other state funds	—	—	—	—
36	Other government funds	—	—	—	—
37	Cash contributions (nongovernment)	10,750.00	43,000.00	12,500.00	50,000.00
38	In-kind contributions (equals Schedule A, Line 24)	—	10,478.00	—	—
39	Program income	2,619.50	—	—	—
40	Other matching revenue	—	—	—	—
41	Total matching revenue funds	13,369.50	53,478.00	12,500.00	50,000.00
42	Other program funds	—	—	—	—
43	Total revenue	13,369.50	53,478.00	12,500.00	50,000.00
	Reconciliation between total expenses and reimbursable expenses				
51	Total expenses (from Schedule A, Line 25)	7,558.75	30,235.00	5,910.75	23,643.00
52	Subtract other unallowable expenses (contractual)	—	—	—	—
53	Subtract excess administration (contractual)	—	—	—	—
54	Subtract matching expenses (equals Line 41)	—	53,478.00	12,500.00	50,000.00
55	Reimbursable expenses (Line 51 Less 52, 53, & 54) (equals Line 33)	7,558.75	(23,243.00)	(6,589.25)	(26,357.00)
56	Total reimbursement to date	,558.75	(23,243.00)	(6,589.25)	(26,357.00)
57	Difference (Line 55 less 56)	7,558.75	(23,243.00)	(6,589.25)	(26,357.00)
58	Advances	—	—	—	—
59	This reimbursement (line 57 less 58)	7,558.75	(23,243.00)	(6,589.25)	(26,357.00)

(Continued)

EXHIBIT 13.3
Uniform Government Grant Report Using Tennessee Policy 03 Format (Continued)

Schedule A, Part 1

CONTRACTOR/GRANTEE NOT-FOR-PROFIT ORGANIZATION

CONTRACT NUMBER
GRANT PERIOD
PROGRAM NAME
SERVICE NAME

CONTRACTING STATE AGENCY

STATE OF TENNESSEE
PROGRAM EXPENSE REPORT
__X__ TOTAL EXPENSES
_____ TOTAL BUDGET
Non Grant

FEDERAL ID Number __62-888888888__
REPORT PERIOD __4/1/20x2—6/30/20x2__
Non Grant

Page __4__ of __7__ Pages

Schedule A

Line Item Number	Expense by Object:	Adult Activity Center — Quarter-to-Date 7/1/20x1—6/30/20x2	Adult Activity Center — Year-to-Date 7/1/20x1—6/30/20x2	Residential Services — Quarter-to-Date 7/1/20x1—6/30/20x2	Residential Services — Year-to-Date 7/1/20x1—6/30/20x2
1	Salaries and wages	19,537.00	78,148.00	7,447.50	29,790.00
2	Employee benefits and payroll taxes	5,585.75	22,343.00	1,697.00	6,788.00
3	*Total personnel expenses*	25,122.75	100,491.00	9,144.50	36,578.00
4	Professional fees	—	—	—	—
5	Supplies	240.25	961.00	73.00	292.00
6	Telephone	188.50	754.00	57.25	229.00
7	Postage and shipping	65.25	261.00	19.75	79.00
8	Occupancy	384.75	1,539.00	117.00	79.00
9	Equipment rental and maintenance	197.25	789.00	60.00	240.00
10	Printing and publications	375.50	1,502.00	114.00	456.00
11	Travel	—	—	—	—
12	Conferences and meetings	308.75	1,235.00	388.50	1,554.00
13	Interest	—	—	—	—
14	Insurance	316.75	1,267.00	96.25	385.00
15	Grants and awards	—	—	—	—
16	Specific assistance to individuals	—	—	—	—
17	Depreciation	576.25	2,305.00	175.00	700.00
18	Other nonpersonnel expenses				
a		122.25	489.00	57.50	230.00
b		22.25	89.00	6.75	27.00
c					
d					
19	*Total nonpersonnel expenses*	2,797.75	11,191.00	1,165.00	4,660.00
20	Reimbursable capital purchases	—	—	—	—
21	*Total direct program expenses*	27,920.50	111,682.00	10,309.50	41,238.00
22	Administrative expenses	—	—	—	—
23	*Total direct and administrative expenses*	27,920.50	111,682.00	10,309.50	41,238.00
24	In-kind expenses		3,295.00		18,500.00
25	*Total expenses*	27,920.50	154,977.00	10,309.50	59,738.00

EXHIBIT 13.3

Uniform Government Grant Report Using Tennessee Policy 03 Format (Continued)

Schedule B, Part 1

CONTRACTOR/GRANTEE NOT-FOR-PROFIT ORGANIZATION _____

CONTRACTING STATE AGENCY _____   CONTRACT NUMBER _____

STATE OF TENNESSEE
PROGRAM REVENUE REPORT
REVENUE AND EXPENSE REPORT
BUDGET _X_ REPORT
Non Grant

FEDERAL ID Number _____ 62-888888888

REPORT PERIOD _____ 7/1/20x2—6/30/20x2
NonGrant

GRANT PERIOD _____
PROGRAM NAME _____
SERVICE NAME _____

Schedule B

Line Item Number	Sources of Revenue	Adult Activity Center 7/1/20x1—6/30/20x2 Quarter-to-Date	Adult Activity Center 7/1/20x1—6/30/20x2 Year-to-Date	Residential Services 7/1/20x1—6/30/20x2 Quarter-to-Date	Residential Services 7/1/20x1—6/30/20x2 Year-to-Date
	Reimbursable program funds:				
31	Reimbursable federal program funds	—	—	—	—
32	Reimbursable state program funds	—	—	—	—
33	Total reimbursable program funds (Equals Line 55)	—	—	—	—
	Matching revenue funds:				
34	Other federal funds	—	—	—	—
35	Other state funds	—	—	—	—
36	Other government funds	—	—	—	—
37	Cash contributions (nongovernment)	15,000.00	60,000.00	7,500.00	30,000.00
38	In-Kind contributions (equals Schedule A, Line 24)	10,823.75	43,295.00	4,625.00	18,500.00
39	Program income	8,422.25	33,689.00	,733.50	26,934.00
40	Other matching revenue				
41	Total matching revenue funds	34,246.00	136,984.00	18,858.50	75,434.00
42	Other program funds	—			
43	Total revenue	34,246.00	136,984.00	18,858.50	75,434.00
	Reconciliation between total expenses and reimbursable expenses				
51	Total expenses (from Schedule A, Line 25)	38,744.25	154,977.00	14,934.50	59,738.00
52	Subtract other unallowable expenses (contractual)				
53	Subtract excess administration (contractual)				
54	Subtract matching expenses (equals Line 41)		136,984.00	18,858.50	75,434.00
55	Reimbursable expenses (Line 51 Less 52, 53, & 54) (equals Line 33)	38,744.25	17,993.00	(3,924.00)	(15,696.00)
56	Total reimbursement to date				
57	Difference (Line 55 Less 56)	38,744.25	17,993.00	(3,924.00)	(15,696.00)
58	Advances				
59	This reimbursement (Line 57 Less 58)	38,744.25	17,993.00	(3,924.00)	(15,696.00)

(Continued)

EXHIBIT 13.3
Uniform Government Grant Report Using Tennessee Policy 03 Format (Continued)

Schedule A, Part 1

STATE OF TENNESSEE
PROGRAM EXPENSE REPORT
X_ TOTAL EXPENSES
___ TOTAL BUDGET
Non Grant

Page _7_ of _7_ Pages

CONTRACTOR/GRANTEE NOT-FOR-PROFIT ORGANIZATION

CONTRACT NUMBER

FEDERAL ID Number _____62-888888888_____
REPORT PERIOD _____4/1/20x2—6/30/20x2_____

CONTRACTING STATE AGENCY

GRANT PERIOD
PROGRAM NAME
SERVICE NAME

Schedule A

Line Item Number	Expense by Object	7/1/20x1—6/30/20x2 FUND RAISING n/a — Quarter-to-Date	7/1/20x1—6/30/20x2 FUND RAISING n/a — Year-to-Date	Quarter-to-Date	Year-to-Date
1	Salaries and wages	1,045.75	4,183.00	—	—
2	Employee benefits and payroll taxes	235.25	941.00	—	—
3	*Total personnel expenses*	1,281.00	5,124.00	—	—
4	Professional fees	—	—	—	—
5	Supplies	27.25	109.00	—	—
6	Telephone	21.50	86.00	—	—
7	Postage and shipping	121.50	486.00	—	—
8	Occupancy	43.75	175.00	—	—
9	Equipment rental and maintenance	22.50	90.00	—	—
10	Printing and publications	234.75	939.00	—	—
11	Travel	—	—	—	—
12	Conferences and meetings	6.25	25.00	—	—
13	Interest	—	—	—	—
14	Insurance	36.00	144.00	—	—
15	Grants and awards	—	—	—	—
16	Specific assistance to individuals	—	—	—	—
17	Depreciation	65.50	62.00	—	—
18	Other nonpersonnel expenses	—	—	—	—
a		8.50	34.00	—	—
b		2.50	10.00		
c					
d					
19	*Total nonpersonnel expenses*	590.00	2,360.00		
20	Reimbursable capital purchases				
21	*Total direct program expenses*	1,871.00	7,484.00	—	—
22	Administrative expenses				
23	*Total direct and administrative expenses*	1,871.00	7,484.00	—	—
24	In-kind expenses	—	—		
25	*Total expenses*	1,871.00	7,484.00	—	—

EXHIBIT 13.3

Uniform Government Grant Report Using Tennessee Policy 03 Format (Continued)

Schedule C, Final Page

CONTRACTOR/GRANTEE NOT-FOR-PROFIT ORGANIZATION _____

STATE OF TENNESSEE
PROGRAM EXPENSE REPORT
X_ TOTAL EXPENSES
___ TOTAL BUDGET

Page _1_ of _1_ Pages

FEDERAL ID Number _____ 62-888888888

REPORT PERIOD _____ 7/1/20x2—6/30/20x2

CONTRACTING STATE AGENCY _____

CONTRACT NUMBER _____
GRANT PERIOD _____
PROGRAM NAME _____
SERVICE NAME _____

Schedule A

Line Item Number	Expense by Object	TOTAL DIRECT GRANT PROGRAM EXPENSES n/a Quarter-to-Date	TOTAL NONGRANT/UNALLOWABLE EXPENSES n/a Nongrant/unallowable Unallowable and Fund raising Year-to-Date	TOTAL ADMINISTRATIVE EXPENSES n/a Administrative Quarter-to-Date	GRAND TOTAL n/a All programs Year-to-Date
1	Salaries and wages	205,291.00	141,006.00	38,703.00	385,000.00
2	Employee benefits and payroll taxes	46,259.00	36,601.00	8,721.00	91,581.00
3	*Total personnel expenses*	251,550.00	177,607.00	47,424.00	476,581.00
4	Professional fees	3,487.00	—	11,853.00	15,340.00
5	Supplies	15,314.00	9,415.00	3,989.00	28,718.00
6	Telephone	4,214.00	1,448.00	794.00	6,456.00
7	Postage and shipping	1,458.00	957.00	275.00	2,690.00
8	Occupancy	8,604.00	2,957.00	1,622.00	13,183.00
9	Equipment rental and maintenance	9,099.00	1,516.00	831.00	11,446.00
10	Printing and publications	12,980.00	3,653.00	5,633.00	22,266.00
11	Travel	9,254.00	—	—	9,254.00
12	Conferences and meetings	1,238.00	3,360.00	2,672.00	7,270.00
13	Interest	—	—	—	—
14	Insurance	7,084.00	2,435.00	1,336.00	10,855.00
15	Grants and awards	6,246.00	—	—	6,246.00
16	Specific assistance to individuals	—	5,432.00	—	5,432.00
17	Depreciation	12,883.00	4,428.00	2,429.00	19,740.00
18	Other nonpersonnel expenses	—	—	4,810.00	4,810.00
a		1,668.00	903.00		2,571.00
b		1,275.00	171.00		1,446.00
c		—	—		—
d		—	—		—
19	Total nonpersonnel expenses	94,804.00	36,675.00	36,244.00	167,723.00
20	Reimbursable capital purchases	—	—	6,246.00	6,246.00
21	*Total direct program expenses*	346,354.00	214,282.00	83,668.00	644,304.00
22	Administrative expenses	49,601.00	34,067.00	(83,668.00)	
23	*Total direct and administrative expenses*	395,955.00	248,349.00	—	644,304.00
24	In-kind expenses		61,795.00	—	61,795.00
25	*Total expenses*	395,955.0	310,144.00	—	706,099.00

Corporate and Foundation Grant Budgeting and Reporting

ONE OF THE MOST important reporting categories, and one of the few that has yet to be addressed in over twenty years of uniform not-for-profit accounting and financial reporting efforts, is grant budgeting and reporting to foundation and corporate grant makers. In 1999, U.S. grant-making foundations and corporations between them gave an estimated $30.83 billion to not-for-profit organizations according to Giving USA.[1] This donor category includes private, independent, and family foundations. The Foundation Center currently tracks over forty-four thousand grant-making foundations; its grants index features over eighty-six thousand grant descriptions covering grant-making programs of over one thousand of the largest foundations in the United States. Grant seekers use their own budget formats when they apply for grants. A single common, required format for grant applications does not exist.

Recommendations for Improving the Quality of Financial Information

Corporations and foundations generally do not specify the expense categories to be used for their grants. They usually accept the budgets as submitted with proposals, provided that the budget categories and formats are consistent with the descriptions in the proposals of how the funds will be used. However, it is important for corporations and foundations to participate in sectorwide collaborative efforts to align internal and external reporting needs of not-for-profit organizations with GAAP, Form 990, and other uniform reports. The goal of these efforts is to improve the quality of

Note: Information in this chapter is aligned with GAAP, Form 990, and other uniform reports.

financial information for all users of not-for-profit organizations' reports and at the same time reduce the cost and burden of such reporting for not-for-profit organizations. Corporate contribution programs and grant-making foundations could considerably accelerate this goal if they were to consider and implement the following seven recommendations.

Recommendation 1: Establish a policy, to be included in grant application guidelines and grant agreements, that the object or line-item expense categories used in interim and final grant reports be the same as those used in the budget submitted with the grant application.

Many corporations and foundations require that the budget categories be used for grant reporting. This is sound grant-making practice.

Recommendation 2: State in grant application guidelines a preference that grant budget line items be consistent with the organization's general chart of accounts.

The program personnel who develop grant proposals often create budget expense categories without aligning them with their organization's chart of accounts or reviewing them with their accounting departments before submitting the grant applications. This is not good program or project budgeting practice and results in the need for special, usually manual, accounting and reporting for each grant. When grant budgets are consistent with an organization's chart of accounts, the accounting department can produce grant reports directly from the accounting system, improving the reliability of the reports and reducing costs.

Recommendation 3: In the grant application guidelines ask for a copy of the most recent Form 990 along with audited financial statements.

The guidelines of many corporations and foundations ask for copies of Form 990. This too is sound grant-making practice. As noted in Chapter Twelve, there is a tremendous amount of information in Form 990, its Schedule A, and its more than twenty-five required attachments. It can be very useful to have this information on file in case it is needed. Once program officers learn how to read Form 990, they can quickly find the specific information needed on the Form 990 of any particular grantee. Not-for-profit organizations are required by federal law to provide copies of their Form 990 on request, so including a Form 990 with their grant applications is not a burden.

Recommendation 4: Impress on grantees the need to improve the quality of grant and other reporting, and to reduce the cost of such reporting, by aligning their accounting systems with GAAP, Form 990, and other uniform reports.

It would be helpful for corporate and foundation supporters to encourage grantees to align their accounting systems, and their grant-reporting systems, with GAAP and Form 990. Corporations and foundations can join with other institutional supporters, boards of directors, CFOs, auditors, umbrella groups, INDEPENDENT SECTOR, NCCS, the research community, the IRS, state charities regulators, and others who are promoting and facilitating this financial management practice.

Not-for-profit organizations are not being asked to replace their accounting systems. They can simply cross-reference their chart of accounts either directly to Form 990 line items and other standard reports or to the UCOA in Chapter Five (which is already cross-referenced to various standard internal and external reports). Some not-for-profit accounting software systems include features that allow users to cross-reference their chart of accounts to special reports and other charts of accounts.

Recommendation 5: Avoid using funding policies that force grantees to create special accounting and reporting procedures for grants.

Some corporations and foundations have funding policies that prohibit the inclusion of certain expense categories in restricted grant budgets. In order to get full cost reimbursement, grantees often find it necessary to create special expense categories that are not consistent with their organization's chart of accounts. This results in two accounting and reporting systems: one for the grant and another for the organization as a whole.

Full reimbursement for indirect costs and some expenses has remained a pervasive and largely unresolved issue for government, corporate, foundation, and other institutional funding agencies and their grantees. The negative impact of this issue on the quality and cost of grant stewardship, accounting, and reporting is substantial. It is doubtful that not-for-profit organizations are going to take steps to improve the quality and reduce the cost of reporting if such steps are going to adversely affect reimbursement for restricted grants. It is a matter of survival for many not-for-profit organizations.

Recommendation 6: Begin experimenting with electronic grant reporting by grantees and electronic grant report processing by grantors.

Government funding agencies are already doing this. Participants in Tennessee's Uniform Government Grant Reporting Project are pursuing electronic reporting by their grantees to reduce grant administration costs and improve the effectiveness of the government grant-making process. Corporate and foundation grant makers need to explore computerization of various aspects of their grant-reporting processes. Some may already be doing so. Effective computerization of corporate and foundation grant report processing may require standardization of corporate and foundation grant reports.

Recommendation 7: Urge regional associations of grant makers to address the issue of grant budgeting and reporting aligned with GAAP, Form 990, and other uniform reports, and include electronic grant reporting and processing.

There is already interest among a number of regional associations of grant makers in standardizing the grant application process. Extending this effort to include the grant budgeting and reporting process would be useful.

Why should corporate and foundation grant makers be supportive of, and cooperate with, efforts to have their grantees align their budgets and grant reports with Form 990, GAAP, and other standard reporting requirements? First, because it is in their interest to improve the quality (reliability, usefulness, and so on) of the grant reports they receive and at the same time reduce the costs to their grantees of accounting for and producing such reports. Second, because it is in their interest to pursue these goals in collaboration with other users of not-for-profit financial information. And third, this will improve the comparability of data being received from multiple grantees and improve the comparability of sectorwide data, both of which will help grant makers in their decision-making process.

Implementation of the above recommendations will result over time in improvements in the grant-making process and will reduce costs to grantees and grantors. The sector is investing billions of dollars each year on budgeting, accounting, auditing, and reporting to an amazing variety of users of financial data. The grant-making community needs to see to it that grantors get better-quality reports at less cost to grantees.

Examples of Corporate and Foundation Restricted Grant Budgeting and Reporting

The examples in this section are based on the following scenario: a not-for-profit organization is applying to the XYZ Foundation for a temporarily restricted $50,000 grant to fund its seniors project. As with all the sample reports in this manual, the financial figures for these illustrations are taken from the functionalized trial balance report in Chapter Seven. The $50,000 grant is found in Table 7.2 under the column for program D, grant 204 (activity code 420) in the row for account number 4230 (Foundation and trust grants). The direct expenses totaling $23,643 are found in Table 7.3 under the same column heading in the row for total direct expenses and assets released from restrictions.

The seniors project in this scenario is assigned an activity code and other accounting system codes and criteria following the sample revenue and expense activity code table in Chapter Six (Table 6.1) as follows:

Activity	Seniors project
Activity code	420
Control account	3310
Function or department	Program D
Funding source	XYZ Foundation
Restriction	Temporary
Project, grant, or cost center	Grant 204

Exhibit 14.1 is the project budget the not-for-profit organization included in its proposal to the XYZ Foundation.

Exhibit 14.2 is the expense report the not-for-profit organization included in its interim progress report to the XYZ Foundation. Note that Exhibit 14.2, line 21, Share of management and general expenses, has an entry of $2,364 (10 percent of line 20, Total direct expenses) that has been included in line 22, Total expenses, for a total of $26,007 of the XYZ Foundation's $50,000 grant expended.

Table 14.1 shows the grant budget and report format that the not-for-profit organization uses, and that the XYZ Foundation accepts, for grant budgeting and reporting. The grant budget and report format is cross-referenced to Form 990, UWAACS, the UCOA, and OMB Circular A-122. The suggested grant budget and report format illustrated in these examples is similar to, and compatible with, the suggested formats found in Chapter Thirteen.

EXHIBIT 14.1

Grant Budget: Seniors Project

Line Number	Expense Category	Project Budget
	Grants	$50,000
	Personnel	
1	Payroll	
	a. Project director	$6,500
	b. Project coordinator	12,000
	c. Support staff	800
	d. Total payroll expenses	$19,300
2	Employee benefits and payroll taxes	$4,500
3	Consulting fees	2,500
4	Total personnel expenses	$26,300
	Other expenses	
5	Supplies	$ 1,000
6	Telephone	400
7	Postage and shipping	200
8	Occupancy	900
9	Equipment rental and maintenance	500
10	Printing and publications	700
11	Travel	300
12	Conferences and meetings	400
13	Interest	0
14	Insurance	800
15	Grants and awards	0
16	Specific assistance to individuals	12,000
17	Depreciation	1,600
18a	Other nonpersonnel expenses—dues	100
b	Membership dues	0
c	Staff development	300
d	Contract temporary help	0
19	Total nonpersonnel expenses	$19,200
20	Total direct expenses	$45,500
21	Share of management and general expenses (10%)	4,500
22	Total expenses	$50,000

TABLE 14.1

Standard Corporate and Foundation Grant Budget and Report Format (Cross-Referenced to Form 990 and Standard Not-for-Profit Accounting Systems)

Line Number	Expense Category	Uniform Form 990 Line Number	United Way Accounts Coding System	Unified Chart of Accounts Account Number	Simplified Grant Budget Format
1	Grants	1a	4000	4210–4250	Include
	Personnel				
	Payroll				
	a. Project director	25, 26	7000	7210, 7220	Include
	b. Project coordinator	25, 26	7000	7210, 7220	Include
	c. Support staff	25, 26	7000	7210, 7220	Include
	d. Total payroll expenses	Sum	Sum	Sum	Include
2	Employee benefits and payroll taxes	27, 28, 29	7100, 7200	7310–7410	Include
3	Consulting fees	30, 31, 32, 43	8000	7510–7550	Include
4	Total personnel expenses	Sum	Sum	Sum	Include
	Other expenses				
5	Supplies	33	8100	7710	
6	Telephone	34	8200	7810	
7	Postage and shipping	35	8300	7910, 7920	
8	Occupancy	36	8400	8010–8080	
9	Equipment rental and maintenance	37	8500	8110	
10	Printing and publications	38	8600	8210, 8220	Group[a]
11	Travel	39	8700	8310	
12	Conferences and meetings	40	8800	8510	
13	Interest	41	9200	8610	
14	Insurance	43	9300	8710	
15	Grants and awards	22	9100	7010, 7020	
16	Specific assistance to individuals	23	8900	7030, 7040	
17	Depreciation	42	9500	8650	
18a–18d	Other nonpersonnel expenses	43	9400	8810–9300	
19	Total nonpersonnel expenses	Sum	Sum	Sum	Include
20	Total direct expenses	Sum	Sum	Sum	Include
21	Share of management and general expenses (10%)	Part II, Col C	Management and general	Management and general (51–69)	Include
22	Total expenses	Sum	Sum	Sum	Include

[a] For a simplified grant budget format, group "Other expenses" (lines 5 to 18) into three or four summary line items, as appropriate; however, do not split UCOA account numbers.

EXHIBIT 14.2

Grant Budget and Report: Seniors Project (Grant 204, Activity Code 420)

Line Number	Expense Category	Project Budget	XYZ Foundation	Foundation B	Foundation C	Actual Total	Budget Balance
1	Foundation Grants	$50,000	$50,000	$0	$0	$50,000	$ 0
	Personnel						
	Payroll						
	a. Project director	$ 6,500	$ 3,568	$0	$0	$ 3,568	$ 2,932
	b. Project coordinator	12,000	7,890			7,890	4,110
	c. Support staff	800	621			621	179
	d. Total payroll expenses	$19,300	$12,079	$0	$0	$12,079	$ 7,221
2	Employee benefits and payroll taxes	4,500	2,778			2,778	1,722
3	Consulting fees	2,500					2,500
4	Total personnel expenses	$26,300	$14,857	$0	$0	$14,857	$11,443
	Other expenses						
5	Supplies	$ 1,000	$323	$0	$0	$323	$677
6	Telephone	400	253			253	147
7	Postage and shipping	200	88			88	112
8	Occupancy	900	517			517	383
9	Equipment rental and maintenance	500	265			265	235
10	Printing and publications	700	504			504	196
11	Travel	300					300
12	Conferences and meetings	400	30			30	370
13	Interest						
14	Insurance	800	426			426	374
15	Grants and awards						
16	Specific assistance to individuals	12,000	5,432			5,432	6,568
17	Depreciation	1,600	774			774	826
18a.	Other nonpersonnel expenses—dues	100	30			30	70
b.	Membership dues		8			8	(8)
c.	Staff development	300	44			44	256
d.	Contract temporary help		92			92	(92)
19	Total nonpersonnel expenses	$19,200	$ 8,786	$0	$0	$ 8,786	$10,414
20	Total direct expenses	$45,500	$23,643	$0	$0	$23,643	$21,857
21	Share of management and general expenses (10%)	4,500	2,364			2,364[a]	2,136
22	Total expenses	$50,000	$26,007	$0	$0	$26,007	$23,993
	Grant funds remaining		$23,993	$0	$0	$23,993[a]	

[a] A share of MRG was not applied in the GAAP examples in Chapter Eleven.

Chapter 15

Reporting to United Ways and Other Grant Makers

EVER SINCE the first United Way campaign in Denver, Colorado, in 1887, local United Way organizations in communities across the nation have been raising funds and distributing them to thousands of tax-exempt health and human services organizations every year. In 1998 over fourteen hundred local United Way organizations raised over $3.58 billion in support of qualified IRC section 501(c)(3) organizations. With the advent of the "donor choice" program (allowing acceptance of donor-designated gifts by United Way organizations), many United Ways today distribute funds to the entire range of tax-exempt section 501(c)(3) organizations, including those involved in arts and culture, hospitals, colleges and universities, and environmental protection organizations.

Undesignated gifts to the "community fund" component of United Ways are distributed by citizen volunteer groups based on funding priorities adopted by the particular United Way. Each independent United Way organization sets its own policy for allocation of funds to a qualified group of agencies in its geographic jurisdiction. Some United Ways require funding requests on prescribed budget forms that are based on GAAP financial statements.

United Way Accounting and Financial Reporting

For over forty years, United Way of America (and its predecessor organization) and local United Ways have played a leading role in establishing and promoting uniform standards of accounting and financial reporting for themselves and for funded agencies. Starting with their leadership in the creation of *1964 Standards of Accounting and Financial Reporting for Voluntary Health and Welfare Organizations*, the national and local United Ways have worked incessantly over the years for full and fair disclosure and for uniformity and comparability in accounting and financial reporting for not-for-profit organizations (see Resource H for details).

In 1974 United Way of America published its comprehensive *Accounting and Financial Reporting: A Guide for United Ways and Not-for-Profit Human Service Organizations* (a second edition was published in 1989). More recently, United Way of America has produced several publications for the guidance of local United Way organizations in financial accounting and reporting in response to recent changes (these are listed in the Bibliography). The 1974 United Way guide contained a new comprehensive chart of accounts—the *United Way of America Accounts Coding System* (UWAACS). The 1989 edition of *Accounting and Financial Reporting* contained revisions that reflect changes in accounting principles and standards. The tables in this chapter cross-reference UWAACS to the financial categories established in 1998 by the National Assembly of National Voluntary Health and Social Welfare Organizations and the National Health Council in *The Black Book Standards of Accounting and Financial Reporting for Voluntary Health and Welfare Organizations*.

Over the past twenty-five years UWAACS has been used as a framework for account structure by many local United Ways and thousands of not-for-profit organizations receiving funding from United Ways and others. It should be noted, however, that the requirements of different accounting software systems often change the account structure and numbering system. UWAACS was used by participants in the 1992 and 1993 annual IRS-NASCO Form 990 meetings as a tool for aligning Form 990 with GAAP. UWAACS was also used by the Nonprofit Management Group at the City University of New York as a point of departure in the development of the 1994 *Model Chart of Accounts: A Cross Reference to Federal/State Form 990 and Other Uniform Financial Reports*. This model chart of accounts in turn was revised for use as the UCOA in the 1997 Tennessee Uniform Government Grant Reporting Project. It has now evolved into the UCOA in Chapter Five of this guide.

The Black Book standards and UWAACS chart of accounts have played, and will no doubt continue to play, an important role in the development of the uniform federal-state Form 990, the UCOA proposed in this manual, uniform financial reporting, public reporting via the Internet, accountability, and electronic reporting.

Combined Federal Campaign

Many United Ways manage the annual Combined Federal Campaign (CFC)—a fundraising campaign conducted among federal government employees at their workplaces. Among several eligibility criteria established by the Office of Personnel Management for participation in CFC, the following are pertinent to this guide:

(a) *To insure that the organizations that wish to solicit donations from Federal employees in the workplace are portraying accurately their programs and benefits, the following public accountability standards must be met by all organizations applying to participate in the CFC.*

(b) *To qualify for inclusion on the list of organizations judged eligible to participate on a national basis, an organization must submit annually to the Director:*

(1) *Documentary evidence that it accounts for its funds in accordance with generally accepted accounting principles and was audited in accordance with generally accepted auditing principles by an independent certified public accountant in the year immediately preceding any year in which it applies for admission to, or its federation certifies its eligibility to receive donations from the CFC. This documentary evidence must include a copy of the organization's audit, prepared in accordance with the above mentioned principles. . . .*

(3) *A statement demonstrating that if its fund-raising and administrative expenses are in excess of 25 percent of total support and revenue, its actual expense for those purposes are reasonable under all the circumstances in this case. For those agencies whose expenses are not in excess of the 25 percent limit, a statement so affirming shall be supplied which also sets forth the actual percentage of their funds that are used for administrative and fund-raising. The Director may reject any application from an agency with fund-raising and administrative expenses in excess of 25 percent of total support and revenue, unless the agency demonstrates to the satisfaction of the Director that its actual expenses for those purposes are reasonable under all circumstances in its case.*[1]

The instructions provided in Chapter Eight for the determination of administration and fundraising expenses, if followed scrupulously, will enable the not-for-profit organization to establish the validity and reliability of the techniques used to accurately reflect those expenses, for CFC eligibility criteria. As mentioned earlier, the required GAAP financial statements and the Form 990 financial statements provide separate expense figures for administration and fundraising functions. In addition, the eligibility criteria for participation in CFC include the requirements that the not-for-profit organization produce an annual report and have its year-end financial statements audited by a CPA (small organizations are excepted).

It should be noted that federal, state, and local governments, corporate and private foundations, and United Ways are not the only grant-making organizations. Other federations (such as the Jewish Welfare Federations) and even major national agencies (such as the American Cancer Society) make grants to other not-for-profit organizations for various programs and projects. Thus, again, the UCOA provided in this guide could serve as a useful tool for both grant makers and grant seekers as they transact the grant-processing function.

Black Book Standards Cross-Referenced to Other Standard Not-for-Profit Accounting Systems

Because many not-for-profit organizations already use the Black Book standards financial categories and UWAACS, it would be useful to have a cross-reference of Black Book standards financial categories to UWAACS, Form 990, the UCOA presented in Chapter Five, and the sample GAAP financial statements shown in Chapter Eleven. Tables 15.1–15.3 provide just such a cross-reference.

TABLE 15.1

1998 Black Book Standards Financial Categories (Cross-Referenced to Form 990 and Other Standard Not-for-Profit Accounting Systems): Assets, Liabilities, and Net Assets

1998 Black Book Standards Financial Categories	United Way Accounts Coding System (Account Name and Number)	Form 990 (Line Number)[a]	Unified Chart of Accounts (Account Number)[b]	Sample GAAP Financial Statements (Line Number)[c]
Assets				
Cash and Cash Equivalents				
Cash	Cash (1000)	45	1010, 1020, 1040	1
Cash equivalents	Short-term investments (1100)	46	1070	2
Investments, at market value	Other current assets (1700)	54	1410	8
Receivables				
Program service fees, less allowance	Accounts receivable (1200)	47a, 47b	1110, 1190, 1270	3
Pledges at fair value, less allowance	Pledges receivable (1300)	48a, 48b	1210, 1220	4
Grants	Pledges receivable (1300)	49	1240	5
From affiliates	Accounts receivable (1200)	51a, 51b	1280, 1290	3
Inventory, at lower of cost or market	Supplies for sale or use (1400)	52	1310, 1320	6
Prepaid expenses and deferred charges	Prepaid expenses and deferred charges (1500)	53	1350, 1360	7
Land, buildings, and equipment, at cost, less accumulated depreciation	Land, buildings, and equipment (1800)	57	1510–1650	11, 12, 13, 14
Assets restricted to investment in land, buildings, and equipment	Other noncurrent assets (1900)	55	1430–1450	
Long-term investments	Other noncurrent assets (1900)	56	1480	
Other assets	Other current assets (1700)	58	1700–1900	9
	Other noncurrent assets (1900)			
Custodian fund	Custodian fund (fund code 501)	58	n/a	n/a
Interfund receivable (payable)	Due from or to other funds (1600)	n/a	n/a	n/a

Liabilities				
Accounts payable and accrued expenses	Accounts payable (2000)	60	2010–2150	21, 22, 23, 24
	Accrued expenses (2100)			
Research grants	Grants payable (2300)	61	2200	n/a
Refundable advances	[United Way] allocations payable (2200)	62	2400, 2310, 2350	25
	Support and revenue Designated for future periods (2500)			
Mortgage payable	Long-term indebtedness (2600)	64b	2730	27
Accounts payable under capital leases	Long-term indebtedness (2600)	64b	2750	n/a
Custodian fund	Custodian fund (fund code 501)	65	2900	n/a
Other liabilities	Other current liabilities (2400)	63, 64a, 64b, 65	2510, 2550, 2600, 2710, 2770, 2800	n/a
	Other noncurrent liabilities (2700)			
Net Assets				
Unrestricted	Fund balances (fund code-account):			
General operating funds	Current unrestricted fund (100-3000)	21, 67	3010	29
Board-designated funds	Current unrestricted fund (101-3010)	21, 67	3020	31
Quasi-endowment funds	Current unrestricted fund (102-3020)	21, 67	3030	30
Program funds	Current unrestricted funds (103-3030)	21, 67	3010	29
Fixed asset funds	Land, buildings, and equipment fund (301-3301)	21, 67	3210	32
Temporarily Restricted				
Donor-restricted funds—purpose	Current restricted fund (201-3201)	21, 68	3300-3399	34
Donor-restricted funds—time	Current restricted fund (202-3202)	21, 68	3500-3599	34
Permanently Restricted	Endowment fund (400-3400)	21, 69	3900-3999	35

Source: *United Way of America, Accounting and Financial Reporting: A Guide for United Ways and Not-for-Profit Human Service Organizations, 2nd ed. (Alexandria, Va.: United Way of America, 1989), app. 19K. Duplicated by permission, United Way of America.*

[a]*See Chapter Twelve.*

[b]*See Chapter Five.*

[c]*See Chapter Eleven.*

TABLE 15.2

1998 Black Book Standards Financial Categories (Cross-Referenced to Form 990 and Other Standard Not-for-Profit Accounting Systems): Revenues, Gains, and Other Support

1998 Black Book Standards Financial Categories	United Way Accounts Coding System (Account Name and Number)	Form 990 (Line Number)[a]	Unified Chart of Accounts (Account Number)[b]	Sample GAAP Financial Statements (Line Number)[c]
Revenue				
Public support received directly	Public support—received directly (4000–4499)	1a	4010–4350	51
Contributions at fair value:				
Individuals	Contributions (4000)	1a	4010, 4080 (contra)	51
Corporations and other businesses	Contributions (4000)	1a	4210	51
Foundations and trusts	Contributions (4000)	1a	4230	51
Other	Contributions (4000)	1a	4250	51
	Contributions to building fund (4100)			
Special events, less direct benefit costs	Special events (4200)	1a, (9a)	4050	52 (contra)
Legacies and bequests	Legacies and bequests (4300)	1a	4070	53
Donated property, equipment, and material	Contributions (4000–4199)	1a	4130	55
Contributed services at fair value	Contributions (4000)	Part III; 82	4110	54
Public support received indirectly	Public support—received Directly (4500–4999)	1b	4410, 4420, 4430	56
Local member units	Collected through Local Member units (4500)	1b	n/a	n/a
Associated organizations	Contributed by associated organizations (4600)	1b	4420	n/a

Federated fundraising organizations	Allocated by federated fundraising organizations (4700)	1b	4410	56
Other	Allocated by unassociated and nonfederated fundraising organizations (4800)	1b	4430	n/a
Revenue and Grants from Government Agencies	Revenue and grants from Governmental agencies (5000)	1c, 2, 93(f), 93(g)	4510–4540, 5010–5040	58
Other Revenue				
Membership dues—individuals	Membership dues—individuals (6000)	3, 94	5310	n/a
Assessments and dues from local member units	Assessments and dues—member units (6100)	3, 94	5320	n/a
Program service fees	Program service fees and net incidental revenue (6200)	2, 93(b)	5210–5280	59
Sales of materials and services to member units	Sales of materials and services To member units (6300)	2, 93(a)	n/a	n/a
Sales to public	Sales to public (6400)	2, 93(a)	5110–5180	59
Investment income	Investment income (6500)	4, 95; 5, 96; 6, 98; 7	5410–5610, 5810	60, 61
Other	Miscellaneous revenue (6900)	8(B), 100; 9a, 101; 10, 102; 11, 103	6180–6810	64
Gains (Losses) on Investments and Sales of Other Assets	Gain (or loss) on investment transactions and sales of other assets (6600)	20; 8(A), 100	5910, 5920, 6110, 6120	62, 63
Net Assets Released from Restrictions				
Satisfaction of program restrictions	n/a (FASB Statement of Financial Accounting Standards no. 117)	n/a	6910, 6920	65
Expiration of time restrictions	n/a (FASB Statement of Financial Accounting Standards no. 117)	n/a	6930	65

Source: *United Way of America, Accounting and Financial Reporting: A Guide for United Ways and Not-for-Profit Human Service Organizations, 2nd ed. (Alexandria, Va.: United Way of America, 1989), app. 19K. Duplicated by permission, United Way of America.*

[a]*See Chapter Twelve.*

[b]*See Chapter Five.*

[c]*See Chapter Eleven.*

TABLE 15.3

1998 Black Book Standards Financial Categories (Cross-Referenced to Form 990 and Other Standard Not-for-Profit Accounting Systems): Object Expenses

1998 Black Book Standards Financial Categories	United Way Accounts Coding System (Account Name and Number)	Form 990 (Line Number)[a]	Unified Chart of Accounts (Account Number)[b]	Sample GAAP Financial Statements (Line Number)[c]
Object Expenses				
Salaries	Salaries (7000)	25, 26	7210, 7220	121
Employee benefits	Employee health and retirement benefits (7100)	27, 28	7310, 7320	122
Payroll taxes and similar	Payroll taxes and similar (7200)	29	7410	122
Professional fees	Professional and other contract service fees (8000)	30, 31, 32, 43	7510, 7520, 7530	124
Contributed services	Donated services (8000–8099)	Part III; 82	7540, 7550, 7580, 7590, 8080	124, 128
Supplies	Supplies (8100)	33	7710	125
Contributed goods	Donated materials (8100–8199)	33	7720	125
Telecommunications services	Telephone (8200)	34	7810	126
Postage and shipping	Postage and shipping (8300)	35	7910, 7920	127
Occupancy	Occupancy (8400)	36	8010, 8020, 8030, 8040	128
Interest	Interest expense (9200)	36, 41	8610, 8050	128
Rental and maintenance of equipment	Rental and maintenance of equipment (8500)	37	8110	129
Printing and publications	Printing and publications (8600)	38	8210, 8220, 8230	130
Travel and transportation	Travel and transportation (8700)	39	8310	131
Conferences, conventions, and meetings	Conferences, conventions, and meetings (8800)	40	8510	132
Specific assistance to individuals	Specific assistance to individuals (8900)	23	7040	136
Membership dues	Membership dues (9000)	43	8810	138
Awards and grants to national organizations	Awards and grants (9100)	22	7010	n/a

Awards and grants to individuals and other organizations	Awards and grants (9100)	22	7005, 7010, 7030	135
Awards and grants—distributions to member units	Allocations to agencies (9600–9690)	22	7020	n/a
Insurance	Insurance (9300)	43	8710	134
Other expenses	Miscellaneous (9400–9499)	43	9300, 8820, 9010, 9020, 9040, 9100, 9110, 9120, 9130, 9140, 9190	138
Depreciation of buildings and equipment	Depreciation or amortization (9500)	42	8650, 8660	137
Unallocated payments to affiliates	Payments to affiliated organizations (9691–9699)	16	9910	n/a
Direct benefit costs	Special events (954)[d]	9b	610[e]	52 (contra)
Functions	United Way Accounts Coding System function name (number):		Unified chart of accounts activity code:	
Program Services:	Program services (001–899)			
Program A	Program A (101)	13; part III, a	100–199	81A, 139A
Program B	Program B (201)	13; part III, b	200–299	82A, 139B
Program C	Program C (301)	13; part III, c	300–399	83A, 139C
Program D	Program D (401)	13; part III, d, e	400–499	84A, 139D
Supporting services:				
Management and general	Management and general (900–949)	14; part II, C	500–699	86A
Fundraising	Fundraising (950–974)	15; part II, D, E	700–899	87A
Payments to affiliates	Payments to affiliates (975–980)	16	9910[f]	n/a
Direct benefit costs	Special events (such as 954)	9b	610	52 (contra)

Source: United Way of America, Accounting and Financial Reporting: A Guide for United Ways and Not-for-Profit Human Service Organizations, 2nd ed. (Alexandria, Va.: United Way of America, 1989), app. 19K. Duplicated by permission, United Way of America.

[a]See Chapter Twelve.
[b]See Chapter Five.
[c]See Chapter Eleven.
[d]United Way of America Accounts Coding System function number.
[e]Unified chart of accounts activity code.
[f]Account number.

Chapter 16

Financial Reporting for Internal Management Purposes

MOST EXTERNAL REPORTS are also useful for internal management purposes. However, there are significant additional and more detailed financial information needs for reporting internally to the board and staff. Thus financial reporting for internal management purposes encompasses all of the reports described so far in this book—and more.

Audited general-purpose financial reports (that is, GAAP reports; see Chapter Eleven) are used by boards and staff as well as contributors, creditors, regulators, and others. During the year, unaudited interim statements of position (balance sheets), statements of activities, functional expense statements, cash flow reports, and supporting notes are provided to boards and staff. These can be monthly or quarterly. Each of these reports can be compared with reports for the previous period, previous year, and corresponding periods in prior years.

Boards and staff also use Form 990 and its Schedule A, from which a variety of useful ratios can be calculated. These ratios, along with specific line items, can be compared against prior years' figures, performance policies of the organization, industry averages based on Form 990 returns, and Form 990 returns of similar organizations.

Restricted grant reports to institutional supporters, such as corporations, foundations, United Ways, and government agencies, are described elsewhere in this guide. They are all of interest and useful to boards and staff. These reports show the budget for each grant, grant funds raised for special projects and specific programs, expenditures charged against each grant by line item expense account, and the budget balances for each line item expense account and for grant amounts still to be raised.

Note: Information in the chapter is aligned with GAAP, Form 990, and other uniform reports.

Two of the most useful internal management reports are prepared monthly (or quarterly) and at the end of the year. These are the *interim unaudited balance sheet* report and the *budget-to-actual* (BTA) report. To keep preparation of both of these reports as simple as possible without sacrificing reliability for decision making, they are prepared on a modified accrual basis.

Modified Accrual Basis Accounting and Reporting

Not-for-profit organizations are generally expected to *report* on an accrual basis. In this method of accounting, contributions are recognized when received or pledged, revenues are recognized when earned, and expenses are recognized when incurred. Large not-for-profit organizations usually do both *accounting and reporting* on an accrual basis. However, many small and midsize not-for-profit organizations do accounting on a cash basis and interim reporting on a modified accrual basis during the fiscal year. They prepare GAAP financial reports on a full accrual basis at the end of the year. The advantage of cash basis accounting and accrual basis reporting is simplicity, which can result in a substantial reduction in the cost and burden of financial management throughout the year. In cash basis accounting, transactions are only recorded in the books when cash is received or disbursed. When financial reports are needed, a cash basis trial balance is prepared. Accruals and adjustments are then added to create an adjusted accrual basis trial balance from which accrual basis financial reports can be prepared.

Interim reports during the year can be prepared on a cash basis. However, they are usually prepared on a modified accrual basis when cash basis reports would present inaccurate and misleading financial information. With the modified accrual basis a few items that might have significant impact, such as accounts receivable or accounts payable, may be reported on an accrual basis while other items are reported on a cash basis.

Budget-to-Actual Reports

BTA reports are among the most important and useful internal management reports. They are used for internal management purposes only and are not distributed externally. BTA reports require that an annual budget be prepared and that the revenue and expense categories used in the budget be consistent with the organization's chart of accounts. The annual budget is the financial part of the annual plan for the organization and includes all of the various board-approved activities to be conducted during the year. Developing and approving the budget, tracking actual revenues and expenses, and comparing them to the budget are primary responsibilities of the board and of those staff members responsible for generating revenues or incurring expenses.

BTA reports include budgeted amounts, actual amounts, balances, and variances (and can reflect budget revisions when applicable). They can present budgeted and actual amounts for both revenue and expenses for the current month or quarter or for the year to date, on a cash or modified accrual basis. (BTA reports do not deal with assets, liabilities, or net assets.) The current year's budget can also be compared with the previous year's budget or actual results.

BTA reports can present summary budget and actual information (as supported by detailed BTA reports) for the overall organization. Detailed BTA reports can present budget and actual revenue and expense data by line item activity (or group of activities), project, program, department, function, and so on. With a comprehensive set of summary and detailed BTA reports, boards and staff do not need to refer to other financial documents for budget or actual revenue and expense data.

Budgeting and Reporting: Examples

The sample BTA reports in Tables 16.1–16.3 are based on the figures from the functionalized trial balance report for the adult activity center (activity codes 110, 120, 130). Table 16.4 shows revenue and expense categories for internal budgeting and reporting. Table 16.5 is an example of a report comparing overall budget to actual for a small organization.

How Budget-to-Actual Reports Lead to Action

The following are the kinds of questions BTA reports address:

- Are actual revenues, overall and by category, behind projections in the budget? Is there a problem? What action is needed? Should the budget be revised?

  If actual revenues are in line with or ahead of projections, no action is required.

- Are actual expenses, overall and by category, ahead of budgeted expenses? Is there a problem? What action is needed? Should the budget be revised?

  If actual expenses are in line with or behind budgeted expenses, no action is required. However, there may be an opportunity to implement or enhance programs that were originally limited because of budget constraints.

TABLE 16.1

Yearly Budget: Adult Activity Center

Revenue or Expense Category	Adult Center (100)	Congregate Meals (120)	Nutrition Education (130)	Total Department Budget
Revenue				
Contributions from individuals				
Special events				
Corporate and foundation grants	$ 50,000			$ 50,000
Government grants		$ 250,000	$ 50,000	300,000
Program service fees and sales	40,000			40,000
Return on investments				
Other revenue				
Total revenue	$ 90,000	$ 250,000	$ 50,000	$ 390,000
Expenses				
Personnel:				
Salaries	$ 75,000	$ 125,000	$ 15,000	$ 215,000
Employee benefits (15.0%)	11,250	18,750	2,250	32,250
Payroll taxes (10.0%)	7,500	12,500	1,500	21,500
Total payroll	$ 93,750	$ 156,250	$ 18,750	$ 268,750
Consulting fees		2,500		2,500
Total personnel expenses	$ 93,750	$ 158,750	$ 18,750	$ 271,250
Nonpersonnel:				
Supplies	$ 10,000	$ 10,000	$ 1,500	$ 21,500
Telephone	1,000	2,500	500	4,000
Postage and shipping	500	800	100	1,400
Occupancy	2,000	4,500	500	7,000
Equipment rental and maintenance	900	7,200	200	8,300
Printing and publications	1,200	9,000	500	10,700
Travel	300	1,000	7,500	8,800
Conferences and meetings	800	300	50	1,150
Interest				
Insurance	1,200	4,200	400	5,800
Grants and awards		6,500		6,500
Specific assistance to individuals				
Depreciation	2,200	8,000	80	10,280
Other nonpersonnel expenses—dues	300	150	450	
Staff development	500	500	1,000	
Contract temporary help		2,500		2,500
Other expenses	200	600	100	900
Total nonpersonnel expenses	$ 21,100	$ 57,750	$ 11,430	$ 90,280
Total expenses	$ 114,850	$ 216,500	$ 30,180	$ 361,530

TABLE 16.2

Year-End Revenue and Expense Report (Actual): Adult Activity Center

Revenue or Expense Category	Adult Center (100)	Congregate Meals (120)	Nutrition Education (130)	Department Total
Revenue				
Contributions from individuals				
Special events				
Corporate and foundation grants	$ 60,000			$ 60,000
Government grants		$ 254,444	$ 33,322	287,766
Program service fees and sales	33,689			33,689
Return on investments				
Other revenue				
Total revenue	$ 93,689	$ 254,444	$ 33,322	$ 381,455
Expenses				
Personnel:				
Salaries	$ 78,148	$ 131,566	$ 13,801	$ 223,515
Employee benefits	12,909	17,062	1,787	31,758
Payroll taxes	9,434	12,468	1,306	23,208
Total payroll	$ 100,491	$ 161,096	$ 16,894	$ 278,481
Consulting fees	274	977	102	1,353
Total personnel expenses	$ 100,765	$ 162,073	$ 16,996	$ 279,834
Nonpersonnel:				
Supplies	$ 9,756	$ 9,109	$ 1,145	$ 20,010
Telephone	754	2,690	282	3,726
Postage and shipping	261	931	97	1,289
Occupancy	1,539	5,493	575	7,607
Equipment rental and maintenance	789	7,504	295	8,588
Printing and publications	1,502	9,945	561	12,008
Travel		678	8,576	9,254
Conferences and meetings	635	319	33	987
Interest				
Insurance	1,267	4,522	474	6,263
Grants and awards		6,246		6,246
Specific assistance to individuals				
Depreciation	2,305	8,225	861	11,391
Other nonpersonnel expenses—dues	215	87	9	311
Staff development	600	472	49	1,121
Contract temporary help		3,487		3,487
Other expenses	89	876	33	998
Total nonpersonnel expenses	$ 19,712	$ 60,584	$ 12,990	$ 93,286
Total expenses	$ 120,477	$ 222,657	$ 29,986	$ 373,120

TABLE 16.3

Budget-to-Actual Report: Adult Activity Center

Revenue or Expense Category	Department Budget	Department Actual	Variance Under/(Over)
Revenue			
Contributions from individuals			
Special events			
Corporate and foundation grants	$ 50,000	$ 60,000	$ (10,000)
Government grants	300,000	287,766	12,234
Program service fees and sales	40,000	33,689	6,311
Return on investments			
Other revenue			
Total revenue	$ 390,000	$ 381,455	$ 8,545
Expenses			
Personnel:			
Salaries	$ 215,000	$ 223,515	$ (8,515)
Employee benefits	32,250	31,758	492
Payroll taxes	21,500	23,208	(1,708)
Total payroll	$ 268,750	$ 278,481	$ (9,731)
Consulting fees	2,500	1,353	1,147
Total personnel expenses	$ 271,250	$ 279,834	$ (8,584)
Nonpersonnel:			
Supplies	$ 21,500	$ 20,010	$ 1,490
Telephone	4,000	3,726	274
Postage and shipping	1,400	1,289	111
Occupancy	7,000	7,607	(607)
Equipment rental and maintenance	8,300	8,588	(288)
Printing and publications	10,700	12,008	(1,308)
Travel	8,800	9,254	(454)
Conferences and meetings	1,150	987	163
Interest			
Insurance	5,800	6,263	(463)
Grants and awards	6,500	6,246	254
Specific assistance to individuals			
Depreciation	10,280	11,391	(1,111)
Other nonpersonnel expenses—dues	450	311	139
Staff development	1,000	1,121	(121)
Contract temporary help	2,500	3,487	(987)
Other expenses	900	998	(98)
Total nonpersonnel expenses	$ 90,280	$ 93,286	$ (3,006)
Total expenses	$ 361,530	$ 373,120	$ (11,590)

TABLE 16.4

Revenue and Expense Categories for Internal Budgeting and Reporting (Cross-Referenced to Form 990, Unified Chart of Accounts, and Sample GAAP Financial Statements)

Revenue or Expense Category	Form 990 (Line Number)	Unified Chart of Accounts (Account Number)	Sample GAAP Financial Statementes
Revenue			
Contributions from individuals	1a	4010, 4070, 4080	51, 53
Special events	1a, 9(a)	4050	52
Corporate and foundation grants	1a	4210–4250	51
Government grants	1c	4510–4540	n/a
Program service fees and sales	2	5010–5280	58, 59
Return on investments	4, 5, 6, 7, 8(A)	5410–5910	60, 61, 62, 63
Other revenue	8(B), 9c, 10, 11	6110–6810	64
Total revenue	Sum	Sum	Sum
Expenses			
Personnel:			
Salaries	25, 26	7210, 7220	121
Employee benefits	27, 28, 29	7310, 7320	122
Payroll taxes	29	7410	122
Total payroll	Sum	Sum	Sum
Consulting fees	30, 31, 32, 43	7510–7550	124
Total personnel expenses	Sum	Sum	Sum
Nonpersonnel:			
Supplies	33	7710	125
Telephone	34	7810	126
Postage and shipping	35	7910, 7920	127
Occupancy	36	8010–8050	128
Equipment rental and maintenance	37	8110	129
Printing and publications	38	8210, 8220	130
Travel	39	8310	131
Conferences and meetings	40	8510	132
Interest	41	8610	133
Insurance	43	8710	134
Grants and awards	22	7020, 7030	135
Specific assistance to individuals	23	7040, 7050	136
Depreciation	42	8650	137
Other nonpersonnel expenses	43	8810–9300	138
Total nonpersonnel expenses	Sum	Sum	Sum
Total expenses	Sum	Sum	Sum

TABLE 16.5

Overall Budget-to-Actual Report for Internal Management

Account Number	Revenue or Expense Category	Total Budget	Total Actual	Percentage of Budget Used	Percentage of Year (Month 12)	Variance Over/ (Under)
	Revenue					
4010	Contributions from individuals	140,000	134,579	96.1	100.0	(5,421)
4230	Foundation grants	12,000	12,000	100.0	100.0	
4510	Government grants	25,000	25,000	100.0	100.0	
5210	Program service fees and sales	75,000	82,678	110.2	100.0	7,678
5410	Interest on savings and temp. cash invest.	8,000	8,679	108.5	100.0	679
6810	Other revenue					
	Total revenue	260,000	262,936	101.1	100.0	2,936
	Personnel expenses					
7210	Salaries of officers, directors, etc.	42,000	42,033	100.1	100.0	(33)
7220	Other salaries and wages	107,500	108,994	101.4	100.0	(1,494)
7310	Pension plan contributions	14,950	15,103	101.0	100.0	(153)
7320	Other employee benefits	7,475	7,551	101.0	100.0	(76)
7410	Payroll taxes	11,960	12,082	101.0	100.0	(122)
	Total payroll	183,885	185,763	101.0	100.0	(1,878)
7540	Professional fees	3,500	3,890	111.1	100.0	(390)
	Total personnel expenses	187,385	189,653	101.2	100.0	(2,268)
	Nonpersonnel expenses					
7710	Supplies	10,400	10,905	104.9	100.0	(505)
7810	Telephone	5,200	4,920	94.6	100.0	280
7910	Postage and Shipping	2,700	3,326	123.2	100.0	(626)
8010	Occupancy (rent, utilities, etc.)	17,000	18,634	109.6	100.0	(1,634)
8110	Equipment rental and maintenance	8,300	7,412	89.3	100.0	888
8210	Printing and publications	10,300	11,043	107.2	100.0	(743)
8310	Travel	5,800	6,329	109.1	100.0	(529)
8510	Conferences and meetings	3,100	3,768	121.5	100.0	(668)
9300	Other nonpersonnel expenses	3,800	2,266	59.6	100.0	1,534
	Total nonpersonnel expenses	66,600	68,603	103.0	100.0	(2,003)
	Total expenses	253,985	258,256	101.7	100.0	(4,271)
	Fiscal year cash-based excess (deficit)	6,014	4,680	77.8	100.0	(1,334)

Hierarchy of Internal Management Reporting

The following example of the hierarchy of internal management reporting illustrates reporting within the organizational structure of a typical not-for-profit organization, from project-level reporting up to board-level reporting.

Imagine a midsize not-for-profit human services organization that has a board of directors, an executive office, and several departments. Each *department* is responsible for one or more programs. Each *program* has one or more services, projects, or grants. Each separate program service, project, and grant is an *activity*.

Levels of Accountability and Reporting

In the hierarchy of accounting and reporting, there are four levels of internal accountability, a fifth level for activity-level accounting and reporting, and a sixth level for line item accounting:

Level 1	The organization (board of directors)
Level 2	Executive office (CEO and CFO)
Level 3	Departments (department heads)
Level 4	Programs (program and project directors)
Level 5	Activities (program services, projects, grants, cost pools)
Level 6	Line items (revenue and expense categories)

Level 5, the *activity level,* is the primary accounting, budgeting, and internal financial control level. It is the level for measuring and tracking revenues and expenses. It is the level of detail at which the accounting system records information on specific grants and other sources of revenue, on how employees, consultants, and volunteers spend their time, and on utilization of other resources, such as equipment, space, supplies, and so on. The activity level is the level of detail at which budgets are prepared.

Level 4, the *program level,* is the primary level for accountability to funding sources. Levels 2 and 3, the *executive office* and *department* levels, are the primary general-purpose (GAAP) and Form 990 financial reporting levels. Revenue and expense information, measured at level 5, is used in reports prepared at level 5 and *aggregated* for the *internal* management reporting requirements of levels 1 through 4. Budgets are also prepared and used at all levels from 1 through 5.

Required Periodic Reporting to Each Level of Management

The financial reporting system provides detailed reports at the activity levels and aggregates these accounting data into relevant summary reports at each higher level in the five-level hierarchy of management reporting.

Program and Project Directors

Program and project directors, the lowest-level managers, require weekly or monthly revenue and expense reports for their overall program (level 4) revenue and expense line item and for each grant, special project, and service or activity conducted under their management (level 5). That is, they need reports for each of their respective areas of responsibility. Examples of programs or grants are nutrition and rehabilitation. Examples of services (activities) under the nutrition program or grant are congregate meals, meals at home, and nutrition education. Revenue and expense reports for program directors are prepared for each activity (service, project, grant) and for activities grouped by program.

Department Heads

Middle-level managers—*department heads*—require monthly revenue and expense reports for their department (level 3) and for each of their programs (level 4). They also need access to all the reports received by the program and project directors who report to them. Department revenue and expense reports are prepared for activities grouped by department and by program within each department.

Executive Director

The *executive director* (CEO or CFO) requires monthly revenue and expense reports for the overall organization (level 2) and for each department (level 3), including central service departments (such as data processing and printing and duplicating services), fundraising departments, and administrative departments. Executive directors also need access to all of the level-4 and level-5 reports received by the department heads who report to them. Revenue and expense reports for the executive director are prepared for all the activities of the organization combined and for activities grouped by program within each department.

Board of Directors

The *board of directors* requires monthly and quarterly *summary* revenue and expense reports for the overall organization (level 1). From time to time they may also need access to all the level-2 through level-5 reports received by and available to the executive director. Summary revenue and expense reports for the board of directors are prepared for all the activities of the organization combined and for activities grouped by department.

Conclusion

THIS GUIDE PROVIDES a conceptual framework and design for financial reporting systems that not-for-profit organizations can implement to achieve three important goals: improving the quality of the financial information they produce, strengthening their accountability, and reducing the cost of producing and using the information. Achieving these goals requires action, cooperation, collaboration, and participation on the part of various stakeholders in not-for-profit reporting and accountability, including those who manage and use the financial information of not-for-profit organizations.

We fervently hope that

- Not-for-profit accounting and financial reporting software developers will implement the systems featured in this guide.

- CPA societies' not-for-profit committees and CPA firms specializing in serving the not-for-profit sector will endorse this guide and assist the sector with the implementation of the unified financial reporting system described here.

- The IRS, NASCO, and the National Association of Attorneys General (NAAG) will join with and encourage all of the other stakeholders to implement the recommendations made in this manual.

- Umbrella and other subsector groups and state and local associations of not-for-profit organizations will use this book to help them design the accounting and financial reporting manuals they provide to their members and the databases they maintain on the financial activities of their members.

- Authors, publishers, trainers, consultants, and management assistance providers will use this unified reporting guide as a reference when they provide not-for-profit financial management tools, services, and guidance.

- Corporate and foundation grant makers and their regional associations will use this manual in designing their guidelines and standards for grantee budgeting and financial reporting. In this regard we hope they will consider distributing this manual to their grantees and other not-for-profit organizations and will provide funding for implementation of unified financial reporting systems.

- Federal, state, and local government agencies that fund not-for-profit organizations will incorporate this guide's unified reporting systems in their grant-reporting requirements.

- Local United Way organizations and other federated fundraising organizations will use this guide in designing budgeting and financial reporting standards for recipients of the funds they raise.

- INDEPENDENT SECTOR, GuideStar, the Nonprofit Academic Center Council, and the National Center for Charitable Statistics (NCCS) at the Urban Institute's Center on Nonprofits and Philanthropy will use this guide in designing their databases, research projects, and information products and services and will encourage others to do the same.

- INDEPENDENT SECTOR, the IRS, NCCS, NAAG, and NASCO will continue to convene these stakeholders in an ongoing project that uses this guide as a point of departure to promote a sectorwide not-for-profit industry standard for unified financial reporting to achieve the goals of quality improvement and cost reduction—*with the click of a mouse.*

In Part One, we stressed that this guide was not only about financial reporting but also about honest and accurate reporting according to prescribed rules and principles. In short it is about accountability. It is about America's not-for-profit sector and its tremendous value to society. Therefore we now reiterate and elaborate on some of the points we made in Part One: why honest, timely, and accurate GAAP financial reporting and filing of IRS Form 990 are so important to the not-for-profit sector and the public it serves.

First, accountability protects and nurtures public trust. Charitable contributions are the fuel that keeps not-for-profit organizations' engines running, and public trust is the lifeblood of these organizations. It is estimated that in 1999 Americans donated in excess of $143 billion to not-for-profit organizations because they believed the organizations represented worthy causes and provided critical public services.[1] And indeed the vast majority of not-for-profit organizations are honest "citizens." Even when their Form

990 returns are not quite accurate or complete, it is usually because of the complexity of the task and the limited resources at their disposal rather than the result of deliberate misrepresentation of facts. The publication of this guide is a step toward educating those engaged in not-for-profit financial accounting and reporting in order to ease the burden and reduce the costs of accurate financial reporting. Greater understanding of not-for-profit accounting systems and reporting requirements, and greater attention to complete and accurate reporting, will benefit both the not-for-profit sector and the public at large.

Second, public scrutiny of not-for-profit organizations has increased significantly over the past few years. This is true not only of state and federal governments but also of voluntary groups and the media. The law now requires full public access to and disclosure of Form 990. Anyone interested in learning about a registered tax-exempt organization is now able to obtain that information relatively easily. Moreover, the coverage of not-for-profit organizations in print and electronic media has increased exponentially compared with only ten years ago. A few sensational scandals have engendered a new interest in charities among investigative reporters.

With respect to Form 990 two areas deserve special mention: Part II, Statement of Functional Expenses, and Part III, Statement of Program Service Accomplishments. Our experience suggests that reporting in these two sections of Form 990 has been particularly weak and problematic. Part II requires not-for-profit organizations to distribute total functional expenses into three broad categories: program services, M&G, and fundraising. Charity regulators, watchdog groups, and the media take special interest in this section of the form. The focus is on the proportion of funds used for program services versus the proportion spent on M&G and fundraising. There is always the temptation to overstate program service expenses and understate M&G and fundraising expenses because—for better or worse—that is often the standard used to measure the efficiency of not-for-profit organizations. This is unfortunate because it is this focus on M&G and fundraising expenses that encourages "creative" accounting and reporting. Not-for-profit organizations must resist this temptation and accurately reflect their functional expenses.

The public and the media need to be made aware that it costs money to raise money and that it costs money to manage a not-for-profit organization just as it costs money to manage a for-profit corporation. In particular, fundraising costs vary according to the age, size, type, and other circumstances of not-for-profit organizations. A single standard for measuring the efficiency and effectiveness of all not-for-profit organizations cannot be valid and should not be used.

Regarding Form 990, Part III, our experience indicates that this section is often poorly completed and sometimes completely ignored. It is here that the not-for-profit organization has the opportunity to communicate to the public its accomplishments succinctly. A properly and carefully completed Part III can go a long way toward communicating the best about the organization. Thus not-for-profit organizations would do well to pay greater attention to this section of Form 990 as more and more people look to Part III to learn what the organization is all about (see Resource I).

Third, NCCS and GuideStar have collaborated to create comprehensive databases on America's not-for-profit organizations and to make the information accessible to anyone. NCCS is the national repository of data on the not-for-profit sector in the United States. It develops and disseminates data for use by researchers, policymakers, and practitioners and conducts research on the sector. GuideStar is a national initiative of Philanthropic Research, Inc., a not-for-profit organization whose mission is to provide objective information about charities to donors and the public at large. The IRS is providing optically scanned Form 990 returns to NCCS, where the data are being digitized and made widely available to the general public on the NCCS and GuideStar Web sites.[2] As this book was being readied for publication, GuideStar posted its charity database on the Internet for the first time, on October 18, 1999.[3] By the time this Guide is published, the Form 990 data should be widely available on Web sites.

Clearly there is interest in information about charities on the Internet. In November 1999 GuideStar reported average weekly Web site hits of 1,104,090. But more important, GuideStar reported that so-called user sessions, those sessions when a user goes beyond the home page, averaged 35,104 per week, with the average user looking at more than twelve pages per visit. In addition to Form 990 information, GuideStar encourages charities to complete a free on-line information form that provides additional data about their mission, programs, and objectives. About five thousand organizations had completed this form through December 1, 1999, with a growth rate of about three hundred new organizations each week. It is not hard to predict that once this vehicle is well established, fine-tuned, and widely publicized, use of this information resource on America's not-for-profit organizations will increase. We can only speculate on the consequences of such easy access to Form 990 returns on the Internet.

Fourth, it is important that not-for-profit organizations use available technology to do accounting and financial reporting. Even relatively small organizations are now able to use technology, and those who cannot are able to purchase such services. Also many not-for-profit management support organizations around the country offer assistance to small and midsize organizations. As part of the 990 in 2000 project we are organizing a network of assistance providers to help small and midsize organizations that need help. Also planned are additional tools, materials, and training workshops around the country. Users of this guide are urged to seek out this organized assistance and take advantage of it.

Finally, not-for-profit organizations by definition are mission driven as opposed to profit motivated. They exist to produce public goods and services and to benefit the public. They enjoy special privileges, such as tax exemption, and contributions to them are tax deductible to the donor. They are expected to uphold the highest standards of ethics and accountability. They must report on their finances and operations honestly and accurately—not for fear of discovery or penalty but because it is the right thing to do. This guide is designed to help them do the right thing.

Resources

Resource A   IRS Form 990 and Schedule A for 1999

Resource B   Content of Unified Chart of Accounts by Account Number

Resource C   Cross-Referencing Your Not-for-Profit Organization's Chart of Accounts to the Unified Chart of Accounts: Cross-Reference Worksheet and Keyword Index

Resource D   Sample Employee Time Sheets

Resource E   Summary of State Registration and Filing Requirements for Not-for-Profit Organizations

Resource F   National Taxonomy of Exempt Entities

Resource G   Voluntary Standard-Setting and Evaluation Groups for Not-for-Profit Organizations

Resource H   A Brief History of Financial Accounting and Reporting Standards for Not-for-Profit Organizations

Resource I   Accountability for Service Efforts and Accomplishments

Resource J   Selected Form 990 and Management and Technical Assistance Web Sites

Resource A

IRS Form 990 and Schedule A for 1999

IRS Form 990 and Schedule A for 1999

Form **990**

Department of the Treasury
Internal Revenue Service

Return of Organization Exempt From Income Tax

Under section 501(c) of the Internal Revenue Code (except black lung benefit trust or private foundation) or section 4947(a)(1) nonexempt charitable trust

Note: *The organization may have to use a copy of this return to satisfy state reporting requirements.*

OMB No. 1545-0047

1999

This Form is
Open to Public
Inspection

A For the 1999 calendar year, OR tax year period beginning _____ , 1999, and ending _____ ,

B Check if:
☐ Change of address
☐ Initial return
☐ Final return
☐ Amended return (required also for state reporting)

Please use IRS label or print or type. See Specific Instructions.

C Name of organization

Number and street (or P.O. box if mail is not delivered to street address) | Room/suite

City or town, state or country, and ZIP+4

D Employer identification number

E Telephone number

F Check ☐ if exemption application is pending

G Type of organization— ☐ Exempt under section 501(c)( ) (insert number) OR ☐ section 4947(a)(1) nonexempt charitable trust

Note: *Section 501(c)(3) exempt organizations and 4947(a)(1) nonexempt charitable trusts MUST attach a completed Schedule A (Form 990).*

H(a) Is this a group return filed for affiliates? ☐ Yes ☐ No

(b) If "Yes," enter the number of affiliates for which this return is filed: _____

(c) Is this a separate return filed by an organization covered by a group ruling? ☐ Yes ☐ No

I If either box in H is checked "Yes," enter four-digit group exemption number (GEN) - - - - - - - - - - - - - - -

J Accounting method: ☐ Cash ☐ Accrual ☐ Other (specify)

K Check here ☐ if the organization's gross receipts are normally not more than $25,000. The organization need not file a return with the IRS; but if it received a Form 990 Package in the mail, it should file a return without financial data. **Some states require a complete return.**

Note: *Form 990-EZ may be used by organizations with gross receipts less than $100,000 and total assets less than $250,000 at end of year.*

Part I **Revenue, Expenses, and Changes in Net Assets or Fund Balances** (See Specific Instructions on page 15.)

1	Contributions, gifts, grants, and similar amounts received:		
a	Direct public support	1a	
b	Indirect public support	1b	
c	Government contributions (grants)	1c	
d	**Total** (add lines 1a through 1c) (attach schedule of contributors) (cash $ _____ noncash $ _____)	1d	
2	Program service revenue including government fees and contracts (from Part VII, line 93)	2	
3	Membership dues and assessments	3	
4	Interest on savings and temporary cash investments	4	
5	Dividends and interest from securities	5	
6a	Gross rents	6a	
b	Less: rental expenses	6b	
c	Net rental income or (loss) (subtract line 6b from line 6a)	6c	
7	Other investment income (describe _____)	7	
8a	Gross amount from sales of assets other than inventory	(A) Securities 8a / (B) Other	
b	Less: cost or other basis and sales expenses	8b	
c	Gain or (loss) (attach schedule)	8c	
d	Net gain or (loss) (combine line 8c, columns (A) and (B))	8d	
9	Special events and activities (attach schedule)		
a	Gross revenue (not including $ _____ of contributions reported on line 1a)	9a	
b	Less: direct expenses other than fundraising expenses	9b	
c	Net income or (loss) from special events (subtract line 9b from line 9a)	9c	
10a	Gross sales of inventory, less returns and allowances	10a	
b	Less: cost of goods sold	10b	
c	Gross profit or (loss) from sales of inventory (attach schedule) (subtract line 10b from line 10a)	10c	
11	Other revenue (from Part VII, line 103)	11	
12	**Total revenue** (add lines 1d, 2, 3, 4, 5, 6c, 7, 8d, 9c, 10c, and 11)	12	
13	Program services (from line 44, column (B))	13	
14	Management and general (from line 44, column (C))	14	
15	Fundraising (from line 44, column (D))	15	
16	Payments to affiliates (attach schedule)	16	
17	**Total expenses** (add lines 16 and 44, column (A))	17	
18	Excess or (deficit) for the year (subtract line 17 from line 12)	18	
19	Net assets or fund balances at beginning of year (from line 73, column (A))	19	
20	Other changes in net assets or fund balances (attach explanation)	20	
21	Net assets or fund balances at end of year (combine lines 18, 19, and 20)	21	

(Revenue — lines 1–12; Expenses — lines 13–17; Net Assets — lines 18–21)

For Paperwork Reduction Act Notice, see page 1 of the separate instructions.   Cat. No. 11282Y   Form **990** (1999)

(Continued)

Form 990 (1999)   Page **2**

| **Part II** | **Statement of Functional Expenses** | All organizations must complete column (A). Columns (B), (C), and (D) are required for section 501(c)(3) and (4) organizations and section 4947(a)(1) nonexempt charitable trusts but optional for others. (See Specific Instructions on page 19.) |

Do not include amounts reported on line 6b, 8b, 9b, 10b, or 16 of Part I.		**(A)** Total	**(B)** Program services	**(C)** Management and general	**(D)** Fundraising
22	Grants and allocations (attach schedule) . (cash $ _____ noncash $ _____)	22			
23	Specific assistance to individuals (attach schedule)	23			
24	Benefits paid to or for members (attach schedule).	24			
25	Compensation of officers, directors, etc. .	25			
26	Other salaries and wages	26			
27	Pension plan contributions	27			
28	Other employee benefits	28			
29	Payroll taxes	29			
30	Professional fundraising fees	30			
31	Accounting fees	31			
32	Legal fees	32			
33	Supplies	33			
34	Telephone	34			
35	Postage and shipping	35			
36	Occupancy	36			
37	Equipment rental and maintenance . . .	37			
38	Printing and publications	38			
39	Travel	39			
40	Conferences, conventions, and meetings .	40			
41	Interest	41			
42	Depreciation, depletion, etc. (attach schedule)	42			
43	Other expenses (itemize): **a** _____	43a			
b	_____	43b			
c	_____	43c			
d	_____	43d			
e	_____	43e			
44	**Total functional expenses** (add lines 22 through 43). *Organizations completing columns (B)-(D), carry these totals to lines 13—15* .	44			

Reporting of Joint Costs. Did you report in column (B) (Program services) any joint costs from a combined educational campaign and fundraising solicitation?   .   .   .   .   ☐ Yes   ☐ No
If "Yes," enter **(i)** the aggregate amount of these joint costs $_____; **(ii)** the amount allocated to Program services $_____;
(iii) the amount allocated to Management and general $_____ ; and **(iv)** the amount allocated to Fundraising $_____

Part III	**Statement of Program Service Accomplishments** (See Specific Instructions on page 22.)		**Program Service Expenses** (Required for 501(c)(3) and (4) orgs., and 4947(a)(1) trusts; but optional for others.)

What is the organization's primary exempt purpose? ---
All organizations must describe their exempt purpose achievements in a clear and concise manner. State the number of clients served, publications issued, etc. Discuss achievements that are not measurable. (Section 501(c)(3) and (4) organizations and 4947(a)(1) nonexempt charitable trusts must also enter the amount of grants and allocations to others.)

a _____
_____
_____
(Grants and allocations $)

b _____
_____
_____
(Grants and allocations $)

c _____
_____
_____
(Grants and allocations $)

d _____
_____
_____
(Grants and allocations $)

e Other program services (attach schedule)   (Grants and allocations $)
f **Total of Program Service Expenses** (should equal line 44, column (B), Program services) .   .   .   .

Form **990** (1999)

(Continued)

Form 990 (1999)   Page **3**

Part IV   Balance Sheets (See Specific Instructions on page 22.)

Note: *Where required, attached schedules and amounts within the description column should be for end-of-year amounts only.*

		(A) Beginning of year		(B) End of year
Assets	45 Cash—non-interest-bearing		45	
	46 Savings and temporary cash investments		46	
	47a Accounts receivable **47a**			
	b Less: allowance for doubtful accounts **47b**		47c	
	48a Pledges receivable **48a**			
	b Less: allowance for doubtful accounts **48b**		48c	
	49 Grants receivable		49	
	50 Receivables from officers, directors, trustees, and key employees (attach schedule)		50	
	51a Other notes and loans receivable (attach schedule) **51a**			
	b Less: allowance for doubtful accounts **51b**		51c	
	52 Inventories for sale or use		52	
	53 Prepaid expenses and deferred charges		53	
	54 Investments—securities (attach schedule)		54	
	55a Investments—land, buildings, and equipment: basis **55a**			
	b Less: accumulated depreciation (attach schedule) **55b**		55c	
	56 Investments—other (attach schedule)		56	
	57a Land, buildings, and equipment: basis **57a**			
	b Less: accumulated depreciation (attach schedule) **57b**		57c	
	58 Other assets (describe _____)		58	
	59 **Total assets** (add lines 45 through 58) (must equal line 74)		59	
Liabilities	60 Accounts payable and accrued expenses		60	
	61 Grants payable		61	
	62 Deferred revenue		62	
	63 Loans from officers, directors, trustees, and key employees (attach schedule)		63	
	64a Tax-exempt bond liabilities (attach schedule)		64a	
	b Mortgages and other notes payable (attach schedule)		64b	
	65 Other liabilities (describe _____)		65	
	66 **Total liabilities** (add lines 60 through 65)		66	
Net Assets or Fund Balances	**Organizations that follow SFAS 117, check here** ☐ **and complete lines 67 through 69 and lines 73 and 74.**			
	67 Unrestricted		67	
	68 Temporarily restricted		68	
	69 Permanently restricted		69	
	Organizations that do not follow SFAS 117, check here ☐ **and complete lines 70 through 74.**			
	70 Capital stock, trust principal, or current funds		70	
	71 Paid-in or capital surplus, or land, building, and equipment fund		71	
	72 Retained earnings, endowment, accumulated income, or other funds		72	
	73 **Total net assets or fund balances** (add lines 67 through 69 OR lines 70 through 72; column (A) must equal line 19 and column (B) must equal line 21)		73	
	74 **Total liabilities and net assets / fund balances** (add lines 66 and 73)		74	

Form 990 is available for public inspection and, for some people, serves as the primary or sole source of information about a particular organization. How the public perceives an organization in such cases may be determined by the information presented on its return. Therefore, please make sure the return is complete and accurate and fully describes, in Part III, the organization's programs and accomplishments.

(Continued)

Form 990 (1999)   Page **4**

| **Part IV-A** | **Reconciliation of Revenue per Audited Financial Statements with Revenue per Return** (See Specific Instructions, page 24.) | | **Part IV-B** | **Reconciliation of Expenses per Audited Financial Statements with Expenses per Return** | |

a Total revenue, gains, and other support per audited financial statements . . | **a** |

b Amounts included on line **a** but not on line 12, Form 990:

(1) Net unrealized gains on investments . $_____

(2) Donated services and use of facilities $_____

(3) Recoveries of prior year grants . . $_____

(4) Other (specify):

------------------ $_____

Add amounts on lines (1) through (4) | **b** |

c Line **a** minus line **b**. . . . . | **c** |

d Amounts included on line 12, Form 990 but not on line **a**:

(1) Investment expenses not included on line 6b, Form 990 . . $_____

(2) Other (specify):

------------------ $_____

Add amounts on lines (1) and (2) | **d** |

e Total revenue per line 12, Form 990 (line **c** plus line **d**) . . . . . | **e** |

a Total expenses and losses per audited financial statements . . | **a** |

b Amounts included on line **a** but not on line 17, Form 990:

(1) Donated services and use of facilities $_____

(2) Prior year adjustments reported on line 20, Form 990 . . . $_____

(3) Losses reported on line 20, Form 990 . $_____

(4) Other (specify):

------------------ $_____

Add amounts on lines (1) through (4) | **b** |

c Line **a** minus line **b** . . . . | **c** |

d Amounts included on line 17, Form 990 but not on line **a**:

(1) Investment expenses not included on line 6b, Form 990 . . $_____

(2) Other (specify):

------------------ $_____

Add amounts on lines (1) and (2) | **d** |

e Total expenses per line 17, Form 990 (line **c** plus line **d**) . . . . | **e** |

| **Part V** | **List of Officers, Directors, Trustees, and Key Employees** (List each one even if not compensated; see Specific Instructions on page 24.) |

(A) Name and address	(B) Title and average hours per week devoted to position	(C) Compensation (If not paid, enter -0-.)	(D) Contributions to employee benefit plans & deferred compensation	(E) Expense account and other allowances
------------------------------------				

------------------------------------				

75 Did any officer, director, trustee, or key employee receive aggregate compensation of more than $100,000 from your organization and all related organizations, of which more than $10,000 was provided by the related organizations?   ☐ **Yes** ☐ **No**

If "Yes," attach schedule—see Specific Instructions on page 25.

Form **990** (1999)

(Continued)

Form 990 (1999)

Page **5**

Part VI Other Information (See Specific Instructions on page 25.)

		Yes	No
76	Did the organization engage in any activity not previously reported to the IRS? If "Yes," attach a detailed description of each activity . **76**		
77	Were any changes made in the organizing or governing documents but not reported to the IRS? . . **77**		
	If "Yes," attach a conformed copy of the changes.		
78a	Did the organization have unrelated business gross income of $1,000 or more during the year covered by this return?. **78a**		
b	If "Yes," has it filed a tax return on **Form 990-T** for this year? **78b**		
79	Was there a liquidation, dissolution, termination, or substantial contraction during the year? If "Yes," attach a statement **79**		
80a	Is the organization related (other than by association with a statewide or nationwide organization) through common membership, governing bodies, trustees, officers, etc., to any other exempt or nonexempt organization? . . **80a**		
b	If "Yes," enter the name of the organization _____		
	_____ and check whether it is ☐ exempt **OR** ☐ nonexempt.		
81a	Enter the amount of political expenditures, direct or indirect, as described in the instructions for line 81. . . . . **81a**		
b	Did the organization file **Form 1120-POL** for this year?. **81b**		
82a	Did the organization receive donated services or the use of materials, equipment, or facilities at no charge or at substantially less than fair rental value? **82a**		
b	If "Yes," you may indicate the value of these items here. Do not include this amount as revenue in Part I or as an expense in Part II. (See instructions for reporting in Part III.). **82b**		
83a	Did the organization comply with the public inspection requirements for returns and exemption applications? **83a**		
b	Did the organization comply with the disclosure requirements relating to quid pro quo contributions? . **83b**		
84a	Did the organization solicit any contributions or gifts that were not tax deductible? **84a**		
b	If "Yes," did the organization include with every solicitation an express statement that such contributions or gifts were not tax deductible? **84b**		
85	*501(c)(4), (5), or (6) organizations.* **a** Were substantially all dues nondeductible by members? . . **85a**		
b	Did the organization make only in-house lobbying expenditures of $2,000 or less? **85b**		
	If "Yes" was answered to either 85a or 85b, **do not** complete 85c through 85h below unless the organization received a waiver for proxy tax owed for the prior year.		
c	Dues, assessments, and similar amounts from members **85c**		
d	Section 162(e) lobbying and political expenditures **85d**		
e	Aggregate nondeductible amount of section 6033(e)(1)(A) dues notices . . **85e**		
f	Taxable amount of lobbying and political expenditures (line 85d less 85e) . **85f**		
g	Does the organization elect to pay the section 6033(e) tax on the amount in 85f?. **85g**		
h	If section 6033(e)(1)(A) dues notices were sent, does the organization agree to add the amount in 85f to its reasonable estimate of dues allocable to nondeductible lobbying and political expenditures for the following tax year?. . **85h**		
86	*501(c)(7) orgs.* Enter: **a** Initiation fees and capital contributions included on line 12 . **86a**		
b	Gross receipts, included on line 12, for public use of club facilities. . . . **86b**		
87	*501(c)(12) orgs.* Enter: **a** Gross income from members or shareholders. . . **87a**		
b	Gross income from other sources. (Do not net amounts due or paid to other sources against amounts due or received from them.) **87b**		
88	At any time during the year, did the organization own a 50% or greater interest in a taxable corporation or partnership, or an entity disregarded as separate from the organization under Regulations sections 301.7701-2 and 301.7701-3? If "Yes," complete Part IX **88**		
89a	*501(c)(3) organizations.* Enter: Amount of tax imposed on the organization during the year under: section 4911 _____ ; section 4912 _____ ; section 4955 _____		
b	*501(c)(3) and 501(c)(4) orgs.* Did the organization engage in any section 4958 excess benefit transaction during the year or did it become aware of an excess benefit transaction from a prior year? If "Yes," attach a statement explaining each transaction. **89b**		
c	Enter: Amount of tax imposed on the organization managers or disqualified persons during the year under sections 4912, 4955, and 4958. . . . . _____		
d	Enter: Amount of tax on line 89c, above, reimbursed by the organization. . . . . _____		
90a	List the states with which a copy of this return is filed _____		
b	Number of employees employed in the pay period that includes March 12, 1999 (See inst.) . **90b** _____		
91	The books are in care of _____ Telephone no. (_____)_____		
	Located at _____ ZIP + 4 _____		
92	*Section 4947(a)(1) nonexempt charitable trusts filing Form 990 in lieu of **Form 1041**—*Check here . . . . . ☐		
	and enter the amount of tax-exempt interest received or accrued during the tax year . . **92**		

Form **990** (1999)

(Continued)

Form 990 (1999)   Page **6**

Part VII Analysis of Income-Producing Activities (See Specific Instructions on page 29.)

Enter gross amounts unless otherwise indicated.

	Unrelated business income		Excluded by section 512, 513, or 514		**(E)** Related or exempt function income
	(A) Business code	**(B)** Amount	**(C)** Exclusion code	**(D)** Amount	
93 Program service revenue:					
a _____					
b _____					
c _____					
d _____					
e _____					
f Medicare/Medicaid payments					
g Fees and contracts from government agencies					
94 Membership dues and assessments . .					
95 Interest on savings and temporary cash investments					
96 Dividends and interest from securities . .					
97 Net rental income or (loss) from real estate:					
a debt-financed property					
b not debt-financed property					
98 Net rental income or (loss) from personal property					
99 Other investment income					
100 Gain or (loss) from sales of assets other than inventory					
101 Net income or (loss) from special events .					
102 Gross profit or (loss) from sales of inventory .					
103 Other revenue: a _____					
b _____					
c _____					
d _____					
e _____					
104 Subtotal (add columns (B), (D), and (E)) . .					

105 Total (add line 104, columns (B), (D), and (E)) . . . . _____

Note: *Line 105 plus line 1d, Part I, should equal the amount on line 12, Part I.*

Part VIII Relationship of Activities to the Accomplishment of Exempt Purposes (See Specific Instructions on page 30.)

Line No.	Explain how each activity for which income is reported in column (E) of Part VII contributed importantly to the accomplishment of the organization's exempt purposes (other than by providing funds for such purposes).

Part IX Information Regarding Taxable Subsidiaries and Disregarded Entities (See Specific Instructions on page 30.)

(A) Name, address, and EIN of corporation, partnership, or disregarded entity	**(B)** Percentage of ownership interest	**(C)** Nature of activities	**(D)** Total income	**(E)** End-of-year assets
	%			
	%			
	%			
	%			

Please Sign Here

Under penalties of perjury, I declare that I have examined this return, including accompanying schedules and statements, and to the best of my knowledge and belief, it is true, correct, and complete. Declaration of preparer (other than officer) is based on all information of which preparer has any knowledge. (**Important:** See General Instruction U, on page 14.)

Signature of officer	Date	Type or print name and title.

Paid Preparer's Use Only

Preparer's signature	Date	Check if self-employed ☐	Preparer's SSN or PTIN
Firm's name (or yours if self-employed) and address		EIN	
		ZIP + 4	

Form **990** (1999)

(Continued)

SCHEDULE A (Form 990)

Department of the Treasury
Internal Revenue Service

Organization Exempt Under Section 501(c)(3)

(Except Private Foundation) and Section 501(e), 501(f), 501(k),
501(n), or Section 4947(a)(1) Nonexempt Charitable Trust

Supplementary Information—(See separate instructions.)

MUST be completed by the above organizations and attached to their Form 990 or 990-EZ

OMB No. 1545-0047

1999

Name of the organization

Employer identification number

Part I   Compensation of the Five Highest Paid Employees Other Than Officers, Directors, and Trustees
(See page 1 of the instructions. List each one. If there are none, enter "None.")

(a) Name and address of each employee paid more than $50,000	(b) Title and average hours per week devoted to position	(c) Compensation	(d) Contributions to employee benefit plans & deferred compensation	(e) Expense account and other allowances

Total number of other employees paid over $50,000 . . . .

Part II   Compensation of the Five Highest Paid Independent Contractors for Professional Services
(See page 1 of the instructions. List each one (whether individuals or firms). If there are none, enter "None.")

(a) Name and address of each independent contractor paid more than $50,000	(b) Type of service	(c) Compensation

Total number of others receiving over $50,000 for professional services . . . .

For Paperwork Reduction Act Notice, see page 1 of the Instructions for Form 990 and Form 990-EZ.   Cat. No. 11285F   **Schedule A (Form 990) 1999**

(Continued)

Part III	**Statements About Activities**		Yes	No

1 During the year, has the organization attempted to influence national, state, or local legislation, including any attempt to influence public opinion on a legislative matter or referendum? . . . . | **1** | | |

If "Yes," enter the total expenses paid or incurred in connection with the lobbying activities $ _____

Organizations that made an election under section 501(h) by filing Form 5768 must complete Part VI-A. Other organizations checking "Yes," must complete Part VI-B AND attach a statement giving a detailed description of the lobbying activities.

2 During the year, has the organization, either directly or indirectly, engaged in any of the following acts with any of its trustees, directors, officers, creators, key employees, or members of their families, or with any taxable organization with which any such person is affiliated as an officer, director, trustee, majority owner, or principal beneficiary:

a Sale, exchange, or leasing of property? . . . . | **2a** | | |

b Lending of money or other extension of credit? . . . . | **2b** | | |

c Furnishing of goods, services, or facilities? . . . . | **2c** | | |

d Payment of compensation (or payment or reimbursement of expenses if more than $1,000)? . . . . . | **2d** | | |

e Transfer of any part of its income or assets? . . . . | **2e** | | |

If the answer to any question is "Yes," attach a detailed statement explaining the transactions.

3 Does the organization make grants for scholarships, fellowships, student loans, etc.? . . . . | **3** | | |

4a Do you have a section 403(b) annuity plan for your employees? . . . . | **4a** | | |

b Attach a statement to explain how the organization determines that individuals or organizations receiving grants or loans from it in furtherance of its charitable programs qualify to receive payments. (See page 2 of the instructions.)

Part IV	**Reason for Non-Private Foundation Status** (See pages 2 through 4 of the instructions.)

The organization is not a private foundation because it is: (Please check only **ONE** applicable box.)

5 ☐ A church, convention of churches, or association of churches. Section 170(b)(1)(A)(i).

6 ☐ A school. Section 170(b)(1)(A)(ii). (Also complete Part V, page 4.)

7 ☐ A hospital or a cooperative hospital service organization. Section 170(b)(1)(A)(iii).

8 ☐ A Federal, state, or local government or governmental unit. Section 170(b)(1)(A)(v).

9 ☐ A medical research organization operated in conjunction with a hospital. Section 170(b)(1)(A)(iii). **Enter the hospital's name, city, and state** ---

10 ☐ An organization operated for the benefit of a college or university owned or operated by a governmental unit. Section 170(b)(1)(A)(iv). (Also complete the **Support Schedule** in Part IV-A.)

11a ☐ An organization that normally receives a substantial part of its support from a governmental unit or from the general public. Section 170(b)(1)(A)(vi). (Also complete the **Support Schedule** in Part IV-A.)

11b ☐ A community trust. Section 170(b)(1)(A)(vi). (Also complete the **Support Schedule** in Part IV-A.)

12 ☐ An organization that normally receives: **(1) more than** 33⅓% of its support from contributions, membership fees, and gross receipts from activities related to its charitable, etc., functions—subject to certain exceptions, and **(2) no more than** 33⅓% of its support from gross investment income and unrelated business taxable income (less section 511 tax) from businesses acquired by the organization after June 30, 1975. See section 509(a)(2). (Also complete the **Support Schedule** in Part IV-A.)

13 ☐ An organization that is not controlled by any disqualified persons (other than foundation managers) and supports organizations described in: **(1)** lines 5 through 12 above; or **(2)** section 501(c)(4), (5), or (6), if they meet the test of section 509(a)(2). (See section 509(a)(3).)

Provide the following information about the supported organizations. (See page 4 of the instructions.)

(a) Name(s) of supported organization(s)	**(b)** Line number from above

14 ☐ An organization organized and operated to test for public safety. Section 509(a)(4). (See page 4 of the instructions.)

(Continued)

Schedule A (Form 990) 1999

Page **3**

Part IV-A **Support Schedule** (Complete only if you checked a box on line 10, 11, or 12.) *Use cash method of accounting.*
Note: *You may use the worksheet in the instructions for converting from the accrual to the cash method of accounting.*

Calendar year (or fiscal year beginning in)	(a) 1998	(b) 1997	(c) 1996	(d) 1995	(e) Total
15 Gifts, grants, and contributions received. (Do not include unusual grants. See line 28.).					
16 Membership fees received					
17 Gross receipts from admissions, merchandise sold or services performed, or furnishing of facilities in any activity that is not a business unrelated to the organization's charitable, etc., purpose					
18 Gross income from interest, dividends, amounts received from payments on securities loans (section 512(a)(5)), rents, royalties, and unrelated business taxable income (less section 511 taxes) from businesses acquired by the organization after June 30, 1975 .					
19 Net income from unrelated business activities not included in line 18 . . .					
20 Tax revenues levied for the organization's benefit and either paid to it or expended on its behalf.					
21 The value of services or facilities furnished to the organization by a governmental unit without charge. Do not include the value of services or facilities generally furnished to the public without charge.					
22 Other income. Attach a schedule. Do not include gain or (loss) from sale of capital assets					
23 Total of lines 15 through 22.					
24 Line 23 minus line 17.					
25 Enter 1% of line 23					

26 **Organizations described on lines 10 or 11:** **a** Enter 2% of amount in column (e), line 24 . . . . | **26a** | |

b Attach a list (which is not open to public inspection) showing the name of and amount contributed by each person (other than a governmental unit or publicly supported organization) whose total gifts for 1995 through 1998 exceeded the amount shown in line 26a. Enter the sum of all these excess amounts. . . . | **26b** | |

c Total support for section 509(a)(1) test: Enter line 24, column (e) . . . . | **26c** | |
d Add: Amounts from column (e) for lines: 18 _____ 19 _____
22 _____ 26b _____ . . . . | **26d** | |
e Public support (line 26c minus line 26d total) . . . . | **26e** | |
f **Public support percentage (line 26e (numerator) divided by line 26c (denominator))** . . . . | **26f** | % |

27 **Organizations described on line 12:** **a** For amounts included in lines 15, 16, and 17 that were received from a "disqualified person," attach a list to show the name of, and total amounts received in each year from, each "disqualified person." Enter the sum of such amounts for each year:

(1998) _____ (1997) _____ (1996) _____ (1995) _____

b For any amount included in line 17 that was received from a nondisqualified person, attach a list to show the name of, and amount received for each year, that was more than the **larger** of (1) the amount on line 25 for the year or (2) $5,000. (Include in the list organizations described in lines 5 through 11, as well as individuals.) After computing the difference between the amount received and the larger amount described in (1) or (2), enter the sum of these differences (the excess amounts) for each year:

(1998) _____ (1997) _____ (1996) _____ (1995) _____

c Add: Amounts from column (e) for lines: 15 _____ 16 _____
17 _____ 20 _____ 21 _____ . . | **27c** | |
d Add: Line 27a total . _____ and line 27b total . _____ . . . | **27d** | |
e Public support (line 27c total minus line 27d total). . . . . | **27e** | |
f Total support for section 509(a)(2) test: Enter amount on line 23, column (e) . . | 27f | | |
g **Public support percentage (line 27e (numerator) divided by line 27f (denominator))**. . . . . | **27g** | % |
h **Investment income percentage (line 18, column (e) (numerator) divided by line 27f (denominator)).** | **27h** | % |

28 **Unusual Grants:** For an organization described in line 10, 11, or 12 that received any unusual grants during 1995 through 1998, attach a list (which is not open to public inspection) for each year showing the name of the contributor, the date and amount of the grant, and a brief description of the nature of the grant. Do not include these grants in line 15. (See page 4 of the instructions.)

Schedule A (Form 990) 1999

(Continued)

Schedule A (Form 990) 1999 | Page **4**

Part V — Private School Questionnaire (See page 4 of the instructions.)
(To be completed ONLY by schools that checked the box on line 6 in Part IV)

		Yes	No
29	Does the organization have a racially nondiscriminatory policy toward students by statement in its charter, bylaws, other governing instrument, or in a resolution of its governing body? **29**		
30	Does the organization include a statement of its racially nondiscriminatory policy toward students in all its brochures, catalogues, and other written communications with the public dealing with student admissions, programs, and scholarships? **30**		
31	Has the organization publicized its racially nondiscriminatory policy through newspaper or broadcast media during the period of solicitation for students, or during the registration period if it has no solicitation program, in a way that makes the policy known to all parts of the general community it serves? **31**		

If "Yes," please describe; if "No," please explain. (If you need more space, attach a separate statement.)

		Yes	No
32	Does the organization maintain the following:		
a	Records indicating the racial composition of the student body, faculty, and administrative staff? **32a**		
b	Records documenting that scholarships and other financial assistance are awarded on a racially nondiscriminatory basis? **32b**		
c	Copies of all catalogues, brochures, announcements, and other written communications to the public dealing with student admissions, programs, and scholarships? **32c**		
d	Copies of all material used by the organization or on its behalf to solicit contributions? **32d**		

If you answered "No" to any of the above, please explain. (If you need more space, attach a separate statement.)

		Yes	No
33	Does the organization discriminate by race in any way with respect to:		
a	Students' rights or privileges? **33a**		
b	Admissions policies? **33b**		
c	Employment of faculty or administrative staff? **33c**		
d	Scholarships or other financial assistance? **33d**		
e	Educational policies? **33e**		
f	Use of facilities? **33f**		
g	Athletic programs? **33g**		
h	Other extracurricular activities? **33h**		

If you answered "Yes" to any of the above, please explain. (If you need more space, attach a separate statement.)

		Yes	No
34a	Does the organization receive any financial aid or assistance from a governmental agency? **34a**		
b	Has the organization's right to such aid ever been revoked or suspended? **34b**		
	If you answered "Yes" to either 34a or b, please explain using an attached statement.		
35	Does the organization certify that it has complied with the applicable requirements of sections 4.01 through 4.05 of Rev. Proc. 75-50, 1975-2 C.B. 587, covering racial nondiscrimination? If "No," attach an explanation **35**		

Schedule A (Form 990) 1999

(Continued)

Schedule A (Form 990) 1999

Page **5**

Part VI-A	**Lobbying Expenditures by Electing Public Charities** (See page 6 of the instructions.)

(To be completed **ONLY** by an eligible organization that filed Form 5768)

Check here   **a**   ☐   if the organization belongs to an affiliated group.

Check here   **b**   ☐   if you checked **"a"** above and "limited control" provisions apply.

Limits on Lobbying Expenditures (The term "expenditures" means amounts paid or incurred.)		**(a)** Affiliated group totals	**(b)** To be completed for ALL electing organizations
36	Total lobbying expenditures to influence public opinion (grassroots lobbying) . . .	36		
37	Total lobbying expenditures to influence a legislative body (direct lobbying)	37		
38	Total lobbying expenditures (add lines 36 and 37)	38		
39	Other exempt purpose expenditures	39		
40	Total exempt purpose expenditures (add lines 38 and 39).	40		

41   Lobbying nontaxable amount. Enter the amount from the following table—

If the amount on line 40 is—   **The lobbying nontaxable amount is—**

Not over $500,000 . . . . 20% of the amount on line 40. . . . .

Over $500,000 but not over $1,000,000 . .$100,000 plus 15% of the excess over $500,000

Over $1,000,000 but not over $1,500,000 . .$175,000 plus 10% of the excess over $1,000,000

Over $1,500,000 but not over $17,000,000 . .$225,000 plus 5% of the excess over $1,500,000

Over $17,000,000 . . . . $1,000,000 . . . .

		41		
42	Grassroots nontaxable amount (enter 25% of line 41)	42		
43	Subtract line 42 from line 36. Enter -0- if line 42 is more than line 36	43		
44	Subtract line 41 from line 38. Enter -0- if line 41 is more than line 38	44		

Caution: *If there is an amount on either line 43 or line 44, you must file Form 4720.*

4-Year Averaging Period Under Section 501(h)

(Some organizations that made a section 501(h) election do not have to complete all of the five columns below. See the instructions for lines 45 through 50 on page 7 of the instructions.)

Lobbying Expenditures During 4-Year Averaging Period

Calendar year (or fiscal year beginning in)	**(a)** 1999	**(b)** 1998	**(c)** 1997	**(d)** 1996	**(e)** Total
45 Lobbying nontaxable amount					
46 Lobbying ceiling amount (150% of line 45(e)).					
47 Total lobbying expenditures					
48 Grassroots nontaxable amount					
49 Grassroots ceiling amount (150% of line 48(e))					
50 Grassroots lobbying expenditures					

Part VI-B	**Lobbying Activity by Nonelecting Public Charities**

(For reporting only by organizations that did not complete Part VI-A) (See page 8 of the instructions.)

During the year, did the organization attempt to influence national, state or local legislation, including any attempt to influence public opinion on a legislative matter or referendum, through the use of:	Yes	No	Amount
a Volunteers.			
b Paid staff or management (Include compensation in expenses reported on lines **c** through **h**.) . . .			
c Media advertisements			
d Mailings to members, legislators, or the public			
e Publications, or published or broadcast statements			
f Grants to other organizations for lobbying purposes			
g Direct contact with legislators, their staffs, government officials, or a legislative body			
h Rallies, demonstrations, seminars, conventions, speeches, lectures, or any other means			
i Total lobbying expenditures (add lines **c** through **h**).			

If "Yes" to any of the above, also attach a statement giving a detailed description of the lobbying activities.

Schedule A (Form 990) 1999

(Continued)

Part VII   **Information Regarding Transfers To and Transactions and Relationships With Noncharitable Exempt Organizations** (See page 8 of the instructions.)

51   Did the reporting organization directly or indirectly engage in any of the following with any other organization described in section 501(c) of the Code (other than section 501(c)(3) organizations) or in section 527, relating to political organizations?

		Yes	No
a Transfers from the reporting organization to a noncharitable exempt organization of:			
(i) Cash	51a(i)		
(ii) Other assets	a(ii)		
b Other transactions:			
(i) Sales or exchanges of assets with a noncharitable exempt organization	b(i)		
(ii) Purchases of assets from a noncharitable exempt organization	b(ii)		
(iii) Rental of facilities, equipment, or other assets	b(iii)		
(iv) Reimbursement arrangements	b(iv)		
(v) Loans or loan guarantees	b(v)		
(vi) Performance of services or membership or fundraising solicitations	b(vi)		
c Sharing of facilities, equipment, mailing lists, other assets, or paid employees	c		

d If the answer to any of the above is "Yes," complete the following schedule. Column (b) should always show the fair market value of the goods, other assets, or services given by the reporting organization. If the organization received less than fair market value in any transaction or sharing arrangement, show in column (d) the value of the goods, other assets, or services received:

(a) Line no.	(b) Amount involved	(c) Name of noncharitable exempt organization	(d) Description of transfers, transactions, and sharing arrangements

52a Is the organization directly or indirectly affiliated with, or related to, one or more tax-exempt organizations described in section 501(c) of the Code (other than section 501(c)(3)) or in section 527?   ☐ **Yes**   ☐ **No**

b If "Yes," complete the following schedule:

(a) Name of organization	(b) Type of organization	(c) Description of relationship

Schedule A (Form 990) 1999

Resource B

Content of Unified Chart of Accounts by Account Number

THIS SECTION PROVIDES a complete listing of the content of each UCOA account in numerical order. Various individual major categories are further defined by showing the content under each category. For example, 1110 (Accounts receivable) includes

Accounts receivable from sales of goods and services

Interest receivable

Receivables—general

Receivables due from affiliates

These definitions are even more important with respect to expense categories (beginning with code 7010) because they provide guidance as to what to include under categories such as salaries, supplies, and occupancy.

Note: UCOA was developed in 1996 by the Quality Reporting Taskforce of the Greater Washington Society of CPAs. UCOA has been vetted by the California Quality Reporting Project and formally endorsed by the California Association of Nonprofits and California Society of CPAs. The National Center for Charitable Statistics at the Urban Institute is providing a permanent home for UCOA.

TABLE B.1

Content of Unified Chart of Accounts: Account Number Index

Unified Chart of Accounts Account Number	Content	Unified Chart of Accounts Account Number	Content
	Assets	1250	Discounts on long-term grants
1010	Cash in bank—operating	1270	Receivables due from trustees and employees
	Bank accounts—non-interest-bearing		Loans and notes due from trustees and employees
1020	Cash in bank—payroll		Salary advances
1040	Petty cash		Travel advances
1070	Savings and temporary cash investments	1280	Other short-term notes and loans receivable
	Certificates of deposit and savings accounts	1290	Allowance for doubtful notes and loans
	Government obligations—up to twelve months	1310	Inventories for sale
	Bank accounts—interest bearing		Donated inventory—sold to clients or public
	Money market funds	1320	Inventories for use
	Savings accounts and certificates of deposit		Donated inventory—given to clients
1110	Accounts receivable		Donated inventory—for use by organization
	Accounts receivable from sales of goods and services	1350	Deferred charges and prepaid expenses
	Interest receivable	1360	Refundable deposits
	Receivables—general accounts receivable	1410	Securities—stocks and bonds
	Receivables due from affiliates		Government obligations—over twelve months
1190	Allowance for doubtful accounts		Investments—marketable securities
	Accounts receivable—allowance for doubtful accounts		Bonds and stocks—marketable
1210	Pledges receivable	1420	Securities—held in perpetuity
	Accounts receivable—pledges receivable		Government obligations—over twelve months
	Pledges receivable from individuals and organizations		Investments—marketable securities
1220	Allowance for doubtful pledges		Bonds and stocks—marketable
	Accounts receivable—allowance for doubtful pledges	1430	Land—held for investment
1230	Discounts on long-term pledges	1440	Buildings—held for investment
1240	Grants receivable		Investments—buildings
	Grants receivable from government, corporations, foundations, federations, and so on	1450	Accumulated depreciation—investment (for 1440)
			Depreciation accumulated for investments
			Investments—accumulated depreciation

(Continued)

Unified Chart of Accounts Account Number	Content
1480	Investments—other
	Bonds and stocks—nonmarketable
1510	Land held for use
1520	Buildings held for use
1530	Accumulated depreciation—buildings for use (for 1520)
1540	Leasehold improvements for use
	Building improvements for use
1550	Accumulated depreciation—improvements for use (for 1540)
1560	Equipment for use
	Furniture and fixtures for use
1570	Accumulated depreciation—equipment for use (for 1560)
1580	Vehicles
1590	Accumulated depreciation—vehicles (for 1580)
1650	Construction in progress
1700	Other long-term assets
1750	Split-interest agreements
1800	Collections of works of art and similar assets
1900	Funds held in trust by others
	Liabilities
2010	Accounts payable
	Payables—general
2110	Accrued expenses—payroll
2120	Accrued expenses—compensated absences
2130	Accrued expenses—payroll taxes
	Accrued expenses—payroll withholding
	Employee withholding (taxes, tax-deferred annuities, etc.)
	Employer payroll taxes payable
2150	Accrued expenses—other
	Interest payable
	Rent payable
2200	Grants and allocations payable
	United Way allocations payable
2310	Control accounts for contracts

Unified Chart of Accounts Account Number	Content
2350	Deferred and unearned revenue
	Dues received for future periods
	Membership dues received for future periods
	Prepaid conference fees
	Revenue designated for future periods
	Subscription fees received for future periods
2400	Refundable advances
2510	Loans from trustees and employees
	Trustee loans
2550	Other short-term notes and loans payable
2600	Annuity obligations
	Liabilities related to split-interest agreements
2710	Bonds payable (such as tax exempt)
2730	Mortgages payable
2750	Obligations under capital leases
2770	Other long-term bonds, notes, and loans payable
2800	Liabilities for government-owned fixed assets
2900	Funds held on behalf of others (custodial)
	Net Assets
3010	Unrestricted available net assets
	Net assets available for general activities
3020	Board designated for special purpose—unrestricted
3030	Board designated endowment—unrestricted
3210	Net assets—land held for use, not investment
	Net assets—buildings held for use, not investment
	Net assets—leasehold improvements
	Net assets—furniture and equipment
3300	Net assets—temporarily restricted for programs

(Continued)

Unified Chart of Accounts Account Number	Content
3400	Net assets—temporarily restricted for fixed asset acquisitions
3500	Net assets—temporarily time-restricted
3910	Permanently restricted net assets Endowment—donor designated Net assets—endowment

Revenue

4010	Contributions from individuals and small businesses Contributions through commercial co-ventures Contributions through direct mail Contributions through door-to-door campaigns Contributions through personal solicitation Contributions through telephone campaigns Contributions through telethons Donations Donor-restricted gifts from individuals Gifts Major gifts from individuals—unrestricted Pledges Unrestricted contributions from individuals
4050	Contributions through special events Special fundraising events (gift portion)
4070	Bequests and legacies Deferred giving Planned gifts and gift agreements
4080	Uncollectible pledges—estimated
4090	Discounts on long-term pledges
4110	Contributed services and use of facilities—GAAP Donated services and use of facilities—GAAP
4120	Contributed services and use of facilities—non-GAAP

Unified Chart of Accounts Account Number	Content
	Donated services and use of facilities—non-GAAP
4130	Gifts in kind—noncash, tangible In-kind contributions
4140	Donated works of art and similar assets Contributed works of art and similar assets
4210	Corporate and other business grants Grants from corporations and other businesses Private foundations—corporate "owned"
4230	Foundation and trust grants
4250	Grants from other nonprofit organizations Grants from churches, civic groups
4270	Discounts on long-term pledges
4310	Contributions from split-interest arrangements
4350	Change in value of split-interest agreements
4410	Allocations from federated fundraising groups Grants from federated fundraising groups Indirect support from federations United Way allocations
4420	Contributions from affiliated organizations Indirect support from affiliated organizations
4430	Contributions from other fundraising agencies Indirect support from other fundraising agencies
4510	Contributions from government agencies Government contributions (including grants) Government grants equivalent to contributions
5010	Contracts and fees from government agencies

(Continued)

Unified Chart of Accounts Account Number	Content	Unified Chart of Accounts Account Number	Content
	Government fees and contracts for services	6310	Sales (gross) to public—non-program-related
5110	Sales of program-related publications	6320	Cost of non-program-related goods sold
5150	Sales of program-related inventory—other	6510	Revenue from advertising in publications
	Cafeteria for clients, visitors, and staff	6520	Revenue from affiliations with other entities
	Concessions at program-related activities	6810	Other revenue
	Gift shop for clients, visitors, and staff		List rental
	Program-related sales		*Net Assets Released from Restriction*
	Bookstore for clients, visitors, and staff	6910	Satisfaction of program restrictions
5180	Estimated uncollectible revenue (for 5110–5180)	6920	Satisfaction of fixed asset acquisition restrictions
5210	Fees for program services	6930	Expirations of time restrictions
5280	Estimated uncollectible revenue (for 5210)		*Expenses*
5310	Dues for individual memberships	7010	Program-related contracts to other entities
	Membership dues—individuals	7020	Grants to other organizations
5320	Dues and assessments from organizations		Grants to research institutions
	Membership dues—organizations		In-kind grants to organizations
5410	Interest on savings and temporary cash investments	7030	Allocations to affiliated organizations
			Allocations by fundraising federations
5420	Dividends and interest from securities		Grants to affiliated organizations
5510	Rents from investment property—gross		In-kind grants to affiliates
5520	Rental expenses for investment property (for 5570)	7040	Awards and grants to individuals
			Allowance for travel under grant
5610	Investment income—other		Allowance for equipment under grant
5810	Unrealized gain (loss) in value of investments		Fellowships
			Graduate fellowships
5910	Gain (loss) on sales of securities—gross		In-kind grants to individuals
5920	Cost and expense for sales of securities		Scholarships and tuition payments
6110	Gain (loss) on sales of other assets		Trainee scholarships
6120	Cost and expense for sales of other assets	7050	Specific assistance to individuals
			Beneficiaries, specific assistance to
6180	Unrealized gain (loss) on value of other assets		Children's board for clients
			Clients, specific assistance to
6210	Special events—gross revenue excluding gifts		Clothing for clients
	Special events—total value to payers		Dental fees of clients

(Continued)

Unified Chart of Accounts Account Number	Content
	Food service for clients
	Homemaker service for clients
	Assistance by others at expense of organization
	Insurance coverage provided clients
	Medical fees of clients
	Medicines for client
	Prosthetic appliances for clients
	Recreation service for clients
	Services by others at expense of organization
	Shelter for clients
	Transportation service for clients
	Wage supplements for clients
7210	Salaries of officers, directors, and trustees
	Chief executive officer's salary
	Directors' salaries, fees
	Executive director's salary
	Executive salaries
	Fees paid to directors and trustees
	Key employee salaries
	Officers' salaries, fees
	Trustees' salaries, fees
7220	Salaries and wages to other employees
	Client salaries and wages
	Maintenance employees' salaries and wages
	Professional staff salaries
	Salaries and wages of clerical and support staff
	Clerical and support staff salaries
	Salaries of temporary help—on payroll
	Technician salaries
7310	Pension plan contributions
	Pension for officers, directors, and trustees
	Retirement plan contributions
7320	Employee benefits—other than pension

Unified Chart of Accounts Account Number	Content
	Benefits—accident insurance cost reimbursement
	Benefits—employment termination expenses
	Benefits—health insurance premiums
	Benefits—health insurance premium reimbursement
	Benefits—life insurance premiums
	Benefits—outplacement expenses
	Benefits—payments to annuitants
	Benefits—payments to pensioned employees
	Benefits for clients on payroll
	Benefits for employees—other than pension
	Benefits for officers, directors, and trustees
	Benefits—accident insurance premiums
	Supplemental payments to pensioned employees
	Termination of employee expenses
7410	Payroll taxes, etc.
	Client payroll taxes and insurance
	Disability insurance premiums
	Federal and state payroll tax and insurance
	FICA. payments (employer's share)
	Insurance—payroll related
	Local payroll tax and insurance
	Payroll disability insurance premiums
	Payroll federal and state taxes and insurance
	Payroll FICA payments (employer's share)
	Payroll insurance related expense
	Payroll taxes and insurance for clients on payroll
	Payroll unemployment insurance and taxes

(Continued)

Unified Chart of Accounts Account Number	Content	Unified Chart of Accounts Account Number	Content
	Payroll worker's compensation insurance		Drugs and medicines (clinic use only)
	State payroll tax and insurance		Donated professional services—GAAP
7510	Professional fees—fundraising	7590	Contributed professional services—non-GAAP
	Fees—fundraising counsel, consultant		Film purchases and processing
	Fees—paid solicitor		First aid supplies for employees
	Development fees—fundraising-related		Food and beverage—non-program-related
7520	Accounting fees		Food and beverage—program-related
	Audit and accounting fees		Food and beverage for employees and visitors
	Bank service charges		Food and beverage services to clients
	Bookkeeping services—outside		Housekeeping, laundry, and linen supplies
	Payroll services—outside		Office supplies
	Professional fees—audit, accounting, etc.		Paper, ink, film, and copying materials
7530	Attorney fees		Prosthetic appliances (clinic use only)
	Legal fees		Recreational supplies
	Professional fees—legal		Stationery, typing, accounting, and similar supplies
7540	Other professional fees		Award plaques, noncash prizes to clients
	Brokerage, commission and collection fees		Supplies—computer, typing, accounting, etc.
	Computer programming fees		Typewriter supplies
	Education fees		Vocational supplies
	Employee recruitment fees	7720	Contributed materials and supplies
	Investment counseling fees		Donated materials and supplies used
	Medical and dental fees	7810	Telephone expense
	Psychological fees		Mailgram
	Public relations fees		Telegram, telex
	Rehabilitation fees		Telegraph expense (mailgram, etc.)
7550	Contract temporary help		Telephone equipment maintenance
	Clerical—contract temporary help		Fax
	Professional—contract temporary help	7910	Postage and shipping (delivery)
7580	Contributed professional services—GAAP		Delivery and messenger service
	Donated professional services—non-GAAP		Federal Express, UPS, other overnight
7710	Supplies		Freight, trucking
	Bookkeeping supplies		Gas and oil—delivery-related
	Classroom supplies		
	Copying and duplicating materials and supplies		
	Craft supplies		

(Continued)

Unified Chart of Accounts Account Number	Content
	Leasing costs—shipping vehicles (not interest)
	Licenses and permits—shipping vehicles
	Maintenance of delivery vehicles
	Overnight (Federal Express, UPS, etc.)
	Parcel post and postage
	Permits and licenses—shipping vehicles
	Postal permit fees
	Rental of trucks for delivery
	Repairs of delivery vehicles
	Shipping—insurance—company vehicles
	Shipping—leasing costs—vehicles (not interest)
	Shipping—licenses and permits for vehicles
	Shipping—tires—company vehicles
	Shipping—gas and oil
	Shipping
	Shipping vehicle maintenance
	Tires—company shipping vehicles
	Trucking, freight
	UPS, Federal Express, other overnight
7920	Mailing services
	Fees—outside mailing service
8010	Rent
	Occupancy
	Office rent
	Housekeeping and janitorial services
	Janitorial and similar service fees
	Occupancy-related licenses and permits
	Building and grounds maintenance and supplies
	Parking fees and building rent
8020	Utilities
	Electricity
	Gas
	Heating oil
	Building rent and parking fees

Unified Chart of Accounts Account Number	Content
	Sewer and water
8030	Real estate taxes
8040	Personal property taxes
	Property taxes
8050	Interest on mortgages
8080	Contributed use of facilities and utilities—GAAP
	Donated use of facilities and utilities—GAAP
	Equipment—donated use of
8090	Donated use of facilities and utilities—non-GAAP
8110	Equipment rental, maintenance, and supplies
	Copy equipment rental and maintenance
	Duplicating equipment rental and maintenance
	Equipment maintenance supplies
	Computers—rental and maintenance
	Postage meters—rental and maintenance
	Rental—copiers, computers, postage meters
	Supplies—equipment maintenance
	Typewriter rental and maintenance
8210	Printing and duplicating
	Copying and duplicating—outside services
	Films—produced by others
	Newsletters, leaflets—purchased
	Photography—purchased
	Artwork—purchased
	Recordings—produced by others
8220	Publications published by others
	Periodicals
	Books and publications—purchased
	Subscriptions to other publications
	Photocopying—purchased
	Subscriptions to periodicals

(Continued)

Unified Chart of Accounts Account Number	Content
	Publications published by organization
8310	Travel
	Airfare, train fare, bus fare
	Auto allowance for employees and volunteers
	Bus, subway, and taxicab fares
	Car rental for travel
	Gas and oil—travel related
	Hotel, meals, and incidental expenses
	Insurance—company travel vehicles
	Leasing costs—travel vehicles (not interest)
	Licenses and permits—travel vehicles
	Local bus, subway, and taxicab fares— travel
	Local and out-of-town travel
	Maintenance—company travel vehicles
	Meetings, etc.—employee and volunteer travel
	Per diem expenses
	Repairs—company travel vehicles
	Tires—company travel vehicles
	Transportation—travel-related
	Travel—auto allowance for employees
	Travel—for volunteers on business
	Travel—hotel, meals, and incidental expenses
	Travel for meetings and conferences
8510	Conventions, meetings, conferences
	Board meetings, luncheons, dinners
	Food and beverage costs for meetings, etc.
	Honoraria and expenses for speakers
	Meeting space and equipment rental
	Meeting supplies
	Meetings—notices, badges
	Meetings—related printing costs
	Equipment rental—meetings, conferences
	Meetings—speakers' honoraria and expenses

Unified Chart of Accounts Account Number	Content
	Meetings, luncheons, dinners with board
	Meetings, luncheons, dinners with volunteers
	Meetings, etc.—registration fees
	Notices, badges for meetings
8610	Interest—general
	Automotive—interest on loans and leases
	Equipment—loan and lease interest
	Interest on equipment loans and leases
	Interest on other long-term debt
	Interest on truck loans and leases
	Shipping—interest on truck loans and leases
	Short-term debt interest
	Travel—interest on auto loans and leases
8650	Depreciaton—allowable
	Amortization—depreciable assets
	Amortization—leasehold improvement
	Automotive equipment depreciation
	Depreciation—buildings
	Depreciation—equipment
	Depreciation, amortization, depletion
8660	Depreciation—not allowable
8710	Insurance
	Automobile insurance
	Business interruption insurance
	General liability insurance
	Insurance—excluding employee-related
	Insurance—malpractice
	Insurance—meeting cancellation
	Insurance—professional liability
	Insurance—property
	Directors' and officers' liability insurance
	Fidelity bonds
	Insurance on shipping and delivery vehicles
	Insurance on travel vehicles (automobiles)

(Continued)

Unified Chart of Accounts Account Number	Content
	Motor vehicle insurance
8810	Membership dues
	Dues for employee and organization memberships
8820	Staff development
	Continuing education for employees
	Degree programs for employees
	Employee development, education, etc.
9010	List rental
	Rental expense for outside lists
9020	Outside computer services
	Electronic data processing service bureau fees
	Computer service bureau fees
9100	Bad debt expense
	Uncollected accounts receivable (bad debt)
9110	Sales taxes
9120	Taxes on unrelated business income (UBIT)

Unified Chart of Accounts Account Number	Content
9150	Other taxes
9210	Fines, penalties, and judgments
9230	Incorporation and other organizational expenses
9240	Advertising expenses of organization
9290	Contingency provisions
9300	Expenses—other
	Credit card fees
	License fees—other
	Moving expenses
	Permit fees—other
	Safety deposit box fees
	State and local charity registration fees
9810	Capital purchases—land
9820	Capital purchases—buildings
	Leasehold improvements
9830	Capital purchases—equipment
9840	Capital purchases—vehicles
9910	Payments to affiliates

Cross-Referencing Your Not-for-Profit Organization's Chart of Accounts to the Unified Chart of Accounts: Cross-Reference Worksheet and Keyword Index

IT IS NOT NECESSARY for your not-for-profit organization to adopt the UCOA account coding system in place of its existing system. When a not-for-profit organization cross-references its chart of accounts to the UCOA, it is in effect cross-referencing its chart of accounts to all the reporting requirements that are aligned with the UCOA. In this way the cross-referencing allows you to use the UCOA as an accounting and reporting tool without having to convert to the UCOA coding system.

In order to do the cross-referencing, you will need the following items:

- A copy of your organization's chart of accounts

- The UCOA cross-reference worksheet (Worksheet C.1)

- The alphabetical UCOA keyword index (Table C.1)

To cross-reference your chart of accounts to the UCOA, follow these steps:

1. Complete the UCOA cross-reference worksheet (Worksheet C.1). At the same time, you can code the copy of your present chart of accounts with corresponding UCOA codes. Refer to the alphabetical UCOA keyword index (Table C.1) as needed to ensure consistency in the content of accounts used.

2. Enter the numbers for your accounts that are the same as or similar to the corresponding UCOA account in the space provided in Worksheet C.1. Leave blank any entries in the worksheet that are not relevant to the financial activities of your organization.

3. When data for two or more UCOA accounts are combined in one of your organization's accounts, note how your organization's account can be subdivided to accommodate the UCOA requirements. There is no limit to the number of your accounts that can be included in one UCOA account. However, the content of your accounts must be consistent with the content of the UCOA account.

4. Once the UCOA cross-reference worksheet is completed and your chart of accounts is coded with UCOA codes, you are ready to revise—*not replace*—your chart of accounts, accounting software, and bookkeeping procedures accordingly.

WORKSHEET C.1

Worksheet for Cross-Referencing Your Organization's Chart of Accounts to the Unified Chart of Accounts

Account Number and Name	Cross-Reference to Your Organization's Chart of Accounts and Comments

Balance Sheet or Statement of Financial Position Accounts (1000–3999)

Asset Accounts (1000–1999):

1010	Cash in bank—operating	_____
1020	Cash in bank—payroll	_____
1040	Petty cash	_____
1070	Savings and temporary cash investments	_____
1110	Accounts receivable	_____
1190	Allowance for doubtful accounts	_____
1210	Pledges receivable	_____
1220	Allowance for doubtful pledges	_____
1230	Discounts on long-term pledges	_____
1240	Grants receivable	_____
1250	Discounts on long-term grants	_____
1270	Receivables due from trustees and employees	_____
1280	Other short-term notes and loans receivable	_____
1290	Allowance for doubtful notes and loans	_____
1310	Inventories for sale	_____
1320	Inventories for use	_____
1350	Prepaid expenses and deferred charges	_____
1360	Refundable deposits	_____
1410	Investments—marketable securities	_____
1420	Marketable securities held in perpetuity	_____
1430	Land held for investment	_____
1440	Buildings held for investment	_____
1450	Accumulated depreciation for 1440	_____
1510	Land—held for use, not investment	_____
1520	Buildings—held for use, not investment	_____
1530	Accumulated depreciation for 1520	_____
1540	Building and leasehold improvements	_____
1550	Accumulated depreciation for 1540	_____
1560	Furniture, fixtures, and equipment	_____
1570	Accumulated amortization for 1560	_____
1580	Vehicles	_____
1650	Construction in progress	_____
1700	Other long-term assets	_____
1800	Split-interest agreement	_____
1850	Collections of works of art and similar assets	_____
1900	Funds held in trust by others	_____

(Continued)

Account Number and Name	Cross-Reference to Your Organization's Chart of Accounts and Comments

Liability and Net Asset Accounts (2000–3999)

2010   Accounts payable

2110   Accrued expenses—payroll

2120   Accrued expenses—compensated absences

2130   Accrued expenses—payroll taxes

2150   Accrued expenses—other

2200   Grants and allocations payable

2310   Control accounts for contracts

2350   Other unearned and deferred revenue

2400   Refundable advances

2510   Loans from trustees and employees

2550   Other short-term notes and loans payable

2600   Liabilities related to split-interest agreements

2710   Bonds payable

2730   Mortgages payable

2750   Obligations under capital leases

2770   Other long-term notes and loans payable

2800   Liabilities for government-owned fixed assets

2900   Funds held on behalf of others—custodial

Unrestricted net assets (3000–3299):

3010   Available for general activities

3020   Board-designated for special purposes

3030   Board-designated endowment

3210   Land—held for use, not investment—net

3220   Buildings—held for use, not investment—net

3230   Building and leasehold improvements—net

3240   Furniture and equipment—net

Temporarily restricted net assets (3300–3899):

3300   Control accounts for grants restricted for program

3400   Control accounts for grants restricted for fixed asset acquisition

3500   Control accounts for time-restricted grants

Permanently restricted net assets (3900–3999):

3910   Endowment

(Continued)

Account Number and Name	Cross-Reference to Your Organization's Chart of Accounts and Comments
Revenues, Gains, and Other Support (4000–6999)	
Contributions Received Directly (Grants, Public Support)	
4010-XXX From individuals and small businesses	_____
4050-XXX Special fundraising events (gift portion)	_____
4070-XXX Legacies and bequests	_____
4080-XXX Estimated uncollectible pledges (for 4000–4070)	_____
4090-XXX Discount on long-term pledges (for 4000–4070)	_____
4110-XXX Donated services or use of facilities—GAAP	_____
4120-XXX Donated services or use of facilities—non-GAAP	_____
4130-XXX Other gifts in kind	_____
4140-XXX Donated works of art and similar assets	_____
4210-XXX Corporate and other business grants	_____
4230-XXX Foundation and trust grants	_____
4250-XXX Grants from other nonprofit organizations	_____
4270-XXX Discount on long-term grants (for 4210–4250)	_____
4310-XXX Contributions from split-interest agreements	_____
4350-XXX Change in value of split-interest agreements	_____
Contributions Received Indirectly (Allocations)	
4410-XXX Allocated by federal fundraising organization	_____
4420-XXX From affiliated organizations	_____
4430-XXX From other fundraising agencies	_____
Government Grants (Equivalent to Contributions)	
4510-XXX Grants from government agencies	_____
4520-XXX Government grants—federal	_____
4530-XXX Government grants—state	_____
4540-XXX Government grants—other	_____
Revenue from Fees and Dues	
5010-XXX Contracts or fees from government agencies	_____
5020-XXX Government contracts—federal	_____
5030-XXX Government contracts—state	_____
5040-XXX Government contracts—other	_____
5110-XXX Sales of program-related publications	_____
5150-XXX Other sales to public, program-related inventory	_____

(Continued)

Account Number and Name	Cross-Reference to Your Organization's Chart of Accounts and Comments
5180-XXX Estimated uncollectible revenue (for 5110–5150)	_____
5210-XXX Other program service sales and fees	_____
5280-XXX Estimated uncollectible revenue (for 5210)	_____
5310-XXX Membership and dues—individuals	_____
5320-XXX Assessments and dues—member units	_____

Revenue from Investments

5410-XXX Interest from savings and temporary cash investments	_____
5420-XXX Dividends and interest from securities	_____
5510-XXX Gross rents	_____
5520-XXX Related rental expense (deduct from 5510)	_____
5610-XXX Other investment income	_____
5810-XXX Unrealized gain (loss) on value of investments	_____
5910-XXX Gross amount from sale of securities	_____
5920-XXX Cost and sales expense (deduct from 5910)	_____

Revenue from Other Sources

6110-XXX Gross amount from sale of other assets	_____
6120-XXX Other cost and sales expense (deduct from 6110)	_____
6180-XXX Unrealized gain (loss) on value of other assets	_____
6210-XXX Special events—gross revenue excluding gifts	_____
6310-XXX Gross sales to public— non-program-related	_____
6320-XXX Cost of goods sold (deduct from 6310)	_____
6510-XXX Revenue from advertising in publications	_____
6520-XXX Revenue from affiliations with other entities	_____
6810-XXX Other revenue	_____

Net Assets Released from Restriction

6910-XXX Satisfaction of program restrictions	_____
6920-XXX Satisfaction of fixed asset acquisition restrictions	_____
6930-XXX Expirations of time restrictions	_____

(Continued)

Account Number and Name	Cross-Reference to Your Organization's Chart of Accounts and Comments

Object Expense Categories (7000–9999)

Grants, Contracts, and Direct Assistance

7010-XXX	Program-related contracts to other entities	
7020-XXX	Grants to other organizations	
7030-XXX	Allocations to affiliated organizations	
7040-XXX	Awards and grants to individuals	
7050-XXX	Specific assistance to individuals	

Salaries and Related Expenses

7210-XXX	Salaries of officers, directors, etc.	
7220-XXX	Other salaries and wages	
7310-XXX	Pension plan contributions	
7320-XXX	Other employee benefits	
7410-XXX	Payroll taxes, etc.	

Other Expenses

7510-XXX	Professional fundraising fees	
7520-XXX	Accounting fees	
7530-XXX	Legal fees	
7540-XXX	Other professional fees	
7550-XXX	Contract temporary help	
7580-XXX	Donated professional services—GAAP	
7590-XXX	Donated professional services—non-GAAP	
7710-XXX	Supplies	
7720-XXX	Donated materials and supplies	
7810-XXX	Telephone	
7910-XXX	Postage and shipping	
7920-XXX	Mailing services	
8010-XXX	Rent	
8020-XXX	Utilities	
8030-XXX	Real estate taxes	
8040-XXX	Personal property taxes	
8050-XXX	Interest on mortgages	
8080-XXX	Donated use of facilities and utilities—GAAP	
8090-XXX	Donated use of facilities and utilities—non-GAAP	
8110-XXX	Equipment rental and maintenance	
8210-XXX	Printing and duplicating	
8220-XXX	Publications published by others	
8230-XXX	Publications published by organization	
8310-XXX	Travel	
8510-XXX	Conferences, conventions, and meetings	
8610-XXX	Interest—general	

(Continued)

Account Number and Name	Cross-Reference to Your Organization's Chart of Accounts and Comments
8650-XXX Depreciation—allowable	
8660-XXX Depreciation—not allowable	
8710-XXX Insurance—excluding employee-related	
8810-XXX Membership dues	
8820-XXX Staff development	
9010-XXX List rental	
9020-XXX Outside computer services	
9100-XXX Bad debt expense	
9110-XXX Sales taxes	
9120-XXX Unrelated business income taxes (UBIT)	
9150-XXX Other taxes	
9210-XXX Fines, penalties, and judgments—organization	
9230-XXX Incorporation and other organizational expenses	
9240-XXX Advertising	
9290-XXX Contingency provisions	
9300-XXX Other expenses	
9810-XXX Capital purchases—land	
9820-XXX Capital purchases—building	
9830-XXX Capital purchases—equipment	
9840-XXX Capital purchases—vehicles	
9910-XXX Payments to affiliates	

TABLE C.1

Unified Chart of Accounts Keyword Index

Keyword	Unified Chart of Accounts Account Number
Assets	
Accounts receivable—allowance for doubtful accounts	1190
Accounts receivable—allowance for doubtful pledges	1220
Accounts receivable—pledges receivable	1210
Accounts receivable due from affiliates	1110
Accounts receivable due from trustees and employees	1270
Accounts receivable from sales of goods and services	1110
Accounts receivable	1110
Accumulated depreciation—buildings for use	1530
Accumulated depreciation—equipment for use	1570
Accumulated depreciation—leasehold improvements for use	1550
Accumulated depreciation—investment	1450
Allowance for doubtful accounts	1190
Allowance for doubtful notes and loans	1290
Allowance for doubtful pledges	1220
Assets—other long-term	1700
Assets—total	Sum
Bank accounts—interest-bearing	1070
Bank accounts—non-interest-bearing	1010
Bank accounts—payroll	1020
Bonds and stocks—marketable	1410
Bonds and stocks—nonmarketable	1480
Buildings—held for investment	1440
Buildings—held for use, not investment	1520
Cash	1010
Certificates of deposit and savings accounts	1070
Collections of works of art and similar assets	1800
Construction in progress	1650

Keyword	Unified Chart of Accounts Account Number
Deferred charges and prepaid expenses	1350
Deposits—rent, utilities	1360
Depreciation—buildings for use	1530
Depreciation—equipment for use	1570
Depreciation—leasehold improvements for use	1550
Depreciation—vehicles for use	1590
Depreciation accumulated for investments	1450
Discounts on long-term grants	1230
Discounts on long-term grants	1250
Donated inventory—for use by organization	1320
Donated inventory—given to clients	1320
Donated inventory—sold to clients or public	1310
Donated works of art and similar assets	1800
Doubtful accounts receivable allowance	1190
Doubtful notes and loans allowance	1290
Doubtful pledge allowance	1220
Due to or from other funds	1980
Equipment for use, not investment	1560
Funds held in trust by others	1900
Government obligations—over twelve months	1410
Government obligations—up to twelve months	1070
Grants receivable	1240
Grants receivable from government, corporations, foundations, federations, etc.	1240
Interest-bearing bank accounts	1070
Interest receivable	1110
Inventories for sale	1310
Inventories for use	1320
Investments—accumulated depreciation	1450
Investments—marketable securities	1410
Investments—other	1480
Land—held for investment	1430

(Continued)

Keyword	Unified Chart of Accounts Account Number
Land held for use, not investment	1510
Leasehold improvements—for use, not investment	1540
Loans and notes due from trustees and employees	1270
Loans and notes receivable—other	1280
Marketable securities—held in perpetuity	1420
Marketable securities held for operatives	1410
Money market funds	1070
Non-interest-bearing bank accounts	1010
Notes and loans receivable—other	1280
Other notes and loans receivable	1280
Payroll bank account	1020
Petty cash	1040
Pledges receivable from individuals and organizations	1210
Pledges receivable	1210
Prepaid expenses and deferred charges	1350
Receivables—general accounts receivable	1110
Receivables—grants	1240
Receivables—other notes and loans	1280
Receivables—pledges	1210
Receivables due from affiliates	1110
Receivables due from trustees and employees	1270
Salary advances	1270
Savings accounts and certificates of deposit	1070
Savings and temporary cash investments	1070
Securities—stocks and bonds	1410
Split-interest agreements	1750
Stocks and bonds—marketable	1410
Stocks and bonds—nonmarketable	1480
Total assets	Sum
Travel advances	1270
Vehicles	1580
Works of art and similar assets	1800

Keyword	Unified Chart of Accounts Account Number
Liabilities	
Accounts payable	2010
Accrued expenses—other	2150
Accrued expenses—payroll	2110
Accrued expenses—payroll taxes	2130
Accrued expenses—payroll withholding	2130
Accrued payroll—compensated absences	2120
Allocations and grants payable	2200
Annuity obligations	2600
Bond liabilities—tax exempt	2710
Capital lease obligations	2750
Compensated absences—accrued payroll	2120
Control accounts for contracts	2310
Deferred and unearned revenue	2350
Dues received for future periods	2350
Employee loans	2510
Employee withholding (taxes, tax-deferred annuities, etc.)	2130
Employer payroll taxes payable	2130
Expenses—accrued payroll	2110
Expenses—other accrued	2150
Funds held on behalf of others (custodial)	2900
Government-owned fixed assets—liabilities	2800
Grants and allocations payable	2200
Interest payable	2150
Liabilities—total	Sum
Liabilities for government-owned fixed assets	2800
Liabilities related to split-interest agreements	2600
Loans and notes payable—long-term	2770
Loans and notes payable—short-term	2550
Loans from trustees and employees	2510
Long-term notes and loans payable	2770
Membership dues received for future periods	2350
Mortgages payable	2730
Notes payable—long-term	2770

(Continued)

Keyword	Unified Chart of Accounts Account Number
Notes payable—short-term	2550
Obligations under capital leases	2750
Payables—accounts payable general	2010
Payroll taxes payable—employer	2130
Prepaid conference fees	2350
Rent payable	2150
Revenue—deferred and unearned	2350
Revenue designated for future periods	2350
Short-term notes and loans payable	2550
Split-interest agreements—related liabilities	2600
Subscription fees received for future periods	2350
Tax exempt bond liabilities	2710
Total liabilities	Sum
Trustee loans	2510
Unearned and deferred revenue	2350
United Way allocations payable	2200
Withholding—employee (taxes, tax-deferred annuities, etc.)	2130

Keyword	Unified Chart of Accounts Account Number
Net Assets	
Available unrestricted net assets	3010
Board designated endowment—unrestricted	3030
Board designated for special purpose—unrestricted	3020
Buildings	3210
Control accounts—fixes asset acquisition restrictions	3400
Control accounts for program-restricted grants	3300
Control accounts for time-restricted grants	3500
Endowment—donor-designated	3910
Fund balances—see net assets	Sum
Furniture and equipment	3210
Land	3210
Leasehold improvements—net assets	3210
Net assets—available, unrestricted	3010
Net assets—buildings	3210
Net assets—endowment	3910
Net assets—furniture and equipment	3210
Net assets—land	3210
Net assets—leasehold improvements	3210
Net assets—temporarily restricted—program	3300
Net assets—temporarily restricted—fixed asset acquisition	3400
Net assets—temporarily restricted—time	3500
Net assets—total	Sum
Net assets—unrestricted	3010
Permanently restricted net assets—see class	3910
Temporarily restricted net assets for fixed asset acquisition	3400
Temporarily restricted net assets for program	3300
Temporarily restricted net assets—time	3500
Total net assets	Sum
Unrestricted net assets—available	3010

(Continued)

Keyword	Unified Chart of Accounts Account Number	Keyword	Unified Chart of Accounts Account Number
Revenue		Cost and expense for sales of other assets	6120
Accretion of discount on long-term pledges	4010	Cost and expense for sales of securities	5920
Advertising in program-related publications	6510	Cost of non-program-related goods sold	6320
Affiliated organization contributions	4420	Deferred giving	4070
Allocations from federated fundraising groups	4410	Direct-mail contributions	4010
Assessments and dues from organizations	5320	Discounts on long-term grants	4270
Bequests and legacies	4070	Discounts on long-term pledges	4090
Bookstore for clients, visitors, and staff	5110	Dividends and interest from securities	5420
Business and corporate grants	4210	Donated services and use of facilities—GAAP	4110
Cafeteria for clients, visitors, and staff	5210	Donated services and use of facilities—non-GAAP	4120
Change in value of split-interest agreements	4350	Donated works of art and similar assets	4140
Commercial co-venture contributions	4010	Donations—see contributions	4010
Concessions at program-related activities	5210	Donor restricted gifts from individuals	4010
Contributed services and use of facilities—GAAP	4110	Door-to-door campaign contributions	4010
Contributed services and use of facilities—non-GAAP	4120	Dues and assessments from organizations	5320
Contributed works of art and similar assets	4140	Dues for individual memberships	5310
Contributions from affiliated organizations	4420	Estimated uncollectible revenue (for 5110)	5180
Contributions from government agencies	4510	Estimated uncollectible revenue (for 5210)	5280
Contributions from individuals .	4010	Expenses for sales of other assets	6120
Contributions from other fundraising agencies	4430	Expenses for sales of securities	5920
Contributions from split-interest agreements	4310	Federal government contracts	5020
Contributions through commercial co-ventures	4010	Federal government grants	4520
Contributions through direct mail	4010	Federated fundraising group allocations	4410
Contributions through door-to-door campaigns	4010	Fees for program services	5210
Contributions through personal solicitation	4010	Fees from government agencies	5010
Contributions through special events	4050	Foundation and trust grants	4230
Contributions through telephone campaigns	4010	Gain (loss) on sales of other assets	6110
Contributions through telethons	4010	Gain (loss) on sales of securities	5910
Corporate and other business grants	4210	Gifts—see contributions	4010
		Gifts in kind—noncash, tangible	4130
		Gift shop for clients, visitors, and staff	5210
		Government contracts—federal	5020
		Government contracts—other	5040
		Government contracts—state	5030
		Government contributions (including grants)	4510
		Government fees and contracts for services	5010

(Continued)

Keyword	Unified Chart of Accounts Account Number	Keyword	Unified Chart of Accounts Account Number
Government grants—federal	4520	Rents from investment property—gross	5510
Government grants—other	4540	Restricted contributions from individuals	4010
Government grants—state	4530	Revenue—other	6810
Government grants equivalent to contributions	4510	Revenue—total	Sum
Grants from churches and civic groups	4250	Revenue from affiliations with other entities	6520
Grants from corporations and other businesses	4210	Sales (gross) to public—non-program-related	6310
Grants from federated fundraising groups	4410	Sales of program-related inventory	5210
Grants from foundation and trusts	4230	Sales of program-related publications	5110
Grants from other nonprofit organizations	4250	Special event contributions	4050
Grants, government equivalent to contributions	4510	Special events—gross revenue excluding gifts	6210
Indirect support from affiliated organization	4420	Special events—total value to payers	6210
Indirect support from federations	4410	Split-interest agreements—change in value	4350
Indirect support from other fundraising agency	4430	Split-interest agreements—contributions	4310
		State government contracts	5030
In-kind contributions	4130	State government grants	4530
Interest and dividends from securities	5420	Sublet income	5510
Interest on savings and temporary cash investments	5410	Telephone campaign contributions	4010
		Telethon campaign contributions	4010
Investment income—other	5610	Total revenue	Sum
Legacies and bequests	4070	Trust and foundation grants	4230
List rental	6810	Uncollectible pledges—estimated	4080
Major gifts from individuals—unrestricted	4010	Uncollectible revenue (for 5110)—estimated	5180
Membership dues—individuals	5310		
Membership dues—organizations	5320	Uncollectible revenue (for 5210)—estimated	5210
Other gifts in kind	4130	United Way allocations	4410
Other government contracts	5040	Unrealized gain (loss) in value of investments	5810
Other government grants	4540		
Other revenue	6810	Unrealized gain (loss) on value of other assets	6180
Planned gifts and gift agreements	4070		
Pledges—see contributions	4010	Unrestricted contributions from individuals	4010
Private foundations—corporate "owned"	4210		
Program-related sales—publications	5110	Works of art and similar assets	4140
Program-related sales	5210		
Program service fees	5210		
Rental expenses for investment property (for 5570)	5520		

(Continued)

Keyword	Unified Chart of Accounts Account Number	Keyword	Unified Chart of Accounts Account Number
Expenses		Benefits—payments to pensioned employees	7320
Accident insurance cost reimbursement	7320	Benefits for clients on payroll	7320
Accident insurance premiums for employees	7320	Benefits for employees—other than pension	7320
Accounting fees	7520	Benefits for officers, directors, and trustees	7320
Advertising expenses of organization	9250	Board meetings, luncheons, dinners	8510
Airfare, train fare, bus fare	8310	Bookkeeping services—outside	7520
Allocations by fundraising federations	7030	Bookkeeping supplies	7710
Allocations to affiliated organizations	7030	Books and publications—purchased	8220
Allowance for equipment under grant	7040	Brokerage, commission, and collection fees	7540
Allowance for travel under grant	7040	Building and grounds maintenance and supplies	8010
Amortization—depreciable assets	8650		
Amortization—leasehold improvement	8650	Building purchases	9820
Artwork—purchased	8210	Building rent and parking fees	8010
Assistance by others at expense of organization	7050	Bus, subway, and taxicab fares	8310
		Business interruption insurance	8710
Attorney fees	7530	Capital purchases—buildings	9820
Audit and accounting fees	7520	Capital purchases—equipment	9830
Auto allowance for employees and volunteers	8310	Capital purchases—land	9810
		Car rental for travel	8310
Automobile insurance	8710	Chief executive officer's salary	7210
Automotive—interest on loans and leases	8610	Children's board for clients	7050
Automotive equipment depreciation	8650	Classroom supplies	7710
Award plaques, noncash prizes to clients	7710	Clerical—contract temporary help	7550
Awards and grants to individuals	7040	Clerical and support staff salaries	7220
Bad debt expense	9100	Client payroll taxes and insurance	7410
Bank service charges	7520	Client salaries and wages	7220
Beneficiaries, specific assistance to	7050	Clients, specific assistance to	7050
Benefits—accident insurance cost reimbursement	7320	Clothing for clients	7050
		Computer programming fees	7540
Benefits—accident insurance premiums	7320	Computer service bureau fees	9020
Benefits—employment termination expenses	7320	Computers—rental and maintenance	8110
		Conferences and conventions—see meetings	8510
Benefits—health insurance premium reimbursement	7320		
		Conferences, conventions, meetings	8510
Benefits—health insurance premiums	7320	Contingency provisions	9290
Benefits—life insurance premiums	7320	Continuing education for employees	8820
Benefits—outplacement expenses	7320	Contract temporary help	7550
Benefits—payments to annuitants	7320		

(Continued)

Keyword	Unified Chart of Accounts Account Number	Keyword	Unified Chart of Accounts Account Number
Contributed materials and supplies	7720	Duplicating and copying—outside services	8210
Contributed professional services—GAAP	7580	Duplicating and copying materials and supplies	7710
Contributed professional services—non-GAAP	7590	Duplicating equipment rental and maintenance	8110
Contributed use of facilities and utilities—GAAP	8080	Education fees	7540
Contributed use of facilities and utilities—non-GAAP	8090	Electricity	8020
Conventions, meetings, and conferences	8510	Electronic data processing service bureau fees	9020
Copy equipment rental and maintenance	8110	Electronic data processing and computer-related service fees	9020
Copying and duplicating—outside services	8210	Employee benefits—other than pension	7320
Copying and duplicating materials and supplies	7710	Employee benefits—see benefits	7320
Craft supplies	7710	Employee benefits for clients on payroll	7320
Credit card fees	9300	Employee development, education, etc.	8820
Degree programs for employees	8820	Employee memberships	8810
Delivery and messenger service—see shipping	7910	Employee recruitment fees	7540
Dental fees of clients	7050	Employment termination expenses	7320
Depreciation—automotive equipment	8650	Equipment—donated use of—GAAP	8080
Depreciation—buildings	8650	Equipment—donated use of—non-GAAP	8090
Depreciation—equipment	8650	Equipment—loan and lease interest	8610
Depreciation, amortization, and depletion—allowable	8650	Equipment allowance under grant	7040
		Equipment depreciation	8650
Depreciation, amortization, and depletion—not allowable	8660	Equipment maintenance supplies	8110
		Equipment purchases	9830
Development fees—fundraising-related	7510	Equipment rental—meetings and conferences	8510
Directors' and officers' liability insurance	8710	Equipment rental, maintenance, and supplies	8110
Directors' salaries, fees	7210	Executive director's salary	7210
Disability insurance premiums	7410	Executive salaries	7210
Donated materials and supplies used	7720	Expenses—other	9300
Donated professional services—GAAP	7580	FICA payments (employer's share)	7410
Donated professional services—non-GAAP	7590	Facilities and utilities—donated—GAAP	8080
Donated use of facilities and utilities—GAAP	8080	Facilities and utilities—donated—non-GAAP	8090
Donated use of facilities and utilities—non-GAAP	8090	Fax	7810
Drugs and medicines (clinic use only)	7710	Federal and state payroll tax and insurance	7410
Dues for employee and organization memberships	8810	Federal Express, UPS, other overnight	7910

(Continued)

Keyword	Unified Chart of Accounts Account Number	Keyword	Unified Chart of Accounts Account Number
Fees—audit, accounting, and bookkeeping	7520	Housekeeping and janitorial services	8010
Fees—fundraising counsel, consultant	7510	Housekeeping, laundry, and linen supplies	7710
Fees—legal	7530	Incorporation and other organizational expenses	9230
Fees—outside mailing service	7920		
Fees—paid solicitor	7510	Individuals, specific assistance to	7050
Fees for outside electronic data processing, computer services	9020	In-kind grants to affiliates	7030
		In-kind grants to individuals	7040
Fees paid to directors and trustees	7210	In-kind grants to organizations	7020
Fellowships	7040	Insurance—business interruption	8710
Fidelity bonds	8710	Insurance—company shipping vehicles	7910
Film purchases and processing	7710	Insurance—company travel vehicles	8310
Films—produced by others	8210	Insurance—directors' and officers' liability	8710
Fines, penalties, and judgments	9210	Insurance—excluding employee-related	8710
First-aid supplies for employees	7710	Insurance—fidelity bonds	8710
Food and beverage—non-program-related	7710	Insurance—general liability	8710
Food and beverage—program-related	7710	Insurance—malpractice	8710
Food and beverage costs for meetings, etc.	8510	Insurance—meeting cancellation	8710
Food and beverage for employees and visitors	7710	Insurance—payroll-related	7410
		Insurance—professional liability	8710
Food and beverage services to clients	7710	Insurance—property	8710
Food service for clients	7050	Insurance coverage provided clients	7050
Freight, trucking	7910	Insurance on shipping and delivery vehicles	8710
Functional expense—total	Sum		
Fundraising counsel, consultant fees	7510	Insurance on travel vehicles (automobiles)	8710
Gas	8020	Interest—general	8610
Gas and oil—shipping (delivery)-related	7910	Interest on automobile loans and leases	8610
Gas and oil—travel-related	8310	Interest on equipment loans and leases	8610
General liability insurance	8710	Interest on mortgages	8050
Government registration fees (state charity)	9300	Interest on other long-term debt	8610
		Interest on other short-term debt	8610
Graduate fellowships	7040	Interest on truck loans and leases	8610
Grants and awards to individuals	7040	Investment counseling fees	7540
Grants to affiliated organizations	7030	Janitorial and similar service fees	8010
Grants to other organizations	7020	Judgments, fines, and penalties	9210
Grants to research institutions	7020	Key employee salaries	7210
Health insurance premium reimbursement	7320	Land purchases	9810
Health insurance premiums—see benefits	7320	Laundry, linen, and housekeeping supplies	7710
Heating oil	8020	Lease interest—see interest	8610
Homemaker service for clients	7050	Leasehold improvement	9820
Honoraria and expenses for speakers	8510	Leasing costs—shipping vehicles (not interest)	7910
Hotel, meals, and incidental expenses	8310		

(Continued)

Keyword	Unified Chart of Accounts Account Number	Keyword	Unified Chart of Accounts Account Number
Leasing costs—travel vehicles (not interest)	8310	Meetings—speakers' honoraria and expenses	8510
Legal fees	7530	Meetings, conferences, and conventions	8510
License fees—other	9300	Meetings, etc.—employee and volunteer travel	8310
Licenses and permits—occupancy-related	8010		
Licenses and permits—shipping vehicles	7910	Meetings, etc.—registration fees	8510
Licenses and permits—travel vehicles	8310	Meetings, luncheons, and dinners with board	8510
Life insurance premiums	7320		
Linen, laundry, and housekeeping supplies	7710	Meetings, luncheons, and dinners with volunteers	8510
List rental expense	9010	Membership dues for employees and organization	8810
Local and out-of-town travel	8310		
Local bus, subway, and taxicab fares—travel	8310	Messenger and delivery service—see shipping	7910
Local payroll tax and insurance	7410	Mortgage interest	8050
Long-term debt interest	8610	Motor vehicle insurance	8710
Mailgram	7810	Moving expenses	9300
Mailing services	7920	Newsletters, leaflets—purchased	8210
Maintenance supplies—copiers, computers, etc.	8110	Notices, badges for meetings	8510
		Occupancy	8010
Maintenance—company travel vehicles	8310	Occupancy-related licenses and permits	8010
Maintenance—copiers, computers, etc.	8110	Office rent	8010
Maintenance and supplies—building and grounds	8010	Office supplies	7710
		Officers' salaries, fees	7210
Maintenance employees' salaries and wages	7220	Oil for heating	8020
		Organization's memberships	8810
Maintenance of shipping (delivery) vehicles	7910	Other expenses	9300
		Outplacement expenses	7320
Malpractice insurance	8710	Outside computer services	9020
Management—contract temporary help	7550	Outside copying and duplicating services	8210
Meals, hotel, and incidental expenses	8310	Outside mailing service fees	7920
Medical and dental fees	7540	Overnight (Federal Express, UPS, etc.)	7910
Medical fees of clients	7050	Paid solicitor fees	7510
Medicine and drugs (clinic use only)	7710	Paper, ink, film, and copying materials	7710
Medicines for client	7050	Parcel post and postage	7910
Meeting cancellation insurance	8710	Parking fees and building rent	8010
Meeting space and equipment rental	8510	Payments to affiliates	9910
Meeting supplies	8510	Payments to annuitants	7320
Meetings—food and beverage costs	8510	Payroll disability insurance premiums	7410
Meetings—notices, badges	8510	Payroll—FICA payments (employer's share)	7410
Meetings—related printing costs	8510		

(Continued)

Keyword	Unified Chart of Accounts Account Number
Payroll—federal and state taxes and insurance	7410
Payroll—insurance-related expense	7410
Payroll services—outside	7520
Payroll taxes and insurance for clients on payroll	7410
Payroll—unemployment insurance and taxes	7410
Payroll—workers' compensation insurance	7410
Penalties, judgments, and fines	9210
Pension for officers, directors, and trustees	7310
Pension plan contributions	7310
Per diem expenses	8310
Periodicals	8220
Permit fees—other	9300
Permits and licenses—occupancy-related	8010
Permits and licenses—shipping vehicles	7910
Permits and licenses—travel vehicles	8310
Personal property taxes	8040
Photocopying—purchased	8210
Photography—purchased	8210
Postage and parcel post	7910
Postage and shipping (delivery)	7910
Postage meters—rental and maintenance	8110
Postal permit fees	7910
Printing and duplicating	8210
Printing costs—meetings, conferences, etc.	8510
Professional—contract temporary help	7550
Professional fees—audit, accounting, etc.	7520
Professional fees—brokerage and commission	7540
Professional fees—computer programming	7540
Professional fees—education	7540
Professional fees—employee recruitment	7540
Professional fees—fundraising	7510
Professional fees—investment counseling	7540
Professional fees—legal	7530
Professional fees—medical and dental	7540
Professional fees—other	7540
Professional fees—psychological	7540

Keyword	Unified Chart of Accounts Account Number
Professional fees—public relations	7540
Professional fees—rehabilitation	7540
Professional fundraising fees	7510
Professional liability insurance	8710
Professional services—donated—GAAP	7580
Professional services—donated—non-GAAP	7590
Professional staff salaries	7220
Program-related contracts to other entities	7010
Property insurance	8710
Property taxes	8040
Prosthetic appliances (clinic use only)	7710
Prosthetic appliances for clients	7050
Psychological fees	7540
Public relations fees	7540
Publications published by organization	8230
Publications published by others	8220
Purchase of books, publications	8220
Purchases—buildings	9820
Purchases—equipment	9830
Purchases—land	9810
Purchases—vehicles	9840
Real estate taxes	8030
Recordings produced by others	8210
Recreation service for clients	7050
Recreational supplies	7710
Registration fees for meetings, etc.	8510
Rehabilitation fees	7540
Rent	8010
Rental—car for travel	8310
Rental—copiers, computers, postage meters	8110
Rental expense for outside lists	9010
Rental of space and equipment for meetings, etc.	8510
Rental of trucks for shipping (delivery)	7910
Repairs—company travel vehicles	8310
Repairs of shipping (delivery) vehicles	7910
Retirement plan contributions	7310
Safety deposit box fees	9300

(Continued)

Keyword	Unified Chart of Accounts Account Number	Keyword	Unified Chart of Accounts Account Number
Salaries and wages of clerical and support staff	7220	Supplemental payments to pensioned employees	7320
Salaries and wages of clients on payroll	7220	Supplies	7710
Salaries and wages to other employees	7220	Supplies—classroom	7710
Salaries of officers, directors, and trustees	7210	Supplies—computer, typing, accounting, etc.	7710
Salaries of professional staff	7220	Supplies—conferences, conventions, and meetings	8510
Salaries of temporary help—on payroll	7220	Supplies—donated materials used	7720
Salary of chief executive officer	7210	Supplies—equipment maintenance	8110
Salary of executive director	7210	Supplies—first aid for employees	7710
Sales taxes	9110	Supplies—housekeeping, laundry, and linen	7710
Scholarships and tuition payments	7040	Supplies—paper, ink, film, and copying materials	7710
Service bureau fees—computer-related	9020	Supplies—plaques, noncash prizes for clients	7710
Services by others at expense of organization	7050	Supplies and maintenance—building and grounds	8010
Sewer and water	8020	Taxes—other	9150
Shelter for clients	7050	Taxes—payroll federal, state, and local	7410
Shipping—insurance—company vehicles	7910	Taxes—personal property	8040
Shipping—interest on truck loans and leases	8610	Taxes—real estate	8030
Shipping—leasing costs—vehicles (no interest)	7910	Taxes—sales	9110
Shipping—licenses and permits for vehicles	7910	Taxes—unrelated business income (UBIT)	9120
Shipping—tires—company vehicles	7910	Taxicab fares	8310
Shipping and delivery vehicle insurance	8710	Technician salaries	7220
Shipping (delivery)—gas and oil	7910	Telegram, telex	7810
Shipping (delivery) and postage	7910	Telegraph expense (mailgram, etc.)	7810
Shipping (delivery) vehicle maintenance	7910	Telephone equipment maintenance	7810
Short-term debt interest	8610	Telephone expense	7810
Speakers' honoraria and expenses for meetings	8510	Telephone-related expense—other	7810
Specific assistance to individuals	7050	Temporary help—contract	7550
Staff development, education, training, etc.	8820	Temporary help salaries—on payroll	7220
State and local charity registration fees	9300	Termination of employee expenses	7320
State payroll tax and insurance	7410	Tires—company shipping vehicles	7910
Stationery, typing, accounting, and similar supplies	7710	Tires—company travel vehicles	8310
Subscriptions to other publications	8220	Total functional expenses	Sum
Subscriptions to periodicals	8220	Trainee scholarships	7040
Subway and taxicab fares	8310	Training seminars and workshops for staff	8820

(Continued)

Keyword	Unified Chart of Accounts Account Number	Keyword	Unified Chart of Accounts Account Number
Transportation—travel-related	8310	Truck rental for shipping (delivery)	7910
Transportation service for clients	7050	Trucking, freight	7910
Travel—airfare, train fare, bus fare	8310	Trustees' salaries, fees	7210
Travel—auto allowance for employees	8310	Tuition and scholarship payments	7040
Travel—for volunteers on business	8310	Typewriter rental and maintenance	8110
Travel—gas and oil	8310	Typewriter supplies	7710
Travel—hotel, meals, and incidental expenses	8310	Unrelated business income taxes (UBIT)	9120
Travel—insurance—company vehicles	8310	Uncollected accounts receivable (bad debt)	9100
Travel—interest on auto loans and leases	8610	Unemployment insurance and taxes	7410
Travel—leasing costs—vehicles (not interest)	8310	UPS, Federal Express, other overnight	7910
		Use of facilities and utilities—donated—GAAP	8080
Travel—licenses and permits on vehicles	8310	Use of facilities and utilities—donated—non-GAAP	8090
Travel—local and out-of-town travel	8310		
Travel—local bus, subway, and taxicab fares	8310	Utilities and use of facilities—donated—GAAP	8080
Travel—per diem payments	8310		
Travel—repairs—company vehicles	8310	Utilities and use of facilities—donated—non-GAAP	8090
Travel—tires—company vehicles	8310		
Travel and travel-related transportation	8310	Vehicle purchases	9840
Travel allowance under grant	7040	Vocational supplies	7710
Travel for meetings and conferences	8310	Wage supplements for clients	7050
Travel vehicle (automobile) insurance	8710	Water and sewer	8020
Truck loan and lease interest	8610	Workers' compensation insurance	7410
Truck maintenance—shipping (delivery)	7910		

Examples of Employee Time Sheets

REGARDLESS OF THE METHOD used, if an organization must substantiate after-the-fact determinations of how staff time is spent, payroll records should include copies of completed monthly time sheets for each employee. Each time sheet should show the number of hours for which the employee was paid each day and how those hours were spent in terms of the valid activity codes you have established for your chart of accounts. See Table D.1 for an example of a completed monthly time sheet.

Individual employee time sheets can be set up on spreadsheet software, if desired. This approach may or may not be the most efficient and effective way for you to maintain monthly time sheet records. A monthly and year-end computer spreadsheet for staff time recording should include

- Monthly time sheets for employees
- Monthly staff time distribution by activity, based on hours spent on each activity
- Monthly staff time distribution by activity, based on percentage of total time spent on each activity
- Monthly staff salary distribution by activity, based on salary dollars allocable to each activity
- Prior month year-to-date staff time distribution by activity, based on hours spent on each activity
- Year-end staff time distribution by activity, based on hours spent on each activity (current month)
- Year-end staff time distribution by activity, based on percentage of total time spent on each activity
- Year-end staff salary distribution by activity, based on salary dollars allocable to each activity

TABLE D.1

Monthly Time Sheet

Activity	Activity Code								Day of Month	
		1	2	3	4	5	6	7	8	9
Program A, general	100			4.0						
Program A, contract 101	120	8.0	8.0	4.0	8.0	4.0			8.0	8.0
Program A, contract 102	130					4.0				
Program B, general	200									
Program A, contract 101	220									
Program C, general	300									
Program A, contract 103	320									
Program D, grant 204	420									
Management and general	510									
Fundraising	710									
Central services	910									
Leave pool	920									
Total		8.0	8.0	8.0	8.0	8.0			8.0	8.0

Activity	Activity Code								Day of Month	
		16	17	18	19	20	21	22	23	24
Program A, general	100		4.0						4.0	
Program A, contract 101	120	8.0	4.0	8.0	4.0			8.0	4.0	8.0
Program A, contract 102	130				4.0					
Program B, general	200									
Program A, contract 101	220									
Program C, general	300									
Program A, contract 103	320									
Program D, grant 204	420									
Management and general	510									
Fundraising	710									
Central services	910									
Leave pool	920									
Total		8.0	8.0	8.0	8.0			8.0	8.0	8.0

[a]Enter percentages for month on page 2.

The following is an example of how computerization can make a complex, detailed accounting procedure easy for the bookkeeping staff to perform. Once the above templates have been established for monthly salary processing, the only data entry required would be the monthly gross salary from the payroll records for each employee and the hours from the time sheets for each employee, distributed by activity (see Table D.2). The prior month's seven-page spreadsheet provides prior-month year-to-date data for the current month's spreadsheet. At the end of each fiscal year, there would be twelve monthly computer spreadsheets in the accounting records for salary processing. All calculations and the production of the seven-page salary processing reports are performed by the spreadsheet soft-

					Period		
10	11	12	13	14	15	Hours	Percent
4.0						8.0	9.1%
4.0	8.0	4.0			8.0	72.0	81.8%
		4.0				8.0	9.1%
						0.0	0.0%
						0.0	0.0%
						0.0	0.0%
						0.0	0.0%
						0.0	0.0%
						0.0	0.0%
						0.0	0.0%
						0.0	0.0%
						0.0	0.0%
8.0	8.0	8.0			8.0	88.0	100.0%

							Period		Month[a]	
25	26	27	28	29	30	31	Hours	Percent	Hours	Percent
							12.0	12.5 %	20.0	10.9 %
				4.0	8.0		56.0	58.3 %	128.0	69.5 %
						8.0	12.0	12.5 %	20.0	10.9 %
							0.0	0.0 %	0.0	0.0 %
							0.0	0.0 %	0.0	0.0 %
							0.0	0.0 %	0.0	0.0 %
							0.0	0.0 %	0.0	0.0 %
							0.0	0.0 %	0.0	0.0 %
							0.0	0.0 %	0.0	0.0 %
							0.0	0.0 %	0.0	0.0 %
							0.0	0.0 %	0.0	0.0 %
8.0	8.0						16.0	16.7 %	16.0	8.7 %
8.0	8.0			8.0	8.0	8.0	96.0	100.0 %	184.0	100.0 %

ware. Tables D.2 through D.8 illustrate this system (which can also be adapted for use in preparing budgets by activity).

For monthly salary processing the spreadsheet can automatically

1. Convert the monthly hours spent by each employee on each activity to time percentages (see Table D.3).

2. Allocate the monthly gross salaries for each employee by activity according to the time percentages (see Table D.4).

3. Tabulate the monthly gross salaries by activity for the two relevant expense accounts: 7210 (Officer salaries) and 7220 (Other salaries). The twenty-four total figures for these two accounts and the twelve activity

TABLE D.2

Monthly Staff Time Distribution Report by Activity (in Hours)

Account Number	Job Title	Monthly Gross Salary (Dollars)	Program A, Unrestricted (100)	Program A, Contract 101 (120)	Program A, Contract 102 (130)	Program B, Unrestricted (200)	Program B, Contract 101 (220)
7210	Executive director, CEO	5,417	50	60			
7210	Director-administrator, CFO, MIS	4,167		84			
7220	Director, Program A	4,167	20	108			
7220	Assistant director, Program A	2,917	168				
7220	Assistant director, Program A	2,917	20	128	20		
7220	Director, Program B	3,750				10	158
7220	Director, Programs C and D	3,750					
7220	Support	2,083	30	30	30	34	
7220	Support	1,667		168			16
7220	Support	1,250	100	68			16
	Total hours—unallocated	32,085	388	646	50	44	158
	Allocation of leave hours—prorated		47	79	6	5	19
	Total hours—with leave allocated		435	725	56	49	177
	Hours as a percentage of total hours		23.7%	39.4%	3.0%	2.7%	9.6%
	Allocation of common hours—prorated		12	20	2	1	5
	Total hours—with common hours allocated		447	745	58	50	182
	Hours as a percentage of total hours		24.3%	40.5%	3.1%	2.7%	9.9%

Note: Three-digit activity codes are shown in parentheses in column headings where applicable.

codes can be posted in the general ledger from this monthly report (see Table D.4).

For year-to-date salary processing the spreadsheet can automatically

1. Add the current monthly hours for each employee for each activity to the prior month's year-to-date hours for each employee for each activity. See Table D.5 for the prior month's year-to-date report in hours and Table D.6 for the current month's year-to-date report in hours.

2. Convert the year-to-date hours for each employee for each activity to time percentages (see Table D.7).

3. Allocate the year-to-date gross salary for each employee by activity according to the time percentages (see Table D.8).

4. Tabulate the year-to-date gross salaries by activity for the two expense accounts, 7210 (Officer salaries) and 7220 (Other salaries) (see Table D.8).

5. Allocate the leave cost pools to the other eleven activity categories for the two salary accounts (see Table D.8).

6. Allocate the central services cost pools for salaries to the other ten activity categories for the two salary accounts (see Table D.8). The figures for total officer salaries (account 7210, common, allocated) and

TABLE D.2

Monthly Staff Time Distribution Report by Activity (in Hours)

Program C, Unrestricted (300)	Program C, Contract 103 (320)	Program D, Grant 204 (420)	Management and General (510)	Fundraising (710)	Other Common Cost Pools, Central Services (910)	Leave Cost Pool, Account Cost Pool (920)	Total
			34	24		16	184
			40		44	16	184
						56	184
						16	184
						16	184
						16	184
			40	80	48	16	184
					44	16	184
						16	184
						16	184
40	80	48	118	24	44	200	1,840
5	10	6	15	3	5	(200)	0
45	90	54	133	27	49	0	1,840
2.4%	4.9%	2.9%	7.2%	1.5%	2.7%		100.0%
1	2	1	4	1	(49)		0
46	92	55	137	28	0		1,840
2.5%	5.0%	3.0%	7.5%	1.5%			100.0%

the total other salaries (account 7220, common, allocated) are transferred by activity code to the functionalized trial balance. This can be done automatically by the spreadsheet software.

7. Add the allocated salaries for the two account numbers together for the total all salaries (allocated) figures for the ten activity categories (see Table D.8).

8. Calculate salaries as percentage of total salaries for each of the ten activity codes (see Table D.8). These percentages can be entered (or automatically transferred by the spreadsheet software) to the functionalized trial balance spreadsheet for use as the basis for allocation of common and indirect or administrative costs.

The seven monthly salary processing reports can be produced by using a computer spreadsheet template programmed along the lines of the one developed for the illustrations in this guide. A word of caution: although spreadsheets can be programmed to do monthly and year-end salary processing and reporting, they are prone to error unless managed very carefully by highly skilled individuals. When accounting software systems or outside payroll processors with the above salary processing capabilities are available, they can be more reliable, be easier to use, and require less skill to operate.

TABLE D.3

Monthly Staff Time Distribution Report by Activity (in Percentages)

Account Number	Job Title	Monthly Gross Salary (Dollars)	Program A, Unrestricted (100, A81, A)	Program A, Contract 101 (120, A81, A)	Program A, Contract 102 (130, A81, A)	Program B, Unrestricted, (200, A82, B)	Program B, Contract 101 (220, A82, B)
7210	Executive director, CEO	5,417	27.2%	32.6%	0.0%	0.0%	0.0%
7210	Director-administrator, CFO, MIS	4,167	0.0%	45.7%	0.0%	0.0%	0.0%
7220	Director, Program A	4,167	10.9%	58.7%	0.0%	0.0%	0.0%
7220	Assistant director, Program A	2,917	91.3%	0.0%	0.0%	0.0%	0.0%
7220	Assistant director, Program A	2,917	10.9%	69.5%	10.9%	0.0%	0.0%
7220	Director, Program B	3,750	0.0%	0.0%	0.0%	5.4%	85.9%
7220	Director, Programs C and D	3,750	0.0%	0.0%	0.0%	0.0%	0.0%
7220	Support	2,083	16.3%	16.3%	16.3%	18.5%	0.0%
7220	Support	1,667	0.0%	91.3%	0.0%	0.0%	0.0%
7220	Support	1,250	54.3%	37.0%	0.0%	0.0%	0.0%
	Totals	32,085	210.9%	351.1%	27.2%	23.9%	85.9%

Note: *Three-digit activity codes, the relevant column and line in the GAAP statement of activity, and the relevant column in the GAAP statement of functional expenses (respectively) are shown in parentheses in column headings where applicable.*

Program C, Unrestricted (300 , A83, C)	Program C, Contract 103 (320 , A83, C)	Program D, Grant 204 (420 , A84, D)	Management and General (510 , A86, F)	Fundraising (710 , A87, G)	Other Common Cost Pools, Central Services (910, Allocated, Allocated)	Leave Cost Pool, Account Cost Pool (920, Allocated, Allocated)	Total
0.0%	0.0%	0.0%	18.5%	13.0%	0.0%	8.7%	100.0%
0.0%	0.0%	0.0%	21.7%	0.0%	23.9%	8.7%	100.0%
0.0%	0.0%	0.0%	0.0%	0.0%	0.0%	30.4%	100.0%
0.0%	0.0%	0.0%	0.0%	0.0%	0.0%	8.7%	100.0%
0.0%	0.0%	0.0%	0.0%	0.0%	0.0%	8.7%	100.0%
0.0%	0.0%	0.0%	0.0%	0.0%	0.0%	8.7%	100.0%
21.7%	43.5%	26.1%	0.0%	0.0%	0.0%	8.7%	100.0%
0.0%	0.0%	0.0%	23.9%	0.0%	0.0%	8.7%	100.0%
0.0%	0.0%	0.0%	0.0%	0.0%	0.0%	8.7%	100.0%
0.0%	0.0%	0.0%	0.0%	0.0%	0.0%	8.7%	100.0%
21.7%	43.5%	26.1%	64.1%	13.0%	23.9%	108.7%	1000.0%

TABLE D.4

Monthly Staff Salary Distribution Report by Activity (in Dollars)

Account Number	Job Title	Monthly Gross Salary (Dollars)	Program A, Unrestricted, (100, A81, A)	Program A, Contract 101 (120, A81, A)	Program A, Contract 102 (130, A81, A)	Program B, Unrestricted, (200, A82, B)	Program B, Contract 101 (220, A82, B)
Officer Salaries:							
7210	Executive director, CEO	5,417	1,472	1,766			
7210	Director-administrator, CFO, MIS	4,167		1,902			
7210(A)	Subtotal—officer salaries	9,584	1,472	3,668			
Other Salaries:							
7220	Director, Program A	4,167	453	2,446			
7220	Assistant director, Program A	2,917	2,663				
7220	Assistant director, Program A	2,917	318	2,027	318		
7220	Director, Program B	3,750				204	3,220
7220	Director, Programs C and D	3,750					
7220	Support	2,083	340	340	340	384	
7220	Support	1,667		1,522			
7220	Support	1,250	679	462			
7220(B)	Subtotal—other employee salaries	22,501	4,453	6,797	658	588	3,220
	Total—all monthly salaries/(unallocated)	32,085	5,925	10,465	658	588	3,220
	Allocation of leave salaries		772	1,364	85	78	418
	Total salaries—with leave allocation		6,697	11,829	743	666	3,638
	Salaries as a percentage of total salaries		20.9%	36.9%	2.3%	2.1%	11.3%
	Allocation of common salaries		243	430	27	24	133
	Total salaries—with common allocated		6,940	12,259	770	690	3,771
	Salaries as a percentage of total salaries		21.6%	38.2%	2.4%	2.1%	11.8%

Note: *Three-digit activity codes, the relevant column and line in the GAAP statement of activity, and the relevant column in the GAAP statement of functional expenses (respectively) are shown in parentheses in column headings where applicable.*

Program C, Unrestricted (300, A83, C)	Program C, Contract 103 (320, A83, C)	Program D, Grant 204 (420, A84, D)	Management and General (510, A86, F)	Fundraising (710, A87, G)	Other Common Cost Pools, Central Services (910, Allocated, Allocated)	Leave Cost Pool, Account Cost Pool (920, Allocated, Allocated)	Total
			1,001	707		471	5,417
			906		997	362	4,167
			1,907	707	997	833	9,584
						1,268	4,167
						254	2,917
						254	2,917
815	1,631	978				326	3,750
						326	3,750
			498			181	2,083
						145	1,667
						109	1,250
815	1,631	978	498			2,863	22,501
815	1,631	978	2,405	707	997	3,696	32,085
107	211	126	314				
922	1,842	1,104	2,719	799	1,126		32,085
2.9%	5.7%	3.4%	8.5%	2.5%	3.5%		100.0%
34	66	41	99	29	(1,126)		
956	1,908	1,145	2,818	828			32,085
3.0%	5.9%	3.6%	8.8%	2.6%			100.0%

TABLE D.5

Prior Month Year-to-Date Time Distribution Report by Activity (in Hours)

Account Number	Job Title	Year-to-Date Gross Salary (Dollars)	Program A Unrestricted, (100)	Program A, Contract 101 (120)	Program A, Contract 102 (130)	Program B, Unrestricted, (200)	Program B, Contract 101 (220)
7210	Executive director, CEO	59,583	279	368	54	374	104
7210	Director-administrator, CFO, MIS	45,833	0	540	0	0	
7220	Director, Program A	45,833	396	1,202	104	0	0
7220	Assistant director, Program A	32,083	1,662	0	0	0	0
7220	Assistant director, Program A	32,083	188	1,328	146	0	0
7220	Director, Program B	41,250	0	0	0	406	1,256
7220	Director, Programs C and D	41,250	0	0	0	0	0
7220	Support	22,917	282	178	178	174	0
7220	Support	18,333	0	1,246	208	0	208
7220	Support	13,750	815	847	0	0	0
	Total hours—unallocated	352,915	3,622	5,709	690	954	1,568
	Allocation of leave hours—prorated		501	788	95	132	216
	Total hours—with leave allocated		4,123	6,497	785	1,086	1,784
	Hours as a percentage of total hours		21.8%	34.3%	4.1%	5.7%	9.4%
	Allocation of common hours—prorated		339	534	65	89	147
	Total hours—with common hours allocated		4,462	7,031	850	1,175	1,931
	Hours as a percentage of total hours		23.5%	37.1%	4.5%	6.2%	10.2%

Note: *Three-digit activity codes are shown in parentheses in column headings where applicable.*

Program C, Unrestricted (300)	Program C, Contract 103 (320)	Program D, Grant 204 (420)	Management and General (510)	Fundraising (710)	Other Common Cost Pools, Central Services (910)	Leave Cost Pool, Line Item Cost Pool (920)	Total
0	0	0	411	72	0	234	1,896
0	0	0	376	0	746	234	1,896
0	0	0	0	0	0	194	1,896
0	0	0	0	0	0	234	1,896
0	0	0	0	0	0	234	1,896
626	606	430	0	0	0	234	1,896
0	0	0	330	0	520	234	1,896
0	0	0	0	0	0	234	1,896
0	0	0	0	0	0	234	1,896
626	606	430	1,117	72	1,266	2,300	18,960
86	84	59	154	10	175	2,300	0
712	690	489	1,271	82	1,441	0	18,960
3.8%	3.6%	2.6%	6.7%	0.4%	7.6%		100.0%
59	57	40	104	7	(1,441)		0
771	747	529	1,375	89	0		18,960
4.1%	3.9%	2.8%	7.2%	0.5%			100.0%

TABLE D.6

Year-End Staff Time Distribution Report by Activity (in Hours)

Account Number	Job Title	Year-to-Date Gross Salary (Dollars)	Program A, Unrestricted (100, A81, A)	Program A, Contract 101 (120, A81, A)	Program A, Contract 102 (130, A81, A)	Program B, Unrestricted, (200, A82, B)	Program B, Contract 101 (220, A82, B)
7210	Executive director, CEO	65,000	329	428	54	374	104
7210	Director-administrator, CFO, MIS	50,000	0	624	0	0	0
7220	Director, Program A	50,000	416	1,310	104	0	0
7220	Assistant director, Program A	35,000	1,830	0	0	0	0
7220	Assistant director, Program A	35,000	208	1,456	166	0	0
7220	Director, Program B	45,000	0	0	0	416	1,414
7220	Director, Programs C and D	45,000	0	0	0	0	0
7220	Support	25,000	312	208	208	208	0
7220	Support	20,000	0	1,414	208	0	2,081
7220	Support	15,000	915	915	0	0	0
	Total hours—unallocated	385,000	4,010	6,355	740	998	1,726
	Allocation of leave salaries		548	867	100	137	235
	Total salaries—with leave allocation		4,558	7,222	840	1,135	1,961
	Salaries as a percentage of total salaries		21.9%	34.7%	4.0%	5.5%	9.4%
	Allocation of common salaries		351	557	64	88	152
	Total salaries—with common allocated		4,909	7,779	904	1,223	2,113
	Salaries as a percentage of total salaries		23.6%	37.4%	4.3%	5.9%	10.2%

Note: *Three-digit activity codes, the relevant column and line in the GAAP statement of activity, and the relevant column in the GAAP statement of functional expenses (respectively) are shown in parentheses in column headings where applicable.*

Program C, Unrestricted (300, A83, C)	Program C, Contract 103 (320, A83, C)	Program D, Grant 204 (420, A84, D)	Management and General (510, A86, F)	Fundraising (710, A87, G)	Other Common Cost Pools, Central Services (910, Allocated, Allocated)	Leave Cost Pool, Line Item Cost Pool (920, Allocated, Allocated)	Total
0	0	0	445	96	0	250	2,080
0	0	0	416	0	790	250	2,080
0	0	0	0	0	0	250	2,080
0	0	0	0	0	0	250	2,080
0	0	0	0	0	0	250	2,080
0	0	0	0	0	0	250	2,080
666	686	478	0	0	0	250	2,080
0	0	0	374	0	520	250	2,080
0	0	0	0	0	0	250	2,080
0	0	0	0	0	0	250	2,080
666	686	478	1,235	96	1,310	2,500	20,800
90	95	65	170	13	180	(2,500)	0
756	781	543	1,405	109	1,490	0	20,800
3.6%	3.8%	2.6%	6.8%	0.5%	7.2%		100.0%
58	60	42	109	9	(1,490)		(0)
814	841	585	1,514	118	0		20,800
3.9%	4.0%	2.8%	7.3%	0.6%			100.0%

TABLE D.7

Year-End Staff Time Distribution Report by Activity (in Percentages)

Account Number	Job Title	Year-to-Date Gross Salary (Dollars)	Program A, Unrestricted (100, A81, A)	Program A, Contract 101 (120, A81, A)	Program A, Contract 102 (130, A81, A)	Program B, Unrestricted, (200, A82, B)	Program B, Contract 101 (220, A82, B)
7210	Executive director, CEO	65,000	15.8%	20.6%	2.6%	18.0%	5.0%
7210	Director-administrator, CFO, MIS	50,000	0.0%	30.0%	0.0%	0.0%	0.0%
7220	Director, Program A	50,000	20.0%	63.0%	5.0%	0.0%	0.0%
7220	Assistant director, Program A	35,000	88.0%	0.0%	0.0%	0.0%	0.0%
7220	Assistant director, Program A	35,000	10.0%	70.0%	8.0%	0.0%	0.0%
7220	Director, Program B	45,000	0.0%	0.0%	0.0%	20.0%	68.0%
7220	Director, Programs C and D	45,000	0.0%	0.0%	0.0%	0.0%	0.0%
7220	Support	25,000	15.0%	10.0%	10.0%	10.0%	0.0%
7220	Support	20,000	0.0%	68.0%	10.0%	0.0%	10.0%
7220	Support	15,000	44.0%	44.0%	0.0%	0.0%	0.0%
	Totals	385,000	192.8%	305.6%	35.6%	48.0%	83.0%

Note: *Three-digit activity codes, the relevant column and line in the GAAP statement of activity, and the relevant column in the GAAP statement of functional expenses (respectively) are shown in parentheses in column headings where applicable.*

Program C, Unrestricted (300, A83, C)	Program C, Contract 103 (320, A83, C)	Program D, Grant 204 (420, A84, D)	Management and General (510, A86, F)	Fundraising (710, A87, G)	Other Common Cost Pools, Central Services (910, Allocated, Allocated)	Leave Cost Pool, Line Item Cost Pool (920, Allocated, Allocated)|	Total
0.0%	0.0%	0.0%	21.4%	4.6%	0.0%	12.0%	100.0%
0.0%	0.0%	0.0%	20.0%	0.0%	38.0%	12.0%	100.0%
0.0%	0.0%	0.0%	0.0%	0.0%	0.0%	12.0%	100.0%
0.0%	0.0%	0.0%	0.0%	0.0%	0.0%	12.0%	100.0%
0.0%	0.0%	0.0%	0.0%	0.0%	0.0%	12.0%	100.0%
0.0%	0.0%	0.0%	0.0%	0.0%	0.0%	12.0%	100.0%
32.0%	33.0%	23.0%	0.0%	0.0%	0.0%	12.0%	100.0%
0.0%	0.0%	0.0%	18.0%	0.0%	25.0%	12.0%	100.0%
0.0%	0.0%	0.0%	0.0%	0.0%	0.0%	12.0%	100.0%
0.0%	0.0%	0.0%	0.0%	0.0%	0.0%	12.0%	100.0%
32.0%	33.0%	23.0%	59.4%	4.6%	63.0%	120.0%	1000.0%

TABLE D.8

Year-End Staff Salary Distribution Report by Activity (in Dollars)

Account Number	Job Title	Year-to-Date Gross Salary (Dollars)	Program A Unrestricted (100, A81, A)	Program A, Contract 101 (120, A81, A)	Program A, Contract 102 (130, A81, A)	Program B, Unrestricted (200, A82, B)	Program B, Contract 101 (220, A82, B)
7210	Executive director, CEO	$65,000	$10,270	$13,390	$1,690	$11,700	$3,250
7210	Director-administrator, CFO, MIS	50,000		15,000			
7210	Subtotal—officer salaries	$115,000	$10,270	$28,390	$1,690	$11,700	$3,250
	Allocation of leave salaries		1,400	3,871	231	1,596	443
	Total officer salaries—leave allocated	115,000	11,670	32,261	1,921	13,296	3,693
	Allocation of common salaries		2,698	7,457	444	3,073	854
7210(A)	Total officer salaries—common allocated	115,000	14,368	39,718	2,365	16,369	4,547
7220	Director, Program A	50,000	10,000	31,500	2,500		
7220	Assistant director, Program A	35,000	30,800				
7220	Assistant director, Program A	35,000	3,500	24,500	2,800		
7220	Director, Program B	45,000				9,000	30,600
7220	Director, Programs C and D	45,000					
7220	Support	25,000	3,750	2,500	2,500	2,500	
7220	Support	20,000		13,600	2,000		2,000
7220	Support	15,000	6,600	6,600			
7220	Subtotal—other employee salaries	$270,000	$54,650	$78,700	$9,800	$11,500	$32,600
	Allocation of leave salaries		7,452	10,732	1,336	1,568	4,446
	Total other salaries—leave allocated	$270,000	$62,102	$89,432	$11,136	$13,068	$37,046
	Allocation of common salaries		1,677	2,416	301	353	1,001
7220(B)	Total other salaries—common allocated	270,000	63,779	91,848	11,437	13,421	38,047
	Total all salaries—allocated	$385,000	$78,147	$131,566	$13,802	$29,790	$42,594
	Salaries as a percentage of total salaries[a]	100.0%	20.3%	34.2%	3.6%	7.7%	11.1%

Note: Three-digit activity codes, the relevant column and line in the GAAP statement of activity, and the relevant column in the GAAP statement of functional expenses (respectively) are shown in parentheses in column headings where applicable.

[a]*This is a frequently used basis for allocating allocable direct and indirect or administrative costs.*

TABLE D.8

Year-End Staff Salary Distribution Report by Activity (in Dollars)

Program C, Unrestricted (300, A83, C)	Program C, Contract 103 (320, A83, C)	Program D, Grant 204 (420, A84, D)	Management and General (510, A86, F)	Fundraising (710, A87, G)	Other Common Cost Pools, Central Services (910, Allocated, Allocated)	Leave Cost Pool, Line Item Cost Pool (920, Allocated, Allocated)	Total
			$13,910	$2,990		$7,800	$65,000
			10,000		19,000	6,000	50,000
			$23,910	$2,990	$19,000	$13,800	$115,000
			3,260	408	2,591	(13,800)	
			27,170	3,398	21,591		115,000
			6,280	785	(21,591)		
			33,450	4,183			115,000
						6,000	50,000
						4,200	35,000
						4,200	35,000
						5,400	45,000
14,400	14,850	10,350				5,400	45,000
				4,500	6,250	3,000	25,000
						2,400	20,000
						1,800	15,000
$14,400	$14,850	$10,350	$4,500		$6,250	$32,400	$270,000
1,964	2,025	1,411	614		852	(32,400)	
$16,364	$16,875	$11,761	$5,114		$7,102		$270,000
442	456	318	138		(7,102)		
16,806	17,331	12,079	5,252				270,000
$16,806	$17,331	$12,079	$38,702	$4,183			$385,000
4.4%	4.5%	3.1%	10.0%	1.1%			100.0%

Summary of State Registration and Filing Requirements for Not-for-Profit Organizations

THE FOLLOWING is a state-by-state summary of registration and filing requirements for not-for-profit organizations. This is not intended to be a complete picture of the various requirements. Several states also require a CPA audit or an independent public accountant's review of financial statements depending on the gross revenue or assets of the organization. Further, several states also have special rules, regulations, and registration and filing requirements for "fundraising counsels" and paid solicitors. These are not covered here. Not-for-profit organizations should consult a qualified legal or accounting professional for a complete set of requirements in their respective locations.

TABLE E.1

State Registration and Filing Requirements

State or District	Registration and Filing Requirements
Alabama	Form 20 or 20F for unrelated business income and copy of Form 990 or 990T, as applicable. $25 fee for annual registration.
Alaska	Form 08-196 is required for all not-for-profit organizations doing business in the state and Form 04-611 for those who solicit contributions; all must file the Annual Charities Statements form with the Department of Law and copies of Form 990, 990-T, or 990-PF, as applicable. No fee.
Arizona	Those incorporated in Arizona must file Form INC0046, and those with business income must file Form 99 or 99T. No fee.
California	Form 19 and Form 109 for those with unrelated business income. Every organization or trustee holding assets for the public must file Form CT-2 if gross receipts or assets exceed $25,000. Trusts must file Forms 541A and 541B.
Colorado	Exempt organizations must file Form CR-1, and those with unrelated business income must file Form 112.
Connecticut	All those soliciting funds in the state must file a onetime registration on Form CPC-63. Form CPC-54 must be filed by those with $25,000 or less in receipts, those who use unpaid fundraisers, or those who have received contributions from ten or fewer persons. $20 fee for initial registration.
Delaware	No filing requirements for tax-exempt organizations.
D.C.	Copies of Form 990, 990T, or 990PF, as applicable and Form DRA25. $80 annual licensing fee.
Florida	IRS determination letter prior to starting fundraising. Form F-1120 for those with unrelated business income. Those with proceeds of $10,000 or more must file Form 990, 990-T, or 990-PF, as applicable. Fees range from $10 to $400, depending on receipts.
Georgia	Form 600T by all exempt organizations with unrelated business income from state sources. Form C-100 and copies of Form 990, 990-T, or 990-PF, as applicable. $25 fee for annual registration.
Hawaii	Form N-70NP for those with unrelated business income.
Idaho	Form 41 for those with unrelated business income.
Illinois	Form I11-990T for those with unrelated business income and Forms C-01 and NP-102.10, as applicable. Initial registration fee $15.
Indiana	Form IT-20NP for those with unrelated business income and Form 990 or 990-T, as applicable. Also Forms IT-35A and IT-35AR.
Iowa	Form IA 1120 for those with unrelated business income and Form IA42-044 and 990-PF, as applicable.
Kansas	No special form; an annual report and a registration statement are required. $20 fee.

(Continued)

TABLE E.1

State Registration and Filing Requirements (*Continued*)

State or District	Registration and Filing Requirements
Kentucky	No special form; an annual report is required.
Louisiana	IRS determination letter for initial qualification for tax-exempt status is required for those desiring tax-exempt status in the state. $25 fee.
Maine	Form 1120-ME for those with unrelated business income and an annual report. $40 initial registration fee.
Maryland	Form 500 for those with unrelated business income and copies of Form 990, 990-T, or 990-PF, as applicable. State registration is required for those with more than $25,000 in solicitations and those who use professional fundraisers. Fees range from $50 to $200, depending on receipts.
Michigan	Form C-8000 for those with unrelated business income in excess of $40,000. Form CT-15 annual report must be filed.
Minnesota	No special form; an annual report is required. If total contributions are less than $25,000 and no professional fundraiser is used, only notice of exemption may be filed. Registration with the attorney general's office is required of all organizations that raise money or hire professional fundraisers. Form 990 must be filed by those with proceeds of $25,000 or more. $25 fee.
Mississippi	Copy of IRS determination letter and Form 990 if income is $25,000 or more. $50 fee.
Missouri	Form 1-A for those who intend to raise funds or plan to employ professional fundraisers and Form 2-A for those with more than $10,000 in proceeds. $15 fee.
Montana	Form CLT-4 and a copy of Form 990-T for those with unrelated business income.
Nebraska	Those that file Form 990-T should file Form 1120N, and those receiving funds from the public should file Form 990.
Nevada	Form 990.
New Hampshire	Organizations that file Form 990 with the IRS must file Form NHCT-2, Annual Report of Charitable Organizations; if filed with Form 990, just a signature will suffice on Form NHCT-2. $25 fee.
New Jersey	Form QCR-101 (several exceptions apply). Those with less than $10,000 in revenue must file Form CO-4, CO-6, or CO-8, as applicable. Fees range from $60 to $250, depending on receipts.
New Mexico	Form CIT-1 for those with unrelated business income. Those soliciting public donations must file with Attorney General Charitable Organization Registry.
New York	New York has a complex set of requirements applicable to different categories of organizations. Form 410, 497, CT-13, CT-247, NYCF-1, NYCF-2A, NYCF-3, and NYCF-4 must be filed, as applicable (consult your legal or accounting professional). $25 fee.

(Continued)

TABLE E.1

State Registration and Filing Requirements (*Continued*)

State or District	Registration and Filing Requirements
North Carolina	Form CD-427 for all exempt organizations and Form CD-464 for those with unrelated business income. Fees range from $50 to $200, depending on receipts.
North Dakota	Form 40 for those with unrelated business income. Form 99 for all exempt organizations and an annual report for those raising funds in the state. Initial fee $25.
Ohio	Charitable Organization Registration Statement and Form CFR-1 must be filed by all those soliciting contributions. Form 990 or a certified copy of financial statements must be filed by those with gross receipts of more than $5,000 or gross assets of more than $15,000. Fees range from $50 to $200, depending on contributions received in the state.
Oklahoma	Form 512-E for those with unrelated business income and an annual report for those soliciting funds from the public. $15 fee.
Oregon	Form CT-12, part I, for all not-for-profit organizations that hold assets in the state; parts II and III must also be filed by all except religious, educational, cemetery, and child-care corporations.
Pennsylvania	Form CC-004 must be filed by all those soliciting funds. Copy of Form 990-PF must be filed by those who file 990-PF with the federal government. $15 to $250 fee.
Rhode Island	Registration with the Division of Tax is required. Form N is required of all exempt organizations. Those soliciting funds in the state must file Forms 115-1-77 and 115-2-78. $75 fee.
South Carolina	Registration is required annually with the Division of Public Charities. Exempt organizations should file Form SC990 (there are some exceptions). $50 fee.
Tennessee	Copy of Form 990-PF must be filed with the attorney general by those who file 990-PF with the federal government. Those soliciting donations from the public must file a tax-exempt organization report with the attorney general. $50 initial fee; subsequently fees range from $100 to $300, depending on receipts.
Texas	A copy of IRS determination letter must be filed with the Franchise Tax Board. Fees range from $150 to $250, depending on recepits.
Utah	Those with unrelated business income must file Form TC-20. All exempt organizations must file an affidavit with the Tax Commission describing the purpose and nature of the organization. $100 fee.
Vermont	A copy of the IRS determination letter must be filed with Vermont Department of Taxes. A status report must be filed with the Corporations Division every fifth year by all exempt organizations.

(Continued)

TABLE E.1

State Registration and Filing Requirements (*Continued*)

State or District	Registration and Filing Requirements
Virginia	Form 500 for those with unrelated business income and Form 990 with Office of Consumer Affairs for those soliciting contributions from the public. Fees range from $30 to $325, depending on previous year's receipts.
Washington	Form Cho-1 must be filed by all those soliciting funds in the state unless the solicitation is for religious or political purposes or solicitation is done by all volunteers and less than $5,000 in gross revenue is raised. $20 initial fee; $10 annually thereafter.
West Virginia	Form CNT-112 for those with unrelated business income. All exempt organizations must file the Charitable Registration Statement and a copy of Form 990 and 990 Schedule A. Fees range from $15 to $50, depending on receipts.
Wisconsin	Form 308 is required of those with contributions of more than $4,000 and employing no paid fundraiser. Those that file federal Form 990-T must file Form 4-T. All corporations registered with the secretary of state must file Form 17, an annual report. $15 fee.
Wyoming	An annual report must be filed with the secretary of state by all exempt organizations. No fee.

Sources: *Mary F. Foster, Howard Becker, and Richard J. Terrano, 1998 Miller GAAP for Not-for-Profit Organizations Plus Tax and Regulatory Reporting (Orlando, Fla.: Harcourt Brace, 1998), and AAFRC Trust for Philanthropy, New York.*

Resource F

National Taxonomy of Exempt Entities: Activity Codes

THIS RESOURCE describes the original version of the National Taxonomy of Exempt Entities (NTEE), which is currently being used by the IRS and the National Center for Charitable Statistics (NCCS) in a slightly condensed version known as NTEE Core Codes (NTEE-CC) for classifying tax-exempt organizations. The adaptation of NTEE presented here is based on the NTEE version used by the Foundation Center (FC) in New York to classify over eighty thousand grants made by various foundations to not-for-profit organizations. In order to maintain consistency with FC grants classification, we have retained the same codes for the same program services (or grants in the case of the Foundation Center). However, we have dropped several codes used by the FC that are applicable to organizational classification only and thus not applicable to program services.

The purpose of the NTEE presented here is to provide a common language and a simple coding scheme to identify the programs and services of most not-for-profit organizations. The NCCS is developing a program services classification system that is linked to the NTEE and can be used to code programs in a standard way. Use of the system will create standard descriptions for nonprofit programs and allow comparisons. The system should be available soon on the NCCS Web site, http://nccs.urban.org.

This FC version of the NTEE has a simple conceptual design: a two-part, three-character alphanumeric code (XXX). The first character is a letter of the alphabet (A through Z), which identifies the *major service group* to which an agency's program belongs. The next two characters (consisting of two numbers or a number and a letter) indicate the specific program *activity* within that major service group. For example, the code A45 represents major service group A (arts, culture, humanities) and program activity 45 (painting). So any agency that provides a program in painting will code the program

A45. A not-for-profit organization using the UCOA presented in Chapter Five and providing a program in painting would code salary expenses allocable to the program as 7120-A45, where 7120 identifies the relevant expense account (Other salaries and wages) and A45 identifies painting as the program activity for which the salary expenses were incurred.

Major Service Groups

The following is a list of the twenty-six major service groups:

A   Arts, culture, humanities

B   Education

C   Environmental improvement and protection

D   Animals

E   Health, general and rehabilitative

F   Mental health, crisis intervention

G   Diseases, medical disciplines

H   Medical research

I   Crime, courts, legal services

J   Employment

K   Food, nutrition, agriculture

L   Housing, shelter

M   Public safety, disaster preparedness and relief

N   Recreation and sports

O   Youth development

P   Human services, other

Q   International affairs

R   Civil rights, social action, advocacy

S   Community development

T   Philanthropy, volunteerism

U   Science

V   Social sciences

W   Public affairs

X   Religion

Y   Mutual aid

Z   Unknown, unclassifiable

Common Activity Codes

Several program service categories are common to all major service groups. Advocacy, research, ethics, and fundraising are examples. For this reason the NTEE assigns *common activity codes* to these activities. Common activity codes are fixed two-digit codes—they are the same for all major service groups. The common activity codes are

01   Alliance, advocacy

02   Management, technical assistance

04   Administration, regulation

05   Research

06   Public policy

07   Reform

08   Ethics

11   Single organization support

12   Fundraising

13   Equal rights

14   Information services

15   Public education

16   Volunteer services

In addition, the number 99 under each major service group is reserved for use when you are not able to find an appropriate program or activity code but you know the major service group. The 99 stands for "not elsewhere classified" (NEC). Thus A99, B99, and C99 are used for arts, culture, humanities NEC, education NEC, and environmental improvement and protection NEC, respectively.

Table F.1 shows the relationship between the major service group categories and the program activities common to them all and provides an easy reference to relevant codes.

TABLE F.1

National Taxonomy of Exempt Entities: Common Activity Codes

Program Activity Common to All Major Service Groups

Major Service Group	Alliance, Advocacy (01)	Management, Technical Assistance (02)	Administration, Regulation (04)	Research (05)	Public Policy (06)	Reform (07)	Ethics (08)	Single Organization Support (11)	Fundraising (12)	Equal Rights (13)	Information Services (14)	Public Education (15)	Volunteer Services (16)
A—Arts, Culture, Humanities	A01	A02	A04	A05	A06	A07	A08	A11	A12	A13	A14	A15	A16
B—Education	B01	B02	B04	B05	B06	B07	B08	B11	B12	B13	B14	B15	B16
C—Environmental Improvement and Protection	C01	C02	C04	C05	C06	C07	C08	C11	C12	C13	C14	C15	C16
D—Animals	D01	D02	D04	D05	D06	D07	D08	D11	D12	D13	D14	D15	D16
E—Health, General and Rehabilitative	E01	E02	E04	E05	E06	E07	E08	E11	E12	E13	E14	E15	E16
F—Mental Health, Crisis Intervention	F01	F02	F04	F05	F06	F07	F08	F11	F12	F13	F14	F15	F16
G—Diseases, Medical Disciplines	G01	G02	G04	G05	G06	G07	G08	G11	G12	G13	G14	G15	G16
H—Medical Research	H01	H02	H04	H05	H06	H07	H08	H11	H12	H13	H14	H15	H16
I—Crime, Courts, Legal Services	I01	I02	I04	I05	I06	I07	I08	I11	I12	I13	I14	I15	I16
J—Employment	J01	J02	J04	J05	J06	J07	J08	J11	J12	J13	J14	J15	J16
K—Food, Nutrition, Agriculture	K01	K02	K04	K05	K06	K07	K08	K11	K12	K13	K14	K15	K16
L—Housing, Shelter	L01	L02	L04	L05	L06	L07	L08	L11	L12	L13	L14	L15	L16
M—Public Safety, Disaster Preparedness and Relief	M01	M02	M04	M05	M06	M07	M08	M11	M12	M13	M14	M15	M16
N—Recreation and Sports	N01	N02	N04	N05	N06	N07	N08	N11	N12	N13	N14	N15	N16
O—Youth Development	O01	O02	O04	O05	O06	O07	O08	O11	O12	O13	O14	O15	O16

TABLE F.1

National Taxonomy of Exempt Entities: Common Activity Codes (*Continued*)

Major Service Group	Alliance, Advocacy (01)	Management, Technical Assistance (02)	Administration, Regulation (04)	Research (05)	Public Policy (06)	Reform (07)	Ethics (08)	Single Organization Support (11)	Fundraising (12)	Equal Rights (13)	Information Services (14)	Public Education (15)	Volunteer Services (16)
					Program Activity Common to All Major Service Groups								
P—Human Services, Other	P01	P02	P04	P05	P06	P07	P08	P11	P12	P13	P14	P15	P16
Q—International Affairs	Q01	Q02	Q04	Q05	Q06	Q07	Q08	Q11	Q12	Q13	Q14	Q15	Q16
R—Civil Rights, Social Action, Advocacy	R01	R02	R04	R05	R06	R07	R08	R11	R12	R13	R14	R15	R16
S—Community Development	S01	S02	S04	S05	S06	S07	S08	S11	S12	S13	S14	S15	S16
T—Philanthropy, Volunteerism	T01	T02	T04	T05	T06	T07	T08	T11	T12	T13	T14	T15	T16
U—Science	U01	U02	U04	U05	U06	U07	U08	U11	U12	U13	U14	U15	U16
V—Social Sciences	V01	V02	V04	V05	V06	V07	V08	V11	V12	V13	V14	V15	V16
W—Public Affairs	W01	W02	W04	W05	W06	W07	W08	W11	W12	W13	W14	W15	W16
X—Religion	X01	X02	X04	X05	X06	X07	X08	X11	X12	X13	X14	X15	X16
Y—Mutual Aid	Y01	YB02	Y04	Y05	Y06	Y07	Y08	Y11	Y12	Y13	Y14	Y15	Y16
Z—Unknown, Unclassifiable	Z01	ZB02	Z04	Z05	Z06	Z07	Z08	Z11	Z12	Z13	Z14	Z15	Z16

How to Use NTEE

An index of NTEE codes appears at the end of this resource. It should be relatively easy to find the correct NTEE code for your organization's programs. First use the alphabetical list of major service groups listed earlier under "Major Service Groups" to find the category into which the program falls. Then go to the corresponding section of the index of NTEE codes and find the code that best describes the program. For example, if your agency provides a program for recycling, you will identify C (Environmental improvement and protection) as the major service group. Then, looking through the C listings in the index of NTEE codes, you will find C27 (Recycling).

If your agency provides one or more program service activities common to all major service groups, refer to both the alphabetical list of major service groups and the list shown earlier under "Common Activity Codes" (Table F.1) to find the appropriate code for such activities. For example, an "employment research" program will be coded J05, where J identifies employment and 05 designates research.

Some multiservice not-for-profit organizations provide program services in more than one major service group area. In these instances they will look under different major service groups to identify specific programs. For example, a multiservice agency might provide the following services:

Program Service	NTEE Code
Dropout prevention	B91
Substance abuse prevention	F21
Delinquency prevention	I21
Domestic violence prevention	I71
Nutrition	K40
Youth development services, general	O50
Foster care	P32

Most organizations will be able to identify their program services using NTEE.

Index of National Taxonomy of Exempt Entities (Edited)

A00: Arts, Culture, Humanities (ACH)

A23—Cultural, ethnic awareness

A24—Folk arts

A25—Arts education

A30—Media, communications

A31—Film, video

A32—Television

A33—Journalism and publishing

A34—Radio

A40—Visual arts

A41—Architecture

A42—Photography

A43—Sculpture

A44—Design

A45—Painting

A46—Drawing

A47—Ceramic arts

A48—Art conservation

A5A—Planetarium

A50—Museums

A51—Museums, art

A52—Museums, children's

A53—Museums, ethnic, folk arts

A54—Museums, history

A55—Museums, marine, maritime

A56—Museums, natural history

A57—Museums, science and technology

A58—Museums, sports, hobby

A59—Museums, specialized

A6A—Opera

A6B—Music, choral

A6C—Music, ensembles and groups

A6D—Music, composition

A6E—Performing arts, education

A6F—Performing arts, multimedia

A6G—Circus arts

A60—Performing arts

A61—Performing arts centers

A62—Dance

A63—Ballet

A64—Choreography

A65—Theater

A66—Theater, playwriting

A67—Theater, musical

A68—Music

A69—Orchestra, symphony

A70—Humanities

A71—Art history

A72—History and archaeology

A73—Language, classical

A74—Language, foreign

A75—Language and linguistics

A76—Literature

A77—Philosophy, ethics

A78—Theology

A80—Historical activities

A82—Historic preservation, historical societies

A83—Genealogy

A84—Centennials and commemorations

A85—Veterans' and war memorials

A90—Arts, services

A91—Arts, artist's services

A99—ACH not elsewhere classified

B00: Education (ED)

B2R—Elementary, secondary school reform

B20—Elementary, secondary education

B21—Early childhood education

B22—Child development, education

B24—Elementary school, education

B25—Secondary school, education

B26—Education, bilingual programs

B27—Education, gifted students

B28—Education, special

B3R—Vocational school reform

B30—Vocational education

B31—Vocational education, postsecondary

B32—Vocational school, secondary

B4R—Higher education reform

B40—Higher education

B41—College, community, junior education

B42—College, four-year liberal arts education

B43—University education

B5A—Public health school, education

B5B—Health sciences school, education

B5R—Graduate school reform

B50—Graduate, professional education

B51—Business school, education

B52—Dental school, education

B53—Law school, education

B54—Medical school, education

B55—Nursing school, education

B56—Teacher school, education

B57—Engineering school, education

B58—Theological school, education

B59—Social work school, education

B60—Adult, continuing education

B61—Adult education, literacy and basic skills

B63—Education, English as a second language

B64—Continuing education, lifelong learning

B70—Libraries, library science

B71—Libraries, public

B72—Libraries, school

B73—Libraries, academic, research

B74—Libraries, medical

B75—Libraries, law

B76—Libraries, special

B77—Archives

B80—Student services

B82—Scholarships, financial aid

B83—Students, sororities, fraternities

B84—Education, alumni groups

B91—Dropout prevention

B92—Reading

B93—Education, testing

B94—Education, parent-teacher associations

B95—Education, community, cooperative

B99—ED not elsewhere classified

C00: Environmental Improvement and Protection (ENV)

C20—Pollution control

C21—Air pollution

C22—Water pollution

C23—Noise pollution

C24—Radiation control

C25—Toxics

C26—Waste management

C27—Recycling

C28—Global warming

C30—Natural resource conservation and protection

C32—Water resources

C34—Land resources

C35—Energy

C36—Forests

C38—Plant conservation

C40—Botanical, landscape

C41—Botanical gardens

C42—Horticulture and garden clubs

C43—Landscaping

C50—Environment, beautification programs

C60—Environmental education

C99—ENV not elsewhere classified

D00: Animals (ANI)

D20—Animal welfare

D21—Animal population control

D30—Wildlife preservation and protection

D31—Wildlife, endangered species

D32—Wildlife, bird preserves

D33—Wildlife, fisheries

D34—Wildlife, sanctuaries

D40—Veterinary medicine

D41—Veterinary medicine, hospital

D50—Zoos, zoological societies

D51—Aquariums

D60—Animals, wildlife, special services

D61—Animals, wildlife, training

D62—Animals, wildlife, exhibition

D63—Animals, wildlife, clubs

D99—ANI not elsewhere classified

E00: Health, General and Rehabilitative (HC)

E20—Medical care, inpatient care

E21—Medicine, medical care, community health systems

E22—Hospitals, general

E24—Hospitals, specialty

E26—Hospitals, intensive care

E30—Medical care, outpatient care

E31—HMOs

E32—Health care, clinics and centers

E33—Health care, infants

E34—Dental care

E35—Optometry and vision screening

E36—Podiatry

E38—Burn centers program

E39—Health care, rural areas

E40—Health care, reproductive health

E41—Obstetrics, gynecology, birthing program

E42—Family planning

E43—Abortion program

E44—Health care, fertility

E45—Health care, sterilization

E46—Health care, prenatal care

E47—Health education, sexuality

E50—Medical care, rehabilitation

E51—Physical therapy

E52—Art and music therapy

E56—Speech and hearing programs

E60—Health care, support services

E61—Health care, blood supply

E62—Health care, emergency transport services

E63—Health care, emergency medical services

E65—Health care, organ, tissue banks

E66—Pharmacology

E70—Public health

E71—Public health, sexually transmitted diseases

E72—Public health, communicable diseases

E73—Public health, occupational health

E74—Public health, epidemiology

E80—Health care, general and financing

E81—Health care, insurance

E82—Health care, cost containment

E83—Health care, financing

E84—Health care, HMO financing

E85—Bioethics

E86—Health care, patient services

E87—Health care, counseling, pastoral care

E90—Nursing care

E91—Nursing home, convalescent facility

E92—Health care, home services

E99—HC not elsewhere classified

F00: Mental Health, Crisis Intervention (MH)

F20—Substance abuse, program

F21—Substance abuse, prevention

F22—Substance abuse, treatment

F30—Mental health, treatment

F31—Hospitals, psychiatric

F33—Mental health, residential care

F34—Mental health, transitional care

F40—Crisis services, hotlines

F41—Crisis services, suicide prevention

F42—Crisis services, rape victim program

F50—Mental health, addictions

F52—Smoking-related

F53—Eating disorders

F54—Gambling addiction

F60—Mental health, counseling, support groups

F61—Mental health, grief, bereavement counseling

F70—Mental health, disorders

F71—Mental health, stress

F72—Mental health, depression

F73—Mental health, schizophrenia

F99—MH not elsewhere classified

G00: Diseases, Medical Disciplines (D, MD)

G20—Birth defects, genetics

G21—Hemophilia

G22—Sickle cell disease

G23—Cerebral palsy

G24—Cystic fibrosis

G25—Down's syndrome

G30—Cancer

G31—Leukemia

G40—Organ diseases

G41—Eye diseases

G42—Ear and throat diseases

G43—Heart and circulatory diseases

G44—Kidney diseases

G45—Lung diseases

G46—Skin disorders

G47—Liver disorders

G48—Brain disorders

G50—Nerve, muscle, bone diseases

G51—Arthritis

G52—Muscular dystrophy

G53—Multiple sclerosis

G54—Epilepsy

G55—Spine disorders

G56—Myasthenia gravis

G60—Allergies

G61—Asthma

G70—Digestive diseases

G8A—Diseases, rare

G81—AIDS

G82—Alcoholism

G83—Alzheimer's disease

G84—Autism

G85—Diabetes

G86—Learning disorders

G87—Parasitic diseases

G88—Tropical diseases

G89—Lupus

G9A—Radiology

G9B—Surgery

G9C—Immunology

G9D—Orthopedics

G91—Anesthesiology

G92—Biomedicine

G93—Chiropractic

G94—Geriatrics

G95—Internal medicine

G96—Neuroscience

G97—Pathology

G98—Pediatrics

G99—D, MD not elsewhere classified

H00: Medical Research (MR)

H20—Birth defects, genetics research

H21—Hemophilia research

H22—Sickle cell research

H23—Cerebral palsy research

H24—Cystic fibrosis research

H25—Down's syndrome research

H30—Cancer research

H31—Leukemia research

H40—Organ research

H41—Eye research

H42—Ear and throat research

H43—Heart and circulatory research

H44—Kidney research

H45—Lung research

H46—Skin disorders research

H47—Liver research

H48—Brain research

H50—Nerve, muscle, bone research

H51—Arthritis research

H52—Muscular dystrophy research

H53—Multiple sclerosis research

H54—Epilepsy research

H55—Spine disorders research

H56—Myasthenia gravis research

H60—Allergies research

H61—Asthma research

H70—Digestive disorders research

H8A—Diseases, rare, research

H80—Medical research, named diseases

H81—AIDS research

H82—Alcoholism research

H83—Alzheimer's disease research

H84—Autism research

H85—Diabetes research

H86—Learning disorders research

H87—Parasitic diseases research

H88—Tropical diseases research

H89—Lupus research

H9A—Radiology research

H9B—Surgery research

H9C—Immunology research

H9D—Orthopedics research

H90—Medical specialty research

H91—Anesthesiology research

H92—Biomedicine research

H93—Chiropractic research

H94—Geriatrics research

H95—Internal medicine research

H96—Neuroscience research

H97—Pathology research

H98—Pediatrics research

H99—MR not elsewhere classified

I00: Crime, Courts, Legal Services (CRI)

I20—Criminal justice, violence prevention

I21—Delinquency prevention

I22—Gun control

I23—Drunk driving

I24—Criminal justice, law enforcement, missing persons

I30—Correctional facilities program

I31—Offenders, ex-offenders, transitional care

I40—Offenders, ex-offenders, rehabilitation

I41—Offenders, ex-offenders, probation, parole

I42—Offenders, ex-offenders, bail issues

I43—Offenders, ex-offenders, services, general

I44—Offenders, ex-offenders, prison alternatives

I50—Courts, judicial administration

I51—Dispute resolution

I60—Criminal justice, law enforcement, police agencies

I70—Abuse prevention

I71—Domestic violence prevention

I72—Child abuse prevention

I73—Sexual abuse prevention

I80—Legal services

I81—Legal services, tenant law

I82—Legal services, guardianship

I83—Legal services, public interest law

I99—CRI not elsewhere classified

J00: Employment (EMP)

J20—Employment, services

J21—Employment, job counseling

J22—Employment, training

J30—Vocational rehabilitation, disabled, aging

J31—Employment, homebound work

J32—Goodwill Industries

J33—Employment, sheltered workshops

J99—EMP not elsewhere classified

K00: Food, Nutrition, Agriculture (F&A)

K20—Agriculture

K21—Agriculture, farm cooperatives program

K22—Agriculture, irrigation program

K24—Agriculture, soil, water-related

K25—Agriculture, farmlands

K26—Agriculture, livestock-related

K28—Agriculture, farm bureaus and granges

K30—Food services, general

K31—Food banks

K32—Food distribution, groceries on wheels

K33—Food services, commodity distribution

K34—Food services, congregate meals

K35—Food services, agency eatery

K36—Food distribution, meals on wheels

K40—Nutrition

K50—Home economics

K99—F&A not elsewhere classified

L00: Housing, Shelter (HOU)

L20—Housing and shelter, development

L21—Housing and shelter, public housing

L22—Housing and shelter, aging

L23—Housing and shelter, single-resident occupancy

L25—Housing and shelter, rehabilitation

L30—Housing and shelter, search services

L40—Housing and shelter, temporary shelter

L41—Housing and shelter, homeless

L50—Housing and shelter, owner, renter issues

L51—Housing and shelter, homeowners

L52—Housing and shelter, tenants

L53—Housing and shelter, co-ops

L81—Housing and shelter, repairs

L82—Housing and shelter, expense aid

L99—HOU not elsewhere classified

M00: Public Safety, Disaster Preparedness and Relief (SAF)

M20—Disasters, preparedness and services

M21—Disasters, civil defense

M22—Disasters, floods

M23—Disasters, search and rescue

M24—Disasters, fire prevention, control

M40—Public safety, education

M41—Public safety, first-aid training

M42—Public safety, automotive safety

M43—Public safety, poisons

M99—SAF not elsewhere classified

N00: Recreation and Sports (REC)

N20—Camps

N30—Recreation, community facilities program

N31—Recreation, centers program

N32—Parks, playgrounds

N40—Athletics and sports, training

N41—Athletics and sports, school programs

N42—Athletics and sports, academies

N50—Recreation, social clubs

N51—Recreation, country clubs

N52—Recreation, fairs and festivals

N6A—Golf

N60—Amateur leagues

N61—Fishing, hunting

N62—Basketball

N63—Baseball

N64—Soccer

N65—Football

N66—Racquet sports

N67—Water sports

N68—Winter sports

N69—Equestrian sports

N70—Amateur competition

N71—Olympics

N72—Special Olympics

N80—Professional leagues

N99—REC not elsewhere classified

O00: Youth Development (YD)

O20—Youth development, centers and clubs

O30—Youth development, adult and child programs

O32—Youth development, intergenerational programs

O50—Youth development services, general

O51—Youth development, community service clubs, programs

O52—Youth development, agriculture

O53—Youth development, business

O54—Youth development, citizenship

O55—Youth development, religion

O99—YD not elsewhere classified

P00: Human Services, Other (HS)

P28—Neighborhood centers program

P29—Thrift shops program

P30—Children and youth services, general

P31—Adoption

P32—Foster care

P33—Children, day care

P34—Children's services, general

P35—Youth, pregnancy prevention

P36—Youth services, general

P37—Child development services, general

P40—Family services, general

P41—Parent education program

P42—Single parents' program

P43—Domestic violence

P44—Home, homemaker aid

P45—Adolescent parents program

P46—Family services, counseling

P50—Human services, personal social services

P51—Human services, financial counseling

P52—Human services, assistance program

P53—Human services, self-help groups

P54—Human services, mind, body enrichment

P58—Human services, gift distribution

P60—Human services, emergency aid

P61—Human services, travelers' aid

P62—Human services, victim aid

P70—Residential, custodial care

P71—Residential, custodial care, special day care

P72—Residential, custodial care, halfway house

P73—Residential, custodial care, group home

P74—Hospices

P75—Senior continuing care community

P80—Human services, special populations

P81—Aging services

P82—Mentally disabled services

P83—Women's services

P84—Minorities', immigrants' services

P85—Homeless, human services

P99—HS not elsewhere classified

Q00: International Affairs (IA)

Q20—International affairs, goodwill promotion

Q21—International exchange, arts

Q22—International exchange, students

Q23—International exchange

Q30—International development

Q31—International agricultural development

Q32—International economic development

Q33—International relief

Q40—Peace

Q41—Arms control

Q42—International affairs, UN-related

Q43—International affairs, national security

Q44—International conflict resolution

Q50—Foreign policy

Q51—International economics, trade policy

Q70—Human rights, international

Q71—International migration, refugee issues

Q99—IA not elsewhere classified

R00: Civil Rights, Social Action, Advocacy (CR)

R20—Civil rights, advocacy

R21—Civil rights, immigrants

R22—Civil rights, minorities

R23—Civil rights, disabled

R24—Civil rights, women

R25—Civil rights, aging

R26—Civil rights, gays, lesbians

R30—Race, intergroup relations

R40—Voter education, rights

R60—Civil liberties, advocacy

R61—Reproductive rights

R62—Civil liberties, right to life

R63—Civil liberties, First Amendment

R64—Civil liberties, freedom of information

R65—Civil liberties, freedom of religion

R66—Civil liberties, right to privacy

R67—Civil liberties, right to die

R68—Civil liberties, due process

R69—Civil liberties, death penalty issues

R99—CR not elsewhere classified

S00: Community Development (CD)

S20—Community development, neighborhood development

S21—Community development, citizen coalitions

S22—Community development, neighborhood associations

S25—Community development, public, private ventures

S30—Economic development

S31—Urban development

S32—Rural development

S33—Economic development, visitor, convention bureau

S40—Business- and industry-related

S41—Community development, business promotion

S43—Community development, small businesses

S47—Community development, real estate

S50—Nonprofit management

S99—CD not elsewhere classified

T00: Philanthropy, Volunteerism (P&V)

T32—Grant making

T40—Volunteerism promotion

T50—Philanthropy and volunteerism, general

T70—Federated giving programs, nonsectarian

T71—Roman Catholic federated giving programs

T72—Jewish federated giving programs

T73—Protestant federated giving programs

T74—Religious federated giving programs

T99—P&V not elsewhere classified

U00: Science (SCI)

U20—Science, general

U21—Marine science

U30—Physical, earth sciences

U31—Astronomy

U32—Space, aviation

U33—Chemistry

U34—Mathematics

U35—Physics

U36—Geology

U40—Engineering and technology

U41—Computer science

U42—Engineering

U50—Biological sciences

U51—Anatomy, human

U52—Botany

U53—Anatomy, animal

U99—SCI not elsewhere classified

V00: Social Sciences (SOC)

V20—Social science, general

V21—Anthropology and sociology

V22—Economics

V23—Psychology, behavioral science

V24—Political science

V25—Population studies

V26—Law, international law

V30—Social science, interdisciplinary studies

V31—Black studies

V32—Women's studies

V33—Ethnic studies

V34—Urban studies

V35—International studies

V36—Gerontology

V37—Labor studies

V38—Rural studies

V39—Poverty studies

V40—Paranormal, mystic studies

V99—SOC not elsewhere classified

W00: Public Affairs (PAF)

W20—Government, public administration

W21—Welfare policy and reform

W22—Public affairs, finance

W23—Public affairs, election regulation

W24—Public affairs, citizen participation

W25—Public affairs, political organizations

W30—Military, veterans' program

W40—Transportation

W50—Telecommunications

W52—Telecommunications, electronic messaging services

W60—Financial services

W61—Credit union program

W70—Leadership development

W80—Utilities

W90—Consumer protection

W99—PAF not elsewhere classified

X00: Religion (REL)

X20—Christian religious programs

X21—Protestant religious programs

X22—Roman Catholic religious programs

X23—Orthodox Catholic religious programs

X24—Mormon religious programs

X30—Jewish religious programs

X40—Islam

X50—Buddhism

X60—Confucianism

X70—Hinduism

X80—Bahai

X90—Religion, interfaith issues

X99—REL not elsewhere classified

Y00: Mutual Aid (MAS)

Y20—Insurance, providers

Y21—Insurance, group

Y22—Insurance, benevolent life

Y23—Insurance, mutual

Y24—Insurance, unemployment compensation

Y30—Pensions

Y33—Pensions, teacher funds

Y34—Pensions, employee trusts

Y35—Pensions, multiemployer plans

Y40—Fraternal societies

Y99—MAS not elsewhere classified

Z00: Unknown, Unclassifiable

Resource G

Voluntary Standard-Setting and Evaluation Groups for Not-for-Profit Organizations

IN THIS RESOURCE we present *standards* promulgated by three national-level groups and two state-level bodies: the National Charities Information Bureau (NCIB), the Philanthropic Advisory Service (PAS) of the Council of Better Business Bureaus (CBBB), the Evangelical Council for Financial Accountability (ECFA), the Maryland Association of Nonprofit Organizations (MANO), and the Charities Review Council of Minnesota (CRCM).[1]

The Groups

First we give a quick overview of each organization; then we look more closely at their standards.

National Charities Information Bureau

Of the five organizations, NCIB is the oldest—founded in 1918—and probably the most often cited in the media. NCIB's work is based on its *Standards in Philanthropy,* nine statements setting forth twenty-eight specific criteria against which charities are consistently evaluated. The standards represent basic, fundamental requirements of good governance, sound board policies, good management, appropriate fundraising, and wise budgeting. These standards have evolved over many years to reflect the counsel of experts in the field of philanthropy and interested donors, as well as changes in the legal, tax, and accounting regulations. NCIB's standards are regularly monitored by its board of directors and its Standards and Reports Committee, made up of unpaid volunteers committed to sound practices in philanthropy.

NCIB requests information on a standardized form from national charities soliciting donations from the public. Its staff then conducts a detailed review of all information provided and checks against its nine *Standards in Philanthropy* for compliance. Individual reports are created for each organization, noting whether or not the organization meets the standards. The report explicitly mentions which, if any, standards were not met. Individual donors, as well as donor organizations such as foundations, corporations, and local United Ways, use NCIB's reports as a guide to their decisions on grant making. NCIB's presence on the Internet at http://www.give.org has been growing in importance as a way of disseminating useful information about charities.

Philanthropic Advisory Service of CBBB

The Philanthropic Advisory Service of the CBBB promotes ethical standards for the charitable community, provides information to the public on charitable organizations, and educates individual and corporate donors on wise giving. It encourages charities to accept responsibility for self-regulation and to adhere to the ethical practices outlined in the CBBB's *Standards for Charitable Solicitations.* These standards were developed over several years with input from executives of charities, professional fundraisers, accountants, government regulators, corporate contribution officers, and CBBB professionals.

In 1996 PAS began posting complete texts of all currently available reports of the most frequently asked-about national charities on the Better Business Bureau's World Wide Web server (www.bbb.org). These detailed reports include information on a national charity's programs, finances, governance, and fundraising efforts, as well as an explanation as to whether the charity meets the twenty-three CBBB *Standards for Charitable Solicitations.*

The twenty-three voluntary CBBB Standards for Charitable Solicitations were first issued in 1974 and last updated in 1981. The Council of Better Business Bureaus' Foundation recently announced plans to begin a revision of these guidelines to ensure their continuing effectiveness. A number of factors have prompted this revision, including but not limited to the growing public interest in charity accountability, changes in nonprofit accounting guidelines, new forms of fundraising such as Internet-based appeals, the growth of cause-related marketing, and the rise in importance of both local charities and organizations that are international in scope. All existing provisions will be reviewed to consider their continued relevancy and effectiveness in addressing ethical issues facing donors and charitable organizations. CBBB is seeking broad input from the charitable community and other interested parties as the standards review process moves forward.

Evangelical Council for Financial Accountability

Since its creation in 1979, ECFA has grown to over 850 member organizations whose collective income is in excess of $5 billion per year. ECFA's accreditation is granted annually and includes a comprehensive review of each organization's representation that it adheres to ECFA's *Seven Standards of Responsible Stewardship.* Each year ECFA has conducted a random site review of a small percentage of its membership. This is in addition to site reviews for high-profile new member applications or on-site compliance reviews of organizations suspected of violating one or more ECFA standards.

ECFA draws its technical expertise from its Standards Committee of experienced professionals, who serve at the pleasure of the board of directors. The board is a diverse collection of prominent high-achievers in their respective fields. The Standards Committee is made up principally of attorneys, certified public accountants, professional fundraisers, and academics, all of whom volunteer their time. A paid staff executes the daily operations of the agency. The organization's structure is a model of effective "peer regulation" with appropriate checks and balances to prevent the abuse of oversight authority.

ECFA grants the use of its seal for display by its member organizations in fundraising and other literature. The seal is a signal to the donor public that the member organization conforms to ECFA's seven standards.

Maryland Association of Nonprofit Organizations

The Maryland Association of Nonprofit Organizations is a relative newcomer to the field of voluntary standards for not-for-profit organizations. In 1998 MANO announced its new Standards for Excellence program, designed to promote excellence and integrity in not-for-profit management. The centerpiece of this program is its position paper *Standards for Excellence: An Ethics and Accountability Code for the Nonprofit Sector.*

The Standards for Excellence program was developed over two years by a team of volunteers from Maryland's not-for-profit community. Based on fundamental values, such as honesty, fairness, respect, trust, responsibility, and accountability, the Standards cover a broad range of topics and show how not-for-profit organizations should act to be ethical and accountable. The Standards also mandate that organizations have procedures in place to evaluate their programs and that board members disclose any conflicts of interest.

To help charities implement the Standards, MANO is developing model policies and educational materials. In addition, MANO is offering a voluntary certification program based on peer review for not-for-profit organizations that wish to demonstrate they are living up to the Standards. Organizations approved by a team of trained peer reviewers will be awarded a Standards of Excellence seal of approval.

Charities Review Council of Minnesota

The Charities Review Council of Minnesota was founded in 1946 as a statewide, independent not-for-profit organization that develops accountability standards for charities and carries out in-depth reviews based on these standards.

CRCM's standards were revised in 1998 in an extensive process that included the participation of nonprofits, foundations, academics, and community leaders. The council maintains an up-to-date database with information on the more than seven thousand nonprofits registered to solicit funds in Minnesota. The council conducts in-depth reviews, applying the accountability standards to approximately one hundred of the most frequently requested charities annually. The information resulting from these reviews is disseminated to the public via the CRCM Web site (www.crcmn.org), in its semiannual *Giving Guide,* in public presentations, and over the telephone. The council's services are free to the public.

The Standards

We reproduce the standards used by these five groups in Exhibits G.1 through G.5. These standards are significant yardsticks for assessing the financial reporting and accountability of not-for-profit organizations.

EXHIBIT G.1

National Charities Information Bureau Standards in Philanthropy

Standards in Philanthropy

NATIONAL CHARITIES INFORMATION BUREAU

The National Charities Information Bureau was founded in 1918 by a group of national leaders who were concerned that Americans were giving millions of dollars to charitable organizations, particularly war relief organizations, that they knew little or nothing about.

Through the years, NCIB has evolved into an organization that promotes informed giving. NCIB believes that donors are entitled to accurate information about the charitable organizations that seek their support. NCIB also believes that well-informed givers should ask questions and make judgments that will lead to an improved level of performance by charitable organizations.

To help givers and charitable organizations, NCIB collects and analyzes information about charities and evaluates them according to the following Standards.

Source: *Copyright© 2000 by National Charities Information Bureau. Reprinted with permission.*

NCIB Standards in Philanthropy

Governance, Policy and Program Fundamentals

1. *Board Governance*: The board is responsible for policy setting, fiscal guidance, and ongoing governance, and should regularly review the organization's policies, programs and operations. The board should have

   a. an independent, volunteer membership;
   b. a minimum of 5 voting members;
   c. an individual attendance policy;
   d. specific terms of office for its officers and members;
   e. in-person, face-to-face meetings, at least twice a year, evenly spaced, with a majority of voting members in attendance at each meeting;
   f. no fees to members for board service, but payments may be made for costs incurred as a result of board participation;
   g. no more than one paid staff person member, usually the chief staff officer, who shall not chair the board or serve as treasurer;
   h. policy guidelines to avoid material conflicts of interest involving board or staff;
   i. no material conflicts of interest involving board or staff;
   j. a policy promoting pluralism and diversity within the organization's board, staff, and constituencies.

2. *Purpose*: The organization's purpose, approved by the board, should be formally and specifically stated.

3. *Programs*: The organization's activities should be consistent with its statement of purpose.

4. *Information*: Promotion, fund raising, and public information should describe accurately the organization's identity, purpose, programs, and financial needs.

5. *Financial Support and Related Activities*: The board is accountable for all authorized activities generating financial support on the organization's behalf:

   a. fund-raising practices should encourage voluntary giving and should not apply unwarranted pressure;
   b. descriptive and financial information for all substantial income and for all revenue-generating activities conducted by the organization should be disclosed on request;
   c. basic descriptive and financial information for income derived from authorized commercial activities, involving the organization's name, which are conducted by for-profit organizations, should be available. All public promotion of such commercial activity should either include this information or indicate that it is available from the organization.

6. *Use of Funds*: The organization's use of funds should reflect consideration of current and future needs and resources in planning for program continuity. The organization should:

   a. spend at least 60% of annual expenses for program activities;
   b. insure that fund-raising expenses, in relation to fund-raising results, are reasonable over time;
   c. have net assets available for use in the following fiscal year not usually more than twice the current year's expenses or twice the next year's budget, whichever is higher;
   d. not have a persistent deficit in net current assets.

Reporting and Fiscal Fundamentals

7. *Annual Reporting*: An annual report should be available on request, and should include:

   a. an explicit narrative description of the organization's major activities, presented in the same major categories and covering the same fiscal period as the audited financial statements;
   b. a list of board members;
   c. audited financial statements or, at a minimum, a comprehensive financial summary that 1) identifies all revenues in significant categories, 2) reports expenses in the same program, management/general, and fund-raising categories as in the audited financial statements, and 3) reports ending net assets. (When the annual report does not include the full audited financial statements, it should indicate that they are available on request.)

8. *Accountability*: An organization should supply on request complete financial statements which:

   a. are prepared in conformity with generally accepted accounting principles (GAAP), accompanied by a report of an independent certified public accountant, and reviewed by the board; and
   b. fully disclose economic resources and obligations, including transactions with related parties and affiliated organizations, significant events affecting finances, and significant categories of income and expense; and should also supply
   c. a statement of functional allocation of expenses, in addition to such statements required by generally accepted accounting principles to be included among the financial statements;
   d. consolidated or combined financial statements for a national organization operating with affiliates prepared in the foregoing manner.

9. *Budget*: The organization should prepare a detailed annual budget consistent with the major classifications in the audited financial statements, and approved by the board.

Preamble

The support of philanthropic organizations soliciting funds from the general public is based on public trust. The most reliable evaluation of an organization is a detailed review. Yet the organization's compliance with a basic set of Standards can indicate whether it is fulfilling its obligations to contributors, to those who benefit from its programs, and to the general public.

Responsibility for ensuring sound policy guidance and governance and for meeting these basic Standards rests with the governing board, which is answerable to the public.

The National Charities Information Bureau recommends and applies the following nine Standards as common measures of governance and management.

NCIB Standards

Governance, Policy and Program Fundamentals

1. **Board Governance:** The board is responsible for policy setting, fiscal guidance, and ongoing governance, and should regularly review the organization's policies, programs, and operations. The board should have

   a. an independent, volunteer membership;

   b. a minimum of 5 voting members;

   c. an individual attendance policy;

   d. specific terms of office for its officers and members;

   e. in-person, face-to-face meetings, at least twice a year, evenly spaced, with a majority of voting members in attendance at each meeting;

   f. no fees to members for board service, but payments may be made for costs incurred as a result of board participation;

   g. no more than one paid staff person member, usually the chief staff officer, who shall not chair the board or serve as treasurer;

   h. policy guidelines to avoid material conflicts of interest involving board or staff;

   i. no material conflicts of interest involving board or staff;

   j. a policy promoting pluralism and diversity within the organization's board, staff, and constituencies.

2. **Purpose:** The organization's purpose, approved by the board, should be formally and specifically stated.

NCIB Interpretations and Applications

Fiscal guidance includes responsibility for investment management decisions, for internal accounting controls, and for short and long-term budgeting decisions.

The ability of individual board members to make independent decisions on behalf of the organization is critical. Existence of relationships that could interfere with this independence compromises the board.

Many organizations need more than five members on the board. Five, however, is seen as the minimum required for adequate governance.

Board membership should be more than honorary, and should involve active participation in board meetings.

Many board responsibilities may be carried out through committee actions, and such additional active board involvement should be encouraged. No level of committee involvement, however, can substitute for the face-to-face interaction of the full board in reviewing the organization's policy-making and program operations. As a rule, the full board should meet to discuss and ratify the organization's decisions and actions at least twice a year. If, however, the organization has an executive committee of at least five voting members, then three meetings of the executive committee, evenly spaced, with a majority in attendance, can substitute for one of the two full board meetings.

Organizations should recruit board members most qualified, regardless of their financial status, to join in making policy decisions. Costs related to a board member's participation could include such items as travel and daycare arrangements. Situations where board members derive financial benefits from board service should be avoided.

In all instances where an organization's business or policy decisions can result in direct or indirect financial or personal benefit to a member of the board or staff, the decisions in question must be explicitly reviewed by the board with the members concerned absent.

Organizations vary widely in their ability to demonstrate pluralism and diversity. Every organization should establish a policy, consistent with its mission statement, that fosters such inclusiveness. An affirmative action program is an example of fulfilling this requirement.

The formal or abridged statement of purpose should appear with some frequency in organization publications and presentations.

3. **Programs:** The organization's activities should be consistent with its statement of purpose.

4. **Information:** Promotion, fund raising, and public information should describe accurately the organization's identity, purpose, programs, and financial needs.

Not every communication from an organization need contain all this descriptive information, but each one should include all accurate information relevant to its primary message.

There should be no material omissions, exaggerations of fact, misleading photographs, or any other practice which would tend to create a false impression or misunderstanding.

5. **Financial Support and Related Activities:** The board is accountable for all authorized activities generating financial support on the organization's behalf:

   a. fund-raising practices should encourage voluntary giving and should not apply unwarranted pressure;

   b. descriptive and financial information for all substantial income and for all revenue-generating activities conducted by the organization should be disclosed on request;

   Such activities include, but are not limited to, fees for service, related and unrelated business ventures, and for-profit subsidiaries.

   c. basic descriptive and financial information for income derived from authorized commercial activities, involving the organization's name, which are conducted by for-profit organizations, should be available. All public promotion of such commercial activity should either include this information or indicate that it is available from the organization.

   Basic descriptive and financial information may vary depending on the promotional activity involved. Common elements would include, for example, the campaign time frame, the total amount or the percentage to be received by the organization, whether the organization's contributor list is made available to the for-profit company, and the campaign expenses directly incurred by the organization.

6. **Use of Funds:** The organization's use of funds should reflect consideration of current and future needs and resources in planning for program continuity. The organization should:

   a. spend at least 60% of annual expenses for program activities;

   b. insure that fund-raising expenses, in relation to fund-raising results, are reasonable over time;

   Fund-raising methods available to organizations vary widely and often have very different costs. Overall, an organization's fund-raising expense should be reasonable in relation to the contributions received, which could include indirect contributions (such as federated campaign support), bequests (generally averaged over five years), and government grants.

   c. have net assets available for use in the following fiscal year not usually more than twice the current year's expenses or twice the next year's budget, whichever is higher;

   Assets available for use are essentially unrestricted and temporarily restricted net assets (excluding property, plant and equipment used in operations, less related liabilities, and assets restricted to investment in property, plant and equipment) adjusted to include deferred income and exclude long-term debt.

   Unless specifically told otherwise, most contributors believe that their contributions are being applied to current program needs identified by the organization. Organizations may accumulate funds in the interest of prudent management. Accumulation of such funds in excess of the Standard may be justified in special circumstances.

   In all cases the needs of the constituency served should be the most important factor in determining and evaluating the appropriate level of available net assets.

   d. not have a persistent deficit in net current assets.

   An organization which incurs a deficit in net current assets should make every attempt to remedy the deficit as soon as possible. Net current assets are essentially unrestricted and temporarily restricted net assets, excluding property, plant and equipment used in operations, less related liabilities, and assets restricted to investment in property, plant and equipment.

   Any organization sustaining a substantial and persistent deficit is at least in demonstrable financial danger, and may even be fiscally irresponsible. In its evaluations, NCIB will take into account evidence of remedial efforts.

Reporting and Fiscal Fundamentals

7. **Annual Reporting:** An annual report should be available on request, and should include

   a. an explicit narrative description of the organization's major activities, presented in the same major categories and covering the same fiscal period as the audited financial statements;

   b. a list of board members;

   c. audited financial statements or, at a minimum, a comprehensive financial summary that 1) identifies all revenues in significant categories, 2) reports expenses in the same program, management/general, and fund-raising categories as in the audited financial statements, and 3) reports ending net assets. (When the annual report does not include the full audited financial statements, it should indicate that they are available on request.)

8. **Accountability:** An organization should supply on request complete financial statements which

   a. are prepared in conformity with generally accepted accounting principles (GAAP), accompanied by a report of an independent certified public accountant, and reviewed by the board;

   and

   b. fully disclose economic resources and obligations, including transactions with related parties and affiliated organizations, significant events affecting finances, and significant categories of income and expense;

   and should also supply

   c. a statement of functional allocation of expenses, in addition to such statements required by generally accepted accounting principles to be included among the financial statements;

   d. consolidated or combined financial statements for a national organization operating with affiliates prepared in the foregoing manner.

9. **Budget:** The organization should prepare a detailed annual budget consistent with the major classifications in the audited financial statements, and approved by the board.

Where an equivalent package of documentation, identified as such, is available and routinely supplied upon request, it may substitute for an annual report.

The listing of board members should include some identifying information on each member.

In particular, financial summaries or extracts presented separately from the audited financial statements should be clearly related to the information in these statements and consistent with them.

To be able to make its financial analysis, NCIB may require more detailed information regarding the interpretation, applications and validation of GAAP guidelines used in the audit. Accountants can vary widely in their interpretations of GAAP guidelines, especially regarding such practices as multi-purpose allocations. NCIB may question some interpretations and applications.

NCIB may provisionally accept compilations of financial reports, if the organization has shown progress toward producing consolidated or combined statements and expects to provide such statements within a reasonable time.

Program categories can change from year to year; the budget should still allow meaningful comparison with the previous year's financial statements, recast if necessary.

NCIB believes the spirit of these Standards to be universally useful for all nonprofit organizations. However, for organizations less than three years old or with annual budgets of less than $100,000, greater flexibility in applying some of the Standards may be appropriate.

National Charities Information Bureau, Inc.
19 Union Square West • New York, NY 10003
Tel: (212) 929-6300 • Fax: (212) 463-7083
http://www.give.org

6/96

EXHIBIT G.2

Philanthropic Advisory Service of the Council of Better Business Bureaus Standards for Charitable Solicitations

COUNCIL OF BETTER BUSINESS BUREAUS, INC.

4200 Wilson Boulevard, Suite 800
Arlington, VA 22203-1838
703.276.0100
703.525.8277 (fax)
www.bbb.org

CBBB Standards for Charitable Solicitations

The Council of Better Business Bureaus (CBBB) promulgates these standards to promote ethical practices by philanthropic organizations. The CBBB believes that adherence to these standards by soliciting organizations will inspire public confidence, further the growth of public participation in philanthropy, and advance the objectives of responsible private initiative and self-regulation.

Both the public and soliciting organizations will benefit from voluntary disclosure of an organization's activities, finances, fund raising practices, and governance--information that donors and prospective donors will reasonably wish to consider.

These standards apply to publicly soliciting organizations that are tax exempt under section 501(c)(3) of the Internal Revenue Code, and to other organizations conducting charitable solicitations.

While the Council of Better Business Bureaus and its member Better Business Bureaus generally do not report on schools, colleges, or churches soliciting within their congregations, they encourage all soliciting organizations to adhere to these standards.

These standards were developed with professional and technical assistance from representatives of soliciting organizations, professional fund raising firms and associations, the accounting profession, corporate contribution officers, regulatory agencies, and the Better Business Bureau system. The Council of Better Business Bureaus is solely responsible for the contents of these standards.

For the Purposes of These Standards:

1. "Charitable solicitation" (or "solicitation") is any direct or indirect request for money, property, credit, volunteer service or other thing of value, to be given now or on a deferred basis, on the representation that it will be used for charitable, educational, religious, benevolent, patriotic, civic, or other philanthropic purposes. Solicitations include invitations to voting membership and appeals to voting members, when a contribution is a principal requirement for membership.

2. "Soliciting organization" (or "organization") is any corporation, trust, group, partnership, or individual engaged in a charitable solicitation; a "solicitor" is anyone engaged in a charitable solicitation.

3. The "public" includes individuals, groups, associations, corporations, foundations, institutions, and/or government agencies.

4. "Fund raising" includes a charitable solicitation; the activities, representations and materials which are an integral part of the planning, creation, production and communication of the solicitation; and the collection of the money, property, or other thing of value requested. Fund raising includes but is not limited to donor acquisition and renewal, development, fund or resource development, member or membership development, and contract or grant procurement.

The Philanthropic Advisory Service (PAS) is a division of the Council of Better Business Bureaus, the umbrella organization for 132 Better Business Bureaus across the U.S. Among other things, PAS produces reports on national charities and promotes ethical standards within the charitable community. The name Better Business Bureau is a registered service mark of the Council of Better Business Bureaus, Inc.

PUBLIC ACCOUNTABILITY

A1 Soliciting organizations shall provide on request an annual report.

The annual report, an annually-updated written account, shall present the organization's purposes; descriptions of overall programs, activities and accomplishments; eligibility to receive deductible contributions; information about the governing body and structure; and information about financial activities and financial position.

A2 Soliciting organizations shall provide on request complete annual financial statements.

The financial statements shall present the overall financial activities and financial position of the organization, shall be prepared in accordance with generally accepted accounting principles and reporting practices, and shall include the auditor's or treasurer's report, notes and any supplementary schedules. When total annual income exceeds $100,000, the financial statements shall be audited in accordance with generally accepted auditing standards.

A3 Soliciting organizations' financial statements shall present adequate information to serve as a basis for informed decisions.

Information needed as a basis for informed decisions generally includes but is not limited to: a) significant categories of contributions and other income; b) expenses reported in categories corresponding to the descriptions of major programs and activities contained in the annual report, solicitations, and other informational materials; c) a detailed schedule of expenses by natural classification (e.g., salaries, employee benefits, occupancy, postage, etc.), presenting the natural expenses incurred for each major program and supporting activity; d) accurate presentation of all fund raising and administrative costs; and e) when a significant activity combines fund raising and one or more other purposes (e.g., door-to-door canvassing combining fund raising and social advocacy, or television broadcasts combining fund raising and religious ministry, or a direct mail campaign combining fund raising and public education), the financial statements shall specify the total cost of the multi-purpose activity and the basis for allocating its costs.

A4 Organizations receiving a substantial portion of their income through the fund raising activities of controlled or affiliated entities shall provide on request an accounting of all income received by and fund raising costs incurred by such entities.

Such entities include committees, branches or chapters which are controlled by or affiliated with the benefiting organization, and for which a primary activity is raising funds to support the programs of the benefiting organization.

USE OF FUNDS

B1 A reasonable percentage of total income from all sources shall be applied to programs and activities directly related to the purposes for which the organization exists.

A reasonable percentage requires that at least 50% of total income from all sources be spent on programs and activities directly related to the organization's purposes.

B2 A reasonable percentage of public contributions shall be applied to the programs and activities described in solicitations, in accordance with donor expectations.

A reasonable percentage requires that at least 50% of public contributions be spent on the programs and activities described in solicitations, in accordance with donor expectations.

B3 Fund raising costs shall be reasonable.

A reasonable use of funds requires that fund raising costs not exceed 35% of related contributions.

B4 Total fund raising and administrative costs shall be reasonable.

A reasonable use of funds requires that total fund raising and administrative costs not exceed 50% of total income.

An organization which does not meet one or more of these percentage limitations (B1, B2, B3, and/or B4) may provide evidence to demonstrate that its use of funds is reasonable. The higher fund raising and administrative costs of a newly created organization, donor restrictions on the use of funds, exceptional bequests, a stigma associated with a cause, and environmental or political events beyond an organization's control are among the factors which may result in costs that are reasonable although they do not meet these percentage limitations.

B5 Soliciting organizations shall substantiate on request their application of funds, in accordance with donor expectations, to the programs and activities described in solicitations.

B6 Soliciting organizations shall establish and exercise adequate controls over disbursements.

CBBB Standards for Charitable Solicitations - 2

SOLICITATIONS & INFORMATIONAL MATERIALS

C1 Solicitations and informational materials, distributed by any means, shall be accurate, truthful and not misleading, both in whole and in part.

C2 Soliciting organizations shall substantiate on request that solicitations and informational materials, distributed by any means, are accurate, truthful and not misleading, both in whole and in part.

C3 Solicitations shall include a clear description of the programs and activities for which funds are requested.

Solicitations which describe an issue, problem, need or event, but which do not clearly describe the programs or activities for which funds are requested will not meet this standard. Solicitations in which time or space restrictions apply shall identify a source from which written information is available.

C4 Direct contact solicitations, including personal and telephone appeals, shall identify: a) the solicitor and his/her relationship to the benefiting organization; b) the benefiting organization or cause; and c) the programs and activities for which funds are requested.

C5 Solicitations in conjunction with the sale of goods, services or admissions shall identify at the point of solicitation: a) the benefiting organization; b) a source from which written information is available; and c) the actual or anticipated portion of the sales or admission price to benefit the charitable organization or cause.

FUND RAISING PRACTICES

D1 Soliciting organizations shall establish and exercise controls over fund raising activities conducted for their benefit by staff, volunteers, consultants, contractors, and controlled or affiliated entities, including commitment to writing of all fund raising contracts and agreements.

D2 Soliciting organizations shall establish and exercise adequate controls over contributions.

D3 Soliciting organizations shall honor donor requests for confidentiality and shall not publicize the identity of donors without prior written permission.

Donor requests for confidentiality include but are not limited to requests that one's name not be used, exchanged, rented or sold.

D4 Fund raising shall be conducted without excessive pressure.

Excessive pressure in fund raising includes but is not limited to solicitations in the guise of invoices; harassment; intimidation or coercion, such as threats of public disclosure or economic retaliation; failure to inform recipients of unordered items that they are under no obligation to pay for or return; and strongly emotional appeals which distort the organization's activities or beneficiaries.

CBBB Standards for Charitable Solicitations - 3

GOVERNANCE

E1 Soliciting organizations shall have an adequate governing structure.

Soliciting organizations shall have and operate in accordance with governing instruments (charter, articles of incorporation, bylaws, etc.) which set forth the organization's basic goals and purposes, and which define the organizational structure. The governing instruments shall define the body having final responsibility for and authority over the organization's policies and programs (including authority to amend the governing instruments), as well as any subordinate bodies to which specific responsibilities may be delegated.

An organization's governing structure shall be inadequate if any policy-making decisions of the governing body (board) or committee of board members having interim policy-making authority (executive committee) are made by fewer than three persons.

E2 Soliciting organizations shall have an active governing body.

An active governing body (board) exercises responsibility in establishing policies, retaining qualified executive leadership, and overseeing that leadership.

An active board meets formally at least three times annually, with meetings evenly spaced over the course of the year, and with a majority of the members in attendance (in person or by proxy) on average.

Because the public reasonably expects board members to participate personally in policy decisions, the governing body is not active, and a roster of board members may be misleading, if a majority of the board members attend no formal board meetings in person over the course of a year.

If the full board meets only once annually, there shall be at least two additional, evenly spaced meetings during the year of an executive committee of board members having interim policy-making authority, with a majority of its members present in person, on average.

E3 Soliciting organizations shall have an independent governing body.

Organizations whose directly and/or indirectly compensated board members constitute more than one-fifth (20%) of the total voting membership of the board or of the executive committee will not meet this standard. (The ordained clergy of a publicly soliciting church's policy-making governing body are excepted from this 20% limitation, although they may be salaried by or receive support or sustenance from the church.)

E4 Soliciting organizations shall have an independent governing body.

Organizations engaged in transactions in which board members have material conflicting interests resulting from any relationship or business affiliation will not meet this standard.

The Philanthropic Advisory Service (PAS) is a division of the Council of Better Business Bureaus (CBBB), the national office of the Better Business Bureau system. The CBBB promotes the highest ethical relationship between businesses and the public through voluntary self-regulation, consumer and business education, and service excellence. It is supported largely through the membership dues of private businesses and is not a government agency.

PAS promotes ethical standards within the charitable community, provides information to the public on charitable organizations, and educates individual and corporate donors on wise giving. PAS never recommends one charity over another, and remains neutral in its selection of organizations for evaluation. These policies allow PAS to serve donors' current information needs better and help donors to make their own decisions regarding charitable giving.

PAS encourages charitable organizations to accept the responsibility of self-regulation and adhere to the ethical practices outlined in the Council of Better Business Bureaus' Standards for Charitable Solicitations. The Standards for Charitable Solicitations were developed with assistance from nonprofit organization executives, professional fund raisers, accountants, government regulators, corporate contribution officers, and Better Business Bureau professionals.

By helping charities earn the confidence of the donating public, PAS contributes to the success of charitable efforts.

CBBB Standards for Charitable Solicitations - 4

EXHIBIT G.3

Evangelical Council for Financial Accountability Standards of Accountability

EVANGELICAL COUNCIL FOR FINANCIAL

ACCOUNTABILITY

STANDARDS OF ACCOUNTABILITY

The ECFA Standards of Responsible Stewardship required for membership:

- **STANDARD #1 – DOCTRINAL STATEMENT**: Every member organization shall subscribe to a written statement of faith clearly affirming its commitment to the evangelical Christian faith and shall conduct its financial and other operations in a manner which reflects those generally accepted Biblical truths and practices.

- **STANDARD #2 – BOARD OF DIRECTORS AND AUDIT REVIEW COMMITTEE**: Every member organization shall be governed by a responsible board of not less than five individuals, a majority of whom shall be other than employees/staff and/or those related by blood or marriage, which shall meet at least semi-annually to establish policy and review its accomplishments. The board shall appoint a functioning audit review committee, a majority of whom shall be other than employees/staff and/or those related by blood or marriage, for the purpose of reviewing the annual audit and reporting its findings to the board.

- **STANDARD #3 – AUDITED FINANCIAL STATEMENTS**: Every member organization shall obtain an annual audit performed by an independent certified public accounting firm in accordance with generally accepted auditing standards (GAAS) with financial statements prepared in accordance with generally accepted accounting principles (GAAP).

- **STANDARD #4 – USE OF RESOURCES**: Every member organization shall exercise management and financial controls necessary to provide reasonable assurance that all resources are used (nationally and internationally) to accomplish the exempt purposes for which they are intended.

- **STANDARD #5 - FINANCIAL DISCLOSURE**: Every member organization shall provide a copy of its current audited financial statements upon written request.

- **STANDARD #6 - CONFLICTS OF INTEREST**: Every member organization shall avoid conflicts of interest. Transactions with related parties may be undertaken only if all of the following are observed; 1) a material transaction is fully disclosed in the audited financial statements of the organization; 2) the related party is excluded from the discussion and approval of such transaction; 3) a competitive bid or comparable valuation exists; and 4) the organization's board has acted upon and demonstrated that the transaction is in the best interest of the member organization.

- **STANDARD #7 - FUND RAISING**: Every member organization shall comply with each of the ECFA Standards for Fund Raising:

- **7.1: TRUTHFULNESS IN COMMUNICATION**: All representations of fact, description of financial condition of the organization, or narrative about the events must be current, complete and accurate. References to past activities or events must be appropriately dated. There must be no material omissions or exaggerations of fact or use of misleading photographs or any other communication which would tend to create a false impression or misunderstanding.

- **7.2: COMMUNICATION AND DONOR EXPECTATIONS**: Fund raising appeals must not create unrealistic donor expectations of what a donor's gift will actually accomplish within the limits of the organization's ministry.

- **7.3: COMMUNICATION AND DONOR INTENT**: All statements made by the organization in its fund raising appeals about the use of the gift must be honored by the organization. The donor's intent is related to both what was communicated in the appeal and to any donor instructions accompanying the gift. The organization should be aware that communications made in fund raising appeals may create a legally binding restriction.

- **7.4: PROJECTS UNRELATED TO A MINISTRY'S PRIMARY PURPOSE**: An organization raising or receiving funds for programs that are not part of its present or prospective ministry, but are proper in accordance with its exempt purpose, must either treat them as restricted funds and channel them through an organization that can carry out the donor's intent, or return the funds to the donor.

- **7.5: INCENTIVES AND PREMIUMS**: Organizations making fund raising appeals which, in exchange for a contribution, offer premiums or incentives (the value of which is not insubstantial, but which is significant in relation to the amount of the donation) must advise the donor of the fair market value of the premium or incentive and that the value is not deductible for tax purposes.

- **7.6: REPORTING**: On request, an organization must provide a report, including financial information, on the project for which it is soliciting gifts.

- **7.7: PERCENTAGE COMPENSATION FOR FUND RAISERS**: Compensation of outside fund raising consultants or an organization's own employees based directly or indirectly on a percentage of charitable contributions raised is not allowed.

- **7.8: TAX DEDUCTIBLE GIFTS FOR A NAMED RECIPIENT'S PERSONAL BENEFIT**: Tax deductible gifts may not be used to pass money or benefits to any named individual for personal use.

- **7.9: CONFLICT OF INTEREST ON ROYALTIES**: An officer, director, or other principal of the organization must not receive royalties for any product that is used for fund raising or promotional purposes by his/her own organization.

- **7.10: ACKNOWLEDGEMENT OF GIFTS IN KIND**: Property or gifts in kind received by an organization should be acknowledged describing the property or gift accurately _without_ a statement of the gift's market value. It is the responsibility of the donor to determine the fair market value of the property for tax purposes. The organization should inform the donor of IRS reporting requirements for all gifts in excess of $5,000.

- **7.11: ACTING IN THE INTEREST OF THE DONOR**: An organization must make every effort to avoid accepting a gift from or entering into a contract with a prospective donor which would knowingly place a hardship on the donor, or place the donor's future well-being in jeopardy.

- **7.12: FINANCIAL ADVICE**: The representative of the organization, when dealing with persons regarding commitments on major estate assets, must seek to guide and advise donors so they have adequately considered the broad interests of the family and the various ministries they are currently supporting before they make a final decision. Donors should be encouraged to use the services of their attorneys, accountants, or other professional advisors.

Research Library/Standards of Responsible Stewardship

EXHIBIT G.4

Maryland Association of Nonprofit Organizations Standards for Excellence

STANDARDS FOR EXCELLENCE:

An Ethics and Accountability Code for the Nonprofit Sector

©1998 Maryland Association of Nonprofit Organizations

PREAMBLE

Maryland's nonprofit sector is committed to public service. Hard at work in communities across the state, nonprofit organizations are serving and meeting the needs of our citizens and strengthening our communities.

The success of Maryland's nonprofit organizations depends upon public confidence and broad public support. Maryland's nonprofits are supported by individuals, corporations and foundations through charitable contributions and volunteer effort; by government through contracts and grants; by consumers through purchases and fees; and by the general public through state and federal tax laws.

The Maryland Association of Nonprofit Organizations (Maryland Nonprofits) is committed to bolstering public confidence in and support for the nonprofit sector. Therefore, Maryland Nonprofits has developed these Standards for Excellence (Standards) to promote ethical practices and accountability in nonprofit organizations across the state.

Nonprofit organizations must comply with applicable local, state, and federal laws. These Standards build on that foundation, and go a step further. Based on fundamental values - such as honesty, integrity, fairness, respect, trust, responsibility, and accountability - these Standards describe how nonprofits should act to be ethical and be accountable in their program operations, governance, human resources, financial management and fundraising. Eight (8) Guiding Principles are provided, along with fifty-five (55) Standards - more detailed performance benchmarks which will enable nonprofits to strengthen their operations.

Maryland Nonprofits is committed to these Standards and all Maryland Nonprofits' members are required to pledge their commitment to the Guiding Principles. Members are supported in their efforts to implement the Standards through training and technical assistance provided by Maryland Nonprofits, as well as through a voluntary self-regulatory program by

http://www.mdnonprofit.org/ethicbook.htm   11/08/1999

Source: *Reprinted with permission. Copyright 1998 by the Maryland Association of Nonprofit Organizations, 190 West Ostend Street, Suite 201, Baltimore, MD 21230, (410) 727-6367.*

An Ethics and Accountability Code for the Nonprofit Sector   Page 2 of 10

which organizations are evaluated based on their compliance with the performance indicators. In addition, Maryland Nonprofits invites non-member nonprofits to subscribe to these Standards.

The Standards for Excellence are intended to describe how the most well managed and responsibly governed organizations should, and do operate. They provide benchmarks to determine how well an organization is fulfilling its obligations to those who benefit from its programs, to contributors, and to the public.

STANDARDS FOR EXCELLENCE - GUIDING PRINCIPLES

1. **MISSION AND PROGRAM**
   Nonprofits are founded for the public good and operate to accomplish a stated purpose through specific program activities. A nonprofit should have a well-defined mission, and its programs should effectively and efficiently work toward achieving that mission. Nonprofits have an obligation to ensure program effectiveness and to devote the resources of the organization to achieving its stated purpose.

2. **GOVERNING BODY**
   Nonprofits are governed by an elected, volunteer board of directors which should consist of individuals who are committed to the mission of the organization. An effective nonprofit board should determine the mission of the organization, establish management policies and procedures, assure that adequate human resources (volunteer or paid staff) and financial resources (earned income, government contracts and grants, and charitable contributions) are available, and actively monitor the organization's financial and programmatic performance.

3. **CONFLICT OF INTEREST**
   Nonprofit board and staff members should act in the best interest of the organization, rather than in furtherance of personal interests or the interests of third parties. A nonprofit should have policies in place, and should routinely and systematically implement those policies, to prevent actual, potential, or perceived conflicts of interest.

4. **HUMAN RESOURCES**
   A nonprofit's relationship to its employees and volunteers is fundamental to its ability to achieve its mission. Volunteers occupy a special place in nonprofit organizations, serving in governance, administrative and programmatic capacities. An organization's human resource policies should address both paid employees and volunteers, and should be fair, establish clear expectations, and provide for meaningful and effective performance evaluation.

5. **FINANCIAL AND LEGAL**
   Nonprofits must practice sound financial management and comply with a diverse array of legal and regulatory requirements. A nonprofit's financial system should assure that accurate financial records are kept and that the organization's financial resources are used in furtherance of the organization's charitable purposes. Organizations should conduct periodic reviews to address regulatory and liability concerns.

6. **OPENNESS**
   Nonprofits are private corporations which operate for public purposes with public support. As such, they should provide the public with information about their mission, program activities, and finances. A nonprofit should also be accessible and responsive to members of the public who express interest in the affairs of the

http://www.mdnonprofit.org/ethicbook.htm   11/08/1999 organization.

7. **FUNDRAISING**

Charitable fundraising provides an important source of financial support for the work of most nonprofit organizations. An organization's fundraising program should be maintained on a foundation of truthfulness and responsible stewardship. Its fundraising practices should be consistent with its mission, compatible with its organizational capacity, and respectful of the interests of donors and prospective donors.

8. **PUBLIC AFFAIRS AND PUBLIC POLICY**

Nonprofits provide an important vehicle through which individuals organize and work together to improve their communities. Nonprofits should represent the interests of the people they serve through public education and public policy advocacy, as well as by encouraging board members, staff, volunteers and constituents to participate in the public affairs of the community.

STANDARDS FOR EXCELLENCE: MISSION AND PROGRAM

Nonprofits are founded for the public good and operate to accomplish a stated purpose through specific program activities. A nonprofit should have a well-defined mission, and its programs should effectively and efficiently work toward achieving that mission. Nonprofits have an obligation to ensure program effectiveness and to devote the resources of the organization to achieving its stated purpose.

A. Mission

- The organization's purpose, as defined and approved by the board of directors, should be formally and specifically stated. The organization's activities should be consistent with its stated purpose.

B. Organizational Evaluation

- A nonprofit should periodically revisit its mission to determine if the need for its programs continues to exist. The organization should evaluate whether the mission needs to be modified to reflect societal changes, its current programs should be revised or discontinued, or new programs need to be developed.

C. Program Evaluation

- A nonprofit should have defined, cost-effective procedures for evaluating, both qualitatively and quantitatively, its programs and projects in relation to its mission. These procedures should address programmatic efficiency and effectiveness, the relationship of these impacts to the cost of achieving them, and the outcomes for program participants.

- Evaluations should be candid, be used to strengthen the effectiveness of the organization and, when necessary, be used to make programmatic changes.

D. Program Service

- In rendering its programs or services, a nonprofit should act with the utmost professionalism and treat persons served with respect. Where appropriate, a nonprofit should have policies in place which protect the confidentiality of personal information and should provide a grievance procedure to address complaints. Nonprofits should regularly monitor the satisfaction of program participants.

GOVERNING BODY

Nonprofits are governed by an elected, volunteer board of directors which should consist of individuals who are committed to the mission of the organization. An effective nonprofit board should determine the mission of the organization, establish management policies and procedures, assure that adequate human resources (volunteer or paid staff) and financial resources (earned income, government contracts and grants, and charitable contributions) are available, and actively monitor the organization's management, financial and programmatic performance.

A. Board Responsibilities

- The board should engage in ongoing planning activities as necessary to determine the mission of the organization, to define specific goals and objectives related to the mission, and to evaluate the success of the organization's programs toward achieving the mission.

- The board should establish policies for the effective management of the organization, including financial and, where applicable, personnel policies.

- The board annually should approve the organization's budget and periodically should assess the organization's financial performance in relation to the budget. As part of the annual budget process, the board should review the percentages of the organization's resources spent on program, administration, and fundraising.

- The board should hire the executive director, set the executive's compensation, and evaluate the director's performance.

- The board should periodically review the appropriateness of the overall salary structure of the organization.

B. Board Composition

- The board should be composed of individuals who are personally committed to the mission of the organization.

- Where an employee of the organization is a voting member of the board, the circumstances must insure that the employee will not be in a position to exercise

Reprinted with permission. Copyright 1998 by the Maryland Association of Nonprofit Organizations, 190 West Ostend Street, Suite 201, Baltimore, MD 21230, (410) 727-6367.

undue influence.

- The board should have no fewer than five (5) unrelated directors. Seven (7) or more directors are preferable.

- The organization's bylaws should set forth term limits for the service of board members.

- Board membership should reflect the diversity of the communities served by the organization.

- Board members should serve without compensation. Board members may be reimbursed for expenses directly related to their board service.

C. Conduct of the Board

- The board is responsible for its own operations, including the education, training and development of board members, annual evaluation of its own performance, and where appropriate, the selection of new board members.

- The board should establish stated expectations for board members, including expectations for participation in fundraising activities, committee service, and program activities.

- The board should meet as frequently as is needed to fully and adequately conduct the business of the organization. At a minimum, the board should meet four times a year.

- The organization should have written policies which address attendance and participation of board members at board meetings, and which include a process to address noncompliance.

- Written meeting minutes reflecting the actions of the board, including reports of board committees when acting in the place of the board, should be maintained and distributed to board and committee members.

CONFLICT OF INTEREST

Nonprofit board and staff members should act in the best interest of the organization, rather than in furtherance of personal interests or the interests of third parties. A nonprofit should have policies in place, and should routinely and systematically implement those policies, to prevent actual, potential, or perceived conflicts of interest.

A. Conflict of Interest Policy

- Nonprofits should have a written conflict of interest policy. The policy should be applicable to board members and staff, and volunteers who have significant independent decision making authority regarding the resources of the organization. The policy should identify the types of conduct or transactions that raise conflict of interest concerns, should set forth procedures for disclosure of actual or potential conflicts, and should provide for review of individual transactions by the uninvolved

Source: *Reprinted with permission. Copyright 1998 by the Maryland Association of Nonprofit Organizations, 190 West Ostend Street, Suite 201, Baltimore, MD 21230, (410) 727-6367.*

members of the board of directors.

B. Conflict of Interest Statements

- Nonprofits should provide board members, staff and volunteers with a conflict of interest statement which summarizes the key elements of the organization's conflict of interest policy. The conflict of interest statement should provide space for the board member, employee or volunteer to disclose any known financial interest which the individual, or a member of the individual's immediate family, has in any business entity which transacts business with the organization. The statement should be provided to and signed by board members, staff, and volunteers, both at the time of the individual's initial affiliation with the organization and at least annually thereafter.

HUMAN RESOURCES

A nonprofit's relationship to its employees and volunteers is fundamental to its ability to achieve its mission. Volunteers occupy a special place in nonprofit organizations, serving in governance, administrative and programmatic capacities. An organization's human resource policies should address both paid employees and volunteers, and should be fair, establish clear expectations, and provide for meaningful and effective performance evaluation.

A. Personnel Policies

- A nonprofit should have written personnel policies and procedures, approved by the board of directors, governing the work and actions of all employees and volunteers of the organization. In addition to covering basic elements of the employment relationship (e.g. working conditions, employee benefits, vacation and sick leave), the policies should address employee evaluation, grievance procedures, confidentiality of employee, client and organization records and information, and employee growth and development.

- With respect to volunteers, the organization's policies and procedures should also address initial assessment or screening, assignment to and training for appropriate work responsibilities, ongoing supervision and evaluation, and opportunities for advancement.

B. Employee Performance Evaluation

- Organizations should have a system in place for regular written evaluation of employees by their respective supervisors, which should take place at least annually.

C. Employee Orientation

- New employees of the organization should receive an orientation, which includes review of the organization's personnel policies and procedures, and an introduction to the Standards for Excellence. Employees should be provided with a copy of the personnel policies and these Standards, and should acknowledge receipt in writing.

FINANCIAL AND LEGAL

Nonprofits must practice sound financial management and comply with a diverse array of legal and regulatory requirements. A nonprofit's financial system should assure that accurate financial records are kept and that the organization's financial resources are used in furtherance of the organization's charitable purposes. Organizations should conduct periodic reviews to address regulatory and liability concerns.

A. Financial Accountability

- A nonprofit should operate in accordance with an annual budget which has been approved by the board of directors.

- A nonprofit should create and maintain financial reports on a timely basis that accurately reflect the financial activity of the organization.

- For nonprofits with annual revenue in excess of $300,000, the accuracy of the financial reports should be subject to audit by a Certified Public Accountant.

- Internal financial statements should be prepared no less frequently than quarterly, should be provided to the board of directors, and should identify and explain any material variation between actual and budgeted revenues and expenses.

- Organizations should provide employees a confidential means to report suspected financial impropriety or misuse of organization resources.

- Organizations should have written financial policies governing: (a) investment of the assets of the organization (b) internal control procedures, (c) purchasing practices, and (d) reserve funds.

B. Legal Compliance and Accountability

- Nonprofits must be aware of and comply with all applicable federal, state, and local laws. This may include, but is not limited to, the following activities: complying with laws and regulations related to fundraising, licensing, financial accountability, human resources, lobbying and political advocacy, and taxation.

- Organizations should periodically assess the need for insurance coverage in light of the nature and extent of the organization's activities and its financial capacity. A decision to forego general liability insurance coverage or Directors and Officers liability insurance coverage shall only be made by the board of directors and shall be reflected in the minutes for the meeting at which the decision was made.

- Nonprofits should periodically conduct an internal review of the organization's compliance with known existing legal, regulatory and financial reporting requirements and should provide a summary of the results of the review to members of the board of directors.

http://www.mdnonprofit.org/ethicbook.htm   11/08/1999

OPENNESS

Nonprofits are private corporations which operate for public purposes with public support. As such, they should provide the public with information about their mission, program activities, and finances. A nonprofit should also be accessible and responsive to members of the public who express interest in the affairs of the organization.

A. Annual Report

- Nonprofits should prepare, and make available annually to the public, information about the organization's mission, program activities, and basic financial data. The report should also identify the names of the organization's board of directors and management staff.

- Public Access
  Nonprofits should provide members of the public who express an interest in the affairs of the organization with a meaningful opportunity to communicate with an appropriate representative of the organization.
  Nonprofits should have at least one staff member who is responsible to assure that the organization is complying with both the letter and the spirit of federal and state laws which require disclosure of information to members of the public.

FUNDRAISING

Charitable fundraising provides an important source of financial support for the work of most nonprofit organizations. An organization's fundraising program should be maintained on a foundation of truthfulness and responsible stewardship. Its fundraising practices should be consistent with its mission, compatible with its organizational capacity, and respectful of the interests of donors and prospective donors.

A. Fundraising Activities

- A nonprofit's fundraising costs should be reasonable over time. On average, over a five year period, a nonprofit should realize charitable contributions from fundraising activities that are at least three times the amount spent on fundraising. Organizations whose fundraising ratio is less than 3:1 should demonstrate that they are making steady progress toward achieving this goal, or should be able to justify why a 3:1 ratio is not appropriate for the individual organization.

- Solicitation and promotional materials should be accurate and truthful and should correctly identify the organization, its mission, and the intended use of the solicited funds.

- All statements made by the nonprofit in its fundraising appeals about the use of a contribution should be honored.

- Nonprofits should honor the known intentions of a donor regarding the use of donated funds.

B. Donor Relationships and Privacy.

- Nonprofits should respect the privacy of donors and safeguard the confidentiality of information which a donor reasonably would expect to be private.

- Nonprofits should provide donors an opportunity to state that they prefer to remain anonymous and that their name, the amount of their gift, or other information not be publicly released.

- Nonprofits should provide donors an opportunity to have their names removed from any mailing lists which are sold, rented, or exchanged.

- Nonprofits should honor requests by a donor to curtail repeated mailings or telephone solicitations from in-house lists.

- Solicitations should be free from undue influence or excessive pressure, and should be respectful of the needs and interests of the donor or potential donor.

C. Acceptance of Gifts

- An organization should have policies in place to govern the acceptance and disposition of charitable gifts that are received in the course of its regular fundraising activities. These policies should include procedures to determine any limits on individuals or entities from which the organization will accept a gift, the purposes for which donations will be accepted, the type of property which will be accepted, and whether to accept an unusual or unanticipated gift in light of the organization's mission and organizational capacity.

D. Employment of Fundraising Personnel

- Fundraising personnel, including both employees and independent consultants, should not be compensated based on a percentage of the amount raised or other commission formula.

- Organizations should only use the services of fundraising consultants who are registered with the Office of the Secretary of State of Maryland.

- Organizations should exercise control over any staff, volunteers, consultants, contractors, other organizations, or businesses who are known to be soliciting contributions on behalf of the organization.

PUBLIC AFFAIRS AND PUBLIC POLICY

Nonprofits provide an important vehicle through which individuals organize and work together to improve their communities. Nonprofits should represent the interests of the people they serve through public education and public policy advocacy, as well as by encouraging board members, staff, volunteers and constituents to participate in the public affairs of the community.

A. Public Policy Advocacy

- Nonprofits should have a written policy on advocacy defining the process by which the organization determines positions on specific issues.

B. Public Education

- Nonprofits should assure that any educational information provided to the media or distributed to the public is factually accurate and provides sufficient contextual information to be understood.

C. Promoting Public Participation

- Nonprofits engaged in promoting public participation in community affairs shall be diligent in assuring that the activities of the organization are strictly nonpartisan.

EXHIBIT G.5

Charities Review Council of Minnesota Accountability Standards

Your source for informed giving.

ACCOUNTABILITY STANDARDS
adopted by the Council's Board of Directors, January 8, 1998

The mission of the Charities Review Council is to promote informed giving by donors who support charities that solicit in Minnesota. The Council's mission is rooted in the belief that charities serve a unique and valuable role in meeting the needs of society, that charities have the right to solicit contributions of time and money in pursuit of their missions, that donors have the right to choose how they spend their charitable dollars and to expect that charities will conduct themselves in an accountable, ethical and effective manner. The Council believes that the responsible actions of both donors and charities will sustain and enhance the climate for charitable giving.

The Council carries its mission forward by creating and applying standards to encourage accountability in the charitable sector; and by providing information to donors that will help them make informed giving decisions. The Council does not have resources sufficient to conduct evaluations of all programmatic aspects of a charity's work. However, the Council's standards are indicators of effective, ethical and accountable management practices. Following are the standards used to evaluate nonprofit organizations, the philosophy behind each standard and guidance on how the standard is applied:

Standards in the areas of -
1. **Public Disclosure**
2. **Governance**
3. **Financial Activity**
4. **Fundraising**

The Philosophy behind each Standard.

Guidance on how the Standard is applied.

PUBLIC DISCLOSURE

PUBLIC DISCLOSURE - STANDARD 1A
Philosophy: To uphold the public's trust in the nonprofit sector, a charity should at a minimum carry out its actions in accordance with Minnesota and federal charity law.

Standard 1A: For the year under review and the preceding two years, the organization has not violated any applicable provisions of Minnesota or federal law relating to the organization's tax exempt status, registration with and reporting to governmental agencies and the public or fundraising practices.

Guidelines for Application: The Council will examine a charity's compliance with applicable laws and regulations including I.R.C. 501(c)(3); Minn. Stat. 309.51; Minn. Stat. 309.52; Minn. Stat. 309.53; Minn. Stat. 309.55; Minn. Stat. 309.556; I.R.C. 170(f)(8); I.R.C. 6115; I.R.C. 6104(e) to determine compliance with public disclosure standard **1A**. In addition, the organization's IRS Form 990 will be obtained from the Attorney General's office as well as any information regarding violation of charity law or actions against the organization by the Attorney General.

Source: *Reprinted with permission. Copyright © 1998, Charities Review Council.*

PUBLIC DISCLOSURE - STANDARD 1B

Philosophy: The Council believes that providing complete information to prospective donors promotes informed, responsible philanthropy.

Standard 1B: The organization provides the following upon request:
- **An annual report** that includes: (a) a description of the organization's purpose; (b) a description of its program activities, accomplishments and geographic area served; (c) a summary of the total cost of each major program (to the extent required in the IRS Form 990); and d) a list of the organization's board of directors.
- **Annual financial statements** prepared in conformance with generally accepted accounting principles, and audited when required by federal or state law or contracts to which the organization is a party.

Guidelines for Application: If an organization fails to provide the Council with a completed Council Disclosure Form within six weeks of the initial request, or demonstrates a pattern of failing to provide information requested by potential donors, the Council will conclude that the organization does not meet public disclosure standard **1B**. Although the annual report is generally a single publication, the Council will consider a collection of documents that when furnished together provides the information requested.

PUBLIC DISCLOSURE - STANDARD 1C

Philosophy: The programs offered by a charity and the results made possible by contributions are of utmost concern to potential donors. Familiarity with the organization's programs and results is essential to any informed giving decision and allows potential donors to match their interests with those of the charities they are supporting.

Standard 1C: Through the annual report or other communications available to donors, the organization provides specific, objective information about its accomplishments related to its stated mission.

Guidelines for Application: The Council will review the organization's annual report or other communications available to donors to determine compliance with public disclosure standard **1C**.

PUBLIC DISCLOSURE - STANDARD 1D

Philosophy: Inconsistencies among a charity's programs, activities and financial information as described in its annual report, audited financial statements and IRS Form 990 prevents donors from meaningfully evaluating the charity's programs and effectiveness.

Standard ID: Program names, activities and financial information listed in the annual report, audited financial statement and IRS Form 990 are consistent.

Guidelines for Application: The Council will review and compare the charity's program names, activities and financial information as stated in its IRS Form 990, audited financial statements and annual report. If irreconcilable differences exist, the charity will not meet public disclosure standard **1D**.

GOVERNANCE

GOVERNANCE - STANDARD 2A

Philosophy: The governing board is one of the most important elements of a well-functioning nonprofit organization. The board sets the strategic agenda for the organization and has overall responsibility for its mission and programs. The board should operate in a way that does not jeopardize clear and responsible decision-making.

Standard: 2A: The governing board meets at least three times per fiscal year with a quorum present, and maintains written minutes of each meeting.

Guidelines for Application: The Council will review the list of board meeting dates and attendance to determine compliance with governance standard **2A**. Meetings of the governing board should be scheduled at regular intervals throughout the year (for example, quarterly), but do not have to be in person.

GOVERNANCE –STANDARD 2B

Philosophy: A well-managed nonprofit organization should have a policy that addresses conflicts of interest of its directors, officers and key staff. Conflict of interest policies help to ensure that no person benefits inappropriately from any transactions in which the organization is involved.

Standard 2B: The organization addresses director, officer, and key staff conflicts of interest pursuant to a written policy that prohibits the interested party from approving or voting on the conflicted transaction and requires full disclosure of all material facts to the appropriate decision makers.

Guidelines for Application: The Council will review the organization's conflict of interest policy to determine compliance with governance standard **2B**. The policy should address conflicts of interest as described in this standard. Key staff is defined as anyone who has the authority to act or enter into contracts on behalf of the organization. Sample policies can be obtained from the Council.

GOVERNANCE – STANDARD 2C

Philosophy: Charity board members' voluntary service is a deeply rooted tradition in the nonprofit sector. Most donors and nonprofit organizations expect that board members serve without compensation.

Standard 2C: Board members receive no compensation for board service other than reimbursement of expenses incurred as a result of board participation.

Guidelines for Application: The Council will ask the organization to disclose its board compensation practices and will review its IRS Form 990 to determine compliance with governance standard **2C.**

GOVERNANCE – STANDARD 2D

Philosophy: The staff of a nonprofit organization is accountable to the governing board. Therefore, when paid staff members also serve on the governing board or as board chair or treasurer, the ability of the board and such officers to act independently is compromised.

Standard 2D: Not more than one member of the governing board is a paid staff person of the organization; no paid staff person serves as board chair or treasurer.

Guidelines for Application: The Council will review the organization's bylaws, articles of incorporation, and list of board and staff members to determine compliance with governance standard **2D**. Only paid positions are considered in applying this standard. Unpaid staff may serve in the capacity of board chair or treasurer.

GOVERNANCE - STANDARD 2E

Philosophy: Limits on board terms help to ensure that the board is accountable. Changes in board membership also allow for greater participation by the community being served.

Standard 2E: No elected member of the governing board serves for more than five years without standing for re-election.

Guidelines for Application: The Council will review bylaws for terms of office and election procedures to determine compliance with governance standard **2E.**

FINANCIAL ACTIVITY

FINANCIAL ACTIVITY – STANDARD 3A

Philosophy: A charity should use its resources in a responsible, effective and efficient manner to achieve results in furtherance of its mission. The Council believes that the ratio of program expenses to total expenses is an indicator of such use. Donors should reasonably expect that substantially more than half of their contribution and the organization's expenses are used for program services. Management and fundraising expenses should be reasonable in relation to the results of the organization and reasonable over time.

Standard 3A: At least 70 percent of the organization's annual expenses are for program activity and not more than 30 percent for management/general and fundraising combined.

Guidelines for Application: The Council will review the organization's audited financial statements (when applicable) and the IRS Form 990 to determine compliance with the financial activity standard **3A.** The Council will determine the percentage allocated for program activity, management and general, and fundraising based on the average of aggregate figures for the three most recent completed fiscal years.

When an organization reports joint cost activities, the Council will examine the activities in comparison with sample fundraising materials and activities described. An organization reporting 50% or more of its program expenses from joint cost activities will be reviewed more closely.

Based on a review of the information gathered, the Council may conclude that joint costs allocated to program are overstated while costs allocated to fundraising are understated. This may cause the Council to conclude that the organization does not meet financial activity standard **3A** and an annotation will indicate a difference in opinion between the Council and the organization regarding its allocation of joint costs.

For charities that have been in operation for fewer than three full years, the Council will analyze the aggregate expenses for all completed years to determine compliance with financial activity standard **3A.** Special consideration may be given to unusual circumstances that affect the organization for a limited period of time.

FINANCIAL ACTIVITY – STANDARD 3B

Philosophy: While the Council believes that organizations should maintain a reasonable level of cash to safeguard against unexpected financial challenges, maintaining excess reserves indicates the organization is not maximizing the use of its resources in pursuit of its charitable mission. In such cases, it may not be appropriate to continue soliciting from the public.

Standard 3B: Unrestricted net assets available for current use are not more than twice the current or next year's budgeted operating expenses.

Guidelines for Application: The Council will review the organization's Statement of Position to determine compliance with financial accountability standard **3B.**

FINANCIAL ACTIVITY – STANDARD 3C

Philosophy: A charity should use its resources prudently and should maintain a healthy financial picture. When making a contribution, donors want to know that the organization has the financial strength to pursue its mission on a long-term basis.

Standard 3C: The organization does not have persistent or increasing operating deficits.

Guidelines for Application: The Council will review the organization's Statement of Activity to determine compliance with financial activity standard **3C**. Persistent is defined as three or more consecutive years. The Council will note if the deficit appears to be decreasing over time.

FINANCIAL ACTIVITY – STANDARD 3D

Philosophy: The governing board is responsible and accountable for the financial management of the corporation.

Standard 3D: The governing board approves an operating budget prior to the beginning of each fiscal year and receives financial reports, at least quarterly, comparing actual to budgeted revenue and expenses.

Guidelines for Application: The Council will ask the organization to disclose the date of the meeting at which the governing board approved an operating budget and the dates financial reports were provided to the governing board to determine compliance with financial activity standard **3D.**

FUNDRAISING

FUNDRAISING – STANDARD 4A

Philosophy: The responsible actions of both donors and charities promote and sustain the climate of giving in Minnesota. To this end, fundraising methods should be ethical and honest and encourage the donor to give voluntarily, based on interest in the purpose and programs of the organization.

Standard 4A: Solicitations and information materials clearly describe the purpose or programs for which the contributed funds will be used and identify the charity that will receive the contribution. The donor is provided with the address or phone number of the charity. All information provided in connection with solicitations is accurate and not misleading.

Guidelines for Application: The Council will review sample fundraising materials (including direct mail solicitations, telemarketing or canvassing scripts), the organization's annual report and financial statements to determine compliance with fundraising standard 4A. The Council will also consider donors' reactions to direct mail appeals. Examples of inaccurate or misleading solicitation practices include:
- statements incorrectly implying local use of donated funds (by callers or letters)
- the use of misleading photos
- misrepresenting the level of program accomplishments
- inaccurate disclosure of programming accomplished through joint cost activities
- activities that are inconsistent with charity mission
- exaggerated or false claims

The organization's name, address and phone number should appear in all written fundraising appeals to donors.

FUNDRAISING – STANDARD 4B

Philosophy: Appeals that are threatening or intimidating are inconsistent with the essential aspects of voluntary charitable giving.

Standard 4B: Solicitations do not cause donors to feel threatened or intimidated. The charity maintains a written policy to discontinue contacting any person upon that person's oral or written request directed to the charity, its professional fundraiser or other agent.

Guidelines for Application: In addition to reviewing sample fundraising materials submitted by the organization, whenever possible the Council will considers donors' reactions to telephone solicitations and door-to-door canvassers to determine compliance with fundraising standard **4B**.

Examples of intimidating or threatening appeals include:
*   insistence by callers after prospect has declined to make a contribution
*   personal criticisms by caller
*   call-backs after prospect has declined to give

The organization's name, address and phone number should be provided immediately to donors upon request by telemarketers or canvassers. The Council will also rely on community volunteers to provide feedback to the Council regarding fundraising appeals.

FUNDRAISING – STANDARD 4C

Philosophy: Donors are entitled to know who is soliciting their gift and what portion of their gift will be received by the charity.

Standard 4C: Solicitors who are not employees or volunteers of the charity identify themselves in each solicitation as professional fundraisers and, upon request, provide the name and address of their employer or contracting party. Upon request, persons authorized by the charity to utilize the charity's name in connection with the sale or marketing of goods or services provide accurate information about the percentage of gross revenue that is paid to the charity.

Guidelines for Application
The Council will review telemarketing scripts, professional fundraising contracts and feedback from donors to determine compliance with fundraising standard **4C**. Complaints by donors regarding the conduct of organizations through their fundraising appeals will be tracked and documented to determine if a pattern exists.

Resource H

A Brief History of Financial Accounting and Reporting Standards for Not-for-Profit Organizations

ALTHOUGH NOT-FOR-PROFIT organizations have existed since the birth of the nation, there was little if any thought given to setting standards for the financial accounting and reporting of those organizations prior to the second half of the twentieth century. In this resource we summarize major landmarks in the evolution of accounting and reporting principles and standards for not-for-profit organizations during the past fifty years with particular reference to the self-regulatory role played by the leadership of these voluntary organizations themselves.

Voluntary Self-Regulatory Efforts

Self-regulatory efforts have contributed greatly to the development and continuing evolution of the accounting and financial reporting of not-for-profit organizations. Here we review the most important milestones.

Ad Hoc Committee Report: 1961

Concerned about the public accountability of voluntary health and welfare organizations and their importance to society, an ad hoc group of twenty-one private citizen leaders were convened at the invitation of the Rockefeller Foundation in 1958 to "reassess the functioning of these agencies in fulfilling their great responsibility."[1] In the foreword to its report, the ad hoc committee observed:

> *Each member was concerned that the multiplicity and complexity of unresolved issues might increasingly confuse the public, undermine*

public confidence, and endanger the support of all private agencies. . . .
Over 100,000 national, regional, and local voluntary health and welfare
agencies now [1961] solicit contributions from the general public—and
the public responds with $1,500,000,000 annually! . . . The principal
findings or conclusions of the Committee are three in number. . . .

> 3. *The obligation of full disclosure and accountability leads to a second*
>   *recommendation of this Committee, namely, that a system of*
>   *uniform accounting be developed by the American Institute of*
>   *Certified Public Accountants. This would greatly facilitate the work*
>   *of budget reviewing bodies, potential contributors, and voluntary*
>   *agencies themselves.*[2]

In recommending the development of standardized accounting and uniform financial reporting by not-for-profit organizations, the ad hoc committee report cited, among others, the following benefit: "Uniform
accounting and financial reporting, if developed and administered properly, would have a profound and beneficial influence on the voluntary
agency movement. It is potentially the most important method for obtaining adequate information about voluntary agencies, for the benefit of both
the agencies and the American public."[3]

Creation of the Black Book: 1964

One of the most important outcomes of the ad hoc committee's report was
the publication of *Standards of Accounting and Financial Reporting for
Voluntary Health and Welfare Organizations,* commonly known as the "Black
Book."

Until 1964 there existed no formal industry-wide accounting or reporting practices for voluntary health and welfare organizations. These organizations followed the accounting and reporting practices generally
employed by trusts, foundations, hospitals, educational institutions, or various other types of organizations to which some of them may have been
indirectly related. In 1964 the National Health Council and the National
Assembly (known at the time as the National Social Welfare Assembly)
published a guide: *Standards of Accounting and Financial Reporting for Voluntary Health and Welfare Organizations.* This project was accomplished with
support from the Avalon Foundation and the Rockefeller Foundation and
with the financial support, full cooperation, and participation of fifty-four
national voluntary health and welfare organizations that were members
of, or affiliated with, either the National Health Council or the National
Assembly. A landmark publication, *Standards of Accounting and Financial
Reporting for Voluntary Health and Welfare Organizations* constituted the first
definitive literature in the not-for-profit accounting field and has, over a

period of thirty-five years, achieved wide acceptance by voluntary health and welfare organizations throughout the nation, as well as by many governmental and regulatory bodies. Until the promulgation of accounting principles by the accounting profession, the publication was recognized by both public bodies and private funders as the authoritative literature in the field.

Filer Commission Report: 1975

Named after its chair, John H. Filer, the Commission on Private Philanthropy and Public Needs was established in November 1973 as a privately initiated, privately funded citizens' panel with two broad objectives: (1) to study the voluntary sector of American society and the role of philanthropic giving in the United States and (2) to make recommendations to the voluntary sector, Congress, and the American public concerning ways in which the sector and the practice of private giving could be strengthened.

In 1975 the commission published its report—*Giving in America: Toward a Stronger Voluntary Sector.* This report provided what was probably the first comprehensive portrait of America's not-for-profit sector. The two-year work of the commission, assisted by scores of scholars, resulted in groundbreaking research: ninety-one individual studies compiled in six volumes in over three thousand pages addressing some of the major questions of the day pertaining to American philanthropy and America's voluntary sector.

Among the commission's numerous topical studies was *A Study of the Inadequacies of Present Financial Reporting by Philanthropic Organizations,* conducted by a special accounting advisory committee. In the introduction to its report the advisory committee wrote:

> *An absence of meaningful financial information leads to concern about the use of charitable funds. This is periodically accented by newspaper headlines of improper use of contributed funds. Possibly, this has resulted in a reduction in the support which would have been available had there been more effective communication by philanthropic organizations.*
>
> *In the Accounting Advisory Committee's opinion, private philanthropy cannot achieve its full potential without completely open, understandable financial reporting based upon uniform principles. The committee is concerned that if private philanthropy does not do a more effective job of financial reporting, regulatory bodies will increasingly assume responsibility to regulate philanthropic organizations. Inadequate reporting, including the absence of uniform accounting principles, will encourage governmental intervention and may lead to decisions regarding philanthropic goals being made more by government and less by the contributor.*

The committee believes that the adoption and use of uniform accounting principles and reporting practices will better serve the contributor, protect the public interest, and facilitate the use of funds in areas where they are needed most.[4]

Based on its study the accounting advisory committee made the following two recommendations:

1. *A single, uniform set of accounting principles . . . should be adopted and followed by all philanthropic organizations.*

2. *A uniform financial report should be adopted by the federal government and each state and municipality which now requires annual financial information from philanthropic organizations. We propose a Standard Accounting Report (SAR) . . . which could be used for this purpose with appropriate supplemental schedules for other information deemed necessary to fulfill the particular regulatory interest.*[5]

It would not be an overstatement to say that the committee's report and recommendations had a powerful impact on the development of uniform standards of accounting and reporting for not-for-profit organizations.

The Role of the Accounting Profession: AICPA and FASB

We now turn to AICPA and FASB, the two authoritative bodies charged with the development of accounting and financial reporting principles and standards for both not-for-profit and for-profit entities.

AICPA

Until the late 1960s there was little interest or incentive for the accounting profession to pay serious attention to accounting and financial reporting for not-for-profit organizations. As a follow-up to the recommendations of the 1961 ad hoc committee's report, the National Health Council and the National Assembly asked the American Institute of Certified Public Accountants (AICPA) to join them as the third sponsor of *Standards of Accounting and Financial Reporting for Voluntary Health and Welfare Organizations*, but AICPA declined. However, in 1966 AICPA published its first audit guide, *Audits of Voluntary Health and Welfare Organizations*. This audit guide provided guidance to independent public accountants with respect to examining and reporting on financial statements of these organizations. However, in strict technical terms the guide stopped short of establishing generally accepted accounting principles (GAAP) for not-for-profit organizations.

Finally, in 1972 AICPA made a start in the not-for-profit arena with the publication of the *Hospital Audit Guide,* which was followed by the *Audit Guide for Colleges and Universities* in 1973 and the *Audit Guide for Voluntary Health and Welfare Organizations* in 1974. This last guide promulgated GAAP for voluntary health and welfare organizations for the first time and recognized the pioneering work of the Black Book, noting that in most cases "these principles are compatible with those set forth in the *Standards of Accounting and Financial Reporting for Voluntary Health and Welfare Organizations.*"[6] The Black Book was concurrently revised to achieve consistency with the *Audit Guide for Voluntary Health and Welfare Organizations.*

This time United Way of America joined the National Health Council and the National Assembly as the third sponsor of the revised second edition of the Black Book. In December 1974 United Way of America published *Accounting and Financial Reporting: A Guide for United Ways and Not-for-Profit Human Service Organizations.* The United Way of America guide incorporated both the Black Book standards and the 1974 AICPA audit guide. The publication of the United Way guide was followed by several workshops around the nation organized by United Way of America to train thousands of organizations in the use of new GAAP and standards. The Black Book and the United Way guide were revised in 1988 and 1989, respectively, to reflect changes in and developments of accounting principles and standards for not-for-profit organizations. Finally, in 1998 a fourth edition of the Black Book was published to incorporate further changes in accounting standards promulgated by the Financial Accounting Standards Board (FASB).

FASB

Until 1973 AICPA's twenty-one-member Accounting Principles Board (APB)—a part-time body—was the sole source of authoritative pronouncements on accounting principles. During the late 1960s various factors converged to cause AICPA to appoint a study group to address some of the prevailing concerns and to determine the future course of standard setting. The work of this study group culminated in the creation of a completely new, independent, and full-time organization—the Financial Accounting Foundation—which in turn created FASB.

In addition to being designated the official rule-making body for financial accounting effective July 1, 1973, FASB was also granted the authority to interpret, amend, or replace existing pronouncements. However, existing APB pronouncements remain in force until they are expressly superseded or amended by actions of FASB.

Since its inception in 1973, FASB has issued over one hundred Statements of Financial Accounting Standards, many of which are relevant to not-for-profit organizations. Several of the statements, including no. 13 (on leases), no. 43 (on compensated absences), no. 74 (on special termination benefits), and no. 87 (on pension plans), address transactions entered into by not-for-profit organizations. FASB Statement no. 32 gives additional authoritative status to AICPA's audit guide by declaring the accounting principles set forth in the audit guide to be preferable when an organization is justifying changes in accounting principles.

Perhaps more important for our purposes are the FASB Statements of Financial Accounting Concepts, which provide a conceptual framework on which uniform accounting principles for all not-for-profit organizations are based. FASB Statement of Financial Accounting Concepts no. 4, *Objectives of Financial Reporting by Nonbusiness Organizations,* issued in December 1980, was the first concepts statement to specifically address financial statements of not-for-profit organizations.

FASB Statement of Financial Accounting Concepts no. 4 opines that general-purpose financial reporting by not-for-profit organizations should supply resource providers and others information that will be useful in

- Making decisions about allocating resources to these organizations

- Assessing the services these organizations provide and their ability to continue to provide those services (financial viability)

- Assessing how managers of these organizations discharge their stewardship responsibilities

This statement also concludes that the information needed to achieve those objectives includes information about:

- Economic resources, obligations, and net resources of an organization and the effects of transactions, events, and circumstances that change resources and interests in those resources.

- The performance of an organization during a specified period. The information most useful for assessing performance is a combination of periodic measurement of changes in the amount and nature of the net resources of a nonbusiness organization plus information about the service efforts and accomplishments of the organization.

In 1985 FASB issued Statement of Financial Concepts no. 6, *Elements of Financial Statements,* which defines ten elements of financial statements, seven of which are applicable to not-for-profit organizations (assets, liabilities, net assets, revenues, expenses, gains, and losses), and which classifies net assets into three categories: unrestricted, temporarily restricted, permanently restricted.

In June 1993 FASB brought sweeping changes to not-for-profit accounting by promulgating standards in two major areas with the publication of its Statements of Financial Accounting Standards no. 116, *Accounting for Contributions Received and Contributions Made,* and no. 117, *Financial Statements of Not-for-Profit Organizations.* Further, in November 1995 FASB published Statement of Financial Accounting Standards no. 124, *Accounting for Certain Investments Held by Not-for-Profit Organizations.*

Most recently, FASB has issued Statement of Financial Accounting Standards no. 136, dealing with situations where one not-for-profit passes gifts through to, or holds assets for the benefit of, another not-for-profit. In addition, it is close to issuing a new standard that will address, among other things, when not-for-profit organizations should consolidate the financial statements of affiliated organizations.

Although much progress has been achieved over half a century, the readers of this guide will undoubtedly recognize that the development of accounting and financial reporting principles and standards for not-for-profit organizations remains a work in progress at the beginning of the twenty-first century.

Accountability for Service Efforts and Accomplishments

THE MOST IMPORTANT INFORMATION a not-for-profit board can provide the organization's supporters, clients, and the public is what the organization did with its money (its service efforts) and what results the organization achieved (its accomplishments). The first question is relatively easy to answer. It requires keeping good records of program inputs, such as the number of people served, meals provided, counseling hours spent, persons counseled, and so on. In most cases these represent program or activity statistics. However, not all program inputs (service efforts) are quantifiable, and not all program statistics are meaningful.

Another problem is the difficulty of obtaining an unduplicated count of persons helped. Many agencies experience the "turnstile phenomenon"— the same client entering and leaving a facility several times a day—which makes it very difficult to keep accurate statistics on the number of clients served. This is particularly true of agencies that serve children and youth. As demand for program accountability increases, many not-for-profit organizations are developing creative ways of measuring and reporting program inputs. Reporting on program inputs is important because reporting on program outcomes (accomplishments) is probably one of the most difficult tasks confronting not-for-profit organizations. Therefore program inputs may sometimes serve as a proxy for program outcomes.

Although challenging, measuring program outcomes is not impossible. The state of the art in program evaluation is sufficiently advanced to enable most organizations to devise some measure—however approximate—of program results.[1] Measuring the results of an agency's program services attempts to answer a simple question: What good did the agency do? The degree of difficulty in measuring results varies according to the type of program service and the criteria used to measure success.

Not-for-profit organizations are confronted with two types of problems in measuring results. In some cases the results are intangible; in other cases it may take several years to truly assess the results. For example, among major federally funded programs it has taken several years and millions of dollars to measure the impact of particular programs, such as poverty reduction, crime and delinquency prevention, or reduction of unwed pregnancies.

Finally, one of the most intractable problems in measuring results is the issue of the relationship between "cause and effect." In the human services or personal social services area, it is particularly difficult to establish that the result—positive or negative—was due exclusively to the service an agency provided. So many external factors influence human behavior and conditions that it is unwise, if not dishonest, to take full credit for a positive change in a client. In most cases, it is not feasible for an average not-for-profit organization to "control for" external factors or influences on a client. Provided this is recognized and honestly communicated, the organization may claim at least some satisfaction or credit for achieving positive outcomes of its program services.

IRS Form 990 specifically requires not-for-profit organizations to provide information on "program service accomplishments." Part III of the form states, "All organizations *must* describe their exempt purpose achievements in a clear and concise manner" (emphasis added). The IRS also recognizes the difficulty most organizations face in accounting for program results. The examples given on Form 990 ("State the number of clients served, publications issued, etc.") clearly indicate that service *efforts* are acceptable.[2]

Resource J

Selected Form 990 and Management and Technical Assistance Web Sites

IN GENERAL see www.qual990.org, a Web site that provides information about nationwide quality reporting efforts related to IRS Form 990 as well as useful links to many other resources. For on-line searchable databases of management assistance providers across the country, visit www.allianceonline.org.

Table J.1 lists Web sites that we believe might be useful to the readers of this guide.

TABLE J.1

Technical Assistance Web Sites

Organization	Web Site
AICPA (American Institute of Certified Public Accountants)	www.aicpa.org
Better Business Bureau	www.bbb.org
Coalition for Nonprofit Healthcare	www.cnhc.org
CompassPoint Nonprofit Services	www.compasspoint.org
Council of Foundations	www.cof.org
Evangelical Council for Financial Accountability	www.crosswalk.com/ecfa/
The Foundation Center	www.fdncenter.org
Financial Accounting Standards Board	www.fasb.org
GuideStar/Philanthropic Research, Inc.	www.guidestar.org
Greater Washington Society of CPAs	www.gwcpa.org
California Society of CPAs	www.calcpa.org
INDEPENDENT SECTOR	www.indepsec.org
Indiana University, Center on Philanthropy	www.tcop.org
IRS Exempt Organizations Division	www.irs.ustreas.gov/prod/tax_stats/exempt.html
National Alliance for Nonprofit Management	www.allianceonline.org
National Assembly of Health and Human Service Organizations	www.nassembly.org
National Center for Nonprofit Boards	www.ncnb.org
National Center of Charitable Statistics at the Urban Institute	www.nccs.urban.org
National Charities Information Bureau	www.give.org
National Council of Nonprofit Associations	www.ncna.org
National Federation of Nonprofits	www.federationofnonprofits.org
National Health Council	www.nhcouncil.org
National Society of Fundraising Executives	www.nsfre.org
Nonprofit Financial Center	www.nonprofitfinancial.org
Nonprofit Sector Research Fund, The Aspen Institute	www.nonprofitresearch.org
OMB Watch	www.ombwatch.org
United Way of America	www.unitedway.net

Notes

Foreword

1. Alicia Meckstroth and Paul Arnsberger, "A 20-Year Review of the Nonprofit Sector, 1975–1995," in *Statistics of Income Bulletin*, Fall 1998, p. 149 (footnotes omitted).

Chapter One

1. Financial Accounting Standards Board, *Accounting for Contributions Received and Contributions Made*, Statement of Financial Accounting Standards, no. 116 (Norwalk, Conn.: Financial Accounting Standards Board, 1994). As cited in American Institute of Certified Public Accountants, *Audit and Accounting Guide: Not for Profit Organizations* (New York: American Institute of Certified Public Accountants, 1998), 1.

2. Ibid., 1–2. Reprinted with permission from AICPA.

3. Ibid., 2. Reprinted with permission from AICPA.

Chapter Two

1. Joel L. Fleishman, "Public Trust in Not-for-Profit Organizations and the Need for Regulatory Reform," in *Philanthropy and the Nonprofit Sector in a Changing America*, ed. Charles T. Clotfelter and Thomas Ehrlich (Bloomington: Indiana University Press, 1999), 172–173. Reprinted with permission.

2. American Association of Fund-Raising Counsel Trust for Philanthropy, "Total Giving Reaches $190.16 Billion," press release, AAFRC Trust for Philanthropy, Indianapolis, May 24, 2000.

3. INDEPENDENT SECTOR, *Giving and Volunteering in the United States: Findings from a National Survey* (Washington, D.C.: INDEPENDENT SECTOR, 1999).

4. Fleishman, "Public Trust in Not-for-Profit Organizations," 174. Reprinted with permission.

5. Meckstroth and Arnsberger, "20-Year Review," p. 149 (footnotes omitted).

6. Fleishman, "Public Trust in Not-for-Profit Organizations," 172. Reprinted with permission.

7. Ibid., 177. Reprinted with permission.

8. American Institute of Certified Public Accountants, *Objectives of Financial Statements* (New York: American Institute of Certified Public Accountants, 1973), 25 (emphasis added). Reprinted with permission from AICPA.

9. See Cyril O. Houle, *Governing Boards* (Washington, D.C.: National Center for Nonprofit Boards, 1989).

10. Malvern J. Gross Jr., Richard F. Larkin, Roger S. Bruttomesso, and John J. McNally, *Financial and Accounting Guide for Not-for-Profit Organizations*, 5th ed. (New York: Wiley, 1995), 2. Reprinted with permission.

11. Evelyn Brody, "A Taxing Time for the Bishop Estate: What Is the IRS Role in Charity Governance?" *University of Hawaii Law Review*, forthcoming.

Chapter Three

1. See a thought-provoking article by Peter Swords, "The Form 990 as an Accountability Tool for 501(c)(3) Nonprofits," *Tax Lawyer*, 1998, *51*(3), 571–618.

2. Gene Steuerle, "The Coming Revolution in the Nonprofit Sector," *Exempt Organization Tax Review*, 1998, *21*(3), 313–315.

3. See the Web sites www.qual990.org and www.guidestar.org.

Chapter Four

1. A good handbook on the subject is Nonprofit Financial Center, *The NFC 1999 Accounting Software Selection Handbook: A Resource for Nonprofit and Religious Organizations* (Chicago: Nonprofit Financial Center, 1999).

Chapter Six

1. Gross and others, *Financial and Accounting Guide,* 356. Reprinted with permission.

2. See ibid., 406–414. Reprinted with permission.

Chapter Eight

1. Mary F. Foster, Howard Becker, and Richard J. Terrano, *Miller GAAP for Not-for-Profit Organizations Plus Tax and Regulatory Reporting* (Orlando, Fla.: Harcourt Brace, 1998), 380–388.

2. Cited in ibid., 379.

3. U.S. Office of Management and Budget, *Cost Principles for Non-Profit Organizations,* OMB Circular A-122, rev. ed. (Washington, D.C.: U.S. Government Printing Office, 1998).

4. Financial Accounting Standards Board, *Financial Statements of Not-for-Profit Organizations,* Statement of Financial Accounting Standards, no. 117 (Norwalk, Conn.: Financial Accounting Standards Board, 1994), 9–10.

5. U.S. Office of Management and Budget, *Cost Principles for Non-Profit Organizations.*

6. American Institute of Certified Public Accountants, *Audit and Accounting Guide: Not for Profit Organizations,* 168.

7. Financial Accounting Standards Board, *Financial Statements of Not-for-Profit Organizations,* 25.

8. American Institute of Certified Public Accountants, *Audit and Accounting Guide: Not for Profit Organizations,* 171.

9. Ibid., n. 12.

10. U.S. Office of Management and Budget, *Cost Principles for Non-Profit Organizations.*

11. American Institute of Certified Public Accountants, *Audit and Accounting Guide: Not for Profit Organizations,* 171–172.

12. U.S. Office of Management and Budget, *Cost Principles for Non-Profit Organizations.*

Chapter Nine

1. U.S. Office of Management and Budget, *Cost Principles for Non-Profit Organizations.*

Chapter Ten

1. American Institute of Certified Public Accountants, *Objectives of Financial Statements,* 50–51.

Chapter Eleven

1. All quotations in this chapter are from Financial Accounting Standards Board, *Financial Statements of Not-for-Profit Organizations,* 2–8.

Chapter Fourteen

1. American Association of Fund-Raising Counsel Trust for Philanthropy, "Total Giving Reaches $190.16 Billion," press release, AAFRC Trust for Philanthropy, Indianapolis, May 24, 2000.

Chapter Fifteen

1. U.S. Office of Personnel Management. "Eligibility Provisions and Public Accountability Standards" *Federal Register,* 1988, *53*(102), 19150–19151.

Conclusion

1. American Association of Fund-Raising Counsel Trust for Philanthropy, "Giving USA: 2000," press release, Indianapolis, May 24, 2000.

2. See the Web sites http://nccs.urban.org/ and http://www.guidestar.org/. The statistics cited in the next paragraph were provided by GuideStar.

3. David Cay Johnston, "Tax Returns of Charities to Be Posted on the Web," *New York Times,* Oct. 18, 1999.

Resource G

1. For a more detailed discussion of governmental and nongovernmental regulation of charities, see Russy D. Sumariwalla, *Charities and Nonprofits in the U.S.: Regulation, Standard-Setting, Accreditation, and Monitoring,* Working Paper, no. 6 (San Francisco: Asia Foundation, 1998).

Resource H

1. Robert H. Hamlin, *Voluntary Health and Welfare Agencies in the United States: An Exploratory Study by an Ad Hoc Citizens Committee* (New York: Schoolmasters' Press, 1961), i.

2. Ibid., iii–iv.

3. Ibid., 40.

4. U.S. Department of the Treasury, *Research Papers Sponsored by the Commission on Private Philanthropy and Public Needs,* Vol. 5 (Washington, D.C.: U.S. Government Printing Office, 1977), 2869.

5. Ibid., 2871.

6. American Institute of Certified Public Accountants, *Industry Audit Guide: Audits of Voluntary Health and Welfare Organizations* (New York: American Institute of Certified Public Accountants, 1988), vi.

Resource I

1. Harry P. Hatry, *Performance Measurement: Getting Results* (Washington, D.C.: Urban Institute Press, 1994).

2. For guidance in identifying program service units, see United Way of America, *UWASIS-II: A Taxonomy of Social Goals and Human Service Programs* (Alexandria, Va.: United Way of America, 1976).

Bibliography

Accounting Advisory Committee. "A Study of the Inadequacies of Present Financial Reporting by Philanthropic Organizations." In U.S. Department of the Treasury, *Research Papers Sponsored by the Commission on Private Philanthropy and Public Needs,* Vol. 5: *Regulation.* Washington, D.C.: U.S. Government Printing Office, 1977.

Adams, J. B., Bossio, R. J., and Rohan, P. *Accounting for Contributed Services: Survey of Preparers and Users of Financial Statements of Not-for-Profit Organizations.* Norwalk, Conn.: Financial Accounting Standards Board, 1989.

American Accounting Association. "Report of the Committee on Accounting Practices of Not-for-Profit Organizations." *Accounting Review,* 1971, *46* (suppl.).

American Institute of Certified Public Accountants. *Accounting for Costs of Activities of Not-for-Profit Organizations and State and Local Governmental Entities That Include Fund Raising.* Statement of Position, no. 98-2. New York: American Institute of Certified Public Accountants, 1998.

American Institute of Certified Public Accountants. *Audit and Accounting Guide: Health Care Organizations.* New York: American Institute of Certified Public Accountants, 1998.

American Institute of Certified Public Accountants. *Audit and Accounting Guide: Not for Profit Organizations.* New York: American Institute of Certified Public Accountants, 1998.

American Institute of Certified Public Accountants. *Objectives of Financial Statements.* New York: American Institute of Certified Public Accountants, 1998.

American Institute of Certified Public Accountants. *Industry Audit Guide: Audits of Voluntary Health and Welfare Organizations.* (2nd ed.) New York: American Institute of Certified Public Accountants, 1988.

Anthony, R. N. *Financial Accounting in Nonbusiness Organizations: An Exploratory Study of Conceptual Issues.* Norwalk, Conn.: Financial Accounting Standards Board, 1978.

Anthony, R. N. "Making Sense of Nonbusiness Accounting." *Harvard Business Review,* May–June 1980, pp. 83–93.

Armishaw, D. P. "Not-for-Profit Organizations: More Disclosure Required?" *Cost and Management,* 1982, *56*(1).

Backer, M. (ed.). *Modern Accounting Theory.* Upper Saddle River, N.J.: Prentice Hall, 1966.

Bedford, N. M. *Introduction to Modern Accounting.* New York: Ronald Press, 1968.

Blazek, J. *Tax Planning and Compliance for Tax-Exempt Organizations: Forms, Checklist, Procedures.* (2nd ed.) New York: Wiley, 1993.

Brace, P. K., Elkin, R., Robinson, D. D., and Steinberg, H. I. *Reporting of Service Efforts and Accomplishments.* Research Report no. R09. Norwalk, Conn.: Financial Accounting Standards Board, 1980.

Brimson, J. A., and Antos, J. *Activity-Based Management for Service Industries, Government Entities, and Nonprofit Organizations.* New York: Wiley, 1994.

Bryan, E. L. *A Finance Reporting Model for Not-for-Profit Associations.* UMI Resources Press, 1981.

Bryce, H. J. *Financial and Strategic Management for Nonprofit Organizations: A Comprehensive Guide to Legal, Financial, Management, Fundraising, and Other Key Nonprofit Issues.* (3rd ed.) San Francisco: Jossey-Bass, 1999.

Calleghan, C. T., and Conners, T. *Financial Management for Nonprofit Organizations.* New York: American Management Institute, 1982.

Commission on Private Philanthropy and Public Needs. *Giving in America: Toward a Stronger Voluntary Sector.* Washington, D.C.: U.S. Government Printing Office, 1975.

Gordon, T. P., Greenlee, J. S., and Nitterhouse, D. "Tax-Exempt Organization Financial Data: Availability and Limitations." *Journal of the American Accounting Association,* June 1999, *13*(2), 113–128.

Council of Better Business Bureaus. *The Responsibilities of a Charity's Volunteer Board.* Publication, no. 24-215. Arlington, Va.: Council of Better Business Bureaus., 1986.

Daughtrey, W. H., Jr., and Gross, M. J., Jr. *Museum Accounting Handbook.* Washington, D.C.: American Association of Museums, 1978.

Dropkin, M., and La Touche, B. *The Budget Building Book for Nonprofits: A Step-by-Step Guide for Managers and Boards.* San Francisco: Jossey-Bass, 1998.

Financial Accounting Standards Board. *Accounting for Leases.* Statement of Financial Accounting Standards, no. 13. Norwalk, Conn.: Financial Accounting Standards Board, 1976.

Financial Accounting Standards Board. *Capitalization of Interest Cost.* Statement of Financial Accounting Standards, no. 34. Norwalk, Conn.: Financial Accounting Standards Board, 1979.

Financial Accounting Standards Board. *Objectives of Financial Reporting by Nonbusiness Organizations.* Statement of Financial Accounting Concepts, no. 4. Norwalk, Conn.: Financial Accounting Standards Board, 1980.

Financial Accounting Standards Board. *Capitalization of Interest Cost in Situations Involving Certain Tax-Exempt Borrowings and Certain Gifts and Grants: An Amendment of FASB Statement No. 34.* Statement of Financial Accounting Standards, no. 62. Norwalk, Conn.: Financial Accounting Standards Board, 1982.

Financial Accounting Standards Board. *Elements of Financial Statements.* Statement of Financial Accounting Concepts, no. 6. Norwalk, Conn.: Financial Accounting Standards Board, 1985.

Financial Accounting Standards Board. *Employers' Accounting for Pensions.* Statement of Financial Accounting Standards, no. 87. Norwalk, Conn.: Financial Accounting Standards Board, 1985.

Financial Accounting Standards Board. "How Accounting Standards Are Set: Due Process and the Decision-Making Process." *FASB Viewpoints,* Oct. 31, 1986.

Financial Accounting Standards Board. *Recognition of Depreciation by Not-for-Profit Organizations.* Statement of Financial Accounting Standards, no. 93. Norwalk, Conn.: Financial Accounting Standards Board, 1987.

Financial Accounting Standards Board. *Statement of Cash Flows.* Statement of Financial Accounting Standards, no. 95. Norwalk, Conn.: Financial Accounting Standards Board, 1987.

Financial Accounting Standards Board. *Deferral of the Effective Date of Recognition of Depreciation by Not-for-Profit Organizations.* Statement of Financial Accounting Standards, no. 99. Norwalk, Conn.: Financial Accounting Standards Board, 1988.

Financial Accounting Standards Board. *Employers' Accounting for Postretirement Benefits Other Than Pensions.* Statement of Financial Accounting Standards, no. 106. Norwalk, Conn.: Financial Accounting Standards Board, 1990.

Financial Accounting Standards Board. *Employers' Accounting for Postemployment Benefits: An Amendment of FASB Statements No. 5 and 43.* Statement of Financial Accounting Standards, no. 112. Norwalk, Conn.: Financial Accounting Standards Board, 1992.

Financial Accounting Standards Board. *Accounting for Contributions Received and Contributions Made.* Statement of Financial Accounting Standards, no. 116. Norwalk, Conn.: Financial Accounting Standards Board, 1994.

Financial Accounting Standards Board. *Disclosure About Derivative Financial Instruments and Fair Value of Financial Instruments.* Statement of Financial

Accounting Standards, no. 119. Norwalk, Conn.: Financial Accounting Standards Board, 1994.

Financial Accounting Standards Board. *Financial Statements of Not-for-Profit Organizations.* Statement of Financial Accounting Standards, no. 117. Norwalk, Conn.: Financial Accounting Standards Board, 1994.

Financial Accounting Standards Board. *Accounting for Certain Investments Held by Not-for-Profit Organizations.* Statement of Financial Accounting Standards, no. 124. Norwalk, Conn.: Financial Accounting Standards Board, 1995.

Financial Accounting Standards Board. *Accounting for the Impairment of Long-Lived Assets and for Long-Lived Assets to Be Disposed Of.* Statement of Financial Accounting Standards, no. 121. Norwalk, Conn.: Financial Accounting Standards Board, 1995.

Financial Accounting Standards Board. *Accounting for Derivative Instruments and Hedging Activities.* Statement of Financial Accounting Standards, no. 133. Norwalk, Conn.: Financial Accounting Standards Board, 1998.

Financial Accounting Standards Board. *Employers' Disclosures About Pensions and Other Postretirement Benefits: An Amendment of FASB Statements No. 87, 88, and 106.* Statement of Financial Accounting Standards, no. 132. Norwalk, Conn.: Financial Accounting Standards Board, 1998.

Fleishman, J. L. "Public Trust in Not-for-Profit Organizations and the Need for Regulatory Reform." In C. T. Clotfelter and T. Ehrlich (eds.), *Philanthropy and the Nonprofit Sector in a Changing America.* Bloomington: Indiana University Press, 1999.

Foster, M. F., Becker, H., and Terrano, R. J. *Miller GAAP for Not-for-Profit Organizations Plus Tax and Regulatory Reporting.* Orlando, Fla.: Harcourt Brace, 1998.

Fox, J. A., and Brown, D. L. (eds.). *The Struggle for Accountability: The World Bank, NGOs, and Grassroots Movements.* Cambridge, Mass.: MIT Press, 1998.

Galloway, J. M. *The Unrelated Business Income Tax.* New York: Wiley, 1982.

Gross, M. J., Jr., Larkin, R. F., Bruttomesso, R. S., and McNally, J. J. *Financial and Accounting Guide for Not-for-Profit Organizations.* (5th ed., 1999 cumulative suppl.) New York: Wiley, 1999.

Hall, M. D. "Financial Condition: A Measure of Human Service Organization Performance." *New England Journal of Human Services,* Winter 1982, pp. 25–34.

Hamlin, R. H. *Voluntary Health and Welfare Agencies in the United States: An Exploratory Study by an Ad Hoc Citizens Committee.* New York: Schoolmasters' Press, 1961.

Hammack, D. C. *Making the Nonprofit Sector in the United States: A Reader.* Bloomington: Indiana University Press, 1998.

Hatry, H. P. *Performance Measurement: Getting Results.* Washington, D.C.: Urban Institute Press, 1994.

Henke, E. O. *Introduction to Nonprofit Organization Accounting.* Boston: Kent, 1980.

Herzlinger, R. E., and Nitterhouse, D. *Financial Accounting and Managerial Control for Nonprofit Organizations.* Cincinnati: South-Western, 1994.

Holck, M., Jr., and Holck, M., Sr. *Complete Handbook of Church Accounting.* Upper Saddle River, N.J.: Prentice Hall, 1978.

Houle, C. O. *Governing Boards.* Washington, D.C.: National Center for Nonprofit Boards, 1989.

Hummel, J. *Starting and Running a Nonprofit Organization.* Minneapolis: University of Minnesota Press, 1980.

INDEPENDENT SECTOR, *Giving and Volunteering in the United States: Findings from a National Survey.* Washington, D.C.: INDEPENDENT SECTOR, 1999.

Kearns, K. P. *Managing for Accountability: Preserving the Public Trust in Public and Nonprofit Organizations.* San Francisco: Jossey-Bass, 1996.

Lang, A. S., and Sorrells, M. *Completing Your IRS Form 990: A Guide for Tax-Exempt Organizations.* Washington, D.C.: American Society of Association Executives, 1999.

Larkin, R. F. "Financial Management of Nonprofit Organizations: Selected Topics." *American Arts,* Jan.–July 1983.

Larkin, R. F. "How to Handle the Unique Audit Problems of Nonprofit Organizations." *Connecticut CPA Quarterly,* Dec. 1987.

Larkin, R. F. *Making Sense of Your Financial Data.* New York: PricewaterhouseCoopers, 1988.

Larkin, R. F. "Accounting." In T. D. Connors (ed.), *The Nonprofit Management Handbook: Operating Policies and Procedures.* New York: Wiley, 1993; suppl. 1994.

Larkin, R. F. "Accounting Issues Relating to Fundraising." In J. M. Greenfield (ed.), *Financial Practices for Effective Fundraising.* New Directions for Philanthropic Fundraising, no. 3. San Francisco: Jossey-Bass, 1994.

Larkin, R. F. "A Timely New Accounting Guide for Religious Groups." *Philanthropy Monthly,* Mar. 1998.

Larkin, R. F. *Wiley Not-for-Profit GAAP 98: Interpretation and Application of Generally Accepted Accounting Principles for Not-for-Profit Organizations 1998.* New York: Wiley, 1998.

Lohmann, R. *Breaking Even: Financial Management in Human Service Organizations.* Philadelphia: Temple University Press, 1980.

Mautz, R. K. "Monuments, Mistakes, and Opportunities." *Accounting Horizons,* June 28, 1988, pp. 123–128.

McMillan, E. J. *Budgeting and Financial Managing Handbook.* Washington, D.C.: American Society of Association Executives, 1994.

Meckstroth, A., and Arnsberger, P. "A 20-Year Review of the Nonprofit Sector, 1975–1995." In *Statistics of Income Bulletin,* Fall 1998.

Moonitz, M. *The Basic Postulates of Accounting.* Accounting Research Studies, no. 1. New York: American Institute of Certified Public Accountants, 1961.

National Assembly and National Health Council. *The Black Book Standards of Accounting and Financial Reporting for Voluntary Health and Welfare Organizations.* (4th ed.) Dubuque, Iowa: Kendall/Hunt, 1998.

National Center for Charitable Statistics and Foundation Center. *National Taxonomy of Exempt Entities Core Codes.* Washington, D.C.: National Center for Charitable Statistics; New York: Foundation Center, 1998.

National Health Council and National Social Welfare Assembly. *Standards of Accounting and Financial Reporting for Voluntary Health and Welfare Organizations.* Washington, D.C.: National Health Council, 1964.

Nelson, C. A., and Turk, F. J. *Financial Management for the Arts: A Guidebook for Arts Organizations.* New York: Associated Councils of the Arts, 1975.

Nonprofit Financial Center. *The NFC 1999 Accounting Software Selection Handbook: A Resource for Nonprofit and Religious Organizations.* Chicago: Nonprofit Financial Center, 1999.

Piersall, R. W. "Depreciation and the Nonprofit Organization." *New York Certified Public Accountant,* Jan. 1971.

President's Council on Integrity and Efficiency. *Questions and Answers on OMB Circular A-133.* Position Statement, no. 6. Washington, D.C.: U.S. Government Printing Office, 1992.

Previts, G. J. *The Scope of CPA Services: A Study of the Development of the Concept of Independence and the Profession's Role in Society.* New York: Wiley, 1985.

PricewaterhouseCoopers. *Position Paper on College and University Reporting.* New York: PricewaterhouseCoopers, 1975.

PricewaterhouseCoopers. *1982 Survey of Financial Reporting and Accounting Practices of Private Foundations.* New York: PricewaterhouseCoopers, 1982.

PricewaterhouseCoopers. *Effective Internal Accounting Control for Nonprofit Organizations.* New York: PricewaterhouseCoopers, 1988.

PricewaterhouseCoopers. *The Audit Committee, the Board of Trustees of Not-for-Profit Organizations, and the Independent Accountant.* New York: PricewaterhouseCoopers, 1992.

PricewaterhouseCoopers. *Not-for-Profit Organizations' Implementation Guide for SFAS Statements 116 and 117.* New York: PricewaterhouseCoopers, 1993.

Roy, R. H., and MacNeill, J. H. *Horizons for a Profession: The Common Body of Knowledge for CPAs.* New York: American Institute of Certified Public Accountants, 1967.

Rubin, S. "The House of GAAP." *Journal of Accountancy,* June 1984, pp. 122–129.

Shim, J. K., Siegel, J. G., and Simon, A. J. *Handbook of Budgeting for Nonprofit Organizations.* Upper Saddle River, N.J.: Prentice Hall, 1996.

Skinner, R. M. *Accounting Standards in Evolution.* Toronto: Holt, Rinehart and Winston, 1987.

State of Tennessee Comptroller of the Treasury. *Accounting and Financial Reporting for Not-for-Profit Recipients of Grant Funds in Tennessee.* Nashville: State of Tennessee Department of Audit, 1998.

Steuerle, G. "The Coming Revolution in the Nonprofit Sector", *Exempt Organization Tax Review,* 1998, *21*(3), 313–315.

Storey, R. K. *The Search for Accounting Principles: Today's Problems in Perspective.* New York: American Institute of Certified Public Accountants, 1964.

Sumariwalla, R. D. *Charities and Nonprofits in the U.S.: Regulation, Standard-Setting, Accreditation, and Monitoring.* Working Paper, no. 6. San Francisco: Asia Foundation, 1998.

Swords, P. "The Form 990 as an Accountability Tool for 501 (c) (3) Nonprofits." *Tax Lawyer,* 1998, *51*(3), 571–618.

Swords, P. "Nonprofit Accountability: The Sector's Response to Government Regulation." Norman A. Sugarman Memorial Lecture, Mandel Center for Nonprofit Organizations, Case Western Reserve University, Cleveland, Ohio, Mar. 16, 1999.

United Community Funds and Councils of America. *Accounting for Community Chests and United Funds: Principles and Methods.* New York: United Community Funds and Councils of America, 1956.

U.S. Department of Health and Human Services. *Guidelines for Audits of Federal Awards to Nonprofit Organizations.* Washington, D.C.: U.S. Government Printing Office, 1989.

U.S. Department of the Treasury. *Research Papers Sponsored by the Commission on Private Philanthropy and Public Needs,* Vol. 5: *Regulation.* Washington, D.C.: U.S. Government Printing Office, 1977.

U.S. General Accounting Office. *Government Auditing Standards.* (rev. ed.) Washington, D.C.: U.S. Government Printing Office, 1994.

U.S. Office of Management and Budget. *Cost Principles for Educational Institutions.* Circular A-21. Washington, D.C.: U.S. Government Printing Office, 1979.

U.S. Office of Management and Budget. *Uniform Administrative Requirements for Grants and Agreement with Institutions of Higher Education, Hospitals, and Other*

Nonprofit Organizations. Circular A-110. Washington, D.C.: U.S. Government Printing Office, 1993.

U.S. Office of Management and Budget. *Audits of States, Local Governments, and Non-Profit Organizations.* Circular A-133. Washington, D.C.: U.S. Government Printing Office, 1997.

U.S. Office of Management and Budget. *Cost Principles for Non-Profit Organizations.* Circular A-122. Washington, D.C.: U.S. Government Printing Office, 1997.

U.S. Office of Personnel Management. "Eligibility Provisions and Public Accountability Standards" *Federal Register,* 1988, *53*(102), 19150–19151.

United Way of America. *Budgeting: A Guide for United Ways and Not-for-Profit Human Service Organizations.* Alexandria, Va.: United Way of America, 1975.

United Way of America. *UWASIS-II: United Way of America Services Identification Systems.* (2nd rev. ed.) Alexandria, Va.: United Way of America, 1976.

United Way of America. *Accounting and Financial Reporting: A Guide for United Ways and Not-for-Profit Human Service Organizations.* (2nd ed.) Alexandria, Va.: United Way of America, 1989.

United Way of America. *Implementation Guide for FASB 116 and 117.* Alexandria Va.: United Way of America, 1996.

United Way of America. *Internal Financial Reporting Guidelines for United Ways.* Alexandria, Va.: United Way of America, 1998.

United Way of America. *Functional Expenses and Overhead Reporting Guidelines for United Ways.* (rev. ed.) Alexandria, Va.: United Way of America, 1998.

Vinter, R. D., and Kish, R. K. *Budgeting for Not-for-Profit Organizations.* New York: Free Press, 1984.

Weinstein, E. A. "Forging Nonprofit Accounting Principles." *Accounting Review,* 1978, *53*(4).

Index

A

Account category, 27

Account number, 26, 27, 28–29

Account number index, 211–220

Account type, 26, 27

Accountability: audits and, 12–13; financial reporting and, 9–10, 190–191, 193; levels of, 186; for program services, 333–334; role of Form 990 in, 14–15; standards for assessing (*See* Standards)

Accounting: activity-level, 40–54, 186; on cash basis, 179; cost, 69; disclosure note on changes in, 126

Accounting and Financial Reporting: A Guide for United Ways and Not-for-Profit Human Service Organizations, 169, 329

Accounting and Financial Reporting for Not-for-Profit Recipients of Grant Funds in Tennessee, 26, 144

Accounting for Costs of Activities of Not-for-Profit Organizations and State and Local Governmental Entities That Include Fund Raising (SOP 98–2), 90, 91

Accounting policies, disclosure note on, 120

Accounting Principles Board (APB), 329

Accounting software, 19–22; benefits of, 19, 22; functionalized trial balance report using, 56–57; general-purpose business, 20; integrated, 19; outsourcing for, 21; salary processing using, 245; sophisticated not-for-profit, 20–21; staff time recording and reporting using, 241, 242–245; transaction coding with chart of accounts in, 19

Accounts receivable: internal controls over, 54; UCOA definition of, 211

Accrual basis accounting and reporting, modified, 179

Activity(ies): classes of (*See* Cost objectives); cost distribution by, 69, 70–72; defined, 40; salary distribution by (*See* Salary distribution); statement of, 115–117, 120–121, 130; time distribution by (*See* Time distribution)

Activity code(s): multiple-level, 45–47; in NTEE, 267–269; single, 29–30, 36

Activity code tables, 30, 42–45

Activity-level accounting, 40–54, 186; budgeting and, 49–52; coding techniques in, 42–47; dimensions of, 40, 41; expense reporting and, 47–49; transaction coding in, 42

Activity-level budgeting, 50–51, 52

Activity-level coding techniques: multiple, 45–47; single, 30, 42–45; for smaller organizations, 43–44

Activity-level cost allocation, 81–82

Administrative activities, classification of, 78

Administrative expenses, CFC eligibility criteria for, 170

AICPA. *See* American Institute of Certified Public Accountants (AICPA)

American Cancer Society, 171

American Institute of Certified Public Accountants (AICPA): not-for-profit organization guide of, 3, 77, 79, 80, 86–87; standard-setting role of, 328–329

Animals (ANI) service group, NTEE codes in, 275

Annual budget, 179, 181

Arts, culture, humanities (ACH) service group, NTEE codes in, 270–272

Asset(s): *Black Book Standards* and cross-references related to, 172; disclosure note on impairment of, 127; disclosure note on transfer of, 124; internal controls over, 53, 54; reporting on, 113–114; UCOA definitions of, 212–213; UCOA keyword index for, 229–230. *See also* Net asset(s)

Asset account codes: in simplified chart of accounts, 37; by type, 29; in UCOA, 27, 31, 212–213

Audience criterion, for allocation of joint costs involving fundraising, 91

Audit and Accounting Guide: Not for Profit Organizations (AICPA): cost allocation bases in, 86–87; cost allocation requirements of, 79, 80; on management and general expenses, 77; organizations covered by, 3

Audit Guide for Colleges and Universities (AICPA), 328

Audit Guide for Voluntary Health and Welfare Organizations (AICPA), 328

Auditing standards, 12

Auditor's opinion, significance of, 13

Audits, accountability and, 12–13

Audits of Voluntary Health and Welfare Organizations (AICPA), 328

Avalon Foundation, 326

B

Balance sheet: in functionalized trial balance report, 58–59, 64; interim unaudited, 179

Balance sheet accounts: cross reference table for, 31–32; UCOA coding of, 27–28, 31–32

Bank statements, reconciliation of, 54

Better Business Bureau, 292

Black Book, 80, 169, 171–177; creation of, 326–327; revisions of, 329

Board-designated unrestricted endowment and reserves, disclosure note on, 122

Board of directors: accounting and reporting for, 186, 187; liability of, 11; training opportunities for, 12

BTA reports. *See* Budget-to-actual (BTA) reports

Budget: by activity, 50–51, 52; annual, 179, 181; functions of, 49, 52; in grant application, 164, 165; sample, 181

Budget categories, for grant reporting, 161

Budget process, 53, 179

Budget-to-actual (BTA) reports, 48–49; action-planning based on, 180; described, 179–180; examples of, 180, 181–185; for smaller organization, 185

C

California Society of CPAs (CalCPA), 15

Capital leases, disclosure note on, 123, 124–125

Capital purchases pool code, 30, 36

Capitalized interest, disclosure note on, 123

Cash: disclosure note on donor-restricted, 121; internal controls over, 54

Cash-based net assets, in functionalized trial balance report, 67

Cash basis accounting, and modified accrual basis reporting, 179

Cash flow, statement of, 117–118, 123

Cause and effect relationship, 334

Central service activities, reporting requirements cross- referenced to, 73

Central service costs, allocation of, 71, 72

Central services cost pool codes, 30, 36

CEOs, stewardship responsibility of, 10–12

Charities Review Council of Minnesota (CRCM), standards of, 293–294, 318–323

Chart of accounts: in computer-based accounting system, 19; cross-referenced to UCOA, 221–240; purpose of, 25–26; revenue and expense budgeting and reporting and, 47–49; simplified, 30, 37–39. *See also* Unified chart of accounts (UCOA)

Checks, internal control rules applicable to, 54

Chief executive officers, stewardship responsibility of, 10–12

Civil rights, social action, advocacy (CR) service group, NTEE codes in, 286–287

Collection items, disclosure note on, 128

Combined Federal Campaign (CFC), eligibility criteria for, 169–171

Commission On Private Philanthropy and Public Needs, 327–328

Commitments, disclosure note on, 124

Common activity codes, in NTEE, 267–269

Common costs: accumulation of, 75; allocation of, 70, 71, 75–76, 90, 91; by central service costs, 71, 72; disclosure of, 91; involving fundraising, 90, 91. *See also* Cost pool(s)

Community development (CD) service group, NTEE codes in, 287

Computer-based accounting system. *See* Accounting software

Computerization, of grant reporting process, 162–163

Content criterion, for allocation of joint costs involving fundraising, 91

Contingencies, disclosure note on, 124

Contractual finance-related violations, disclosure note on, 126

Contributions: *Black Book Standards* and cross-references related to, 174–175; disclosure notes on, 120–121; donor-restricted, 116–117, 121; in statement of activities, 116–117

Control accounts, 29

Controls, internal, 52–54

Corporate grant budgeting and reporting, 160–167

Cost accounting, 69

Cost accumulation, 70

Cost allocation: activity-level, 81–82; bases for, 86–88; cost center approach to, 89; dimensions of, 82–88; direct-staff salaries as basis for, 88–89; methods of, 81–93; by object expense category, 82, 83–85; objectives of, 81; recommended policies on, 81; reducing burden of, 88–89; requirements for, 78–81; terminology and definitions for, 69–78; timing of, 86; by type of cost pool, 82, 86. *See also* Cost pool allocation

Cost categories, 70, 74–76

Cost distribution, 69, 70–72

Cost objectives: classes of, 70, 72–74; defined, 70, 72; distribution of account costs to, 69, 70–72; reporting requirements cross-referenced to, 73

Cost pool(s), types of, 76, 82, 86

Cost pool allocation: by account, 75–76; cost centers for, 89; sequence of, 82, 86; by service department, 76, 82; for smaller organizations, 90, 92–93; year-to-date, 75

Cost pool codes, 30, 36

Cost Principles for Nonprofit Organizations. See OMB Circular A-122, *Cost Principles for Nonprofit Organizations*

Council of Better Business Bureaus (CBBB), Philanthropic Advisory Service's standards of, 292, 301–304

Crime, courts, legal services (CRI) service group, NTEE codes in, 281

Cross-reference worksheet, UCOA, 223–228

D

Databases on not-for-profit organizations, 141, 192, 335–336

Debt, disclosure note on, 125–126

Department codes, multiple-level, 45–46

Department heads, accounting and reporting for, 186, 187

Depreciation, disclosure note on, 123

Derivatives, disclosure note on, 128

Direct costs: allocation of, 70, 71, 74–75; allocation percentages based on, 72; in OMB Circular A-122, 74, 80

Direct-staff salaries, as basis for cost allocation, 88–89

Disbursements, internal controls over, 54

Disclosure note: on accounting changes, 126; on board-designated unrestricted endowment and reserves, 122; on commitments, 124; on concentration of risks, 128; on contingencies, 124; on contributions receivable, 121; on correction of an error, 126–127; on debt, 125–126; on donated materials and services, 122; on donor-restricted contributions and net assets, 120–121; on finance-related legal and contractual violations, 126; on financially interrelated organizations, 126; on functional classification of expenses, 123–124; on investments, 122, 128; on leases, 123, 124–125; on nonmonetary transactions, 124; on pensions and other postemployment employee benefits, 127; on property, equipment, and depreciation, 123; on subsequent events, 127; on summary of significant accounting policies, 120; on use of estimates, 128

Diseases, medical disciplines (D,MD) service group, NTEE codes in, 278–279

Donated materials and services: disclosure note on, 122; in Form 990 versus GAAP financial statements, 132

Donor-restricted contributions, 116–117, 121

Donor-restricted net assets, 115, 120–121

Double-entry bookkeeping, automatic, 20

E

Education service group, NTEE codes in, 272–274

Electronic grant reporting, 162–163

Embezzlement, prevention of, internal controls for, 53–54

Employee benefits: cost pools for, 76, 82; disclosure note on postemployment, 127

Employee time recording. *See* Staff time recording and reporting

Employment (EMP) service group, NTEE codes in, 281–282

Endowment and reserves, disclosure note on, 122

Environmental improvement and protection (ENV) service group, NTEE codes in, 274–275

Equipment, disclosure note on, 123

Equity, 114. *See also* Net asset(s)

Error correction, disclosure note on, 126–127

Estimates, disclosure note on use of, 128

Evaluation, program, 333–334

Evangelical Council for Financial Accountability (ECFA), 292–293, 305–307

Excel, 20

Executive director, accounting and reporting for, 186, 187

Expense(s): activity-level accounting for, 40–54; functional classification of, 123–124, 133; in functionalized trial balance report, 62–63, 65–66; UCOA definitions of, 28, 34–35, 215–220; UCOA keyword index for, 234–240. *See also* Revenue and expense

Expense account codes: activity coding for, 29–30, 36; in simplified chart of accounts, 39; in UCOA, 28, 34–35, 215–220

Expense categories: in grant budgeting and reporting, 161; object (*See* Object expense categories)

F

FASB (Financial Accounting Standards Board): creation of, 329; on definition of governmental organization, 4–5; on definition of not-for-profit organization, 3; standard-setting role of, *xxiv*, 329–331

FASB Statement No. 4, *Objectives of Financial Reporting*, 330

FASB Statement No. 6, *Elements of Financial Statements*, 330

FASB Statement No. 34, *Capitalization of Interest Cost*, 123

FASB Statement No. 62, *Capitalization of Interest Cost in Situations Involving Certain Tax-Exempt Borrowings and Certain Gifts and Grants*, 123

FASB Statement No. 87, *Employers' Accounting for Pensions*, 127

FASB Statement No. 106, *Employers' Accounting for Postretirement Benefits Other Than Pensions*, 127

FASB Statement No. 112, *Employers' Accounting for Postemployment Benefits*, 127

FASB Statement No. 116, *Accounting for Contributions Received and Contributions Made*, 116–117, 331

FASB Statement No. 117, *Financial Statements of Not-for-Profit Organizations*, 331; cost allocation requirements in, 78–79, 80; cost objective descriptions in, 72–74; financial statement requirements in, 113; on purpose of financial statements, 112

FASB Statement No. 119, *Disclosure About Derivative Financial Instruments and Fair Value of Financial Instruments*, 128

FASB Statement No. 121, *Accounting for the Impairment of Long-Lived Assets and for Long-Lived Assets to Be Disposed Of*, 123

FASB Statement No. 124, *Accounting for Certain Investments Held by Not-for-Profit Organizations*, 331

FASB Statement No. 132, *Employers' Disclosures About Pensions and Other Postretirement Benefits*, 127

FASB Statement No. 136, 331

FASB Statements of Financial Accounting Standards, 329–330

Filer, J. H., 327

Filer Commission Report, 327–328

Financial Accounting Standards Board. *See* FASB (Financial Accounting Standards Board)

Financial and Accounting Guide for Not-for-Profit Organizations, internal control rules in, 54

Financial position, statement of, 113–115, 119, 129

Financial reporting: accountability and, 9–10, 190–191, 193; information technology and, 19–22, 192–193; standards for assessing (*See* Standards); unified (*See* Unified financial reporting)

Financial statements: disclosure notes accompanying, 120–128; FAS-117 required, 113–118; Form 990 (*See* Form 990); fund accounting model for, 112–113; GAAP (*See* GAAP financial statements); purpose of, 105–106, 112; sample, 119–121; for smaller organizations, 128–131. *See also* specific statements

Financially interrelated organizations, disclosure note on, 126

Financing agreement, disclosure note on, 126

Fixed asset purchases pool code, 30, 36

Fixed asset records, internal controls over, 54

Food, nutrition, agriculture (F&A) service group, NTEE codes in, 282

Form 990: for 1999, 198–209; accountability and public disclosure role of, 14–15; as attachment to grant applications, 161; attachments and explanations for, 133, 140; *Black Book Standards* cross-referenced to, 171–177; board and staff use of, 178; cost allocation requirements of, 79–80, 81; on definition of management and general expenses, 77; filing requirements for, 14; grant budget and report format cross-referenced to, 166; importance of reporting accuracy in, 191–192; program service accomplishments information required in, 334; public disclosure requirements for, 141–142; quality reporting efforts related to, 335; quality resolution related to, 15, 16–18; revenue and expense categories for internal budgeting and reporting cross-referenced to, 184; sample (Parts I–VII), 134–139; Schedule A of, 204–209; simplified activity coding system cross-referenced to, 44; simplified chart of accounts cross-referenced to, 37–39; UCOA cross-referenced to, 31–35; versus GAAP financial statements, 132–133

Form 1023 exemption application, public disclosure requirements for, 141–142

Foundation Center (FC), 265–266

Foundation grant budgeting and reporting, 160–167

Functional-basis financial package, 41

Functional expenses: disclosure note on, 123–124; in Form 990 versus GAAP financial statements, 133; statement of, 118, 122, 131, 191

Functionalized trial balance report, 55–67; balance sheet in, 58–59, 64; changes in cash-based net assets in, 67; development of, 55–56; expenses in, 62–63, 65–66; revenues in, 60–61, 65; sample, 58–63; simplified, 64–67; using accounting software, 56–57; using spreadsheet software, 56

Fund accounting model, for GAAP financial statements, 112–113

Fund balance, 114. *See also* Net asset(s)

Funding source codes, multiple-level, 46

Fundraising activities: allocation of joint costs involving, 90, 91; FASB description of, 73; reporting requirements cross-referenced to, 73

Fundraising activity codes, 30, 36

Fundraising expenses: CFC eligibility criteria for, 170; importance of reporting accuracy for, 191

G

GAAP financial statements: *Black Book Standards* cross-referenced to, 171–177; board and staff use of, 178; cost allocation requirements of, 78–79; functionalized trial balance report cross-referenced to, 58–63; fund accounting model for, 112–113; requirements for, 108–130; revenue and expense categories for internal budgeting and reporting cross-referenced to, 184; types of costs in, 74; UCOA cross-referenced to, 31–35; versus Form 990 financial statements, 132–133

Gains and losses reporting: *Black Book Standards* and cross-references related to, 175; in statement of activities, 116–117

General. *See* Management and general

General ledger revenue and expense account manual, 21–22

Giving Guide (CRCM), 294

Giving in America: Toward a Stronger Voluntary Sector (Commission On Private Philanthropy and Public Needs), 327–328

Governmental organization, definition of, 4–5

Grant budgeting and reporting, 160–166, 171; electronic, 162–163; examples of, 163–167; recommendations for improving quality of, 160–163; regional standardization of, 163; using Tennessee Policy 03 Format, 143–159

Grantee accounting systems, alignment of, 161–162

Greater Washington Society of CPAs (GWSCPA), 15, 144–145

GuideStar Web site, 141, 192

H

Harassment, public disclosure requirements and, 142

Health, general and rehabilitative (HC) service group, NTEE codes in, 275–277

Hospital Audit Guide (AICPA), 328

Housing, shelter (HOU) service group, NTEE codes in, 282–283

Human services, other (HS) service group, NTEE codes in, 284–285

I

Information technology, and financial reporting, 19–22, 192–193

Interim reports, 179

Internal controls, 52–54

Internal management reporting, 178–187; budget-to-actual, 179–185; hierarchy of, 186–187; on modified accrual basis, 179; revenue and expense categories for, 184. *See also* Budget-to-actual (BTA) reports

Internal Revenue Code Section 501(c), tax-exempt organizations under, 6–7

International affairs (IA) service group, NTEE codes in, 285–286

Internet: for public disclosure of financial information, 141, 192; technical assistance Web sites on, 335–336

Investments: disclosure note on, 122, 128; in Form 990 versus GAAP financial statements, 132; internal controls over, 54

IRS Form 990. *See* Form 990

IRS Form 1023 exemption application, public disclosure requirements for, 141–142

J

Jewish Welfare Federations, 171

Joint costs. *See* Common costs

K

Kamehameha Schools/Bishop Estate, liability of trustees of, 11

Keyword index, UCOA, 229–240

L

Leases, disclosure note on, 123, 124–125

Legal finance-related violations, disclosure note on, 126

Levis, W. C., *xvii–xviii*

Liabilities: after financial statement date, 127; *Black Book Standards* and cross-references related to, 173; reporting on, 114; UCOA definitions of, 213; UCOA keyword index for, 230–231

Liability account codes: in simplified chart of accounts, 37; by type, 29; in UCOA, 27, 32, 213

Loss contingency, disclosure note on, 124

Losses and gains reporting: *Black Book Standards* and cross-references related to, 175; in statement of activities, 116–117

Lotus 1-2-3, 20

M

Management and general activities: FASB description of, 73; reporting requirements cross-referenced to, 73

Management and general activity codes, 30, 36

Management and general cost(s): administrative, 78; allocation of, 70, 72, 73, 77; Form 990 definition of, 77; importance of reporting accuracy for, 191

Management and general cost pool, 76, 82

Maryland Association of Nonprofit Organizations (MANO), standards of, 293, 308–317

Materials and services, donated, 122, 132

Medical research (MR) service group, NTEE codes in, 279–281

Membership-development activities, FASB description of, 73–74

Mental health, crisis intervention (MH) service group, NTEE codes in, 277

Minnesota, Charities Review Council standards for, 293–294, 318–323

Modified accrual basis accounting and reporting, 179

Month-end cost allocation, 86

Mutual aid (MAS) service group, NTEE codes in, 290

N

NACS (Nonprofit Accounts Coding System), 26–27

NACS account numbers, 26

NACS activity codes: described, 26–27; multiple activity-level codes cross-referenced to, 46–47; revenue and expense budgeting and reporting and, 47–49; for smaller organizations, 43–44; tables for, 42–45

National Assembly, 326

National Center for Charitable Statistics (NCCS), 192, 265

National Charities Information Bureau (NCIB), standards of, 291–292, 295–300

National Grants Management Association (NGMA), 144–145

National Health Council, 326

National Taxonomy of Exempt Entities (NTEE), 265–290; common activity codes in, 267–269; condensed version of, 265; core codes in, 265; how to use, 270; index of, 270–290; major service groups in, 266

Net asset(s): *Black Book Standards* and cross-references related to, 173; donor-restricted, 115, 120–121; permanently restricted, 115; temporarily restricted, 115; UCOA definitions of, 213–214; UCOA keyword index for, 231; unrestricted, 114–115

Net asset account codes: in simplified chart of accounts, 37; in UCOA, 27–28, 32, 213–214

Net asset reporting: in statement of activities, 115–117; in statement of financial position, 114–115

Nonmonetary transactions, disclosure note on, 124

Nonprofit Accounts Coding System. *See* NACS

Not-for-profit organizations: definition of, 3–4; public disclosure requirements for, 141–142, 191; standards for (*See* Standards); state registration and filing requirements for, 259–263; as term of choice, 5

Not-for-profit sector: accountability of, 9–13, 190–193; growth of, 9; names for, 8

NTEE. *See* National Taxonomy of Exempt Entities (NTEE)

O

Object expense categories: *Black Book Standards* and cross-references related to, 176–177; cost accumulation by, 70; cost allocation by, 82, 83–85; suggested allocation bases for, 87

Objectives of Financial Statements (AICPA), 105–106

OMB Circular A-122, *Cost Principles for Nonprofit Organizations:* cost allocation requirements of, 80–81; on cost objectives, 72; on direct costs, 74, 80; staff time recording requirements in, 94–95; Tennessee reporting requirements alignment with, 144; types of costs in, 74; UCOA cross-referenced to, 31–36

OMB Circular A-133, *Audits of Institutions of Higher Education and Other Nonprofit Organizations,* 144

Operating leases, disclosure note on, 125
Operations classification, in statement of activities, 117
Organizational administration, 78

P

Payroll services, outsourcing for, 21, 245
Pensions, disclosure note on, 127
Philanthropic Advisory Service of the Council of Better Business Bureaus, standards of, 292, 301–304
Philanthropic Research Inc., 141, 192
Philanthropy, volunteerism (P&V) service group, NTEE codes in, 287
Planning, budgeting and, 49, 53
Program administration, 78
Program directors, accounting and reporting for, 186, 187
Program evaluation, 333–334
Program-related activity codes, 30, 36
Program services: accountability for, 333–334; FASB description of, 73; importance of accomplishments in, 192; reporting requirements cross-referenced to, 73
Project codes, multiple-level, 46
Project directors, accounting and reporting for, 186, 187
Property, disclosure note on, 123
Public affairs (PAF) service group, NTEE codes in, 289
Public disclosure requirements, 141–142, 191
Public safety, disaster preparedness and relief (SAF) service group, NTEE codes in, 283
Public trust, financial reporting and, 9–10, 190–191
Purpose criterion, for allocation of joint costs involving fundraising, 90, 91

Q

Quality Form 990 Resolution, 15, 16–18

R

Receipts, internal controls over, 54
Records, safekeeping of, 54
Recreation and sports (REC) service group, NTEE codes in, 283–284
Regional grant makers, standardization of grant budgeting and reporting by, 163
Religion (REL) service group, NTEE codes in, 289–290
Rentals. *See* Leases
Restricted contributions, 116–117, 121
Restricted grant reports, board and staff use of, 178
Restricted net assets, 115, 120–121
Restriction codes, multiple-level, 46
Revenue(s): activity-level accounting for, 40–54; *Black Book Standards* and cross-references related to, 174–175; in functionalized trial balance report, 60–61, 65; UCOA definitions of, 214–215; UCOA keyword index for, 232–233
Revenue account codes: activity coding for, 29–30, 36; in simplified chart of accounts, 38; in UCOA, 28, 33–34, 214–215
Revenue and expense account manual, general ledger, 21–22
Revenue and expense activity code tables, 42–45

Revenue and expense reporting: BTA comparisons in, 48–49; categories for, 184; chart of accounts and, 47–49; grant, 164, 167; sample year-end, 182; in statement of activities, 116–117
Risks, disclosure note on concentration of, 128
Rockefeller Foundation, 325–326

S

Salaries, establishing amounts for, 96
Salary distribution, 96; monthly, 100, 248–249; year-end, 256–257; year-to-date, 101
Salary processing, 94–101, 241–257
Science (SCI) service group, NTEE codes in, 287–288
Securities, marketable, internal controls over, 54
Service department: cost pools for, 76, 82; examples of, 76
Service groups: in NTEE, 266–267; NTEE codes indexed by, 270–290
Seven Standards of Responsible Stewardship (ECFA), 292–293, 305–307
Shared costs. *See* Common costs
Social sciences (SOC) service group, NTEE codes in, 288–289
Split-interest agreements, disclosure note on, 128
Spreadsheets: benefits of, 20; for functionalized trial balance report, 56; for staff time recording and reporting, 241, 242–245
Staff time recording and reporting, 94–101, 241–257; OMB A-122 requirements for, 94–95; salary allocations for, 95, 96, 100, 101; spreadsheets for, 241, 242–245; time sheets for, 95, 96–98, 241, 242–243. *See also* Salary distribution; Time distribution
Standards, 291–323; of Charities Review Council of Minnesota, 293–294, 318–323; of Evangelical Council for Financial Accountability, 292–293, 305–307; history of, 325–331; of Maryland Association of Nonprofit Organizations, 293, 308–317; of National Charities Information Bureau, 291–292, 295–300; of Philanthropic Advisory Service of the Council of Better Business Bureaus, 292, 301–304; role of accounting profession in development of, 328–331; voluntary self-regulatory efforts in development of, 325–328
Standards for Charitable Solicitations (CBBB), 292, 301–304
Standards for Excellence: An Ethics and Accountability Code for the Nonprofit Sector (MANO), 293, 308–317
Standards in Philanthropy (NCIB), 291–292, 295–300
Standards of Accounting and Financial Reporting for Voluntary Health and Welfare Organizations. See Black Book Standards of Responsible Stewardship (ECFA), 292–293, 305–307
State charities regulation offices: cost allocation requirements of, 79–80; financial information required by, 14
State charity supplements, uniform, 107
State registration and filing requirements for not-for-profit organizations, 259–263
Statement of activities: described, 115–117; purpose of, 116; sample, 120–121; simplified, 130

Statement of cash flow, 117–118, 123

Statement of financial position: described, 113–115; sample, 119; simplified, 129

Statement of functional expenses: described, 118; importance of reporting accuracy in, 191; sample, 122; simplified, 131

Statement of program service accomplishments, importance of, 192

Stewardship responsibility, financial reporting and, 10–12

A Study of the Inadequacies of Present Financial Reporting by Philanthropic Organizations, 327–328

Sumariwalla, R. D., *xvii*

Supporting services, FASB description of, 73–74

T

Tax-exempt organizations: classification of (*See* National Taxonomy of Exempt Entities (NTEE)); under Internal Revenue Code Section 501(c), 6–7

Technical assistance Web sites, 335–336

Technology, and financial reporting, 19–22, 192–193

Tennessee: national groups assisting, 144–145; reporting requirements of, 145

Tennessee Uniform Reporting Policy Statement 03: revision of, 144–145; sample, 150–159; Schedule A, 146–147; Schedule B, 148–149; UCOA cross-referenced to, 31–35

Time distribution: in hours, 244–246, 250–251, 252–253; monthly, 96, 99, 244–247; in percentages, 246–247, 254–255; prior month, 250–251; year-end, 252–255

Time sheets, 95, 96–98, 241, 242–243

Time tracking threshold, 96

Transaction coding, activity-level, 42

Transfer of assets, disclosure note on, 124

Treasurer: stewardship responsibility of, 10–12; training opportunities for, 12

Trial balance report. *See* Functionalized trial balance report

U

Unified chart of accounts (UCOA): account number examples for, 28–29; account number index for, 211–220; balance sheet accounts in, 27–28, 31–32;

Black Book Standards cross-referenced to, 171–177; coding system used in, 26–27; cross-reference worksheet for, 223–228; cross-referencing procedure for, 221–222; grant budget and report format cross-referenced to, 166; keyword index for, 229–240; outline of, 27–30; proposed, 30, 31–35; revenue and expense accounts in, 28, 33–35; revenue and expense categories for internal budgeting and reporting cross-referenced to, 184; simplified activity coding system cross-referenced to, 44; simplified chart of accounts cross-referenced to, 37–39; specific activity codes in, 29–30

Unified financial reporting: accountability and, 9–10, 190–191; with the click of a mouse, *xxiii–xxiv*; conclusions on, 189–193; overview of, 105–107

Uniform government grant reports using Tennessee Policy 03 Format, 143–159; sample, 150–159; Schedule A, 146; Schedule B, 148

Uniform Grant Budgeting and Reporting Program (Tennessee), 144

Uniform state charity financial summaries and supplements, 107

United Way: accounting and financial reporting guide of, 169, 329; accounting and financial reporting to, 168–169; and Combined Federal Campaign, 169–171

United Way of America Accounts Coding System (UWAACS): *Black Book Standards* cross-referenced to, 171–177; grant budget and report format cross-referenced to, 166; role of, 169; UCOA cross-referenced to, 31–35

V

Voluntary sector. *See* Not-for-profit organizations

W

Web sites: for public disclosure of financial information, 141, 192; technical assistance, 335–336

Y

Year-end cost allocation, 86

Youth development (YD) service group, NTEE codes in, 284